Collaborative Teams for
Students with Severe Disabilities

Collaborative Teams for Students with Severe Disabilities
Integrating Therapy and Educational Services

Second Edition

by

Beverly Rainforth, Ph.D., PT
State University of New York at Binghamton

and

Jennifer York-Barr, Ph.D., PT
University of Minnesota
Minneapolis

·P A U L·H·
BROOKES
PUBLISHING CO.

Baltimore • London • Toronto • Sydney

Paul H. Brookes Publishing Co.
Post Office Box 10624
Baltimore, Maryland 21285-0624

Typeset by PRO-Image Corporation, Techna-Type Division, York, Pennsylvania.
Manufactured in the United States of America by
Thomson-Shore, Inc., Dexter, Michigan.

Preparation of this book was supported in part by Grant #HO86V40007 from the U.S. Department
of Education to Allegheny-Singer Research Institute and State University of New York at
Binghamton and by Grant #HO86R40012 and subcontract #MNEd/022-INCL-094 of Grant
#HO86J20010 from the U.S. Department of Education to the Institute on Community Integration at
the University of Minnesota. The positions presented herein do not necessarily represent policies of
the U.S. Department of Education, and no official endorsement should be inferred.

The cases described in this book are based on the authors' actual experiences. Names have been
changed and identifying details have been altered to protect confidentiality.

Readers are granted permission to photocopy the forms in the appendix of this volume for use in
the course of their service provision to students with disabilities and their families.

Library of Congress Cataloging-in-Publication Data

Rainforth, Beverly, 1949–
    Collaborative teams for students with severe disabilities: integrating therapy and educational
services/by Beverly Rainforth and Jennifer York-Barr.—2nd ed.
      p.   cm.
    Includes bibliographical references and index.
    ISBN 1-55766-291-6 (pbk.)
      1. Handicapped children—Education—United States.   2. Handicapped
children—Rehabilitation—United States.   3. Teaching teams—United States. I. York-Barr,
Jennifer, 1958– II. Title.
LC4031.R35   1997
371.9—dc21
                                                                         97-207
                                                                            CIP

British Library Cataloguing in Publication data are available from the British Library.

Contents

About the Authors

Beverly Rainforth, Ph.D., PT, Associate Professor of Special Education, School of Education and Human Development, State University of New York at Binghamton, Post Office Box 6000, Binghamton, New York 13902-6000

Beverly Rainforth has worked as a physical therapist and special education teacher with infants, children, and adults with developmental disabilities in residential, special school, and public school settings since 1971. She works with school districts to develop inclusive education opportunities for students with disabilities and to build a culture of collaboration among educators, related services professionals, and families. As a teacher educator, Dr. Rainforth also works at interdisciplinary collaboration in the university. She chairs the Related Services Interest and Action Group for TASH, The Association for Persons with Severe Handicaps.

Jennifer York-Barr, Ph.D., PT, Associate Professor, Department of Educational Policy and Administration, University of Minnesota, 410B Wulling Hall, 86 Pleasant Street, SE, Minneapolis, Minnesota 55455

Jennifer York-Barr has worked in the area of interdisciplinary collaboration since 1980. She works with numerous schools in Minnesota to facilitate more collaborative partnerships among general educators, special educators, and other support personnel. Dr. York-Barr also coordinates the Teacher Leadership Program in the College of Education at the University of Minnesota. She has published and presented extensively on topics of collaboration and inclusive schooling.

Also contributing to this volume:

Winnie Dunn, Ph.D., OTR, FAOTA, Professor and Chairperson, Department of Occupational Therapy Education, School of Allied Health, University of Kansas Medical Center, 3901 Rainbow Boulevard, Kansas City, Kansas 66160-7602

Winnie Dunn has worked on community-based programs for children and families since the 1970s. She has conducted research and written about service provision throughout her career. In addition, Dr. Dunn has provided many workshops and seminars with interdisciplinary audiences about recommended practices for children and family services.

Carl J. Dunst, Ph.D., Research Scientist, Orelena Hawks Puckett Institute, 189 East Chestnut Street, Asheville, North Carolina 28801

Carl J. Dunst has worked in the fields of early intervention, developmental psychology, and family support for more than 2 decades. He has conducted basic and applied research focusing on the ecological factors associated with positive outcomes in children who have or are at risk for disabilities and their families and the application of the research findings for practice and policy. Dr. Dunst and his colleagues have written extensively about child development, family support, community development, and helpgiving practices in the field of developmental disabilities.

Cathy Macdonald, M.A., Program Planner/Facilitator, Educational Cooperative Service Unit of the Metropolitan Twin Cities Area, 3499 Lexington Avenue North, St. Paul, Minnesota 55126

Cathy Macdonald has worked as a speech-language clinician, a curriculum writer, a legal advocate for people with severe disabilities, and an education specialist for the Institute on Community Integration at the University of Minnesota. She has continued her interest in collaborative teams in education, both professionally and personally, with involvement in site-based decision making and other school improvement efforts.

Christine L. Salisbury, Ph.D., Director, Child and Family Studies Program, Allegheny University of the Health Sciences, One Allegheny Square, Suite 510, Pittsburgh, Pennsylvania 15212

Christine L. Salisbury has worked in the field of severe disabilities and early childhood intervention since the early 1970s as a teacher, a community-based program administrator, a faculty member, and a researcher. In each capacity she has made efforts to work collaboratively with families, professionals, and policy makers to improve the quality of services and supports for children with a full range of disabilities and their families. Dr. Salisbury directs the Consortium on Inclusive Schooling Practices and a participatory action research project. In both initiatives, there is a prevailing emphasis on collaborative problem solving and meaningful involvement of key constituent groups.

Preface

Last spring (coincidentally, about the time we committed to writing this second edition of our book), while driving home from child care, Jen's 7-year-old son, Sam, announced he was going to write a book about teams. Here's how the conversation went:

Sam: *Mom, I want to write a book about teams.* [His class had been publishing books all year.] *Maybe you and I could write it, and Mrs. Hanover* [Sam's first-grade teacher] *could publish it for us.*

Mom: *Hm. That's an interesting idea. What made you think of it? Why do you want to do that?*

Sam: *To help some kids in my class. They don't all know how to work in a team very well.*

Mom: *What does it mean to you—to work on a team?*

Sam: *It means you work together, no matter what.*

Mom: *Why do you think it's a good idea to work on teams?*

Sam: *Because two people can come up with better ideas than just one person. Like me and Kapou. We have some really good ideas together, and we helped Carolina with her project, too.*

Mom: *What happens if people on your team disagree or see things differently?*

Sam: *You figure it out without fighting.*

So, there you have it—the condensed version of our book. Teaming means you work together, no matter what. You do it because you'll come up with better ideas. And, if (or when) you disagree, you just figure it out—without fighting.

We place this story in our book's preface as a reminder of the wisdom and intuitive understandings that many young people bring to the realms of collaboration and diversity. If we extend our collaborative efforts to include children as valued members of our teams who bring relevant and important perspectives, undoubtedly our learning will be enriched, and the process of moving forward will be greatly facilitated. The children have much to offer us grown-ups, and they provide us with great hope for inclusive futures. If we do our jobs well, perhaps we can expand, instead of extinguish, some of the children's intuitive understandings.

Publication of this second edition of *Collaborative Teams for Students with Severe Disabilities* marks almost 2 decades of shared, professional life experiences for us. In 1980, we met in Urbana, Illinois, and had the good fortune to learn and work with colleagues in a cooperative educational program for students with severe and multiple disabilities. Progressive at the time, these students were bused from a relatively large geographic area to regular public schools. They attended special classes but had daily interactions with peers who did not have disabilities using a *reverse mainstreaming* approach; that is, students without disabilities regularly spent time in the special classes. Some of the youngest students with severe disabilities also spent time in general education classes during physical education or music. Intermediate and junior high school–age students also experienced community-based instruction in real work, home, and recreation settings.

There were no therapy rooms, so the contexts for service provision were the places and activities in which the students with severe disabilities normally participated on a daily basis: classrooms, lunchrooms, playgrounds, bus-loading areas, neighboring grocery stores and malls, and local employment sites. Particularly for these students, it was crystal clear that the context of instruction must be meaningful to increase the likelihood of both establishing and maintaining new abilities. Being present and sharing an entire day with a child in the context of her or his experience brought an essential understanding of the many situations throughout the school day in which "therapy" intervention was necessary to maximize learning and interaction. Thirty minutes twice a week in a separate context would be of questionable meaning.

The underlying support for the integrated school and community learning opportunities offered to children in this program were staff deeply committed to the belief that all students need and are entitled to opportunities to live and learn in the real world. Equally important, there was a strong belief and commitment that the best, if not the only, way to figure out how to do this was by working together—sharing the resources of energy, discipline-specific knowledge and skill, creativity, and fun. The language of *transdisciplinary teamwork* had both personal meaning and practical significance to the teachers, parents, therapists, paraprofessionals, and administrators. By working together and focusing on providing integrated instruction, a strong ethic of collaboration emerged. Without a doubt, this foundation of collaboration was responsible for the integrated and supported learning experiences for the children and young adults in the program.

This was Jen's first professional employment experience as a newly licensed physical therapist. She naively thought that these collaborative and integrated approaches were the way of education for most, if not all, students with severe disabilities everywhere. Bev, being a more experienced teacher and therapist (in Urbana doing graduate work at the time), knew better. She had been fortunate to learn about the rationale for and meaning of the transdisciplinary model as it was first being conceptualized in funded projects in the 1970s. She had worked with teams that called themselves "transdisciplinary" but were not, and she had worked with teams that collaborated extensively without labeling it as such. Bev had learned, as Jen did, that collaboration did not just happen because it sounded like a good thing to do or it was the newest educational fad. Collaboration happened because of shared meaning in the values of family and student focus, integration, teamwork, and equal opportunity. It happened because meaningful roles for the staff evolved as we worked together. Structures changed (e.g., weekly, large chunks of time in each classroom, regularly scheduled team meetings) to support our roles as cofacilitators of learning in integrated contexts. Our skills as collaborators developed. Just as context was an important condition of learning for students, the context and focus of our work was a necessary condition to learn new ways of working together.

With her varied experiences as a team member, Bev was intrigued with figuring out what makes teams work. She recognized a good team when she saw it in Urbana and found Jen to be an enthusiastic partner in clarifying their process. As requests for information about Urbana's integrated model came from other school districts and state departments, we decided perhaps we should compile all of the materials we had and write a book . . . a workbook . . . a cookbook? The thought of writing a book about teamwork seemed good, right, and relatively simple. For a long time we called it "the transdisciplinary cookbook," reflecting our half-joking, half-serious thinking that there were recipes that people could follow to create an effective team. When we finally began the arduous process of putting our thoughts and experiences into writing, we entered new realms of thought and understanding about the processes of collaboration and about ourselves as team members. In the new context of book writing, we continually relearned what we already knew about collaboration in educational settings. First, we realized that two people with similar education and experience did not have sufficient breadth to write a book with a transdisciplinary perspective. So Cathy Macdonald (a speech-language pathologist), Christine L. Salisbury (a special educator with expertise in working with families), and Winnie Dunn (an occupational therapist) were asked to assist with the task. After creating the first edition, we recognized that Chris and Winnie were valued consultants without whom the team could not have achieved its goal. At that time, we also knew that Bev, Jen, and Cathy were the core team; we had made a long-term commitment, and therefore, we felt great pride in small triumphs and deep frustration with ongoing struggles, just as do the core members of educational teams. We rediscovered that achieving a shared goal required us to communicate with one another frequently, honestly, and respectfully. Our interdependence required each of us to fulfill our commitments; it also required us to be patient and trusting when any of us needed to pull back from this commitment and attend to other needs. We reaffirmed that working together is a way of belonging, and belonging is an important ingredient in fulfilled lives. We rediscovered that relationships of this kind are likely to become personal as well as professional. We continually reaffirmed that work is more fun when working together as a team, particularly when team members like one another.

We knew that each of us brought unique professional expertise to the book; we also discovered the personal talents that each person brought to the book. We learned to maximize our talents and expertise and to laugh about our quirks (we discovered many). We rediscovered that working collaboratively is slower and more difficult than working independently, but the products of collaboration far surpass anything we could produce individually. Our collaboration both enabled and encouraged us to reassess our direction and methods, and we frequently corrected our course, continually striving for improvement and always involved in the process of growing.

In this, our second edition, we regret that one of our original core team members, Cathy Macdonald, has moved on to other life pursuits. With the addition or loss of any one team member, the newly formed or remaining team reconfigures and creates new, shared meaning and aligns new roles and responsibilities for task completion. Cathy's passion, creativity, expertise, fun, and extraordinary capacity for detail have been missed this time around. Because her prior contributions remain so evident in this second edition, however, Cathy is recognized as a contributor to Section II of the book. An addition to our team is

Carl J. Dunst, who brought his current research and efforts with families to Chapter 3, coauthored with Chris.

As we finish writing this Preface, the last task in completing our second edition, our thinking continues to change. As with our first edition, we review the chapters and see many possibilities for revision and improvement. Unlike the lifelong process of learning for children and adults with severe disabilities, writing a book is necessarily a finite process (or so our publisher continues to remind us). And so, complete with imperfections, incomplete understandings, and partially developed structures to support collaboration, we move this book forward to you. Join with others—parents, educators, community members—or at least one other person who either shares your beliefs about integration and collaboration or who is open to considering the possibilities. Use this book not as a cookbook, but as a guide. The resulting process and outcomes will be uniquely yours. Learn from others, share your own discoveries, and continue in your process of growing.

Acknowledgments

Creating this second edition represented collaborations with countless people, some of whom are easier to identify than others. A few people who are easy to name are Jill England, Inclusive Education Consultant at Wayne State University, who offered suggestions on chapter content; Elissa Stupp, graduate assistant at the State University of New York at Binghamton, who assisted with proofreading chapters and reference lists; and Erin Simunds, doctoral student at the University of Minnesota, who located current guidelines from professional organizations. We appreciate your assistance in developing and preparing the manuscript. We also thank Melissa A. Behm, Scott Beeler, and the staff of Paul H. Brookes Publishing Co., who encouraged us to prepare a second edition and worked with us to make that a reality.

We thank our families, who have been listeners, teachers, balancers, guides, cheerleaders, and supporters in our collaborative learnings. We especially appreciate their understanding during times when "the book, the book, the book" became a very present reality in our family lives.

We also recognize our many colleagues and friends who have contributed beyond words life experiences and perspectives about collaboration—those with whom we share the very real challenges, insights, and delights that emerge in the process of joining together.

Finally, we dedicate this book to the many people we have yet to meet in person but who we know are kindred spirits in schools and communities throughout the country—students, families, community members, and educators. You have demonstrated the courage to embark on a collaborative journey to improve education and life outcomes for children, including those children with the most significant challenges and unique capacities. Without you, your talent, and your creative energy, there would be no collaborative realities in schools. We all know "it" doesn't just happen. It happens because a committed group of people decides that it will.

Collaborative Teams for Students with Severe Disabilities

I

PHILOSOPHICAL, LEGAL, AND PROGRAMMATIC FOUNDATIONS

Section I of this book provides the philosophical, legal, and programmatic foundations of collaborative teamwork for students with severe disabilities. In Chapter 1, the educational and social context in which students with severe disabilities and their families find themselves is explored. Included are updated definitions of *severe disabilities, inclusive settings,* and *related services.* Since the first edition of this book was published in 1992, there have been substantial changes in the meanings of these terms. Emphasized in the definition of *severe disabilities* is recognition of assets and support needs in the lives of individuals, as opposed to an almost exclusive focus on deficits. *Inclusive settings* in public schools have become more broadly recognized as the least restrictive environment of choice for students with severe disabilities. Lending even greater support for inclusiveness are a variety of innovations in general education as well as special education. More individuals in the fields of general and special education are beginning to view diversity and collaboration as shared issues of importance, resulting in greater interactions and shared resources. Finally, the roles of physical therapists, occupational therapists, and speech-language pathologists as *related services* professionals are increasingly provided as direct supports for successful learning in inclusive settings. Chapter 1 clarifies the target population of the book, the settings in which these individuals receive their education and related services, and the role of related services professionals in their lives.

In Chapter 2, the foundations of collaborative teamwork for students with severe disabilities in educational settings are described. An evolution and rationale of collaborative services is presented, which explains how related services professionals increasingly find themselves on teams that operate interdependently for the benefit of children and families.

1

Underlying assumptions include the need to look individually at students in the real-world contexts in which they function on a daily basis and the need to consider individually their unique capacities and desires in order to create a meaningful educational experience. Roles and responsibilities of related services providers in general and of speech-language pathologists and occupational and physical therapists specifically are discussed in Chapter 2.

Given the central role of families in the lives of students with severe disabilities, Chapter 3 focuses exclusively on families' membership on collaborative teams. The nature of partnerships with families is explored with the position of equal status advocated; legal, research, and practical considerations are discussed. Factors that affect family participation and strategies for improving partnerships with families are presented.

After the foundations of collaborative services are presented in Section I, Section II of this book provides strategies and examples for creating individualized programs in which students with severe disabilities are supported to learn in inclusive settings. Section III, the final section of this book, provides strategies and examples for putting in place the structures and supports that promote effective collaboration among members of students' teams.

1

Terminology, Motivations, and Concerns of a Collaborative Approach

In 1990, when we began preparation of the first edition of *Collaborative Teams for Students with Severe Disabilities,* some educational teams serving students with severe disabilities were just beginning to integrate these students in regular schools and in general education classes for portions of the school day. As we write this second edition, many teams are involved in supporting students in inclusive settings for most, if not all, of the school day. This more inclusive educational design reflects a desire on the part of families to have their sons and daughters remain at home, attend their local neighborhood schools, and become woven into the fabric of surrounding community life. More broadly, it reflects a larger societal shift in which people with disabilities are present and integrated into society to an ever-increasing extent. Large medically oriented residential facilities continue to be replaced by a range of community living op-

tions, including supports for families to care for their children with disabilities at home. Just like other family members, children with disabilities are recognized as participants in their communities who go on family social outings, run errands to stores and other businesses, eat in restaurants, visit museums and libraries, play with other children, and attend religious services. Young adults with severe disabilities are learning to perform real work in community businesses through supported work efforts, enabling them to become contributing members of society and enhancing their dignity, confidence, and self-esteem.

Increased community opportunity and participation have resulted from federal and state mandates guaranteeing a free appropriate public education for all children with disabilities. In the 1980s, a significant component of educational services for students with severe disabilities was instruction referenced to community participation. Having experienced many successes and benefits of community participation for children and youth with even the most severe disabilities, the 1990s are yielding requests by parents and advocates and program initiation by forward-thinking educators for even greater community presence: education of children with disabilities in the same school they would attend if they did not have disabilities and alongside general education peers. Frequently lacking in the earlier era of programs emphasizing community-based instruction (see, e.g., Falvey, 1989) was meaningful and ongoing connection and interaction with same-age peers. More children with severe disabilities can now be seen attending their neighborhood schools, taking regular classes, riding the same buses as siblings and neighbors, participating in regular after-school activities, and taking part in the same graduation ceremonies as students who are not identified as having disabilities. In addition to families, many teachers and therapists have been pivotal in creating and supporting inclusive learning opportunities.

Not surprisingly, this increasing school and community inclusion has been met with varied responses. Some educators and parents maintain oppositional perspectives, which include concerns about inadequate support in general education classes, unwelcoming attitudes of teachers and students, insufficient time for meaningful collaboration, increased financial costs, and decreased quality of education for students without disabilities. Some maintain positive perspectives, asserting the potential benefits of increased and varied learning opportunities for students with disabilities, greater program coherence and consistency, social and emotional growth for all students, and collegial support from team members. Experience is a powerful teacher. To be sure, in many situations there is validity to the aforementioned concerns and benefits—all are possible. Our perspective, which serves as the primary assumption underlying this book, is that education plays an essential societal role in shaping current and future community life. We have chosen to direct our energy and discipline on the side of figuring out ways to increase meaningful inclusion in school, home, and community life. We believe that difference is not just a reality to be "tolerated" or "dealt with" but an asset if individuals are supported effectively to learn and act on the value of diversity (Turner & Louis, 1996). As educators, we believe the health and viability of communities in the future will be affected, in part, by how well we facilitate positive social interdependence among children in schools and how well we demonstrate it among ourselves. Johnson and Johnson (1989) eloquently articulate a rationale for such interdependence:

> Humans do not have a choice. We have to cooperate. Cooperation is an inescapable part of our lives. It is built into our biology and is the hallmark of our species. Cooperation is the building block of human evolution and progress. It is the heart of interpersonal relationships, families, economic systems, and legal systems. World interdependence is now a reality based on technology, economics, ecology, and politics that go beyond national boundaries and tie all countries in the world together. The management of human interdependence . . . is one of the most pressing issues of our time. Understanding the nature of interdependent systems and how to operate effectively within them is an essential quality of future citizens. The question is not whether we will cooperate. The question is, "how well will we do it?" (p. 167)

With the reality of increasing student diversity, educational team members have increasing opportunities, if not responsibilities, to assume significant roles in learning about, figuring out, and facilitating positive social, intellectual, and physical growth so that children and youth, including those with severe disabilities, realize fulfilling, integrated lives. Frequently, these roles are assumed in the absence of a road map. Inclusive and effective educational experiences result from creative, collaborative, and passionate effort. It is not a journey on which to embark alone.

As students with disabilities have become more fully included, educational teams have recognized the need to adopt more integrated and collaborative approaches to service provision. Teachers and therapists are more likely to analyze student needs and to determine capacities in actual general education, community, and home environments. Team members are developing creative strategies to apply their expertise in real-world situations, to increase participation and contributions by students with severe disabilities. Teachers and therapists are actively pursuing collaboration with one another, both because students can achieve greater outcomes and because staff experience professional growth and satisfaction. For the same reasons, the professionals who compose the educational team are recognizing the importance of collaborating with family and friends of the student with disabilities, who know the student best.

The primary responsibility of physical therapists, occupational therapists, and speech-language pathologists[1] in public education is to work collaboratively with other team members to assist students with disabilities to benefit from their educational programs. This means that therapists must be knowledgeable about the actual challenges experienced by students in their educational programs and that teachers and therapists together must create and put in place supports for students with severe disabilities in typical school, classroom, home, recreation, work, and community environments. This is no small charge, but, when teachers and related services personnel work as members of a collaborative team, many advantages and new opportunities are presented. Team members can assess student performance in actual daily routines, allowing more accurate determinations of service needs and priorities. Team members have access to professionals with complementary areas of expertise, enabling the entire team to recognize the complex needs of students with severe disabilities and to design more comprehensive and effective interventions. Team members can evaluate effectiveness of their interventions in direct relation to students' abilities to respond to demands of real-world environments and activities. When there are questions about the feasibility or effectiveness of interventions, team members share responsibility for problem solving and decision making, which produces more creative solutions and strategies. Working with students with severe disabilities in their daily routines allows teachers and therapists to teach, learn from, and engage in mutual support with others who support the students, including parents, siblings, classmates, paraprofessionals, general educators, and librarians. As teachers and therapists become more actively involved in these activities, they find that they value and are valued by other team members to an increasing extent.

---

[1]In this book, we use the terminology of physical therapists, occupational therapists, and speech-language pathologists in referring to elements of these specific disciplines, as recommended by their professional organizations. Where readability would be compromised, however, we refer to these professionals collectively as therapists, as distinguished from teachers and other related services providers. For ease of discussion throughout this book, we refer to these services collectively as therapies.

DEFINITIONS OF CORE TERMINOLOGY

A cardinal rule for effective teamwork is to communicate clearly. We have attempted to follow this rule by avoiding jargon and defining concepts as they are introduced. Three terms that hold different meanings for readers from different backgrounds are *severe disabilities, inclusive settings,* and *related services.* Because these terms define the scope of the book, it is appropriate to start by specifying their intended meanings for our purposes here.

Severe Disabilities

This discussion of meanings ascribed to the term *severe disabilities* is prefaced with acknowledgment of our discomfort with offering "group" or generalized definitions and with using descriptions that emphasize areas of personal challenge. Neither generalized knowledge nor information about challenges is sufficient in the determination of an appropriate individualized education program. Unfortunately, the provision of educational supports that are "more than usual" requires identification of challenges or deficits that result in unique educational needs. Diagnostic, deficit-driven eligibility criteria and their corresponding funding allocations continue to make deficit descriptions a reality in service systems. In day-to-day life and practice, however, many parents and service providers have realized or are discovering the importance of recognizing strengths and building on capacities to maximize participation (O'Brien & Mount, 1991; Strully & Strully, 1989). In fact, positive changes in the perceptions of individuals with severe disabilities are evident in recently published professional literature. Shifting away from an exclusive focus on deficits and challenges, definitions of the term *severe disabilities* sometimes now include more valuing descriptors that affirm the growth potential

and unique capacities of individuals with disabilities. Since the mid-1970s, there have been clear and repeated demonstrations that participation and contribution increase when individuals are provided with meaningful learning opportunities and appropriate support (Langone, 1996).

Numerous definitions have been offered for the heterogeneous group of students referred to as having severe disabilities. Presented here are several of those more frequently referenced. Since the mid-1970s, most federal and state definitions have emphasized cognitive limitations and adaptive behavior deficits as the exclusive defining characteristics. The U.S. Department of Education, Office of Special Education and Rehabilitative Services (Assistance to States, 1996) defines two relevant terms, *mental retardation* and *multiple disabilities:*

> "Mental retardation" means significantly subaverage general intellectual functioning existing concurrently with deficits in adaptive behavior and manifested during the developmental period that adversely affects a child's educational performance. (34 C.F.R. §300.7[b][5])

> "Multiple disabilities" means concomitant impairments (such as mental retardation–blindness, mental retardation–orthopedic impairment, etc.), the combination of which causes such severe educational problems that they cannot be accommodated in special education programs solely for one of the impairments. The term does not include deaf-blindness. (34 C.F.R. §300.7[b][6])

Brown et al. (1983), longtime advocates for individuals with severe disabilities and their families, offered a narrow definition, in part to advocate for funding specially allocated to support this most vulnerable class of citizens. Similar to the federal definitions, the Brown et al. (1983) definition focuses on measures or perceptions of intellectual capacity:

The label "severely handicapped" refers to approximately the lowest functioning 1% of the school-age population. This 1% range includes students who also have been ascribed such labels as moderately/severely/profoundly retarded, trainable level retarded, physically handicapped, multiply handicapped, deaf/blind, psychotic, and autistic. Certainly a student can be ascribed one or more of these labels and still not be referred to as severely handicapped for purposes here, as she or he may not be currently functioning intellectually within 1% of a particular age. (p. 71)

The Education for All Handicapped Children Act of 1975 (PL 94-142) defined this population, in part, by the services its members need:

A severely handicapped child is one who, because of the intensity of physical, mental, or emotional problems, or a combination of such problems, needs educational, social, psychological, and medical services beyond those which have been offered by traditional regular and special educational programs, in order to maximize his full potential for useful and meaningful participation in society and for self-fulfillment. (45 C.F.R. §121.2)

Expressing a more value-enhanced definition of people with severe disabilities, The Association for Persons with Severe Handicaps (TASH, 1989) emphasized the concept of supports required for integrated life functioning as paramount. TASH considers individuals with severe disabilities as

individuals of all ages who require extensive ongoing support in more than one major life activity in order to participate in integrated community settings and to enjoy the quality of life that is available to citizens with fewer or no disabilities. Support may be required for life activities such as mobility, communication, self-care, and learning as necessary for independent living, employment, and self-sufficiency. (p. 30)

In 1992, the American Association on Mental Retardation (AAMR) published a substantially reconceptualized definition of *mental retardation,* which includes many individuals considered as having severe disabilities (Luckasson et al., 1992). Although the original AAMR language of "subaverage intellectual functioning" (as determined by intelligence testing) remains, "adaptive behavior" has been more specifically operationalized as including 10 skill areas: communication, self-care, home living, social skills, community use, self-direction, health and safety, functional academics, leisure, and work (Luckasson et al., 1992). Similar to the TASH definition, a significant component of the new AAMR classification emphasizes that the purpose of assessment is determination of the level and type of individualized supports required for a person to function in community settings. The traditional subcategories of *mild, moderate, severe,* and *profound* have been eliminated and replaced with classifications of support needed to promote community participation. The support categories are identified as *intermittent, limited but consistent, extensive,* and *pervasive.* Additional improvements are located in the specified assumptions that underlie the definition: 1) assessments must be conducted in ways that are culturally and communicatively compatible, 2) adaptive skill limitations are determined in the community contexts that are age appropriate, and 3) there must be recognition of strengths coexisting with limitations in adaptive skill functioning.

The evolution of meanings associated with the term *severe disabilities* toward more accepting, if not valuing, human conceptions reflects progress not only in the field of disabilities but in society's overall perceptions of diversity. Considered in this broader perspective, individuals with disabilities and their many advocates have been part of an important shift in thinking about the many differences among people. We hope this shift will lead us to become communities of people, local and global, who are more expecting, accepting, and valuing of human difference. Appreciation of the courage, perseverance, and, sometimes, outrage of the many individuals involved in this social movement is appropriate, if not long overdue. To provide additional perspective on the magnitude of the social and attitudinal barriers faced by people with disabilities, we quote from Bogdan and Knoll (1995):

> The meaning of disability in special education goes far beyond alleged physical, behavioral, and psychological differences. Disability has symbolic meaning that must be looked at in terms of what society honors and what it degrades. Society's thoughts about intelligence, confidence, beauty, and winning must be understood to understand what we mean when we mockingly call someone "retarded" or "blind as a bat." Our society traditionally has been structured to bring shame to people with alleged disabilities. . . only a small part of the problems of discrimination—providing physical access to wheelchairs. . . is technical. The problems of disability are much more social, located much deeper in the seams of our society. (p. 694)

A sociological perspective, therefore, suggests that some of the greatest challenges experienced in the pursuit of opportunity, participation, and contribution are pervasive societal values of attractiveness, intelligence, athletic ability, and wealth. With this perspective held clearly in mind, let us not err by focusing all our efforts on facilitating growth within individuals, but also exert effort toward breaking down the larger barriers to access and opportunity—societal attitudes and values. Specific to the context of schooling, we affirm the value of individuals with varied and unique characteristics in today's schools and view such diversity as essential in the development of citizens and future community members who perceive difference as strength for our communities.

Until 1992, most of the authors' work was with children and adolescents with severe

disabilities, their families, and their educational teams. Although the focus of this book is on that population, we have discovered that many of the same principles and strategies have direct applications to early intervention and adult services. Furthermore, as we work more within general education settings and with more diverse student populations, we are learning that many students with milder disabilities or other unique learning challenges can also benefit from an ecological perspective and from collaborative efforts of an educational team. Trying to discuss students of all ages and abilities would expand the focus of this book beyond a manageable level. We urge readers, however, to consider the strategies presented here to meet the needs of the individuals whom they support. The strategies shared in this book are intended to operationalize the philosophy of discovering and building on capacities, in addition to addressing unique challenges.

Inclusive Settings

As described more fully in Chapter 2, *inclusion* has its legal precedence in the Least Restrictive Environment clause of the federal Education for All Handicapped Children Act of 1975 (PL 94-142) and Individuals with Disabilities Education Act (IDEA) of 1990 (PL 101-476). Other words that stem from this legal mandate are *mainstreaming* and *integration,* although mainstreaming, integration, and inclusion are not terms used in federal law. *Mainstreaming* has referred to the placement of students with disabilities, usually mild disabilities, in general education settings for part of the school day, especially during nonacademic classes. When students were mainstreamed in academic classes, it was because they had earned their way in by doing the same academic work as students in the regular class. Although mainstreamed students were still coached "on shore" in special classes, once in the mainstream, the students needed to swim on their own. If they started to drown, they were rescued and returned to the safety of the special class. Because the support of special educators in mainstream classes (direct or indirect) was not an operational part of the model, many educators considered mainstreaming a disappointing failure.

Integration has referred to students with the full range of disabilities interacting with peers without disabilities during specified portions of a school day, for social rather than curricular benefits. As in mainstreaming, the special class was the primary affiliation and "home base" for students with disabilities. Although students with and without disabilities benefited from social integration when appropriate supports were provided, social gains were not enough. Parents and educators began to realize that students could make gains in social, academic, and other curricular areas when supports were provided in general education rather than special education settings.

Inclusion refers to placement and membership in general education, with both social and curricular goals and with special education and related services provided as essential supports. In inclusive settings, all students are members of the general education system. Falvey, Grenot-Scheyer, Coots, and Bishop (1995) outline key components of an inclusive program:

Placement of *all* students in age-appropriate general education classrooms in neighborhood schools;

Comprehensive assessment of students' individual learning styles, strengths, and needs, and the development of individualized education programs based upon those assessment results;

Collaboration among families, general education teachers, special education teachers, administrators, paraprofessionals, and related service personnel to apply each of their areas of expertise in effectively meeting the needs of *all* students;

Classroom management strategies to motivate students and create supportive and caring educational environments;

Systematic arrangement of general education instructional settings and specialized support, along with adaptations of general education curriculum to meet these individual needs;

Positive behavior management strategies to motivate students and create supportive educational environments;

Infused teaching of basic motor, personal care, communication, social interaction, and academic skills within general education activities and routines;

Use of age-appropriate settings, activities, and materials provided to students in preschools, elementary and secondary schools, and through their post-secondary years; and

Collaborative and innovative strategies to assist schools to make the systemic "paradigm shift" that is necessary to create schools that effectively include and teach *all* of its students. (pp. 34–35)

Whereas some view the emergence of inclusion as extreme, others view it as the next logical step forward in a history of progressive desegregation and inclusion. Many express concern that students with significant disabilities and educational needs will be "dumped" into general education classes. Important components of an inclusive approach to schooling include individualized social and curricular goals and appropriate support (e.g., adaptations, special education and related services) provided in the general education context so that goals are achieved. Placement alone does not constitute an inclusive program, and placement without appropriate supports will almost certainly work counter to the goals of inclusion.

The key components of *inclusion* offered by Falvey et al. (1995) are structures, strategies, and supports that are likely to be in place when inclusive outcomes are realized for students. Assuming a different yet complementary perspective, York-Barr, Kronberg, and Doyle (1996) assert meanings of inclusion that extend beyond structure and process to focus on personal relevance. Table 1.1 lists words that individuals have offered to communicate personal meanings of inclusion and exclusion. Each of us knows what it feels like to be included and that this is a necessary state of being to be fully open to new learning. Each of us also knows what it feels like to be excluded (not by choice) and how devastating that is to our psychological well-being. Advances in brain research offer empirical evidence that legitimizes these intuitions we have always had (Caine & Caine, 1994). When feeling rejected, afraid, insecure, or angry, our brains downshift to lower processing centers where our fight-or-flight mechanisms take over. Openness to new information and higher-level processing of the information is simply not possible.

Table 1.1.   Meanings of inclusion and exclusion

What Does It Mean to Be Fully Included in a Community?

- Opportunities
- Contributing
- Participating
- Being respected
- Acceptance
- Taking risks
- Friendship
- Success
- Security
- Belonging
- Making choices
- Being needed
- Cooperating
- Feeling useful
- Happiness
- Freedom
- Confidence
- Being valued

What Does It Mean to Be Excluded from a Community?

- Rejection
- Discrimination
- Denied participation
- Feeling weird
- Being alone
- Anger
- Sadness
- Fear
- Viewed as different
- Denied opportunity
- Being ignored
- Feeling inferior
- Feeling powerless
- Resentment
- Frustration
- Depression

From York-Barr, J., Kronberg, R., & Doyle, M.E. (1996). *Creating inclusive school communities: A staff development series for general and special educators: Module 1. A shared agenda for general and special educators* (p. 21). Baltimore: Paul H. Brookes Publishing Co.; reprinted by permission.

Offering unequivocal support for including all individuals in society is the American Occupational Therapy Association (1995) public position on full inclusion:

Full inclusion means that all individuals, regardless of ethnicity, race, age, religion, gender, sexual orientation, or disability, should be able to be a part of the naturally occurring activities of society. Full inclusion addresses the need for all individuals to have the same opportunities. It also recognizes the benefits to everyone of being with individuals who are different from themselves.

Occupational therapy supports full inclusion throughout all practice areas of the profession. Occupational therapy practitioners provide adaptive and compensatory strategies to increase an individual's performance in activities of daily living, work, play, or leisure. Interventions include the use of activities designed to improve performance, as well as the identification of adaptive equipment, environmental modifications, and alternative methods necessary to support improved function. Occupational therapy practitioners assume a collaborative partnership with the person served and their significant others to support the individual's rights to self-direction. Also, occupational therapy practitioners work collaboratively with other professionals to help ensure access to interventions and services in support of full inclusion.

Occupational therapy advocates that society has an obligation to provide reasonable accommodations necessary to allow individuals to access social, vocational, educational, and recreational opportunities. By embracing an attitude of full inclusion, all individuals will benefit from the opportunities afforded by a diverse society.

Considering the social, psychological, and structural perspectives of inclusion offers a more holistic understanding of this most important foundation of schooling. To maximize positive engagement in learning opportunities, students must be in environments in which they feel psychologically safe, accepted, and cared about, and in which curriculum and instruction are skillfully designed to meet their unique learning capacities and needs. Physical proximity (i.e., presence in the general education setting) is a necessary but insufficient condition. Team members also require a psychologically safe environment if they are to do their best work to realize inclusive and effective schooling for all students. Working in the context of a collegial and collaborative team can offer this support.

Related Services

This book focuses on integrating occupational therapy, physical therapy, and speech-language pathology services in the context of educational programs. These specific services are three of many referred to in federal law as related educational services (IDEA, 1990):

> The term "related services" means transportation, and such developmental, corrective, and other supportive services (including speech pathology and audiology, psychological services, physical and occupational therapy, recreation, including therapeutic recreation and social work services, and medical and counseling services, including rehabilitation counseling, except that such medical services shall be for diagnostic and evaluation purposes only) as may be required to assist (a) child with a disability to benefit from special education, and includes the early identification and assessment of disabling conditions in children. (20 U.S.C. §1401(a)(17))

Related services, such as occupational therapy, physical therapy, and speech-language pathology services, are available only to students who first qualify for special education services. The intent of the legislation is clear: Services must be focused on directly supporting students to be successful in their special education programs, wherever those programs are provided, including general education, home, or community environments.

Therapy services are required by many students with severe disabilities. Too often, however, these services are designed and provided separately from other parts of students' educational programs. It is not uncommon to have therapy objectives separate from educational objectives, to have therapy services provided only in separate environments, or to have therapists never observe or work with students in their classroom environments. Moreover, the logistical barriers to providing support in integrated environments continue to increase as students are more decentralized in neighborhood schools. New designs of service provision are desperately needed if therapists are to know enough about students' programs to offer effective support and if therapists are to realize a sense of purpose and cohesion in the sometimes fragmented reality of being a related services professional. These needs are heightened even further when therapists provide itinerant services.

When parents, teachers, and therapists do collaborate to integrate related services and education, the resulting programs can be more comprehensive, consistent, well informed, and effective. As discussed later in this book, preliminary research indicates that team members are more satisfied and students realize greater benefits when occupational therapists, physical therapists, and speech-language pathologists collaborate with other members of the educational team to provide integrated related services.

ADOPTING A COLLABORATIVE APPROACH

Since writing our first edition, we have experienced, studied, and read much about collaboration in the context of general education restructuring. We found much about which to be hopeful in terms of schools becoming more collaborative for all students and educators. In fact, it is rare to review the work of major authors and change agents in the field of education (e.g., Fullan, 1991, 1993a, 1993b; Lieberman & Miller, 1991; Louis & Kruse, 1995; Sergiovanni, 1994) without finding direct reference to the need for schools to be communities, for educators to learn with and from one another, for colleagues to join together locally in creating new instructional designs to better accommodate student diversity, and for teachers to team teach for portions of each day. Leaders in the field of organizational development and change further assert the need for facilitating positive and collaborative working relationships among the people in organizations to maximize effectiveness; and outcomes (see, e.g., Covey, 1989, 1992; Senge, Kleiner, Roberts, Ross, & Smith, 1994; Wheatley, 1994).

Johnson and Pugach (1996) describe three waves of collaboration between the systems of general and special education. The first wave focused on expert consultation by special educators (and sometimes related services professionals) to general educators. Often this resulted in general educators returning to their classrooms feeling more overwhelmed because of the increased expectations in the absence of "real" support in their daily classroom realities. In addition, special educators and related services personnel did not always understand the context variables operating in the general education settings. Sometimes this led to making suggestions that were irrelevant or difficult to implement without support in the classroom. A second wave of collaboration was characterized by more mutual interaction in which joint problem solving was the focus. In the third emerging wave, collaboration is viewed as a foundation of educational restructuring. With general education moving toward more collaborative ways of working, Johnson and Pugach suggest that special education has an important and potentially

central role in creating effective schools for all students. Clearly, many special educators and related services personnel possess extensive and positive collaboration experiences that could be brought to bear in the larger system of education. Evelyn Deno's (1970) early conceptualizations of special education as *development capital* for general education may be approaching reality.

Some readers might think the promise of benefits to both the students and team members would be sufficient to motivate teams to pioneer their way to a collaborative team approach. Unfortunately, this expectation is not supported by the research on systems change in education. The dominant culture of professional isolation in schools continues and is not easily changed. The culture of isolation decreases the risk taking and personal responsibility that are necessary to adopt innovations. Through extensive study of the adoption of innovations in educational programs, Hord, Rutherford, Huling-Austin, and Hall (1987) concluded that each individual reacts differently to change and needs support and training that respond to individual concerns about the innovation and change process. Hord et al. found that educators moved through several stages of concern, which fall into three categories: self-concerns, task concerns, and impact concerns. *Self-concerns* reflect the desire for more information about what the innovation is, the type of support available, and the personal risks involved if the innovation is to be adopted. *Task concerns* reflect the need for more information about how to use the innovation, and frustration with the effects of using the innovation inefficiently. *Impact concerns* reflect the desire to determine the benefits of the innovation and to identify strategies that would improve use. Movement through these stages of concern typically occurs in a developmental fashion, although the intensity of each stage and the rate of movement through stages vary considerably among individuals. Recycling through earlier stages also occurs as new challenges emerge in the process of innovation. Educational team members who are contemplating or currently working to adopt a collaborative team approach can probably identify with one or more of these concerns. Recognizing these concerns as valid and part of the process can ease somewhat the adoption process. In addition, as new ways of thinking and behaving emerge, team members are likely to experience feelings of loss that occur with any significant life transition.

Educational team members are encouraged to use this book as a guide and support as they create a more collaborative approach to providing educational services for students with severe disabilities. Although teams and their students will benefit from the practices described herein, team members are reminded that concerted effort is required for initial adoption, and considerable practice is required before new strategies feel comfortable and efficient. Furthermore, the "recommended practices" described here continue to evolve as teams seek improvements over what they did yesterday. Finally, this book is about fluid and spiraling processes, which, in efforts to address "task concerns" effectively, have been translated into a rather linear set of procedures; therefore, teams are encouraged to reexamine the bases for their actions frequently. Rather than adopt a rigid set of procedures, readers are encouraged to adopt a collaborative team approach as a process that continues to evolve just as the knowledge, abilities, goals, and needs of students and their teams evolve, continually asking "Is this working for the children? What is best for the students?" The evolution of service provision must be driven and guided by maintaining a focus on the desired outcomes of collaboration: student membership and participation in home and community life.

REFERENCES

American Occupational Therapy Association Commission on Practice. (1995). *Full Inclusion Position Paper: Occupational therapy: A profession in support of full inclusion.* Rockville, MD: American Occupational Therapy Association.

Assistance to States for the Education of Children with Disabilities Regulations, 34 C.F.R. §§ 300.7(b)(5) and (b)(6), (1996).

Bogdan, R., & Knoll, J. (1995). The sociology of disability. In E.L. Meyen & T.M. Skrtic (Eds.), *Special education and student disability* (pp. 677–711). Denver: Love Publishing.

Brown, L., Nisbet, J., Ford, A., Sweet, M., Shiraga, B., York, J., & Loomis, R. (1983). The critical need for nonschool instruction in educational programs for severely handicapped students. *The Journal of The Association for the Severely Handicapped, 8*(3), 71–77.

Caine, R.N., & Caine, G. (1994). *Making connections: Teaching and the human brain.* Menlo Park, CA: Addison-Wesley.

Covey, S.R. (1989). *The seven habits of highly effective people: Powerful lessons in personal change.* New York: Fireside.

Covey, S.R. (1992). *Principle-centered leadership.* New York: Fireside.

Deno, E. (1970). Special education as development capital. *Exceptional Children, 37,* 229–237.

Education for All Handicapped Children Act of 1975, PL 94-142, 20 U.S.C. §§1400 *et seq.*

Falvey, M.A. (1989). *Community-based curriculum: Instructional strategies for students with severe handicaps* (2nd ed.). Baltimore: Paul H. Brookes Publishing Co.

Falvey, M.A., Grenot-Scheyer, M., Coots, J.J., & Bishop, K.D. (1995). Services for students with disabilities: Past and present. In M.A. Falvey (Ed.), *Inclusive and heterogeneous schooling: Assessment, curriculum, and instruction* (pp. 23–40). Baltimore: Paul H. Brookes Publishing Co.

Fullan, M.G. (1991). *The new meaning of educational change.* New York: Teachers College Press.

Fullan, M.G. (1993a). *Change forces: Probing the depths of educational reform.* Bristol, PA: Falmer Press.

Fullan, M.G. (1993b). Innovation, reform, and restructuring strategies. In G. Cawelti (Ed.),

Challenges and achievements of American education: 1993 ASCD Yearbook (pp. 116–133). Alexandria, VA: Association for Supervision and Curriculum Development.

Hord, S.M., Rutherford, W.L., Huling-Austin, L., & Hall, G.E. (1987). *Taking charge of change.* Alexandria, VA: Association for Supervision and Curriculum Development.

Individuals with Disabilities Education Act (IDEA) of 1990, PL 101-476, 20 U.S.C. §§ 1400 *et seq.*

Johnson, D.W., & Johnson, R.T. (1989). *Cooperation and competition: Theory and research.* Edina, MN: Interaction Book Company.

Johnson, L.J., & Pugach, M.C. (1996). The emerging third wave of collaboration: Beyond problem-solving. In W. Stainback & S. Stainback (Eds.), *Controversial issues confronting special education: Divergent perspectives* (pp. 197–204). Newton, MA: Allyn & Bacon.

Langone, J. (1996). Mild mental retardation. In P.J. McLaughlin & P. Wehman (Eds.), *Mental retardation and developmental disabilities* (2nd ed., pp. 113–142). Austin, TX: PRO-ED.

Lieberman, A., & Miller, L. (Eds.). (1991). *Staff development for education in the '90s* (2nd ed.). New York: Teachers College Press.

Louis, K.S., & Kruse, S. (1995). *Professionalism and community: Perspectives on reforming urban schools.* Thousand Oaks, CA: Sage Publishers and Corwin Press.

Luckasson, R., Coulter, D.L., Polloway, E.A., Reiss, S., Schalock, R.L., Snell, M.E., Spitalnik, D.M., & Stark, J.A. (1992). *Mental retardation: Definition, classification, and systems of supports.* Washington, DC: American Association on Mental Retardation.

O'Brien, J., & Mount, B. (1991). Telling new stories: The search for capacity among people with severe handicaps. In L.H. Meyer, C.A. Peck, & L. Brown (Eds.), *Critical issues in the lives of people with severe disabilities* (pp. 89–92). Baltimore: Paul H. Brookes Publishing Co.

Senge, P., Kleiner, A., Roberts, C., Ross, R.B., & Smith, B.J. (1994). *The fifth discipline fieldbook: Strategies and tools for building a learning organization.* New York: Doubleday and Dell Publishing Group.

Sergiovanni, T.J. (1994). *Building community in schools.* San Francisco: Jossey-Bass.

Strully, J.L., & Strully, C.F. (1989). Friendships as an educational goal. In S. Stainback, W. Stainback, & M. Forest (Eds.), *Educating all students in the mainstream of regular education* (pp. 59–68). Baltimore: Paul H. Brookes Publishing Co.

The Association for Persons with Severe Handicaps. (1989). *TASH resolutions and policy statements.* Seattle, WA: Author.

Turner, C.S.V., & Louis, K.S. (1996). Society's response to differences: A sociological perspective. *Remedial and Special Education, 17*(3), 134–141.

Wheatley, M.J. (1994). *Leadership and the new science: Learning about organization from an orderly universe.* San Francisco: Barrett-Koehler Publishers.

York-Barr, J., Kronberg, R., & Doyle, M.E. (1996). *Creating inclusive school communities: A staff development series for general and special educators: Module 1. A shared agenda for general and special educators.* Baltimore: Paul H. Brookes Publishing Co.

2

Foundations of
Collaborative Teamwork

Students with severe disabilities are entitled to related educational services under the provisions of PL 101-476, the Individuals with Disabilities Education Act (IDEA) of 1990. As a result, it has become relatively commonplace since the mid-1970s to include physical therapists, occupational therapists, and speech-language pathologists on educational teams in the public schools. The educational domain has become a common arena of practice for professionals who, historically, were associated with medical models of service provision. Increasingly, therapists and other related services personnel are providing services in ways that complement the movement to integrate students with severe disabilities into their local public schools and into general education environments with special education support (Falvey, 1986, 1989, 1995; Stainback & Stainback, 1992, 1996; Thousand et al., 1986; Williams, Fox, Thousand, & Fox, 1990). This evolution of service provision is reflected in the "Position Statement on the Provision of Related Services" of The Association for Persons with Severe Handicaps (TASH), which asserts that the role of related services personnel is to collaborate with one another and with teachers and families in the design and implementation of programs that support the participation of individuals with severe disabilities in typical family, school, and community life (TASH, 1986) (see Figure 2.1). Other national organizations also have promoted an integrated model of therapy that supports the educational programs of students with disabilities in the public schools (American Occupational Therapy Association, 1989; American Physical Therapy Association [APTA], 1990; American Speech-Language-Hearing Association Committee on Language Learning Disorders, 1991).

Many educators and therapists generally recognize the potential benefits of collaboration, but mere recognition does not involve in-depth didactic or experiential learning op-

15

The Association for Persons with Severe Handicaps (TASH) is an international organization whose primary purpose is to advocate for and support exemplary models of service delivery for persons with severe handicaps.

Many persons with severe handicaps have complex and challenging needs. The expertise of related services professionals, such as physical therapists, occupational therapists, and speech and language pathologists is frequently required.

TASH believes that related services personnel have expertise and can contribute in the process of integrating persons with severe handicaps into typical home community life. A high degree of collaboration and sharing of information and skills must occur among families, direct services providers, and related services personnel.

The provision of integrated services requires that related services personnel:
1. Establish priorities with parents/advocates and other team members.
2. Observe and assess persons with handicaps in natural settings.
3. Collaborate with family and team members to provide intervention strategies and adaptations that optimize participation in natural settings.
4. Teach specific and individualized procedures to enhance functional positioning, movement, and communication abilities in natural settings.
5. Evaluate the effectiveness of intervention procedures based on performance outcomes in natural settings.

Figure 2.1.   TASH position statement on the provision of related services to people with severe handicaps. (From The Association for Persons with Severe Handicaps. [1986]. *Position statement on the provision of related services.* Seattle, WA: Author; reprinted by permission.)

portunities directed at enhancing collaborative dispositions, knowledge, and skills. Furthermore, once employed, it is not uncommon for practicing therapists to work in a school environment in which the broader school culture does not facilitate collaborative interactions among staff. Professionals who are members of educational teams have been prepared in different approaches to service provision, with one of the biggest differences being that teachers are trained in an educational model and therapists in a medical model. There are philosophical, theoretical, and practical differences between these models (Hanft & Place, 1996; Ottenbacher, 1982) that can serve as challenges to collaboration among professionals from educational and medical disciplines. Some authors (e.g., McEwen & Sheldon, 1995) assert that the distinctions are no longer relevant, but in practice differences have not been addressed or reconciled. Although professional preservice education generally includes didactic information about teamwork, few preservice training programs provide instruction or experiences that prepare graduates for truly collaborative models of service provision (Aksamit & Alcorn, 1988; Rainforth, 1985; Sapon-Shevin, 1988; Stainback & Stainback, 1987; York, Rainforth, & Dunn, 1990). Furthermore, few professional training programs model or expect interdisciplinary or transdisciplinary themes (Cross, Collins, & Boam-Wood, 1996); rather, they perpetuate unidisciplinary thinking, with assessment, program planning, and service provision approached in isolation from a single-discipline perspective. Given the lack of preservice or professional practice support, it is not surprising that the personal, professional, and contextual challenges faced in the process of creating collaborative ways of working often exceed the desire or capacity of individual professionals from various disciplines to work together effectively.

When working in isolation from one another, team members may communicate about a child only at annual and periodic review meetings; rarely do they collaborate in ways that result in effective, integrated programs and supports that enhance student participation in family, school, and community life. Herein lies a disconcerting paradox in the design of educational programs for students with long-term, intensive, and multiple disabilities. When professionals do not assume responsibility for the synthesis, integration, application, and generalization of fragmented, sometimes conflicting, program components (e.g., special education, physical therapy, speech-language pathology), they inadvertently shift the responsibility of synthesis and integration onto the very people who require their assistance to "pull it all together" in meeting daily life opportunities and challenges: students with severe disabilities and their families. Traditional isolated and fragmented approaches to service provision have been problematic for students, their families, and service providers. Such approaches seem to be maintained more by default than by a deliberate, well-informed choice to continue separate ways of working. Special educators and therapists have consistently reported favoring greater degrees of integrated services than realized in their own educational settings (Effgen & Klepper, 1994; McWilliam & Bailey, 1994), suggesting that practitioners need assistance translating philosophies and general principles into day-to-day practice.

This chapter establishes the foundations of a collaborative teamwork approach for integrating related services into educational programs for students with severe disabilities. Specifically, the chapter offers 1) meanings of collaborative teamwork, 2) a comprehensive rationale for collaborative teamwork, 3) an overview of team member roles and contributions, and 4) unifying assumptions of collaborative teamwork in ed-

ucational programs for students with severe disabilities. This information provides the overarching framework for the remainder of the book. Following this chapter are chapters focused more specifically on creating individualized student programs. The final two chapters of the book, Chapters 8 and 9, return to an explicit discussion on collaboratively designing strategies for establishing teamwork practices that support an integrated program design.

MEANINGS OF COLLABORATIVE TEAMWORK

According to *Webster's Ninth New Collegiate Dictionary* (1987), "collaborate" is from the Latin derivatives *com* and *laborare,* which means to "labor together." Other definitions from this source include "to work jointly with others," and "to cooperate with." Teamwork is defined as "work done by several associates with each doing a part but all subordinating personal prominence to the efficiency of the whole" (*Webster's,* 1987). Collaboration has definitely become a buzzword in the 1990s. In the special education and related services literature, collaboration is generally considered to be a process in which problems or goals are addressed by a team of individuals, each of whom contributes his or her knowledge and skills and is viewed as having equal status (Dettmer, Dyck, & Thurston, 1996; Morsink, Thomas, & Correa, 1991; Pugach & Johnson, 1995; Vandercook & York, 1990; Whelan, 1996; York, Giangreco, Vandercook, & Macdonald, 1992). A specific application of collaboration, referred to as collaborative consultation, is defined as "an interactive process that enables people with diverse expertise to generate creative solutions to mutually defined problems" and presumes the desired outcome is enhanced student learning in the most appropriate integrated context (Idol, Nevin, & Paolucci-Whitcomb, 1994, p. 1).

Emphasizing the interpersonal nature of collaboration, Friend and Cook (1996) state that "interpersonal collaboration is a style for direct interaction between at least two co-equal parties voluntarily engaged in shared decision-making as they work toward a common goal" (p. 6). They contrast a collaborative style of interaction with styles that are more directive or authoritative and with those that are more passive or accommodating. Also offered are characteristics that more fully describe the essence of collaboration, including voluntary, involving parity among participants, based on mutual goals, dependent on shared responsibility for participation and decision making, sharing resources, and sharing accountability for outcomes (Friend & Cook, 1996).

Drawing from aspects of each of these meanings of collaboration and adding to them our own, we express *collaboration* as an interactive process in which individuals with varied life perspectives and experiences join together in a spirit of willingness to share resources, responsibility, and rewards in creating inclusive and effective educational programs and environments for students with unique learning capacities and needs. A high degree of collaboration has been considered the hallmark of the transdisciplinary and integrated therapy approaches to teamwork advocated for students with severe disabilities for more than 20 years (e.g., Albano, Cox, York, & York, 1981; Dunn, 1991; Effgen, 1995; Giangreco, York, & Rainforth, 1989; Hart, 1977; Nietupski, Scheutz, & Ockwood, 1980; Orelove & Sobsey, 1987, 1991, 1996; Patterson et al., 1976; Peterson, 1980; Rainforth & York, 1987; Sternat, Messina, Nietupski, Lyon, & Brown, 1977; York, Rainforth, & Giangreco, 1990). In this book, collaborative teamwork is conceptualized as

embracing both the transdisciplinary and integrated therapy approaches for students with severe disabilities. Although these two approaches have evolved in a complementary manner, there are several distinctions between them.

Transdisciplinary Teamwork

Historically, early intervention services and habilitation services for infants, children, and adults with disabilities have been deeply rooted in a medical orientation in which individuals with disabilities are perceived as sick or able to be "fixed" (see Lane, 1976). This history, paired with the preparation of many team members as health or allied health professionals, has sustained the predominance of the medical model in special education programs. A medical orientation is reflected in the practice of individual disciplines focusing on separate aspects of performance (e.g., gross motor, fine motor, vision, health, language) and taking children for "treatment" with the assumption that the treatment, even though episodic and fragmented, will yield improved isolated performance that will eventually generalize in meaningful ways to everyday life. In a medical model, if isolated performance is not achieved, children are judged "unable to benefit" from therapy and treatment is discontinued. Prior to the legal education mandate for related services, therapy for children with severe disabilities frequently was discontinued not necessarily because these children were incapable of further growth but because services that were episodic and isolated did not tap the child's potential. Unfortunately, some still advocate those isolated models and subsequent student exclusion (Parette, Hourcade, & Brimer, 1996), but this situation started improving somewhat with introduction of the transdisciplinary approach. *Paramount to the transdisciplinary approach is an understanding that the multiple needs of children are inter-related.* The medical model is better suited to treatment of people with acute illness and isolated injuries than to long-term education of children with significant learning difficulties.

Transdisciplinary teamwork models emerged in recognition of the fact that children do not perform isolated skills irrespective of function and environmental demands. That is, to function in any daily environment, activity, or routine requires efficient and integrated use of sensorimotor, cognitive, and communication abilities. Attempting to elicit communication without regard for motoric influence, for example, is likely to impede optimal performance. Understanding the varied influences on function and the ability to integrate this understanding into instruction requires cross-disciplinary sharing of information and skills. Herein lies a defining characteristic of transdisciplinary team function: *role release.* Role release is a process of transferring information and skills traditionally associated with one discipline to team members of other disciplines (Lyon & Lyon, 1980; Patterson et al., 1976).

The role release construct as defined by Lyon and Lyon (1980) involves three levels: 1) sharing general information about basic concepts, approaches, and practices; 2) sharing informational skills, which includes more detailed information about specific practices or methods; and 3) sharing performance competencies, which involves actually teaching specific interventions or methods to other team members. The nature and degree of information that must be shared among team members are related directly to individual student needs in educational activities. For example, all team members may be appropriate recipients of general information about the sensorimotor or communication abilities of a student with severe disabilities. Only selected team members may need to learn specific intervention methods that facilitate and improve sensorimotor and communication skills of students. Team members collaborate in determining the nature and scope of role release to ensure that the people who implement interventions have the necessary information, skills, and support to do so effectively.

More recently, Hanft and Place (1996) offered specific guidelines for making decisions about strategies, methods, and interaction styles to use when therapists serve in a consulting role, which necessarily involves some degree of role release. As part of the process for planning a student's program and determining related services members' roles, the team determines the intervention strategies that can best achieve desired outcomes for students. If the expertise of a related services provider is required, decisions are made about the best methods and styles of interaction for transferring information and actions from the related services provider to an individual who will be working on a regular basis with the student. Patterson et al. (1976) emphasized the importance of ongoing involvement and accountability, which are never abandoned, throughout all stages of role release. That is, even when team decisions are made such that therapists teach others varied interventions, therapists do not release responsibility for ensuring that students are appropriately supported. It is delegation, not abdication.

The transdisciplinary approach originally was conceived as a framework for professionals to share important information and skills with primary caregivers, including parents of infants with complex disabilities and aides in residential institutions (Hutchison, 1978). This enabled primary caregivers to develop greater consistency in meeting the integrated needs of children by developing competence in addressing motor, communication, health, and other needs. This approach also decreased the sometimes large number of different service providers with whom the individual with disabilities, or his or her family, had to interact on an intensive basis. The transdisciplinary concept had a revolutionary and positive effect on services for people with disabilities because it initiated the sharing of skills that previously had been considered the exclusive domain of individual disciplines. Parents, educators, occupational therapists, physical therapists, speech-language pathologists, psychologists, nurses, and others began implementing role release to design more integrated programs for children with disabilities. These transdisciplinary services involved a much greater degree of collaboration than traditional models that employed unidisciplinary, multidisciplinary, and occasionally interdisciplinary practices (see Table 2.1).

Although the transdisciplinary teamwork model resulted in many positive changes in service provision and interactions among individuals with varied discipline backgrounds, an important element was missing from its conceptualization. The transdisciplinary approach addressed who provides services and how multiple needs can be addressed by virtually any team member given training and ongoing support, but the *context* of service provision (i.e., where and in what circumstances services are provided) was not a key element of the approach. As a result, parents, teachers, and health and residential service providers often became pseudotherapists by implementing methods associated with various disciplines; however, a major struggle continued when sensorimotor, communication, or other skills were taught in contexts that were not particularly interesting or relevant for the child. Many professionals who initially were excited by the potential of the transdisciplinary approach became disillusioned in its application when context was not considered. Almost simultaneously, however, an ap-

Table 2.1.   Evolution of the transdisciplinary model

Model	Objective
Unidisciplinary	Developing competency in one's own field
Intradisciplinary	Believing that the effort you and others make in your field can make contributions to individuals with disabilities
Multidisciplinary	Recognizing the important contributions of other disciplines to individuals with disabilities. Enunciating a philosophy that comprehensive services based on individual needs must be made available to all individuals with disabilities
Interdisciplinary	Working with other disciplines in the development of jointly planned programs for individuals with disabilities
Transdisciplinary	Committing oneself to teaching, learning, and working with others across traditional disciplinary boundaries to better serve individuals with disabilities

From Patterson, E.G., D'Wolff, N., Hutchison, P., Lowry, M., Schilling, M., & Siepp, J. (1976). *Staff development handbook: A resource for the transdisciplinary process.* New York: United Cerebral Palsy Associations, Inc.; adapted by permission.

proach that addressed the context for therapy services was evolving in many educational programs. This approach is referred to as integrated therapy.

Integrated Therapy

The integrated therapy approach (Albano et al., 1981; Campbell, 1987; Giangreco et al., 1989; Rainforth & York, 1987; Sternat et al., 1977) evolved to emphasize providing services within contexts considered meaningful or functional for an individual (student), and thus has become an important complement to transdisciplinary service provision. When implementing an integrated approach to therapy, a student who is developing mobility skills, for example, receives instruction during the times of the day when he or she needs to make transitions, such as when moving between activities in the classroom or when traveling to and from the bus or cafeteria. Mobility instruction might be provided by the physical therapist or by other members of the student's educational team who have been trained and supported by the physical therapist.[1] Regardless of who provides the instruction, the intervention methods are instructionally and contextually integrated. That is, the instruction integrates strategies from varied disciplines as appropriate and is provided in the contexts in which students need to demonstrate motor, communication, and other skills so that participation in everyday life is enhanced.

There are several benefits to providing services in these real-life situations. First, the team takes responsibility for identifying relevant contexts in which students might use emerging skills and then designs interventions to elicit desired performance in those contexts, rather than leaving generalization to chance. Second, therapy services do not have to compete with the important formative aspects of schooling experiences because typical school activities and routines are recognized as rich with social, cognitive, communication, and motor learning opportunities. Students do not have to be removed from the typical educational context. Third, by integrating therapy services into everyday contexts, children learn to respond to the natural cues and contingencies that exist in most home, school, and community environments. The net effect is that children acquire new motor and communication skills in more meaningful situations, which are also more likely to support and encourage continued use.

Many agree that it makes sense to provide direct instruction in real-life situations, but some would argue that only therapists should provide the direct instruction (therapy) for sensorimotor and communication skill acquisition in those situations. Two major problems arise when integrated therapy provided only by a therapist is the exclusive approach to service provision. First, it presumes that a therapist will always be available to teach a student during natural learning opportunities, and that no other students will need intervention during those time periods and activities. For example, if the speech-language pathologist is scheduled on a daily basis to facilitate communication during the transition to first-period class, that therapist cannot be in any other situation with any other students during that

---

[1]State laws governing the practice of physical therapy, occupational therapy, and speech-language therapy often specify that physical therapy services, for example, can be provided only by a physical therapist or designated paraprofessional. Therefore, when adhering to a transdisciplinary and integrated approach to "therapy," it is appropriate to say that a teacher (or other "nontherapist") is teaching motor skills or reinforcing the physical therapy program, but it is inaccurate to communicate that a teacher is providing physical therapy services. By definition, only the activities performed directly by the physical therapist are considered physical therapy.

time. Second, such an approach is based on the inaccurate presumption that students have circumscribed disabilities and needs that can be addressed in isolation from one another—for example, that the speech-language pathologist can facilitate communication without regard to interfering sensorimotor abilities. As is discussed in Chapter 4, it is most effective to provide instruction in clusters of motor, communication, social, and cognitive skills in the context of everyday activities. To do so requires that team members with expertise in these areas pool their knowledge to design comprehensive and integrated instructional methods. In other words, providing effective integrated therapy services almost always requires the role release that typifies the transdisciplinary team approach.

Collaborative Teamwork

To realize the benefits of the perspectives, knowledge, and skills of numerous disciplines throughout a student's educational program, we advocate a combination of transdisciplinary and integrated therapy approaches to service provision. In this book, we use the term *collaborative teamwork* to reflect essential and complementary components of both integrated therapy and transdisciplinary approaches to service provision. *Integrated therapy* refers to the services that provide students with severe disabilities frequent opportunities to learn functional motor, communication, and other skills as part of natural routines in integrated school and community environments (Sternat et al., 1977). *Transdisciplinary* refers to the sharing of information and skills among team members across traditional discipline domains (Hutchison, 1978; Patterson et al., 1976). This enables the team to implement an integrated therapy approach to service provision. Defining characteristics of a *collaborative team* approach that combines integrated therapy and transdisciplinary services are presented in Table 2.2. Implementation is flexible and incorporates both direct and indirect services from therapists.

Team members who are not therapists are likely to provide the majority of sensorimotor and communication instruction on a daily basis. To maintain program integrity, however, therapists must maintain direct, "hands-on" involvement with students on a regular basis. APTA, for example, specifies that

when therapists provide specific child/procedure consultation, direct service in the educational environments is required:
To evaluate the child's initial abilities and needs;
To determine appropriate intervention procedures;
To train other team members to use the procedures;
To confirm that others use the procedures properly;
To confirm that procedures are promoting the desired outcome for the child;
To revise procedures when the child achieves objectives or is not making satisfactory progress; and
To provide ongoing supervision (including retraining) to team members who use the procedures. (1990, p. 3.8)

An essential component of a collaborative model of program support, therefore, is a structure that provides opportunities for therapists to remain involved directly with students. The major differences between the collaborative model and traditional service provision models are where, how frequently, and in what capacities or roles the therapists have that direct involvement. Therapists' roles shift to spending more time observing and analyzing student abilities in educational activities and more time collaborating with classroom staff to integrate instructional methods (Hanft & Place, 1996).

Table 2.2.   Defining characteristics of collaborative teamwork

1. Equal participation in the collaborative teamwork process by family members and the educational service providers on the educational team

2. Equal participation by all disciplines determined to be necessary for students to achieve their individualized educational goals

3. Consensus decision making about priority educational goals and objectives related to all areas of student functioning at school, at home, and in the community

4. Consensus decision making about the type and amount of support required from related services personnel

5. Attention to motor, communication, and other embedded skills and needs throughout the educational program and in direct relevance to accomplishing priority educational goals

6. Infusion of knowledge and skills from different disciplines into the design of educational methods and interventions

7. Role release to enable team members who are involved most directly and frequently with students to develop the confidence and competence necessary to facilitate active learning and effective participation in the educational program

8. Collaborative problem solving and shared responsibility for student learning across all aspects of the educational program

There are many ways to implement collaborative teamwork services in educational programs. Because teachers, paraprofessionals, and parents are the most likely individuals to accompany and support students with severe disabilities during natural learning opportunities at home, at school, and in the community, they are logical implementers or facilitators of ongoing instruction to promote improved motor and communication skills. Perhaps the most frequent strategy, therefore, involves teachers and paraeducators learning to incorporate methods traditionally associated with the therapy disciplines throughout daily educational activities. Many parents, special education teachers, and paraeducators have developed competence in implementing methods traditionally associated with the practices of physical and occupational therapy and speech-language pathology (Albano, 1983; Coufal, 1993; Giangreco, 1986; Inge &

Snell, 1985; McCollum & Stayton, 1985; Peck, Killen, & Baumgart, 1989).

Another strategy is team teaching, such as a teacher and a speech-language pathologist conducting reading class together, or a physical therapist and a physical education teacher teaching a physical education unit together. A variety of team teaching and other adult collaboration strategies have evolved recently in an effort to combine and integrate expertise so that students with diverse needs can learn well in general education and other integrated environments (Bauwens & Hourcade, 1995; Friend & Cook, 1996; Stainback, Stainback, & Harris, 1989). All collaborative teamwork approaches require team members to engage in joint planning and role release. The exact way in which team members collaborate to design and implement effective educational plans, including related services, will vary according to local resources, logistical considerations, local school district program design, and particular experience and expertise of team members. Strategies for making these determinations are presented in Chapter 8.

A third strategy is to recruit support from classmates and friends who are available to provide support throughout daily school activities (Jorgensen, 1992; Kronberg, York-Barr, & Doyle, 1996; Thousand, Villa, & Nevin, 1994; Villa & Thousand, 1992). Many peers are interested, willing, and competent in assisting their classmates and friends with disabilities to participate, to learn, and to contribute in daily life. Although we do not advocate delegating professional responsibilities to students, we recognize the important contributions and mutual benefits that can be realized and so encourage their participation in the educational process. Fostering positive interdependence, caring, and a sense of community among students during their public schooling is emerging as a critical component in the broader arena of educational and social reform as well (Noddings, 1992).

RATIONALE FOR COLLABORATIVE TEAMWORK

The collective work, or goal, of individuals joining together as members of collaborative teams is the design and facilitation of curricular, instructional, and social support so that students achieve their individually meaningful, thoughtfully considered educational goals. Broadly conceptualized, the goals of each student's education are presence, participation, achievement, contribution, and satisfaction in home and community life (National Center for Educational Outcomes, 1995; Ysseldyke & Thurlow, 1994). Such goals or outcomes of education are found in state statutes and regulations and in mission statements and graduation outcomes articulated by state

departments, school districts, and building-based personnel. For example, in Minnesota

> The legislature declares that the purpose of public education in Minnesota is to help all individuals acquire knowledge, skills, and positive attitudes toward self and others that will enable them to solve problems, think creatively, continue learning, and develop maximum potential for leading productive, fulfilling lives in a complex and changing society. (Education Code: Prekindergarten–Grade 12, Minn. Stat. § 120.011 [1985])

The mission of education is articulated as follows:

> The mission of public education in Minnesota, a system of lifelong learning, is to ensure individual academic achievement, an informed citizenry, and a highly productive work force. This system focuses on the learner, promotes and values diversity, provides participatory decision-making, ensures accountability, models democratic principles, creates and sustains a climate for change, provides personalized learning environments, encourages learners to reach their maximum potential, and integrates and coordinates human services for learners. (Education Code: Prekindergarten–Grade 12, Minn. Stat. § 120.011 [1991])

Also in Minnesota statutes is a clear statement as to the purpose of the Individualized Education Plan:

> The Individualized Education Plan for each child with disabilities shall address the student's needs to develop skills to live and work as independently as possible in the community. (Education Code: Prekindergarten–Grade 12, Minn. Stat. § 120.17 [1985])

Articulated in these excerpts are assertions that a child's time in public education is intended to support, if not maximize, her or his capacity to live and contribute in society. Michael Fullan (1993), an internationally renowned scholar on school change, emphasizes that "education has a moral purpose . . . to make a difference in the lives of students regardless of background, and to help produce citizens who can live and work productively in increasingly dynamically complex societies'' (p. 4). Schools have been created and personnel hired for this purpose. Increasing numbers of schools are designing large-scale participatory efforts to establish locally owned and supported specific outcomes. Clarity and ownership regarding outcomes serves as an important basis for designing and redesigning educational service delivery systems.

This section articulates a comprehensive rationale for why collaborative teamwork is an essential support for achieving educational outcomes, especially for those children whose abilities are unique and whose life experiences often are challenging (Table 2.3). Included in this rationale are 1) school culture and the potential of collegiality; 2) diverse perspectives enhancing quality directions and outcomes; 3) the influence of context on learning; 4) learning characteristics of students with severe disabilities; 5) recommended educational practices for students with severe disabilities; 6) legal mandates and precedents, including *educational relevance;* and 7) guidelines for therapy practice in educational environments.

School Culture and the Potential of Collegiality

The environments in which we work have a large impact on how we work, how we feel about our work, and what we are able to accomplish. Isolation as a pervasive characteristic of school culture is reason for great concern. Fullan and Hargreaves (1991) explain:

> Teaching has long been called "a lonely profession," always in pejorative terms. The professional isolation of teachers limits access to new ideas and better solutions, drives stress inward to fester and accumulate, fails to recognize and praise success, and permits incompetence to exist and persist to the detriment of students, colleagues and the teachers themselves. . . . The problem of isolation is a deep-seated one. Architecture often supports it. The timetable reinforces it. Overload sustains it. History legitimizes it. (pp. 5–6)

Collaboration is increasingly viewed as a source of hope, if not inspiration, to address the presence of isolation. In Rosenholtz's (1989) study of "stuck" and "moving" schools, she found that, in "moving" schools, teachers viewed teaching as difficult and expected that they needed to be continually learning with and from one another and using outside resources to effectively do their jobs. Seeking assistance and support was seen not as a sign of weakness but as a recognition of the need for continuous learning. "It is assumed that improvement in teaching is a collective rather than an individual enterprise, and that analysis, evaluation, and experimentation in concert with colleagues are conditions under which teachers improve" (p. 73).

As collaborative interactions among faculty expand, schools begin to emerge as communities with strong connections among

Table 2.3. Major reasons for a collaborative teamwork model of service provision for students with severe disabilities

School culture and the potential of collegiality
Diverse perspectives enhancing quality directions and outcomes
The influence of context on learning
Learning characteristics of students with severe disabilities
Recommended educational practices for students with severe disabilities
Legal mandates and precedents, including *educational relevance*
Guidelines for therapy practice in educational environments

members. Sergiovanni (1994) points out the pervasiveness of the language of *community* in school restructuring literature and dialogue—*community of learners, professional communities,* and *caring and inclusive communities* are just some examples. He provides insight about the meaning and significance of *community* in everyone's lives, and perhaps especially in the lives of today's children and youth given this time of great social, family, and community challenges: "When students experience a loss of community they have two options: to create substitutes for this loss or to live without community, with negative psychological consequences. Unfortunately, the substitutes that young people create are often dysfunctional or distorted" (p. 11). In his book, *Building Community in Schools,* Sergiovanni asserts and substantiates the position that the establishment of community is an essential precursor to maximizing learning potential, for children and adults.

Perhaps one of the most exciting aspects of becoming involved with change in general education is realizing that creating collaborative cultures in schools is a shared endeavor, which can also unite general education and special education and related services. Increasingly, educators and leaders of school reform are recognizing the deleterious effects of isolation on learning and growth of professionals, which goes on to interfere with professional renewal. Central to many restructuring initiatives is greater collegiality and meaningful connections among members of the school community (Louis & Kruse, 1996). Gossen and Anderson (1995) describe the benefits of a *collegial school* over *conventional schools* or *congenial schools. Conventional schools* operate with traditional hierarchical structures and staff isolation dominates. In *congenial schools,* there are strong interpersonal relationships but professional complacency.

Collegial schools are characterized by co-operative goal structures, vigorous dialogue about educational practices in light of beliefs and current knowledge, no surprise or fear about disagreement, and a deepened sense of belonging as a result of meaningful professional interactions.

Special educators and related services personnel have a procedural, if not structural, advantage over many classroom teachers in that the very nature of their work requires interactions with adult colleagues. What are frequently absent, however, are meaningful interactions and consideration of varied perspectives that extend beyond mere greetings, exchanges of paper, and one-way sharing of discipline-specific information. Given the necessity of related services professionals working with and through teachers and other team members, the potential exists to deepen the interactions and promote ongoing professional support and renewal.

Diverse Perspectives Enhancing Quality Directions and Outcomes

Closely aligned with the previous discussion is recognition that sharing diverse perspectives has the potential to greatly increase the quality of creative solutions developed to address issues that emerge in the daily work in schools. Practicing educators live the daily reality of ambiguity, uncertainty, and complexity in their classrooms and schools. Recognizing the lack of "textbook answers" to dilemmas, *reflective practice* with colleagues is emerging as an important process in school reform (Montie, 1996). Although consensus is lacking about a meaning of *reflection,* Sparks-Langer and Colton (1991) note that "the opposite of reflective action is the mindless following of unexamined practices or principles" (p. 37). When team members consider diverse perspectives, they can critically examine their own assumptions (Johnston, 1994; Smyth, 1989). "Hearing other perspectives can affirm one's current efforts or situation. At other times, hearing other views may be an inspiration for change by providing a compelling, alternative action" (Montie, 1996, p. 28). Schon (1987) provides an illustrative metaphor by which to consider the need for ongoing reflection in the daily practice of schooling. He contrasts "high hard ground" knowledge, that which is empirically and analytically derived, with "swamp" knowledge. The reality of many practicing professionals in schools is "the swamp"—a context in which answers are not readily apparent but must be created and re-created as the ambiguities and uncertainties of daily practice unfold. Although recognizing a place for "high hard ground" knowledge, clearly there is a need for support and varied perspective in daily, of-the-moment work. Collegial relationships can provide such support.

Specific to the practice of integrating therapy and education are the interwoven benefits of seeking and integrating unique perspectives and the collegial support realized through such interactions. There are two primary benefits of collaboration among members of the educational team. First, there are the benefits realized because of the diverse perspectives, skills, and knowledge available from the variety of disciplines represented on the educational team. This creates a tremendous resource for problem solving and support and can result in effective, integrated, instructive networks for students. A second benefit of collaboration is derived from the group interaction if structured for cooperative, as opposed to individualistic or competitive, interactions (Johnson & Johnson, 1989).

Each team member brings a unique perspective about an individual student's strengths and challenges. For example, parents have the greatest information about the student's daily life outside of school; teachers are most knowledgeable about requirements and opportunities in the classroom and about curricular and instructional adaptations; physical and occupational therapists bring to the team their knowledge of sensorimotor functioning; and speech-language pathologists contribute strategies for alternative and augmentative communication, including use of language for social interactions. Because of the diversity of the team composition, a wide array of information is brought to bear on common problems and provides the basis for a relevant and effective curricular and instructional design.

Several authors provide examples from practice of both the disciplinary diversity and the benefits of collaboration available through collaborative teamwork. Albano and colleagues (1981) reported that collaboration among disciplines for students with severe disabilities can serve to "unite the highly specialized and fragmented array of professional services with the information and concerns of the family" (p. 23). They went on to report that integrating the knowledge, skills, and services of individual team members can result in reduced duplication of services, more consistent attention to areas of student need throughout the school day, more relevant application of the knowledge and skills of individual disciplines to educational difficulties experienced by students, and ongoing professional growth and development by learning from professionals with differing knowledge and skills. These assertions were subsequently verified in a comprehensive case study for a program that implemented a collaborative teamwork approach to service provision (Albano, 1983). McCormick, Cooper, and Goldman (1979) found that integrating therapy methods in functional daily activities (e.g., dressing, using the rest room) increased the amount of instructional time for students with severe and multiple disabilities, primarily by decreasing the time spent in transport and by replacing passive caregiving with active instruction in daily living activities. Furthermore, they found that efficiency was particularly increased for teachers because they typically assumed primary responsibility for routine caregiving needs. Campbell, McInerney, and Cooper (1984) and Giangreco (1986) found that, by integrating therapy methods in functional activities, skill acquisition increased for individual students.

A second major benefit of collaboration is realized for the group members themselves. Collaborative efforts to achieve mutual goals promote caring and committed relationships and skills critical for psychological health, including developing social competencies, helping others achieve, coping with failure, controlling anxiety, managing conflict, confiding feelings, and expressing needs (Johnson & Johnson, 1989). Positive interdependence among team members can develop such that they recognize the need for and seek out the perspectives of other team members when a problem must be solved. Group problem solving, specifically, has numerous advantages over individual approaches: group membership stimulates greater interest in the problem, collective contributions bring more information to bear on the problem, individual contributions have a summative effect, and a group has a greater capacity to recognize and reject poorly conceived solutions (Kruger, 1988). Brandt (1988) asserted that adults and children have basic needs for belonging, support, and power. Being a member of a collaborative educational team enhances one's sense of belonging. Support is realized when fellow team members listen and acknowledge contributions. Power, in a very positive sense, is felt when team members not only acknowledge contributions but

value and incorporate contributions into problem resolution. Learning teams (Glasser, 1986, 1992) and cooperative teams (Johnson & Johnson, 1987a, 1987b; Johnson, Johnson, & Maruyama, 1983; Slavin, Madden, & Leavey, 1984), and various other collegial and professional teams (Louis & Kruse, 1996; Thousand & Villa, 1992), have been advocated to realize the benefits of group process and collaboration.

For most teams, adopting a collaborative mode of interaction, as opposed to individualistic or competitive modes, requires change in existing organizational structures, as well as in existing job roles and responsibilities. Many of the existing structures in educational programs foster individualistic efforts, such as teachers teaching alone behind closed doors, therapists conducting back-to-back therapy sessions in separate rooms throughout the entire school day, lack of regularly scheduled team meetings, lack of professional development on collaboration skills (e.g., problem solving, conflict resolution, decision making), and individualized education programs (IEPs) organized to require separate reports and objectives from each discipline. In general, schools are not structured to support collaboration among service providers. When educators and therapists primarily work in isolation, they do not realize the support available when ownership and responsibility for student learning is shared.

The Influence of Context on Learning

There is a growing body of literature that emphasizes the profound influence of context on learning. Support is found in educational literature that focuses on advances in learning research. Evidence is also steadily emerging from literature on practices of therapy professionals.

Research in teaching and learning indicates that learning is maximized when participants interact with one another and when they can construct personal meaning from the material or other instructional circumstances (Colton & Sparks-Langer, 1993; Englert, Tarrant, & Mariage, 1992; Grennon & Brooks-Grennon, 1993; Schon, 1987). Until recently, research on teaching focused almost exclusively on the instructional exchange between teacher and student (i.e., teacher behaviors and corresponding student responses). More recent research on *constructivist theory* confirms that "each of us makes sense of our world by synthesizing new experiences into what we have previously come to understand" (Grennon & Brooks-Grennon, 1993, p. 4). Englert and colleagues (1992) offer principles of instruction that have emerged from social constructivist theory and research: 1) embedding instruction in meaningful activities, 2) promoting classroom dialogue for self-regulated learning, 3) demonstrating instructional responsiveness to individual learner needs and realities, and 4) establishing learning communities in classrooms. These principles relate directly to the overarching assumptions of this book:

- Establishing a sense of connectedness among members of the learning community (e.g., general education classroom environment)
- Facilitating positive interdependence among students and among adult team members
- Embedding communication and sensorimotor skill instruction in naturally occurring daily activities and routines

Constructivist principles are violated when teachers and therapists fragment student learning by working on isolated skills in separate environments devoid of purpose or meaning for the student. In new learning paradigms, diversity and collaboration are considered valuable resources for effective learning. Together, new insights are gained,

new knowledge is created, and new solutions emerge to context-specific challenges.

The therapy literature now speaks to the impact of context on learning. Dunn, Brown, and McGuigan (1994) describe a framework for considering the effect of context in the practice of occupational therapy. They refer to this framework as the Ecology of Human Performance (EHP):

Context is described as the lens from which persons view their world. The interrelationship of person and context determines which tasks fall within the person's performance range . . . occupational therapy has many assessments that examine muscle strength, social skills, vestibular, function, dressing, or uses of leisure time. However, contextual features such as the physical qualities of an environment, the cultural background of the person, or the effect of friendship on performance are often missing from assessment tools typically used in occupational therapy . . . [The EHP] was developed to provide a framework for investigating the relationship between important constructs in the practice of occupational therapy: person, context (temporal, physical, social, cultural), tasks, performance, and therapeutic intervention. The primary theoretical postulate is that performance cannot be understood outside of context. (pp. 595–598)

Drawing from motor learning research, McEwen and Sheldon (1995) provide an excellent summary and application to the practice of pediatric therapy. They identify a major shift in practice from neuromaturational and reflex-hierarchical models of assessment and intervention to systems models that employ motor learning principles. Drawing from the work of motor learning researchers, McEwen and Sheldon (1995) state

motor behavior is organized to accomplish specific tasks within a particular context (Haley, Baryza & Blanchard, 1993; Heriza, 1991). . . . [U]seful motor behaviors are more likely to result from functional tasks than from working on movement patterns for movement's sake alone (Shumway-Cook & Woolacott, 1995).

As Gordon said, it is easy to facilitate movement patterns; what is difficult is to get people
to use the pattern during some functional activities (Gordon, 1987). It is unlikely, for example, that movement organized to maintain
balance while sitting on a ball will be helpful
in maintaining balance while sitting on a chair
to work at a computer or standing in line at a
drinking fountain. Sitting on a ball, sitting on
a chair, and standing in line are different tasks
and movement is uniquely organized to accomplish each of them (Harris & McEwen, 1996).
(McEwen & Sheldon, 1995, p. 35)

Their guidelines for therapy include an emphasis on providing opportunities to practice
in real contexts in which motor behavior is
required; plan for trials to be distributed
across learning environments and activities;
and practice tasks as a whole, instead of in
their fragmented composite parts (McEwen
& Sheldon, 1995). From the realm of
speech-language pathology, Hixson (1993)
and Coufal (1993) promote the alignment of
an integrated approach to service provision
with understandings of the development of
language as holistic in that children are con-
stantly interacting with their environments.

Several studies with children who have
disabilities indicate a positive effect of
meaningful context on motor performance.
When teachers were instructed in gross motor facilitation, there was a sustained increase in their encouragement of children to
perform gross motor activities (Preito,
1992). Similarly, using nondirective consultation to increase implementation of
language intervention in mainstreamed
preschools, Peck et al. (1989) found that
teachers effectively facilitated language in
targeted situations and also generalized facilitation to new situations. Campbell et al.
(1984) documented the effectiveness of embedding therapeutic goals in natural settings
for children with multiple disabilities, stating that the inherent motivation and consistent implementation by all individuals

resulted in higher rates of skill acquisition.
A study conducted by Giangreco (1986) indicated increased accuracy from 63% to
100% for the behavior of reaching when the
child was in a natural environment. Examining the effect of motivation, Kircher
(1984) found that exertion was perceived
less readily when a child was engaged in
purposeful, as opposed to nonpurposeful, activities.

Two studies have compared the effect of
providing therapy in an isolated setting (e.g.,
therapy room) with the effect of providing
therapy in classroom, natural settings. Karnish, Bruder, and Rainforth (1995), using an
alternating treatment design for three children with cerebral palsy, found that the integrated context yielded superior results in
terms of movement speed and quality. Cole,
Harris, Eland, and Mills (1989) found no
differences in motor performance between
children treated in classrooms or therapy
rooms, possibly because the standardized assessment tool was not sensitive enough to
measure differences. A survey administered
to classroom staff, however, indicated their
preference for the in-class approach. Dunn
(1990) compared direct therapy with consultation for preschoolers with developmental delays. The goal attainment was the same
across approaches; however, with the consultative approach teachers recognized and
attributed more of the success to integrated
methods.

Learning Characteristics of
Students with Severe Disabilities

The *developmental principle* asserts that all
people are capable of learning, regardless of
age, ability, or extent of disabilities (Perske,
1981). In designing educational programs
for students with severe disabilities, educational team members assume that all children are capable of learning, if for no other
reason than that it is impossible to prove,

and irresponsible to assume, otherwise (Baer, 1981). To assume that some students are not capable of learning increases the probability that these individuals will not be provided with opportunities to learn. It is the responsibility of educational teams to design programs that address the learning abilities and needs of all students. In designing effective educational programs, it is important to consider the implications of learning characteristics, including individual assets, capacities, and difficulties.

All students have characteristics that are strengths in the learning process. Team members of students with severe disabilities engage in a *capacity search* (O'Brien & Mount, 1991) to identify general and specific assets or strengths, such as perseverance, pleasantness, high energy, adherence to routines, and good eye–hand coordination, that can be useful in designing the educational program and intervention methods. For example, a ninth grader with severe disabilities became quite adept at moving between the supplies area and his work table in an industrial technology class. Recognizing this as an asset, lab partners figured out a way this student could be responsible for transporting needed supplies and materials using his wheelchair. Another high school student was pleasant, enjoyed people, and was very mobile. In a futures planning session, delivering mail in an office building was identified as a potential employment direction that would capitalize on his strengths. Another student who interacted best when structures and routines were rigidly adhered to did well with the repetitive, structured work task of stamping travel agency labels on vacation brochures. A first grader who required and appreciated physical assistance to participate in art was teamed up with a student who previously had not participated well in art but who enjoyed working together with the student on

art projects. These are examples of how unique characteristics can be viewed as strengths and turned into capacities for participation in natural environments.

Team members address learning challenges of individual students by considering the impact of those challenges on educational performance in actual contexts. When compared with individuals who do not have identified disabilities, most students with severe disabilities experience greater difficulty with skill acquisition, retention, generalization, and synthesis (Brown, Nietupski, & Hamre-Nietupski, 1976; Gearheart, Weishahn, & Gearheart, 1992; Hunt & Marshall, 1994; Peterson, 1980). These learning difficulties and their implications are described in greater detail here. The team designs and implements curricular and instructional strategies that capitalize on student strengths while addressing and minimizing the effects of learning challenges.

Skill Acquisition First, children having severe disabilities typically learn certain skills more slowly and, therefore, are likely to acquire fewer skills than their peers without labels. Both the quantity and the quality of their performance frequently differ from those of children without identified disabilities. A child with severe cerebral palsy, for example, will learn motor skills more slowly and will demonstrate less efficient movement patterns than children without cerebral palsy. Movement quantity and quality usually can improve to some extent, but many children will continue to have motor skill difficulties even as adults. A child with autism and mental retardation would be expected to learn language more slowly than peers without labels and to continue to have communication challenges even as an adult. Because children and adults with severe disabilities acquire fewer skills over a lifetime than do peers without identified disabilities, educational teams must focus instruction on each student's most crucial needs, maximizing assets and strengths while minimizing and accommodating for challenges. In doing so, teams also must make the most of the natural learning opportunities that arise throughout each day's activities.

Retention   Another learning characteristic of students with severe disabilities is that they tend to forget skills they do not practice. Horner, Williams, and Knobbe (1985) found that the greatest single predictor of whether students would retain skills they had mastered was whether or not they continued to practice the skills. Even children and adults without apparent disabilities have difficulty remembering the Pythagorean theorem or Hamlet's soliloquy given the infrequent demands for these skills in daily life. Frequent practice, which increases the probability of skill retention, is most likely to occur when students perceive skill performance to be purposeful (Steinbeck, 1986), and when skills are natural components of their daily routines (Brown, Evans, Weed, & Owen, 1987; Holvoet, Guess, Mulligan, & Brown, 1980). Educational teams must select for instruction skills that students have a high probability of using frequently in current and future school, home, and community environments.

Generalization   A third learning characteristic of students with severe disabilities is difficulty generalizing skills from one situation to another. Some children, for example, have large repertoires of skills at home that they never demonstrate at school, and vice versa. Even at school, a student who reliably points to communication symbols in a speech therapy room may not point to the same symbols when he or she has information to share in the classroom or cafeteria. In many situations, lack of generalization results from poor instructional design. There is considerable evidence that generalization is thwarted for students with severe

disabilities when skills are taught in isolated, controlled environments (Haring, 1988). The motor learning research discussed previously provides further support. Teaching functional motor and communication skills in many naturally occurring daily routines increases the likelihood of generalization to new situations (Stokes & Baer, 1977). Furthermore, research indicates that skills can be taught just as effectively through distributed practice within daily routines as through the traditional approach of predominantly massed practice (Mulligan, Lacy, & Guess, 1982). The implication for therapists and other team members in educational settings is, once again, to direct most of their effort toward student acquisition and performance of skills in naturally occurring environments and functional routines and activities throughout therapy.

Synthesis   A fourth learning characteristic of students with severe disabilities is difficulty synthesizing skills learned separately. For example, a child may learn to maintain upright postures in physical therapy, gaze at preferences in speech-language therapy, and bite and chew in occupational therapy. During an actual mealtime, however, the child may experience extreme difficulty sequencing or combining these skills for meaningful use. To ensure skill synthesis in naturally occurring daily routines, educational team members must analyze each student's daily activities, identify the skill clusters that are most important to teach, and integrate relevant knowledge and methods from each discipline to design effective instructional procedures. Although teachers and therapists initially find this process of integrating diverse intervention methods challenging, failure to do so places the responsibility for skill synthesis on the students. If the educational team members have difficulty with synthesis, is it realistic to expect students with significant learning challenges to synthesize skills on their own?

Multiple Challenges One final characteristic of many students with severe disabilities is the multiplicity of their challenges. Many students not only have intellectual challenges but have needs related to medical, health, orthopedic, sensory, and affective conditions as well. Given the varied knowledge and skills required to meet multiple and complex needs, a very high degree of service coordination is necessary. For an individual student, the team may include professionals from many disciplines and often from many agencies (Orelove & Sobsey, 1996). A collaborative and integrated approach to service provision is necessary both to manage the number of professionals with whom students with disabilities and their families must interact routinely and to increase the coordination and consistency across disciplines and agencies. Bricker (1976) recommended that the teacher assume the role of *educational synthesizer*, to integrate input from other members of the educational team and to serve as the primary contact person for the family. As more students with severe and multiple disabilities are included in general education environments, the most effective way to coordinate services will need to be determined on an individual basis given local resources and circumstances. Any team member, including the parent, could serve as program coordinator, team leader, case manager, or inclusion facilitator.

Conclusion The learning challenges of students with disabilities, which are compounded when these students have multiple and complex needs, require carefully designed and implemented educational programs and extraordinary coordination of service provision. As discussed in Chapter 1, current definitions of disability focus not so much on identification and labeling of defi-

cits as on determination of supports required for a person to participate in and contribute to society. To this end, team members must spend time together on a regular basis to collaborate in the design and implementation of educational services.

Recommended Educational Practices for Students with Severe Disabilities

More than two decades ago, Brown and colleagues (1976) presented *the criterion of ultimate functioning* as a standard against which to evaluate educational program components for students with severe disabilities. They asserted that the goal of an education for students with severe disabilities is preparation for participation in regular community life, but that the practices in the education of students with severe disabilities frequently were not consistent with this goal. In their article, they posed a series of questions to be addressed prior to initiating instruction on any skill or activity:

> Why should the student engage in the activity?
> Is this activity necessary to prepare the student to ultimately function in complex, heterogeneous community settings?
> Could the student function as an adult just as well if he/she did not acquire the skill?
> Is there a different activity that would allow the student to approximate realization of the criterion of ultimate functioning more quickly or efficiently?
> Will the activity impede, restrict, or reduce the probability that the student will ultimately function in community settings?
> Are the skills, materials, tasks, and criteria similar to those encountered in real life? (p. 6)

These questions, and the related criteria, were progressive in 1976; today they are just as relevant and constitute minimum criteria for an appropriate program. Consider the following scenarios, which illustrate applications of these criteria to the provision of educationally related services.

Diego is a 6-year-old boy who loves to move and is fascinated with mobile toys that have wheels. He also happens to have severe developmental delays. Because he tends to "bunny hop," the physical therapist has designed a program to teach Diego to creep reciprocally. Recently, Diego started pulling to stand spontaneously. The physical therapist instructed Diego's parents and teacher to discourage this because Diego does not yet have the foundation of reciprocal movement needed to rise from the floor to stand and to walk. After much discussion, the team agreed that discouraging Diego from spontaneously rising to stand could actually impede his already slow progress toward walking. Instead, they decided to shape Diego's spontaneous movement. During designated transition times throughout the school day, when Diego had opportunities to initiate pulling to stand and lowering to kneel, team members trained by the physical therapist would facilitate Diego's movement to emphasize quality reciprocal movement patterns and weight shifting. They also decided to facilitate reciprocal creeping when Diego was playing on the floor and to teach him to ride a tricycle. Although the team could only theorize that tricycle riding might help promote acquisition of some reciprocal movement skills needed for walking, they agreed that, at a minimum, riding a tricycle would provide Diego another option for playing with his friends, and thus met several of the criteria of ultimate functioning.

Melanie is a young woman who enjoys hanging out at the mall with her girlfriends, especially when she has money to buy accessories. She has developed an increased interest in work since she has learned that, through working, she can earn money. Melanie has severe disabilities and has difficulty with eye–hand coordination and motor planning. In an attempt to address Melanie's perceptual-motor needs, the occupational therapist taught Melanie to put graduated pegs in a board and rings on a cone. When the team reviewed Melanie's performance, they found that she did learn the pegs and rings tasks, but the skills had not translated to improved performance related to the priority educational goals identified by Melanie's parents, teacher, and occupational therapist. These goals were working at the neighborhood grocery store, going out to the mall with friends, and engaging in independent leisure activities in and around her home. To address the lack of generalization, the occupational therapist first identified the perceptual-motor demands of the priority activities in the grocery store, in the mall, and at home. For example, at work, Melanie had to stock various items on shelves and hooks; at the mall, she and her friends browse through clothing and accessories and play video games; and at home, Melanie preferred yarn and needlework craft activities and using a Walkman-type cassette player. With the perceptual-motor demands of priority goal activities identified, the occupational therapist and other members of the team devised strategies to teach the requisite skills as part of the instruction provided in the neighborhood grocery store, mall, and other relevant designated community environments.

Frank is an outgoing middle school student. Although he is challenged by severe physical disabilities, he displays extraordinary charm, making him a favorite of friends and family alike. When identifying learning opportunities in his seventh-grade science class, the team considered teaching grasp and manipulation skills required to engage in various lab activities. Upon further consideration, however, the team realized that direct instruction to increase fine motor skill efficiency had not proven effective for functional participation during the past 10 years. Therefore, they decided that a more functional option was to teach Frank to identify the materials needed for the lab sessions and to request the assistance of classmates in gathering the materials. The team reasoned that 1) it was likely that Frank would always require assistance in tasks requiring fine motor skills; and 2) as an adult, Frank was likely to have personal care attendants with whom he would need to communicate his needs and desires. Teaching Frank to identify needed materials and to direct others to provide assistance are self-determination skills that serve as a foundation for participation and control in his home and integrated community life.

The *criterion of ultimate functioning* construct highlighted the need to shift away from strictly developmental and prerequisite curricular paradigms toward practices that maximize adaptive functioning in regular home and community environments. Since the mid-1970s, discussion of recommended or best practices has dominated special education literature (see Browder, 1991; Brown et al., 1979; Brown & Lehr, 1989; Falvey, 1989; Ford et al., 1989; Gaylord-Ross, 1989; Horner, Meyer, & Fredericks, 1986; Orelove & Sobsey, 1996; Sailor et al., 1989; Sailor & Guess, 1983; Sailor, Wilcox, & Brown, 1980; Snell, 1993; Sontag, Smith, & Certo, 1977; Thomas, 1976; Wilcox & Bellamy, 1982). Researchers have identified, defined, and validated nine "best practices" in education of students with severe disabilities (Williams et al., 1990): age-appropriate placement in local public schools, integrated delivery of services, social integration, transition planning, community-based training, functional curricular expectations, systematic data-based instruction, home–school partnership, and systematic program evaluation. These practices are defined in Table 2.4 and referenced in subsequent chapters of this book.

Representing the emerging thought and practice of many educators involved in inclusive schooling efforts, Jorgensen and Calculator (1994) describe the development of a new paradigm of schooling inclusive of *all students*—full inclusion in a restructured school. They describe beliefs and corresponding practices (Table 2.5). Coots, Bishop, Grenot-Scheyer, and Falvey (1995) review practices in general education and offer the following as characteristics of good schools for all children:

All students are provided *free access* to schools that are safe, attractive, and without prejudice;
Educational settings are *integrated, heterogeneous,* and *responsive* to different learning styles and abilities;
Equal educational opportunity is supported by the provision of necessary resources for all children;

A *broad range of support services* are provided to address the individual needs of all students;
Teachers, other personnel, and parents *collaborate* to deliver educational services;
Teachers hold *high expectations* for all students and are *prepared* to meet the challenges presented by diverse classrooms;
Comprehensive, sensible, culturally supportive, and *developmentally appropriate teaching strategies and curricula* are presented;
All students have access to a *common body of knowledge* and the opportunity to acquire *higher order skills;*
Assessment of progress is broad-based and evaluation structures enhance individual strengths and potential; and
Peer interactions and relationships are valued and facilitated. (pp. 13–14)

The alignment between recommended or best practices for students with severe disabilities (see, e.g., Table 2.5) and the characteristics of a quality education for all students lends additional support to our recurring assertion that relevant and carefully designed curricular, instructional, and social interaction practices are essential conditions of effective schooling for everyone. Furthermore, in both frameworks, collaboration is explicitly identified as an essential element.

As recommended educational practices have evolved to support the education of children with severe disabilities in the full range of typical activities in neighborhood public schools, the models of educational and related services provision have necessarily changed. Teachers and therapists increasingly recognize that they cannot ensure educational relevance through isolated, pull-out assessments and services. To promote educational relevance, related services personnel must observe and work with the students in the context of educational programs in order to 1) identify functional, educationally relevant challenges that could be addressed through the provision of related educational services; and 2) determine interventions that could be both effective and ap-

Table 2.4.   Best educational practices for students with severe disabilities

1. Age-appropriate placement in local public schools
The placement of choice for all students (with and without handicaps) should be within chronologically age-appropriate regular classrooms in the student's local public schools.

2. Integrated delivery of services
IEPs and instructional programs should indicate the integration of instruction on education and related service goals into everyday school, home, and community activities. Related service providers should offer consultation and assistance to special and regular educators, parents, and others on developing, implementing, and integrating instruction on related service goals.

3. Social integration
Students with handicaps should have access to the same environments as non-handicapped peers of similar chronological age. Primary goals of social integration should be to increase the number of integrated community and school environments and to improve the quality of interactions in those environments.

4. Transition planning
Transition planning should occur well in advance of major moves (e.g., early education/special education to elementary school, elementary to high school, high school to adult services). Transition objectives should be included in IEPs and reflect the input of significant parties affected by the transition.

5. Community-based training
Students should have the opportunity to acquire and demonstrate specific skills within appropriate community settings. Conditions and criteria of IEP goals and objectives should include performance in natural environments.

6. Curricular expectations
There should be curricula or curriculum guidelines which progress from no skills to adult functioning in all areas of integrated community life. There should be a system for longitudinal monitoring of student progress.

7. Systematic data-based instruction
There should be written schedules of daily activities, clearly defined objectives, reliably implemented instructional programs, and systematic data collection and analysis. Instructional decisions should be based upon documentation of students' progress.

8. Home-school partnership
Parents should have ongoing opportunities to participate in the development of their child's IEP and the delivery of educational and related services. There should be a clearly delineated system for regularly communicating with parents and providing parents with information. Parental concerns should be reflected in IEP goals and objectives.

9. Systematic program evaluation
Educational and related services should be evaluated on a regular basis. Evaluations should actively involve the entire program staff and provide administrators and staff with information regarding the achievements of program goals; student progress; discrepancies needing remediation; directions for future programs change; and program impact upon students, their families, and the community.

From Williams, W., Fox, T.J., Thousand, J., & Fox, W. (1990). Level of acceptance and implementation of best practices in the education of students with severe handicaps in Vermont. *Education and Training in Mental Retardation, 25*(2), 121; reprinted by permission.

Table 2.5.   Relationship between beliefs and practices in inclusive, restructured schools

Beliefs	Practices
All students have value and have something to offer the school.	Diversity is celebrated through different holidays, recognition of a variety of types of achievement—athletic, academic, volunteering, and so on.
All students benefit from learning together with others who have different talents and needs.	There is an emphasis on cooperative learning and helping one another.
Teaching practices must be adapted to fit the heterogeneous nature of the student body.	Teaching practices are utilized that are proven effective for diverse groups of learners; cooperative learning; reading and writing process; coaching rather than lecturing; active learning; individualized instruction is available to all students, not just those with disabilities.
Collaboration among teachers enhances the teaching and the learning environments.	The school provides time for teachers to work together and teachers utilize collaborative skills to develop curriculum, deliver instruction, and resolve problems.
Unless students have friends and feel worthwhile, they will be unprepared for learning and their education will be incomplete.	Intentional community building strategies are used such as devoting considerable time and energy to advisee–advisor relationships and developing circles of friends for students.
Separating students into groups based on characteristics that are traditionally devalued is counterproductive.	There are no separate classes for students with disabilities and homogeneous instructional grouping is utilized with care.

From Jorgensen, C.M., & Calculator, S.N. (1994). The evolution of best practices in educating students with severe disabilities. In S.N. Calculator & C.M. Jorgensen (Eds.), *Including students with severe disabilities in schools: Fostering communication, interaction, and participation* (p. 13). San Diego: Singular; reprinted by permission.

propriate in the context of educational activities. It is exceedingly difficult, if not impossible, for related services personnel to contribute in a meaningful way to the design and implementation of an effective educational program without firsthand knowledge of the student's performance in educational environments and activities. A collaborative teamwork approach that provides the structure and opportunity for therapists to provide services (direct and indirect) in integrated educational environments and activities is a complementary model of service provision for implementing recommended educational practices designed to achieve integrated life outcomes (Giangreco et al., 1989).

Legal Mandates and Precedents, Including Educational Relevance

Legal mandates and precedents sometimes are considered a primary reason for collaborative teamwork, with the logic being, "You should collaborate because the law says you have to." In reality, "statutes, the formal legislative component of the law, are developed and approved when sufficient case law and changing societal trends cause legislators to accept a 'call' for action" (Rapport, 1995, p. 7). Parents, joined by many professionals, recognized the need for children with disabilities to receive a quality education. Their strong advocacy resulted in the passage of PL 94-142, the Education for All Handicapped Children Act (EHA), in 1975. This major federal legislation guaranteed special education and related services in least restrictive environments to children with disabilities ages 6–21, at no cost to parents. In 1986, the EHA amendments (PL 99-457) extended these provisions to children ages 3–21, with incentives offered to states to further extend provisions to birth. In 1990, the act was reauthorized as the Individuals with Disabilities Education Act (IDEA). The mandates in federal law provide both legal and programmatic bases for the design of special education and related services, which are to be provided in least restrictive environments. Understanding this mandate requires understanding how the component services are defined. For example, *special education* is defined by the EHA as "specially designed instruction, at no cost to the parent, to meet the unique needs of a handicapped child" (20 U.S.C. § 140[16], 1975). *Related services* are defined as

transportation and such developmental, corrective, and other supportive services (including speech pathology and audiology, psychological services, physical and occupational therapy, recreation, and medical and counseling services, except that such medical services shall be for diagnostic and evaluation purposes only) as may be required to assist a handicapped child to benefit from special education, and includes the early identification and assessment of handicapping conditions in children. (20 U.S.C. § 1401[17], 1975)

Note that the definitions of *special education* and *related services* do not include any reference to the location of services. Traditionally, special education and related services have been associated with or even defined in terms of special places where children with disabilities go to receive ser-

vices (e.g., "Tony is at P.T." or "Alisha goes to special ed every day for a half hour"). In many school districts, children can only receive special education and related services by going to special education classes, therapy rooms, or even separate schools. As students with disabilities are included more fully in neighborhood schools and general education classes, special education and related services are increasingly conceptualized as services and supports rather than programs or places (Taylor, 1988). Both special education and related services can be implemented in a variety of places, including general education classes and off campus in integrated community settings.

Considering the issue of place, the legal directive toward more integrated and inclusive services stems from the *least restrictive environment (LRE)* clause of the federal law. The LRE mandate requires assurances that

to the maximum extent appropriate, handicapped children . . . are educated with children who are not handicapped, and that special classes, separate schooling, or other removal of handicapped children from the regular education environment, occurs only when the nature or severity of the handicap is such that education in regular classes with supplementary aids and services cannot be achieved satisfactorily. (EHA, 20 U.S.C. § 1412[5], 1975)

Although the preference for services in "regular" environments seems apparent, Taylor (1988) articulated some of the confusion or "pitfalls" that have emerged in interpreting the LRE mandate. His LRE pitfalls have direct application to the misconception that special education and related services are places that children go to receive services and are services that are mutually exclusive of general education. Most relevant to our discussion here are five of Taylor's (1988) seven pitfalls:

The LRE principle legitimizes restrictive environments. As long as a continuum exists, every point on the continuum is legitimized and therefore can be used in practice.

The LRE principle confuses segregation and integration on the one hand with intensity of services on the other. In other words, to get intensive services (or any services at all), one must be in a more restrictive (less integrated) environment.

The LRE principle is based on a "readiness model." This assumes that individuals get ready for less restrictive environments by learning appropriate behavior in a more restrictive environment.

The LRE principle implies that people must move as they develop and change. Following from the previous pitfall, once new skills are learned, individuals must move.

The LRE principle directs attention to physical settings rather than to the services and supports people need to be integrated into the community. (pp. 45–48)

Increasingly, the concept of "ordinary environments . . . extraordinary supports" is advocated as the basis of service design. In other words, all students with disabilities can participate in and benefit from the same educational environments as students without labels, but to do so may require that they receive more support than typically provided to students without labels. Although IDEA does not use the term "inclusion," two recent court cases, *Oberti v. Board of Education of the Borough of Clementon School District* (New Jersey) and *Sacramento City Unified School District v. Rachel H.* (California) have affirmed that general education classes with supports are the least restrictive environment for students with severe disabilities.

Like special education, related services must be provided in the least restrictive environment and must be provided as a support to the educational program, not as services unto themselves (Bateman, 1996; Effgen, 1995; Hanft & Place, 1996; Rainforth & Roberts, 1996; Rapport, 1995; Strickland & Turnbull, 1990). The notion of *educational relevance* has emerged as a central issue in the provision of therapy services. The related services of physical and occupational therapy and speech-language pathology must relate directly to the child's educational program and must be provided in such a way that the child receives a greater benefit from the educational program than if related services were not provided. It is important to note, however, that the intent of providing related services is not to guarantee an "optimal" education but to provide reasonable opportunity for educational benefit (Strickland & Turnbull, 1990).

The related services mandate of PL 94-142 has been one of the most litigated aspects of the legislation, largely because of questions concerning the parameters of educational relevance (Osborne, 1984). Giangreco (1989) presented a chronology of major legislation and litigation affecting the provision of related services (Table 2.6). Central to the outcome in each case was deference to services that allow both access to and participation in an educational program in the most integrated settings deemed reasonable. One additional case not included in Giangreco's synopsis, *Roncker v. Walter* (1983), established the "standard of portability," a precedent with significant impact on the provision of related services. In the *Roncker* case, the court ruled that the availability of special services only in segregated settings did not justify excluding a child from integrated settings. The decision explicitly identified related services, special equipment, and specially designed (i.e., accessible) environments as provisions that could be, and would be, arranged in integrated environments.

Reports of a decade ago cited by Strickland and Turnbull (1990) indicate that schools provided the majority of occupational therapy, physical therapy, speech-language pathology, and counseling services received by students with disabilities. For many students with severe disabilities the

Table 2.6.   Chronology and synopsis of major related services legislation and litigation

PARC v. Pennsylvania (1972)

Established the legal right of students with severe handicaps to receive public education.

Education for All Handicapped Children Act (1975)

In addition to ensuring a free, appropriate, public education for all students with handicapping conditions, this legislation established that students have a right to receive related services that "...may be required to assist a handicapped child to benefit from special education." Related services are developmental, corrective, or other supportive services including, but not limited to, speech pathology, audiology, psychological services, physical therapy, occupational therapy, counseling, and medical services. Medical services shall be for diagnostic and evaluation purposes only. The Code of Federal Regulations (1987) Section 300.13 extended this list to include school health services, social work services in schools, and parent counseling and training.

Espino v. Besteiro (1981)

School was ordered to provide an air conditioned classroom as a related service for a 7-year-old child who could not regulate his own body temperature. The school had previously agreed to provide an air conditioned cubicle to be placed in a classroom that was not air conditioned, but the court ruled that the cubicle restricted the student's interactions with peers.

Hymes v. Harnett Board of Education (1981)

Court ruled that the school must provide management of a student's tracheostomy tube during the school day to allow access to school-based education. The school's plan to provide homebound instruction because of the tracheostomy was deemed unduly restrictive.

Tokarick v. Forest Hills School District (1981)

School was ordered to provide clean intermittent catheterization (CIC) as a related service because the "...absence of such a service would prevent the child from participating in the regular school program."

Board of Education of the Hendrick Hudson Central School Board v. Rowley (1982)

In this Supreme Court decision, a sign-language interpreter was denied as a related service to a student with a hearing impairment because the Court ruled that she was, and had been, benefiting from instruction. Justice Renquist ruled that, "Free appropriate public education is satisfied when state provides personalized instruction with sufficient support services to permit the handicapped child to benefit educationally from instruction" (p. 3034) and that the requirement of free appropriate public education does not require the state to maximize the potential of each child.

Stacy G. v. Pasadena Independent School District (1982)

In this case regarding a student with severe retardation and behavioral problems, the court ruled that related services must be provided in the form of parent training in behavioral management techniques and counseling to the parents to help relieve emotional stress.

PARC V. Pennsylvania Consent Decree of Enforcement Petition in Fialkowski v. School District of Philadelphia (1982)

In anticipation of the outcome of court proceedings, the Philadelphia City School District settled out of court with plaintiffs in 1982. The agreement bound the school district to provide extensive retraining and

(continued)

Table 2.6.   *(continued)*

instructional support to staff in classrooms for students with severe handicaps. In part, this agreement called for the provision of transdisciplinary services including: a) "For students receiving related services, collaboration between the teacher and specialist for planning and evaluating programs," and b) "For students with therapeutic goals, techniques are carried over into educational activities with input from the therapist."

Birmingham & Lamphere School Districts v. Superintendent (1982)

Court ruled that a local hearing officer did have the right to order the school district to provide related services in the form of summer enrichment activities that were essentially noninstructional in nature.

Department of Education, State of Hawaii v. Katherine D. (1983)

In this case regarding a student with cystic fibrosis and tracheomalacia, the court ruled that the school recommendation for homebound instruction did not meet the requirement of a free appropriate public education. The court ordered placement in regular public school with staff being trained in management of the student's tracheostomy tube (dispense medication, suction lungs, reinsert tube if dislodged). The court tempered its position by saying the schools were required to make accommodations "within reason" and that budgetary constraints and realistic resources are considered by the court.

Hurry v. Jones (1983)

The court ruled that the school must provide transportation as a related service for a student with mental and physical handicaps. This transportation was inclusive from the child's home to the school bus and from the bus to the classroom.

Rettig v. Kent City (1983)

In part, this decision ordered a school to provide related services in the form of one hour per week of extracurricular activities to a 10-year-old student with severe handicaps. This decision was based in part on the Code of Federal Regulations Section 300.306 (Nonacademic Services) "Each public agency shall take steps to provide nonacademic and extracurricular activities in such a manner as is necessary to afford handicapped children an equal opportunity for participation in those services and activities" and that "...they be exposed on an equal basis as nonhandicapped children."

Irving Independent School District v. Tatro (1984)

This Supreme Court ruling designated clean intermittent catheterization as a related service. It distinguished it as a support school health service, not a medical service. The Court explained that provision of such a service did not place an undue burden or expense on the school district.

Detsel v. Sullivan (1990)

This case began with a local hearing officer determining that constant in-school nursing care was a related service for a child with a life threatening lung condition who requires 24-hour day nursing services. The decision was overruled by the State Commissioner of Education whose decision was upheld through the courts. The Supreme Court refused to hear the case. While nursing has been considered a "school health service" and appropriately provided as a related service, the courts ruled that the constancy and nature of this service qualified it as "medical" and thus excluded it as a related service because it was beyond the competence of the school nurse. The service also was denied because it placed an undue financial burden on the school district. The family then sued Medicaid for payment of nursing services. The United States Court of Appeals (second circuit) determined that Medicaid would pay for nursing services while the student was attending public school.

(continued)

Table 2.6.   *(continued)*

Individuals with Disabilities Education Act (IDEA, PL 101-476) (1990)

This amendment to the Education for All Handicapped Children Act of 1975 (PL 94-142) adds rehabilitation counseling and recreation, including therapeutic recreation and social work services, to the federal definition of related services.

From Giangreco, M.F. (1989). Making related service decisions for students with severe handicaps in public schools: Roles, criteria, and authority. *Dissertation Abstracts International, 50,* 1624A. (University Microfilms No. 89-19, 561); reprinted by permission.

need for such related services seems readily apparent. Decisions on the appropriateness of services, however, must continue to be made on an individual basis. Hanft and Place (1996) offer specific guidelines for making such determinations:

1. Identify *how* specific therapeutic domains (for example, sensory processing, neuromuscular function, motor perception, and adaptive behaviors) contribute to and/or challenge a student's performance in school.
2. Assess and describe a *student's performance* in specific areas of the school, such as the classroom, lunchroom, halls, playground, art class, and gymnasium, rather than solely on the basis of formal test results.
3. Discuss how intervention will *improve* the student's performance in academic subjects and other school activities.
4. Communicate, both verbally and through written reports, in *jargon-free* language that all team members can understand. (p. 17)

These authors also make the important distinction that therapy provided in a classroom is not necessarily educationally relevant. Some therapists simply change the location of their services from a separate room to a classroom but continue with interventions of questionable relevance to a student's IEP. Providing teachers or paraprofessionals with suggestions for interventions to implement in the classroom also does not necessarily meet the criteria for educational relevance.

A checklist of practices that are likely to indicate the educational relevance of related services provided to students with severe disabilities in educational settings is provided in Figure 2.2. Therapists and other related services personnel can engage in practices specified only if they work as members of collaborative educational teams and are knowledgeable about the contextually relevant educational demands and opportunities for each student. The requirements of educational relevance and least restrictive environment are likely to be addressed when therapists integrate their knowledge and skills into instruction provided in the context of routine daily activities that comprise the student's educational program, whether at school, in the community, or at home.

Guidelines for Therapy Practice in Educational Environments

Publications by the APTA (1990), the American Occupational Therapy Association (1989), the American Speech-Language-Hearing Association Committee on Language Learning Disorders (1991), and the Neurodevelopmental Treatment Association (DeMauro, 1988) reflect the unique nature of therapy practice in educational settings that is due, at least in part, to the special education mandates cited previously that guide the provision of related services. Contained within professional policies and guidelines are statements that endorse alternatives to the traditional models of therapy service provision (Table 2.7). (*Note:* At the time of this writing, the professional practice

✓   The need for collaboration with related services personnel is determined by that person's potential contribution to student achievement of priority educational goals.

✓   Related services personnel assess student capabilities in the context of the educational program, including the typical school, home, and community environments, routines, and activities determined to be priorities for each student.

✓   Related services personnel work directly with students within the context of the educational program.

✓   Related services personnel work with teachers and other team members to identify motor and communication priorities within the educational program.

✓   Objectives related to improving motor and communication abilities are embedded throughout the IEP, as opposed to being separate components.

✓   Related services personnel and teachers work together to design instructional methods for teaching students to participate to a greater degree and with more success in the educational program.

✓   Therapists teach others to use the instructional methods they have found effective in facilitating improved motor, communication, or other competencies.

✓   Related services personnel work on an ongoing basis with students and other team members to evaluate student progress in educational activities.

Figure 2.2. Checklist for discussion of educational relevance of related services provided to students with severe disabilities in educational settings.

guidelines cited in this chapter were in the process of being revised. Unfortunately, the latest revisions were not available for excerpted publication. Readers are encouraged to contact the respective therapy associations for updated guidelines.)

Two documents of the APTA offer further evidence of this organization's support of physical therapists in promoting enhanced participation in natural environments. The *Position on Practice in Educational Environments* (APTA, 1995b) asserts that the role of physical therapists is assisting children to "attain their optimal educational potential and benefit from special education" and "establishing working relationships . . . in order to integrate physical therapy services into school systems." The *Guidelines for Pediatric Content in Professional Physical Therapist Education* (APTA, 1995a) state

The Pediatric Section of the APTA recognizes there is an increasing need for graduates of physical therapy programs to assist in meeting the needs of children and families in our society. The Section believes that physical therapists should provide services . . . in a manner that is consistent with the philosophy of family-centered care . . . that is respectful of cultural diversity, occurs in natural environments when possible, and fosters collaborative partnerships. (p. ii)

The Pediatric Section goes on to recommend that professional preparation include competencies in the areas of communication and collaboration with families and with other service providers. As noted in Chapter 1, the American Occupational Therapy Association (1995) has strongly affirmed the role of occupational therapists in supporting full inclusion.

Educationally relevant services are a required professional practice and must be

Table 2.7.   Excerpts from professional policies and guidelines on the provision of related services

Source	Major provisions in support of collaborative teamwork
American Physical Therapy Association. (1990). *Physical therapy practice in educational environments.*	Physical therapy traditionally has been considered something that occurs in a specially equipped and private room during a scheduled block of time. The LRE requirement means that physical therapists need to 1) emphasize intervention strategies rather than places and 2) make every effort to identify strategies that team members can use in the course of the child's daily routines, when postural control, mobility, and sensory processing are really required. When related services focus first on the natural opportunities for children to develop and practice motor competence in routine activities in integrated environments, there is greater assurance that the related services will fulfill their mandated purpose: "to assist a handicapped child to benefit from special education."
American Occupational Therapy Association. (1989). *Guidelines for occupational therapy services in the public schools.*	Intervention refers to all activities performed by occupational therapy personnel to carry out the IEP. In the educational setting, intervention includes direct therapy, monitoring, and several types of consultation. "Occupational therapy treatment refers to the use of specific activities or methods to develop, improve, and/ or restore the performance of necessary functions; compensate for dysfunction; and/or minimize debilitation." The intervention must be planned and provided within the child's least restrictive environment.
American Speech-Language-Hearing Association Committee on Language Learning Disorders. (1991). *A model for collaborative service delivery for students with language-learning disorders in the public schools.*	The collaborative service delivery model affords the speech-language pathologist the opportunity to 1) observe and assess how the student functions communicatively and socially in the regular classroom, 2) describe the student's communicative strengths and weaknesses in varied educational contexts, and 3) identify which curricular demands enhance or interfere with the student's ability to function communicatively, linguistically, and socially.

provided in a way that ensures direct application of team member knowledge and skills to students' educational programs. Previously in this chapter, routine activities and environmental demands were identified as the natural and functional contexts in which to teach motor and communication skills (discussed in greater detail in Chapter 4). The need for a particular related service is determined by the need for knowledge and skills from that discipline to improve student participation in the educational program.

COLLABORATIVE TEAM MEMBERS AND THEIR ROLES

In schools throughout the United States, an increasing number of parents of children with disabilities, including children labeled as having profound and multiple disabilities, have requested that their children be educated exclusively in general education and other integrated settings, with no "pull-out" services. Because most related services personnel were trained to provide direct services in segregated settings, it is challenging (if not frightening) to shift to other models of service provision (e.g., to integrate physical therapy services for a child with severe disabilities into a regular fourth-grade class). Similarly, as children with disabilities become more fully included in general education, the role of special education teachers is beginning to shift to a more indirect model of service provision also (Stainback et al., 1989; Thousand, Nevin-Parta, & Fox, 1987). Increasingly, therapists and special educators will be required to shift from a model of providing service and support in self-contained environments to collaborating with general educators and community members in integrated environments.

With the outcomes, characteristics, and reasons for collaborative teamwork articulated, individuals who frequently are members of collaborative teams for students with severe disabilities are identified and their respective roles and contributions are described. In Chapter 8, we discuss in more operational terms the team member practices, strategies, and skills.

Defining Who Is on the Collaborative Team

Participation on a collaborative educational team can and should vary depending on current educational priorities for individual students. First, there are usually team members who are involved very directly in the design and implementation of the day-to-day educational program. These members are referred to as the *core team* (Giangreco, Cloninger, & Iverson, 1993). For many students with severe disabilities, the core team consists of the student, family members, teachers (special and general educators), a communication specialist (speech-language pathologist with expertise in augmentative and alternative communication), a physical or occupational therapist or both, and a para-

professional or teaching associate who provides instructional and management support to the student and class (Giangreco & Eichinger, 1990; Orelove & Sobsey, 1996). When students have extensive sensory or medical needs, a vision or hearing specialist and a nurse may be members of the core team. In addition, some school districts have case managers or social workers who assist with coordination of services. In such situations, these individuals also would be logical members of the core team.

Second, there are individuals who serve as team members on a more itinerant basis; that is, their roles do not support as intensively or directly the day-to-day educational program. Individuals with this level of involvement are referred to as the *support team* (Giangreco et al., 1993). For students who have no functional sensorimotor limitations or for whom motoric difficulties are deemed a very low priority in the educational program, physical and occupational therapists may be support rather than core team members. Frequently, vision specialists, audiologists, psychologists, social workers, nurses, dietitians, and orientation and mobility specialists serve as support team members and are called in to consult as needed (Orelove & Sobsey, 1996).

Distinguishing between core and support team members is helpful from a practical standpoint. Coordination efficiency declines as the number of team members increases. Members of the core team need frequent access to each other for problem solving, decision making, and support. Ensuring this access is foremost in scheduling (see Chapter 8). Members of both the core and the support teams need flexible schedules to allow for consultation and formal involvement in team meetings when their expertise and other contributions are deemed necessary. For support team members, we suggest involvement at least annually with contributions directed to priority educational goals.

As students' priorities change, the degree and nature of individual team member participation should change accordingly. For example, the team of a student who is making a transition from a self-contained early childhood special education program to an inclusive kindergarten might decide that the highest priority for that student during the first month of school will be successful inclusion in the social culture of the kindergarten class. The speech-language pathologist, therefore, initially might be intensively involved in the kindergarten classroom to serve the following functions: modeling effective communication strategies, teaching classmates to use the student's augmentative communication system, determining social opportunities and demands requiring instructional emphasis, facilitating interactions with classmates, supporting the classroom teacher with strategies for student participation, and assessing the effectiveness of communication interventions. The speech-language pathologist might be involved almost daily for the first 2 weeks of school and then reduce his or her time to provide weekly in-classroom consultation and support. During the initial transition time to kindergarten, other support personnel (e.g., physical therapist) might not be involved in an effort to minimize the number of people present in and influencing the kindergarten.

Team Member Roles and Contributions

All of the collaborative team members contribute general assistance as well as discipline-specific knowledge and skills. Common responsibilities, such as participating in problem solving and assisting team members with applying therapy strategies, are roles that are also shared among related services personnel.

Generic Team Member Roles There are roles and contributions of a generic nature that are shared by all team members. These include 1) participating in team decisions about educational priorities and interventions for each student, 2) contributing to problem-solving efforts across all aspects of a student's educational program, 3) sharing discipline-specific knowledge and skills to promote student participation in the educational program and staff understanding of student capabilities, 4) supporting the contributions and efforts of fellow team members, and 5) continuing to grow and learn about practices that support the participation and contribution of individuals with severe disabilities in regular family, school, and community life.

Discipline-Specific Roles In addition to the general roles and contributions shared by all team members, there are specific contributions in terms of knowledge and skill areas associated with different disciplines. There is, however, overlap of knowledge and skills among disciplines given the specific training, experience, and interests of each individual professional. Furthermore, although each discipline claims a core set of skills, two people with the same discipline credentials do not necessarily have the same skills. Table 2.8 presents areas of expertise often associated with specific disciplines (Campbell, 1987). Hanft and Place (1996) identify and describe five therapeutic domains of occupational and physical therapy and describe their potential impact on student participation in educational settings: 1) sensory awareness and processing, 2) neuromuscular functions, 3) motor (gross, fine, and oral-motor) skills, 4) perceptual skills, and 5) adaptive behavior.

Focused on the provision of appropriate communication services for students with severe disabilities, Calculator and Jorgensen (1994) strongly advocate a zero exclusion

Table 2.8. Areas of expertise of team members

Discipline	Areas of expertise

Occupational Therapy	Sensory factors related to posture and movement
	Muscle tone
	Range of motion
	Posture/postural alignment
	Functional use of movement
	    1. Self-care
	    2. Recreation/leisure
	    3. Work
	Adaptive positioning equipment
	Adaptive devices for learning
	Materials and task adaptation
	Splinting

Physical Therapy	Sensory factors related to posture and movement
	Muscle tone
	Range of motion
	Muscle strength
	Joint mobility
	Endurance
	Flexibility
	Posture/postural alignment
	Balance and automatic movement
	Functional use of movement
	    1. Mobility (e.g., walking)
	    2. Recreation/leisure
	Adaptive positioning equipment
	Lower limb bracing/splinting/inhibitive casting
	Task adaptation

Speech-Language Pathology	Neuromotor factors related to oral musculature and respiration/phonation
	Hearing (screening)
	Functional use of movement
	    1. Communication
	    2. Social
	    3. Self-care (prespeech and feeding)
	Cognition
	Communication devices
	Communicative/social interactions

Education	Sensory factors related to learning and performance
	    (Instructional methods for students with visual, auditory, or multisensory impairment)
	Functional use of movement
	    1. Environmental problem solving
	    2. Social
	    3. Communication
	    4. Self-care
	    5. Recreation/leisure
	    6. Work

Audiology	Hearing (and aural rehabilitation) Hearing aids
Vision	Vision (and training procedures to enhance vision) Vision prostheses

Parent	Functional use of movement
	    1. Communication
	    2. Social
	    3. Recreation/leisure
	    4. Self-care
	Determining motivators

Adapted from Campbell, P.H. (1987). The integrated programming team: An approach for coordinating multiple discipline professionals in programs for students with severe and multiple handicaps. *Journal of The Association for Persons with Severe Handicaps, 12,* 107–116; adapted by permission.

model of communication services, which has not been practiced in the past. They make the point that many students who traditionally would not have been considered candidates for speech or language intervention are high priorities for communication services. Calculator and Jorgensen (1994) generally describe major contributions of speech-language pathologists in natural settings as determining how a student communicates, the purposes and communicative intents of the student's messages, and whether a student's communicative behavior is intentional.

In determining the need for specific support personnel, educational teams first must identify student needs or challenges and then determine which specific team members (regardless of discipline label) can contribute the necessary knowledge and skills (see Chapter 8). As asserted throughout this chapter, to make such determinations, knowledge of student performance in natural settings is essential.

Related Services Personnel Roles   In addition to generic team member roles and discipline-specific contributions, there are common roles among related services personnel. Snell and Raynes (1995) reported on interviews conducted with various elementary school staff about their roles and responsibilities in inclusive schools. Responsibilities of related services providers included

> Being part of the student's team, participating in problem-solving with other professionals;
> Promoting the generalization of student skills by helping team members apply therapy strategies throughout the student's day;
> Being creative in weaving therapy objectives and equipment adaptations into planned classroom activities and "specials" (art, music, physical education, etc.); and
> Utilizing flexible schedules so that therapy and consultation can be available when needed during class activities. (p. 107)

Giangreco (1990) identified 10 roles of related services personnel from a review of professional literature. Through ratings from 312 parents, special educators, and therapists, he then established the perceived relative importance of each role in the processes of assessing, planning, implementing, and evaluating programs for students with severe disabilities in public schools. Although there were some variations among the perceptions of the parents, educators, and therapists, he found general agreement as to the importance of the 10 roles.

The six roles ranked most important were classified as *outcome/enabling roles* because "they are used by school personnel to achieve functional outcomes for students and/or to enable students to pursue those outcomes" (p. 26). These roles were 1) developing adaptations, equipment, or both to encourage functional participation; 2) facilitating functional skills and activities; 3) engaging in reciprocal consultation with colleagues; 4) removing or modifying barriers to participation; 5) preventing regression, deformity, and/or pain; and 6) being a resource and support to families. The four roles ranked as least important were classified as *discretionary roles* because therapists engaged in them as individual circumstances made them appropriate and necessary. These roles were 1) remediating/restoring identified deficits, 2) promoting normal developmental sequences, 3) serving as an advocate for the students, and 4) being a liaison between the medical community and the school team.

These rankings suggest that members of the educational teams for students with severe disabilities in Giangreco's sample recognized the major tenet of service provision and the legal precedents outlined earlier in this chapter: Related services personnel on educational teams function to support the

Table 2.9. Assumptions of a collaborative teamwork approach to education and related services for students with severe disabilities

1. All students can learn given the opportunity and appropriate support.
2. The desired educational outcomes for all students are participation in, contribution to, and enjoyment of family, school, and community life, now and in the future.
3. All students, regardless of abilities, interests, and needs, must grow up and learn together in the same school and community environments in order to achieve desired educational outcomes.
4. It is the explicit responsibility of the collaborative educational team to assist students in achieving desired educational outcomes.
5. The collaborative team is composed of the student, significant family members, friends, and the relevant and related services personnel required to assist students in achieving desired educational outcomes.
6. Positive social interdependence among team members must be structured to realize the benefits of collaborative teamwork.
7. Discipline-referenced knowledge and skills are shared among team members so that relevant expertise is available to students in all aspects of their educational program.
8. An ecological curricular design is required to assist students in achieving desired educational outcomes.
9. An IEP is developed jointly by the collaborative educational team and reflects an integrated approach to service, design, and provision.
10. Collaborative teamwork strategies must remain flexible in order to meet changing needs of students and families.

educational program. In contrast with the ranked priorities, however, the therapists in the Giangreco (1990) study reported that they continued to invest most of their professional energies in discretionary roles, which are their lowest priorities. Similarly, Effgen and Klepper (1994) and McWilliam and Bailey (1994) found discrepancies between what therapists (and some other providers) considered to be ideal (desired) and actual ways in which therapy services are provided. In general, respondents were supportive of more integrated approaches to therapy than they currently practiced. These findings suggest that priorities and practices do not necessarily match, and that merely identifying priorities does not ensure that they actually receive priority attention. Changing old models of service provision requires substantial professional and organizational change, which takes understanding,

commitment, support, and long-term systematic efforts.

Assumptions of Collaborative Teamwork for Students with Severe Disabilities

This chapter has provided foundational information that supports a collaborative teamwork approach to integrating related services in educational programs for students with severe disabilities. The day-to-day actions of individual team members are shaped by a combination of foundational knowledge and personal values and competence. Effective teams explore the knowledge and values of their members and work to articulate a set of beliefs that all members can support. It is these shared beliefs, then, that largely determine the nature and scope of the collaborative teamwork employed in the design and implementation of education, including the provision of related services.

When teamwork breaks down, it is often because team members have not established this foundation and each individual team member operates from a different set of beliefs and assumptions.

Table 2.3 and Figure 2.1, presented earlier in this chapter, contain principles involved in collaborative teamwork and educational relevance of services. These constitute important assumptions about these aspects of service provision. Table 2.9 presents a third set of assumptions for the design and provision of education and related services for students with severe disabilities. These assumptions are shared by the authors and, collectively, they form the basis for the information and strategies offered in the remainder of this book. Readers are encouraged to discuss these assumptions with teammates as a first step toward understanding one another's individual perspectives and for beginning to articulate a shared set of assumptions about a collaborative teamwork approach for supporting the educational program of students with severe disabilities.

REFERENCES

Aksamit, D., & Alcorn, D. (1988). A preservice mainstream curriculum infusion model: Student teachers' perceptions of program effectiveness. *Teacher Education and Special Education, 11,* 52–58.

Albano, M., Cox, B., York, J., & York, R. (1981). Educational teams for students with severe and multiple handicaps. In R. York, W.K. Schofield, D.J. Donder, D.L. Ryndak, & B. Reguly (Eds.), *Organizing and implementing services for students with severe and multiple handicaps* (pp. 23–34). Springfield: Illinois State Board of Education.

Albano, M.L. (1983). *Transdisciplinary teaming in special education: A case study.* Urbana: University of Illinois–Urbana/Champaign.

American Occupational Therapy Association. (1989). *Guidelines for occupational therapy services in the public schools* (2nd ed.). Rockville, MD: Author.

American Occupational Therapy Association Commission on Practice. (1995). *Occupational therapy: A profession in support of full inclusion.* Rockville, MD: American Occupational Therapy Association.

American Physical Therapy Association. (1990). *Physical therapy practice in educational environments.* Alexandria, VA: Author.

American Physical Therapy Association. (1995a). *Guidelines for pediatric content in professional physical therapist education.* Alexandria, VA: Author.

American Physical Therapy Association. (1995b). *Position on practice in educational environments.* Alexandria, VA: Author.

American Speech-Language-Hearing Association Committee on Language Learning Disorders. (1991). A model for collaborative service delivery for students with language-learning disorders in the public schools. *Asha, 3*(33)(Suppl.).

Baer, D. (1981). A hung jury and a Scottish verdict: "Not proven." *Analysis and Intervention in Developmental Disabilities, 1*(1), 91–97.

Bateman, B.D. (1996). *Better IEPs: How to develop legally correct and educationally useful programs* (2nd ed.). Longmont, CO: Sopris West.

Bauwens, J., & Hourcade, J.J. (1995). *Cooperative teaching: Rebuilding the schoolhouse for all students.* Austin, TX: PRO-ED.

Brandt, R. (1988). On students' needs and team learning: A conversation with William Glasser. *Educational Leadership, 45*(6), 38–45.

Bricker, D. (1976). Educational synthesizer. In M.A. Thomas (Ed.), *Hey, don't forget about me! Education's investment in the severely, profoundly and multiply handicapped* (pp. 84–89). Reston, VA: Council for Exceptional Children.

Browder, D.M. (1991). *Assessment of individuals with severe disabilities: An applied behavior approach to life skills assessment* (2nd ed.). Baltimore: Paul H. Brookes Publishing Co.

Brown, F., Evans, I., Weed, K., & Owen, V. (1987). Delineating functional competencies: A component model. *Journal of The Association for Persons with Severe Handicaps, 12*(2), 117–124.

Brown, F., & Lehr, D.H. (Eds.). (1989). *Persons with profound disabilities: Issues and practices.* Baltimore: Paul H. Brookes Publishing Co.

Brown, L., Branston, M.B., Hamre-Nietupski, S., Pumpian, I., Certo, N., & Gruenwald, L. (1979). A strategy for developing chronological age appropriate and functional curricular content for severely handicapped adolescents and young adults. *Journal of Special Education, 13*(1), 81–90.

Brown, L., Nietupski, J., & Hamre-Nietupski, S. (1976). The criterion of ultimate functioning. In M.A. Thomas (Ed.), *Hey, don't forget about me! Education's investment in the severely, profoundly and multiply handicapped* (pp. 2–15). Reston, VA: Council for Exceptional Children.

Calculator, S.N., & Jorgensen, C.M. (1994). *Including students with severe disabilities in schools: Fostering communication, interaction, and participation.* San Diego: Singular.

Campbell, P.H. (1987). The integrated programming team: An approach for coordinating multiple discipline professionals in programs for students with severe and multiple handicaps. *Journal of The Association for Persons with Severe Handicaps, 12,* 107–116.

Campbell, P.H., McInerney, W., & Cooper, M. (1984). Therapeutic programming for students with severe handicaps. *American Journal of Occupational Therapy, 38,* 594–602.

Cole, K.N., Harris, S.R., Eland, S.F., & Mills, P.E. (1989). Comparison of two service delivery models: Integrated and out-of-class therapy approaches. *Pediatric Physical Therapy, 1,* 49–54.

Colton, A., & Sparks-Langer, G. (1993). A conceptual framework to guide the development of teacher reflection and decision-making. *Journal of Teacher Education, 44*(1), 45–54.

Coots, J.J., Bishop, K.D., Grenot-Scheyer, M., & Falvey, M. (1995). Practices in general education: Past and present. In M.A. Falvey (Ed.), *Inclusive and heterogeneous schooling: Assessment, curriculum, and instruction* (pp. 7–22). Baltimore: Paul H. Brookes Publishing Co.

Coufal, K.L. (1993). Collaborative consultation for speech-language pathologists. *Topics in Language Disorders, 14*(1), 1–114.

Cross, D.P., Collins, B.C., & Boam-Wood, S. (1996). A survey of interdisciplinary personnel preparation. *Physical Disabilities: Education and Related Services, 14*(2), 13–32.

DeMauro, G. (1988, January). Member's hotline. *NDTA Newsletter, 5.*

Dettmer, P.A., Dyck, N.T., & Thurston, L.P. (1996). *Consultation, collaboration, teamwork for students with special needs.* Newton, MA: Allyn & Bacon.

Dunn, W. (1990). A comparison of service provision models in school-based occupational therapy services. *Occupational Therapy Journal of Research, 10*(5), 300–320.

Dunn, W. (1991). Integrated related services. In L.H. Meyer, C.A. Peck, & L. Brown (Eds.), *Critical issues in the lives of people with severe disabilities* (pp. 353–377). Baltimore: Paul H. Brookes Publishing Co.

Dunn, W., Brown, C., & McGuigan, A. (1994). The ecology of human performance: A framework for considering the effect of context. *American Journal of Occupational Therapy, 48,* 595–607.

Education Code: Prekindergarten–Grade 12, Minn. Stat. § 120.011 (1985).

Education Code: Prekindergarten–Grade 12, Minn. Stat. § 120.17 (1985).

Education Code: Prekindergarten–Grade 12, Minn. Stat. 120.011 (1991).

Education for All Handicapped Children Act (EHA) of 1975, PL 94-142, 20 U.S.C. § 1400 *et seq.*

Education of the Handicapped Act Amendments of 1986, PL 99-457, U.S.C. § 1400 *et seq.*

Effgen, S. (1995). The educational environment. In S.K. Campbell (Ed.), *Physical therapy for children* (2nd ed., pp. 847–872). Philadelphia: W.B. Saunders.

Effgen, S., & Klepper, S.E. (1994). Survey of physical therapy practice in educational settings. *Pediatric Physical Therapy, 6*(1), 15–21.

Englert, C.S., Tarrant, K.L., & Mariage, T.V. (1992). Defining and redefining instructional practice in special education: Perspectives on good teaching. *Teacher Education and Special Education, 15*(2), 62–85.

Falvey, M.A. (1986). *Community-based curriculum: Instructional strategies for students with severe handicaps.* Baltimore: Paul H. Brookes Publishing Co.

Falvey, M.A. (1989). *Community-based curriculum: Instructional strategies for students with severe handicaps* (2nd ed.). Baltimore: Paul H. Brookes Publishing Co.

Falvey, M.A. (Ed.). (1995). *Inclusive and heterogeneous schooling: Assessment, curriculum, and instruction.* Baltimore: Paul H. Brookes Publishing Co.

Ford, A., Schnorr, R., Meyer, L., Davern, L., Black, J., & Dempsey, P. (Eds.). (1989). *The Syracuse community-referenced curriculum guide for students with moderate and severe disabilities.* Baltimore: Paul H. Brookes Publishing Co.

Friend, M., & Cook, L. (1996). *Interactions: Collaboration skills for professionals* (2nd ed.). White Plains, NY: Longman.

Fullan, M. (1993). *Change forces; Probing the depths of education reform.* Bristol, PA: Falmer Press.

Fullan, M., & Hargreaves, A. (1991). *What's worth fighting for? Working together for your school.* Andover, MA: Regional Laboratory for Educational Improvement.

Gaylord-Ross, R. (Ed.). (1989). *Integration strategies for students with handicaps.* Baltimore: Paul H. Brookes Publishing Co.

Gearheart, B.R., Weishahn, B.R., & Gearheart, C.J. (1992). *The exceptional student in the regular class.* New York: Macmillan.

Giangreco, M. (1986). Effects of integrated therapy: A pilot study. *Journal of The Association for Persons with Severe Handicaps, 11,* 205–208.

Giangreco, M. (1989). Making related service decisions for students with severe handicaps in public schools: Roles, criteria, and authority. *Dissertation Abstracts International, 50,* 1624A. (University Microfilms No. DA8919516)

Giangreco, M.F. (1990). Making related service decisions for students with severe disabilities: Roles, criteria, and authority. *Journal of The Association of Persons with Severe Handicaps, 15,* 22–31.

Giangreco, M.F., Cloninger, C.J., & Iverson, V.S. (1993). *Choosing options and accommodations for children (COACH): A guide to planning inclusive education.* Baltimore: Paul H. Brookes Publishing.

Giangreco, M., & Eichinger, J. (1990). *Related services and the transdisciplinary approach: Parent training module.* Seattle, WA: The Association for Persons with Severe Handicaps, TASH–Technical Assistance for Services to Children with Deaf-Blindness.

Giangreco, M., York, J., & Rainforth, B. (1989). Providing related services to learners with severe handicaps in educational settings: Pursu-

ing the least restrictive option. *Pediatric Physical Therapy, 1*(2), 55–63.

Glasser, W. (1986). *Control theory in the classroom.* New York: Harper & Row.

Glasser, W. (1992). *The Avalon School: Managing students without coercion* (2nd ed.). New York: Harper Collins.

Gordon, J. (1987). Assumptions underlying physical therapy intervention: Theoretical and historical perspectives. In J.H. Carr & R.B. Shepherd (Eds.), *Movement science: Foundations for physical therapy and rehabilitation* (pp. 1–30). Rockville, MD: Aspen Publishers, Inc.

Gossen, D., & Anderson, J. (1995). *Creating the conditions: Leadership for quality schools.* Chapel Hill, NC: New View.

Grennon, J., & Brooks-Grennon, M. (1993). *The case for the constructivist classroom.* Alexandria, VA: Association for Supervision and Curriculum Development.

Haley, S.M., Baryza, M.J., & Blanchard, Y. (1993). Functional and naturalistic frameworks in assessing physical and motor disablement. In I.J. Wilhelm (Ed.), *Physical therapy assessment in early infancy* (pp. 225–256). New York: Churchill Livingstone.

Hanft, B.E., & Place, P.A. (1996). *The consulting therapist: A guide for OTs and PTs in schools.* San Antonio, TX: Therapy Skill Builders.

Haring, N.G. (Ed.). (1988). *Generalization for students with severe handicaps: Strategies and solutions.* Seattle: University of Washington Press.

Harris, S.R., & McEwen, I.R. (1996). Assessing motor skills. In M.L. McLean, D. Bailey, & M. Wolery (Eds.), *Assessing infants and toddlers with special needs* (pp. 305–333). Columbus, OH: Charles E. Merrill.

Hart, V. (1977). The use of many disciplines with the severely and profoundly handicapped. In E. Sontag, J. Smith, & N. Certo (Eds.), *Educational programming for the severely and profoundly handicapped* (pp. 391–396). Reston, VA: Council for Exceptional Children.

Heriza, C. (1991). Motor development: Traditional and contemporary theories. In M.J. Lister (Ed.), *Contemporary management of motor control problems: Proceedings of the II STEP Conference* (pp. 99–126). Alexandria, VA: Foundation for Physical Therapy.

Hixson, P.K. (1993). An integrated approach to program development. *Topics in Language Disorders, 14*(1), 41–57.

Holvoet, J., Guess, D., Mulligan, M., & Brown, F. (1980). The individualized curriculum sequencing model (II): A teaching strategy for severely handicapped students. *Journal of The Association for the Severely Handicapped, 5,* 337–352.

Horner, R.H., Meyer, L.H., & Fredericks, H.D.B. (Eds.). (1986). *Education of learners with severe handicaps: Exemplary service strategies.* Baltimore: Paul H. Brookes Publishing Co.

Horner, R.H., Williams, J.A., & Knobbe, C.A. (1985). The effect of "opportunity to perform" on the maintenance of skills learned by high school students with severe handicaps. *Journal of The Association for Persons with Severe Handicaps, 10,* 172–175.

Hunt, N., & Marshall, K. (1994). *Exceptional children and youth.* Boston: Houghton Mifflin.

Hutchison, D.J. (1978). The transdisciplinary approach. In J.B. Curry & K.K. Peppe (Eds.), *Mental retardation: Nursing approaches to care* (pp. 65–74). St. Louis: C.V. Mosby.

Idol, L., Nevin, A., & Paolucci-Whitcomb, P. (1994). *Collaborative consultation* (2nd ed.). Austin, TX: PRO-ED.

Individuals with Disabilities Education Act (IDEA) of 1990, PL 101-476, 20 U.S.C. §§ 1400 *et seq.*

Inge, K., & Snell, M. (1985). Teaching positioning and handling techniques to public school personnel through inservice training. *Journal of The Association for Persons with Severe Handicaps, 10,* 105–110.

Johnson, D.W., & Johnson, F.P. (1987a). *Joining together: Group theory and group skills* (3rd ed.). Englewood Cliffs, NJ: Prentice-Hall.

Johnson, D.W., & Johnson, R.T. (1987b). Research shows the benefit of adult cooperation. *Educational Leadership, 45*(3), 27–30.

Johnson, D.W., & Johnson, R.T. (1989). *Cooperation and competition: Theory and research.* Edina, MN: Interaction Book Company.

Johnson, D.W., Johnson, R.T., & Maruyama, G. (1983). Interdependence and interpersonal attraction among heterogeneous and homogeneous individuals: A theoretical formulation and a meta-analysis of the research. *Review of Educational Research, 53,* 5–54.

Johnston, M. (1994). Contrasts and similarities in case studies of teacher reflection and change. *Curriculum Inquiry, 24*(1), 9–26.

Jorgensen, C. (1992). Natural supports in inclusive schools: Curricular and teaching strategies. In J. Nisbet (Ed.), *Natural supports in school,* at work, and in the community for people with severe disabilities (pp. 179–215). Baltimore: Paul H. Brookes Publishing Co.

Jorgensen, C., & Calculator, S. (1994). The evolution of best practices in educating students with severe disabilities. In S. Calculator & C. Jorgensen (Eds.), *Including students with severe disabilities in schools: Fostering communication, interaction, and participation* (pp. 1–25). San Diego: Singular.

Karnish, K., Bruder, M.B., & Rainforth, B. (1995). A comparison of physical therapy in two school based treatment contexts. *Physical and Occupational Therapy in Pediatrics, 15*(4), 1–25.

Kircher, M.A. (1984). Motivation as a factor of perceived exertion in purposeful versus non-purposeful activity. *American Journal of Occupational Therapy, 38,* 165–170.

Kronberg, R.M., York-Barr, J., & Doyle, M.E. (1996). *Creating inclusive school communities: A staff development series for general and special educators: Module 2: Classrooms as caring communities.* Baltimore: Paul H. Brookes Publishing Co.

Kruger, L. (1988). Programmatic change strategies at the building level. In J.L. Graden, J.E. Zins, & M.J. Curtis (Eds.), *Alternative educational delivery systems: Enhancing instructional options for all students* (pp. 491–512). Washington, DC: National Association of School Psychologists.

Lane, H. (1976). *The wild boy of Aveyron.* Cambridge, MA: Harvard University Press.

Louis, K.S., & Kruse, S. (1996). *Professionalism and community: Perspectives on reforming urban schools.* Thousand Oaks, CA: Corwin Press.

Lyon, S., & Lyon, G. (1980). Team functioning and staff development: A role release approach to providing integrated educational services for severely handicapped students. *Journal of The Association for the Severely Handicapped, 5,* 250–263.

McCollum, J., & Stayton, V. (1985). Infant–parent interaction: Studies and intervention based on the SIAI model. *Journal of the Division for Early Childhood, 9*(2), 125–135.

McCormick, L., Cooper, M., & Goldman, R. (1979). Training teachers to maximize instructional time provided to severely and profoundly handicapped children. *AAESPH Review, 4,* 301–310.

McEwen, I.R., & Sheldon, M.L. (1995). Pediatric therapy in the 1990s: The demise of the educational versus medical dichotomy. *Physical and Occupational Therapy in Pediatrics, 15*(2), 33–45.

McWilliam, R.A., & Bailey, D.B. (1994). Predictors of service delivery models in center-based early intervention. *Exceptional Children, 61,* 56–71.

Montie, J.K. (1996). *Critical reflection with others: Teacher practices that support growing community for everybody's children.* Unpublished master's thesis, University of Minnesota, Minneapolis.

Morsink, C.V., Thomas, C.C., & Correa, V.I. (1991). *Interactive teaming: Consultation and collaboration in special programs.* Columbus, OH: Charles E. Merrill.

Mulligan, M., Lacy, L., & Guess, D. (1982). Effects of massed, distributed, and spaced trial sequencing on severely handicapped students' performance. *Journal of The Association for the Severely Handicapped, 7,* 48–51.

National Center for Educational Outcomes. (1995). *Foundations for NCEO's outcomes and indicators series.* University of Minnesota: Author.

Nietupski, J., Scheutz, G., & Ockwood, L. (1980). The delivery of communication therapy services to severely handicapped students: A plan for change. *Journal of The Association for the Severely Handicapped, 5,* 13–23.

Noddings, N. (1992). *The challenge to care in schools: An alternative approach to education.* New York: Teachers College Press.

Oberti v. Board of Education of the Borough of Clementon School District, 995F.2d 1204 (3rd Cir., 1993).

O'Brien, J., & Mount, B. (1991). Telling new stories: The search for capacity among people with severe handicaps. In L.H. Meyer, C.A. Peck, & L. Brown (Eds.), *Critical issues in the lives of people with severe disabilities* (pp. 89–92). Baltimore: Paul H. Brookes Publishing Co.

Orelove, F.P., & Sobsey, D. (1987). *Educating children with multiple disabilities: A transdisciplinary approach.* Baltimore: Paul H. Brookes Publishing Co.

Orelove, F.P., & Sobsey, D. (1991). *Educating children with multiple disabilities: A transdisciplinary approach* (2nd ed.). Baltimore: Paul H. Brookes Publishing Co.

Orelove, F.P., & Sobsey, D. (1996). *Educating children with multiple disabilities: A transdisciplinary approach* (3rd ed.). Baltimore: Paul H. Brookes Publishing Co.

Osborne, A.G., Jr. (1984). How the courts have interpreted the related services mandate. *Exceptional Children, 51,* 249–252.

Ottenbacher, K. (1982). Occupational therapy and special education: Some issues and concerns related to Public Law 94-142. *American Journal of Occupational Therapy, 36,* 81–84.

Parette, H.P., Jr., Hourcade, J.J., & Brimer, R.W. (1996). Degree of involvement and young children with cerebral palsy. *Physical Disabilities: Education and Related Services, 14*(2), 33–59.

Patterson, E.G., D'Wolff, N., Hutchison, D., Lowry, M., Schilling, M., & Siepp, J. (1976). *Staff development handbook: A resource for the transdisciplinary process.* New York: United Cerebral Palsy Associations.

Peck, C.A., Killen, C.C., & Baumgart, E. (1989). Increasing implementation of special education instruction in mainstream preschools: Direct and generalized nondirective consultation. *Journal of Applied Behavior Analysis, 22,* 197–210.

Perske, R. (1981). *Hope for the families.* Nashville, TN: Abingdon Press.

Peterson, C. (1980). Support services. In B. Wilcox & R. York (Eds.), *Quality education for the severely handicapped: The federal investment* (pp. 136–163). Washington, DC: U.S. Department of Education, Office of Special Education and Rehabilitative Services.

Preito, G.M. (1992). *Effects of physical therapist instruction on the frequency and performance of several assorted gross motor activities for students with motor disabilities.* Unpublished master's thesis, Hanhnemann University, Philadelphia.

Pugach, M., & Johnson, L. (1995). *Collaborative practitioners, collaborative schools.* Denver: Love Publishing.

Rainforth, B. (1985). *Collaborative efforts in the preparation of physical therapists and teachers of students with severe handicaps.* Unpublished doctoral dissertation, University of Illinois at Urbana-Champaign.

Rainforth, B., & Roberts, P. (1996). Physical therapy. In R.A. McWilliam (Ed.), *Rethinking pull-out services in early intervention: A professional resource* (pp. 243–265). Baltimore: Paul H. Brookes Publishing Co.

Rainforth, B., & York, J. (1987). Integrating related services into community instruction. *Journal of The Association for Persons with Severe Handicaps, 12,* 188–198.

Rapport, M.J.K. (1995). Laws that shape therapy services in educational environments. In I.R. McEwen (Ed.), *Occupational and physical therapy in educational environments* (pp. 5–32). Binghamton, NY: Haworth Press.

Roncker v. Walter, 700 F.2d 1058, *cert. denied,* 104 S.Ct. 196, 464 U.S. 864, 78 L.Ed.2d 171. (6th Cir. 1983).

Rosenholtz, S. (1989). *Teachers' workplace: The social organization of schools.* New York: Teachers College Press.

Sacramento City Unified School District v. Rachel H., 14 F.3rd 1398 (9th Cir. 1994).

Sailor, W., Anderson, J.L., Halvorsen, A.T., Doering, K., Filler, J., & Goetz, L. (1989). *The comprehensive local school: Regular education for all students with disabilities.* Baltimore: Paul H. Brookes Publishing Co.

Sailor, W., & Guess, D. (1983). *Severely handicapped students: An instructional design.* Boston: Houghton Mifflin.

Sailor, W., Wilcox, B., & Brown, L. (Eds.). (1980). *Methods of instruction for severely handicapped students.* Baltimore: Paul H. Brookes Publishing Co.

Sapon-Shevin, M. (1988). Working toward merger together: Seeing beyond the distrust and fear. *Teacher Education and Special Education, 11,* 103–110.

Schon, D.E. (1987). *Educating the reflective practitioner.* San Francisco: Jossey-Bass.

Sergiovanni, T.J. (1994). *Building community in schools.* San Francisco: Jossey-Bass.

Shumway-Cook, A., & Woolacott, M. (1995). *Motor control: Theory and practical applications.* Baltimore: Williams & Wilkins.

Slavin, R.E., Madden, N.A., & Leavey, M. (1984). Effects of cooperative grouping and individualized instruction on mainstreamed students. *Exceptional Children, 50,* 434–443.

Smyth, J. (1989). Developing and sustaining critical reflection in teacher education. *Journal of Teacher Education, 40*(2), 2–9.

Snell, M.E. (Ed.). (1993). *Systematic instruction of persons with severe handicaps* (3rd ed.). Columbus, OH: Charles E. Merrill.

Snell, M.E., & Raynes, M. (1995). Changing roles in inclusive schools: Staff perspectives at Gilbert Linous Elementary. *Kappa Delta Pi Record, 31*(3), 104–109.

Sontag, E., Smith, J., & Certo, N. (1977). *Educational programming for the severely and profoundly handicapped.* Reston, VA: Council for Exceptional Children.

Sparks-Langer, G.M., & Colton, A.B. (1991). Synthesis of research on teachers' reflective thinking. *Educational Leadership, 48*(6), 37–44.

Stainback, S., & Stainback, W. (1987). Facilitating merger through personnel preparation. *Teacher Education and Special Education, 10,* 185–190.

Stainback, S., & Stainback, W. (Eds.). (1992). *Curriculum considerations in inclusive classrooms: Facilitating learning for all students.* Baltimore: Paul H. Brookes Publishing Co.

Stainback, S., & Stainback, W. (Eds.). (1996). *Inclusion: A guide for educators.* Baltimore: Paul H. Brookes Publishing Co.

Stainback, S.B., Stainback, W.C., & Harris, K.C. (1989). Support facilitation: An emerging role for special educators. *Teacher Education and Special Education, 12,* 148–153.

Steinbeck, T. (1986). Purposeful activity and performance. *American Journal of Occupational Therapy, 40,* 529–541.

Sternat, J., Messina, R., Nietupski, J., Lyon, S., & Brown, L. (1977). Occupational and physical therapy services for severely handicapped students: Toward a naturalized public school service delivery model. In E. Sontag, J. Smith, & N. Certo (Eds.), *Educational programming for the severely and profoundly handicapped* (pp. 263–287). Reston, VA: Council for Exceptional Children.

Stokes, T., & Baer, D. (1977). An implicit technology of generalization. *Journal of Applied Behavior Analysis, 10,* 349–367.

Strickland, B.B., & Turnbull, A.P. (1990). *Developing and implementing individualized education programs* (3rd ed.). Columbus, OH: Charles E. Merrill.

Taylor, S.J. (1988). Caught in the continuum: A critical analysis of the principle of the Least Restrictive Environment. *Journal of The Association for the Severely Handicapped, 13,* 41–53.

The Association for Persons with Severe Handicaps. (1986). *Position statement on the provision of related services.* Seattle, WA: Author.

Thomas, M.A. (Ed.). (1976). *Hey, don't forget about me! Education's investment in the severely, profoundly and multiply handicapped.* Reston, VA: Council for Exceptional Children.

Thousand, J., Fox, T., Reid, R., Godek, J., Williams, W., & Fox, W. (1986). *The homecoming model: Educating students who present intensive educational challenges within regular education environments.* Burlington: University of Vermont.

Thousand, J., Nevin-Parta, A., & Fox, W. (1987). Inservice training to support the education of learners with severe handicaps in their local public schools. *Teacher Education and Special Education, 10,* 4–13.

Thousand, J.S., & Villa, R.A. (1992). Collaborative teams: A powerful tool for school restructuring. In R.A. Villa, J.S. Thousand, W. Stainback, & S. Stainback (Eds.), *Restructuring for caring and effective education: An administrative guide to creating heterogeneous schools* (pp. 73–108). Baltimore: Paul H. Brookes Publishing Co.

Thousand, J.S., Villa, R.A., & Nevin, A.I. (Eds.). (1994). *Creativity and collaborative learning: A practical guide to empowering students and teachers.* Baltimore: Paul H. Brookes Publishing Co.

Vandercook, T., & York, J. (1990). A team approach to program development and support. In W. Stainback & S. Stainback (Eds.), *Support networks for inclusive schooling: Interdependent integrated education* (pp. 95–122). Baltimore: Paul H. Brookes Publishing Co.

Villa, R.A., & Thousand, J.S. (1992). Student collaboration: An essential for curriculum delivery in the 21st century. In S. Stainback & W. Stainback (Eds.), *Curriculum considerations in inclusive classrooms: Facilitating learning for all students* (pp. 117–142). Baltimore: Paul H. Brookes Publishing Co.

Webster's ninth new collegiate dictionary. (1987). Springfield, MA: Merriam-Webster.

Whelan, R.J. (1996). Collaboration: From oversight to shared vision. In E.L. Meyen, G.A. Vergason, & R.J. Whelan (Eds.), *Strategies for teaching exceptional children in inclusive settings* (pp. 391–400). Denver: Love Publishing.

Wilcox, B., & Bellamy, G.T. (1982). *Design of high school programs for severely handicapped students.* Baltimore: Paul H. Brookes Publishing Co.

Williams, W., Fox, T., Thousand, J., & Fox, W. (1990). Level of acceptance and implementation of best practices in the education of students with severe handicaps in Vermont. *Education and Training in Mental Retardation, 25*(2), 120–131.

York, J., Giangreco, M.F., Vandercook, T., & Macdonald, C. (1992). Integrating support personnel in the inclusive classroom. In S. Stainback & W. Stainback (Eds.), *Curriculum considerations in inclusive classrooms: Facilitating learning for all students* (pp. 101–116). Baltimore: Paul H. Brookes Publishing Co.

York, J., Rainforth, B., & Dunn, W. (1990). Training needs of physical and occupational therapists who provide services to children and youth with severe disabilities. In A.P. Kaiser & C.M. McWhorter (Eds.), *Preparing personnel to work with persons with severe disabilities* (pp. 153–180). Baltimore: Paul H. Brookes Publishing Co.

York, J., Rainforth, B., & Giangreco, M.F. (1990). Transdisciplinary teamwork and integrated therapy: Clarifying some misconceptions. *Pediatric Physical Therapy, 2*(2), 73–79.

Ysseldyke, J.E., & Thurlow, M.L. (1994). What results should be measured to decide whether instruction is working for students with disabilities? *Special Services in the Schools, 9*(2), 39–49.

3

Home, School,
and Community Partnerships
Building Inclusive Teams

Christine L. Salisbury and Carl J. Dunst

The nature of the relationship between schools and families has changed since the mid-1970s. These changes have had at least three sources of influence. First, federal legislation in the early 1970s provided an entrée for parents of children with disabilities into the program-planning process. Subsequent amendments to those earlier pieces of legislation strengthened the opportunities for involvement afforded to parents and created expectations that schools would conceptualize their roles to support the entire family system. Consequently, the field has witnessed an evolution from parent involvement, to home–school partnerships, to

family involvement, to a recognition of the essential role that communities play in supporting education. Recent program and policy initiatives have gone even further, underscoring the importance of understanding and addressing community resources and supports in the design of systems of support for children, families, and schools (Dryfoos, 1994; Stone, 1993; U.S. Department of Education, 1994a). Second, school restructuring and reform initiatives in general education have begun to create opportunities for parents to become more substantively involved in school decision making (Newmann & Wehlage, 1995). Ac-

Preparation of this chapter was supported, in part, by grant H086D90006 from the U.S. Department of Education, Office of Special Education Programs, to the State University of New York at Binghamton and by Cooperative Agreement H086V0007 from the U.S. Department of Education, Office of Special Education Programs, to Allegheny University of the Health Sciences. The opinions expressed herein do not necessarily reflect the position or policy of the U.S. Department of Education, and no official endorsement should be inferred.

cording to research conducted by the Center on Organization and Restructuring in Schools (Newmann & Wehlage, 1995), schools that have distinguished themselves as making significant strides in restructuring educational practices are those that tend to have a high level of parent participation. However, the nature of the interactions between schools and families seems to vary, and high levels of participation may not be universally positive. There is, in fact, a rising concern among general education professionals that schools must change historical patterns of interaction with families and be more responsive to diverse family and child needs (Newmann & Wehlage, 1995; Powell, 1989). Third, parents have become more vocal in their desire for accountability and student achievement. The need to reach, empower, and mobilize not only parents, but families, is now actively being addressed by the general education community, with a particular focus on workable strategies applicable to families from diverse backgrounds now comprising local educational communities (U.S. Department of Education, 1994a). Evidence exists that parents play substantive roles in setting the conditions for improved school and postschool performance (Henderson & Berla, 1994) and that alliances that include school, home, and community groups are necessary for children, families, and schools to be successful.

There is, then, a growing recognition that historical conceptions must change regarding the composition of the team and its role and purview in meeting the needs of children and families. Whether referred to as comprehensive, inclusive, complete, or full-support schools, their intent is to link educational, psychological, social, and other supportive resources to children and families so that they are optimally prepared to benefit from their educational experiences. The unifying element across school, home, and

community initiatives is the family. Given the diversity of child and family needs within the educational community, schools can no longer narrowly define their mission as a solely academic enterprise without also acknowledging the myriad other issues that affect the performance of children in today's public schools (Melaville & Blank, 1994; U.S. Department of Education, 1994b). The ultimate success of meeting student needs will, in fact, rest on the educational system's ability to link effectively with home and community. Such reconceptualizations will require that professionals and educational systems organize themselves differently and alter traditionally defined policies and practices.

Underlying the call for home–school–community partnerships is the assumption that parents are afforded meaningful opportunities to function as equal team members in the educational communities that support their children. Despite the convergence of these three influences and the consonance with disability education policy, schools continue to struggle with how to meaningfully involve parents and families in the educational process. Although there are many day-to-day challenges, strategies do exist to address implementation issues at the level of both policy and practice. The purposes of this chapter are threefold: first, to briefly review the nature of home–school–community partnerships; second, to identify factors that affect the quality of these partnerships; and finally, to describe strategies, approaches, and practices for developing partnerships that include schools, families, and communities in the educational process.

Three values ground how we have chosen to structure this chapter. First, we believe that systems change is necessary to the development of meaningful home–school–community partnerships. The context in which children are educated and families live provides important supports, and sometimes challenges, to their interactions with educational systems. How those systems respond to the needs of families can significantly affect the quality of the interaction and the extent to which the outcome is truly a partnership. Second, we believe that schools must strive to be family centered to adequately address and respond to the myriad factors affecting children and families. Schools and programs that are family-centered are ones that are responsive to family concerns, desires, and priorities; employ parent–professional partnerships and collaborative strategies for achieving desired goals and outcomes; and place families in pivotal decision-making roles as part of children's education. Finally, we believe that schools have a responsibility to develop a broad array of supports that are responsive to the diverse needs of children, families, and the professionals who support them. This means that schools must not only recognize, but also accept and value, the differences represented in their classrooms and communities. No longer can schools "do it all." Partnerships with other agencies in their local communities are becoming increasingly necessary to help support the array of needs presented by children and their families (Melaville & Blank, 1994). Effective schools cultivate those extended partnerships so that instruction, family support, and professional resources flow fluidly between home, school, and the community.

NATURE OF PARENT
AND FAMILY PARTNERSHIPS

Children whose parents are involved in their education experience more success in school than students whose parents are not as involved (Epstein, 1993; Guralnick, 1989; Powell, 1989). Epstein (1993) describes five types of parent involvement: parenting, communicating, volunteering, learning at home, and representing other parents. We add to this list the contention that parents' involvement in their local community is equally important in mobilizing resources that can support not only their own children but also other children and the educational programs throughout their community. Parent involvement in each of these areas has the potential to produce positive outcomes for parents, students, and educators (Epstein, 1993). However, that potential can only be realized if schools are willing to explore the development of partnerships in ways that are both responsive and flexible. Given the contributions that parents can make toward their child's achievements, we believe it is important for schools to think broadly about the ways in which they can work with families and use a variety of means in which parents can be meaningfully involved in their child's education (Shevin, 1983; Vincent, Laten, Salisbury, Brown, & Baumgart, 1980).

Traditional Parent Involvement

Decision making has been the prevailing and traditional form of parent participation on teams constituted to support children with disabilities. Although the incorporation of parents on such teams is acknowledged in the educational (Turnbull & Turnbull, 1986a; Turnbull & Winton, 1984) and related services (Bazyk, 1989; Campbell, 1987; Rainforth & York, 1987) literatures, much of what transpires during team meetings does not meaningfully include parents in the decision-making process, nor yield collaboratively derived outcomes. This point becomes critical when parents are expected to support decisions of the team that directly affect the family as well as the child, such as recommendations for how to implement activities in the home or what goals will be addressed first.

Throughout the 20th century, a number of role changes have emerged for parents of children with disabilities. Parents have moved from being perceived as the source of their child's problems to having more proactive roles as service developers, learners, teachers of their child, advocates, and educational decision makers (Summers, Behr, & Turnbull, 1989; Turnbull & Turnbull, 1986a). Unfortunately, in our zealousness to create more substantive roles and responsibilities for parents within the educational context, we have forgotten the primary role of these individuals—parents as family members. Parents' abilities to function effectively as integral members of an educational team will, in large part, be mediated by a variety of other factors—principally their responsibilities to their child and family. Failure to acknowledge and address these factors in the design and development of educational programs and policies will minimize the willingness and ability of parents to participate and hamper the development of collaborative home–school relationships.

The link between home and school is an essential one that can be optimized when professionals understand how families function and why it is necessary to match program practices to family needs. Dunst, Trivette, and Deal (1988) noted that the mismatch between what professionals and families see as needs can create conflict and can result in families failing to follow professionally prescribed interventions. Specifically, they suggest that

> what may be viewed as either oppositional or apathetic behavior may have less to do with contempt for professional opinion and more to do with lack of consensus regarding the nature of the presenting problem, the need for treatment (medical, educational, therapeutic), and the course of the action that should be taken. (p. 3)

It is therefore important that professionals engage in a consensus-building process within the team, acknowledge and value differences among families, and address discrepancies between professional and parent agendas.

WHY SHOULD PARENTS BE INVOLVED?

There are legal, empirical, and practical motivations for promoting the inclusion of parents and families in educational programs. Federal and state policies provide a backdrop of minimum standards for involving parents in decisions about their child's educational plan and services. Findings from school- and community-based research indicate that parent involvement can positively affect the growth and development of the child and the integrity of educational programs. Beyond these two sources of information, there are practical issues that make it imperative that schools, communities, and families work together to improve the nature and quality of service delivery systems.

Legal Basis for Participation

PL 94-142 (the Education for All Handicapped Children Act of 1975) and subsequent amendments including the Individuals with Disabilities Education Act (IDEA) of 1990 (PL 101-476) and the Individuals with Disabilities Education Act Amendments of 1991 (PL 102-119) stipulate that parents be afforded the opportunity to actively participate in planning for their child's educational program and that such participation be as equal members of the individualized education program (IEP) and individualized family service plan (IFSP) teams. Turnbull and Turnbull (1986a) cited a policy interpretation of IEP requirements prepared by the Office of Special Education Programs, U.S. Department of Education, that clarifies expectations for state and local education agencies related to the inclusion of parents in the decision-making process:

> The parents of a child [with a disability] are expected to be equal participants, along with school personnel, in developing, reviewing,

and revising the child's IEP. This is an active role in which the parents (a) participate in the discussion about the child's need for special education and related services, and (b) join with the other participants in deciding what services the agency will provide the child. (p. 226)

Parent participation on teams and in the educational process would therefore seem to constitute a desired priority. However, compliance with legal and legislative requirements should be the last reason we choose to include parents. Rather, the most defensible arguments are based on adoption of a set of values, principles, and practices that compel us to include parents because it is good for children, families, schools, and communities.

Although there is a clear mandate requiring the active participation of parents in the IEP and IFSP process, problems with interpretation of these regulations have hindered implementation efforts. Research on the nature of parent involvement in the IEP process since the passage of PL 94-142 indicates that participation has largely been passive rather than active (Goldstein, Strickland, Turnbull, & Curry, 1980; Turnbull & Turnbull, 1986a). These studies indicate that, in at least half of the cases cited, IEPs were completed by the staff prior to meeting with the parents and that parents had little knowledge of the content of the IEP document. For these parents, "participation" meant listening to professionals and approving the IEP already prepared for their review. Such practices are clearly inconsistent with the intent of the legislation.

Findings of limited participation may also be linked to the reality of who actually attends the IEP meetings and how professionals view the involvement of parents. Scanlon, Arick, and Phelps (1981) found that the special education teacher and the mother attended the IEP meetings 75% of the time, whereas professionals from other

disciplines attended only about 30% of the time. It clearly becomes difficult to function as a "team" when attendance disparities such as this exist. General and special education research indicates that school staff often rank parent contributions as less important than their own (Elam, Lowell, & Gallup, 1994; Gilliam & Coleman, 1981; Morgan & Rhode, 1983; Yoshida, Fenton, Kaufman, & Maxwell, 1978), or view the involvement of parents as an encroachment into the school's area of expertise (Allen & Hudd, 1987).

Recent federal legislation in the field of early intervention significantly broadened the scope of responsibilities for professionals working with infants and toddlers who are at risk for developmental disabilities or who evidence disabling conditions. The Individuals with Disabilities Education Act Amendments of 1991 (PL 102-119) and its predecessor (the Education of the Handicapped Act Amendments of 1986, PL 99-457) amended PL 94-142 to create Part H, the Program for Infants and Toddlers with Disabilities. This law requires each state to develop a statewide system that includes provisions for addressing all required components. A multidisciplinary evaluation and an IFSP are among the required components of Part H.

Conceptually similar to the IEP, the IFSP is a central component in the implementation of the Part H program and, therefore, must be addressed by professionals at the direct services level. However, the focus of services under Part H is on the capacity of families to meet the needs of their infants and toddlers, making it necessary that teams become family centered, rather than solely child focused, in their orientation. Walsh, Campbell, and McKenna (1988) pointed out that the IFSP, like the IEP, is based on information derived from a multidisciplinary assessment of child and family needs and includes an assessment of family priorities and concerns.

Conceptual and Research Bases for Participation

Children do not exist in isolation. They function as members of interdependent systems within the family, school, and community. Within each system exist forces and supports that influence the child's behavior both within and among a variety of environments (Bronfenbrenner, 1979; Minuchin, 1974). Placing the child within an ecological context, it then becomes clear that the child's performance in school will be affected, in large part, by what transpires at home as well as in school and in the community at large. However, parents are the only people who will be able to contribute information about the values, priorities, and supports available within the home environment. Because research indicates that parents are reliable sources of information (Beckman, 1984; Gradel, Thompson, & Sheehan, 1981), the formulation of ecologically valid and educationally functional goals is logically dependent on the participation of parents in the planning and decision-making process.

Home and community environments represent important learning contexts in which children with disabilities will need to demonstrate skills acquired at school. If professionals are to adequately prepare students to successfully function in future environments (Brown, Nietupski, & Hamre-Nietupski, 1976; Salisbury & Vincent, 1990; Vincent, Salisbury et al., 1980), they will need to teach students in such a way that skills can be effectively generalized to settings beyond the school context. An ecologically grounded, home- and community-referenced curriculum provides information about those natural contexts that professionals can use to develop appropriate intervention strategies

(Rainforth & Salisbury, 1988; Salisbury & Vincent, 1990; Vincent, Salisbury, Strain, McCormick, & Tessier, 1990).

There are at least two significant trends emerging from recent empirical and conceptual work in the field of special education and related services that have implications for the parent as a team member. First, although there are considerable data to support the efficacy of didactic (adult-initiated and -directed) interventions using parents as "therapists" or "teachers," there is also evidence to support the efficacy of naturally occurring, ecologically based intervention strategies that deemphasize the direct instruction role for parents. These data indicate that children learn well when adults capitalize on child-initiated activities. Activities selected by the child, rather than the parent, are inherently motivating to children and create opportunities in which adults can reinforce and extend important skills within naturally occurring routines in ways that minimize the role of "teacher" or "therapist" (Bazyk, 1989; Bricker & Cripe, 1989; Lucca & Settles, 1981; MacDonald & Gillette, 1986; Mahoney & Powell, 1988; Rainforth & Salisbury, 1988; Salisbury & Vincent, 1990; Vincent, Salisbury, Laten, & Baumgart, 1979; Warren & Kaiser, 1986). By emphasizing the value and use of incidental and other responsive teaching strategies, it is possible to preserve the primary role of parent while helping the parents promote their child's development.

Second, naturally occurring, ecologically based intervention programs have the potential of preserving and strengthening the positive reciprocal qualities of parent–child relationships that can otherwise be negatively affected when the parent is placed in a more directive "therapist" or "teacher" role (Bazyk, 1989; Humphry, 1989; Seitz & Provence, 1990; Simeonsson & Bailey, 1990; Summers et al., 1989; Turnbull &

Turnbull, 1986b; Tyler & Kogan, 1972). By vesting the control for the interaction with the child and encouraging parents to interact with their child "naturally," it is possible to minimize some of the frustrations, stress, and resentment that can occur when the parents feel pressed to have their child "make progress" (Bazyk, 1989; Turnbull & Turnbull, 1986b).

The American Occupational Therapy Association (1989) recommended giving parents the freedom to determine the extent and nature of their involvement in therapy and home activities (Bazyk, 1989). Altheide and Livermore (1987) reported that the American Speech-Language-Hearing Association (ASHA) also highlighted the importance of giving consideration to the needs of families in the development of communication systems. According to the authors, ASHA went further by endorsing the inclusion of families on the interdisciplinary evaluation team. Positive parent–child relationships are viewed by these two professional organizations as an important outcome of therapy with the child.

Practical Considerations

Beyond the conceptual, empirical, and legal arguments for parent inclusion lies the practical reality that parents serve as long-term advocates and supports to their son or daughter. Because team membership is subject to change on a frequent basis, parents provide a source of continuity and stability essential for smooth transitions during and after the school years. This continuity becomes critical during the postschool years as young adults become "integrated" into a variety of residential, vocational, and leisure environments.

Without question, parents have influenced the course of educational policy in the United States more than any other group. Although the importance of their contribu-

tions has been endorsed at both the state and federal levels, it is ironic that parent involvement and inclusion in local program planning remains an area of some concern.

FACTORS AFFECTING FAMILY PARTICIPATION

If teams of professionals are to move beyond compliance to the encouragement, commitment, and meaningful inclusion of parents as equal team members, it will be necessary for all school personnel to identify those policies and practices that function as barriers to family participation. This section briefly reviews some of the key factors that parents and professionals identify as influences on affecting the quality of home–school relationships. This overview is not intended to be exhaustive and draws on our own work (Dunst & Trivette, 1996; Dunst, Trivette, & Deal, 1994; Dunst, Trivette, & Hamby, 1996; Dunst et al., 1988; Salisbury, 1987; Salisbury & Evans, 1988; Salisbury & Vincent, 1990; Salisbury, Vincent, & Gorofa, 1987; Vincent et al., 1990) and that of others in the fields of special education and related services (e.g., Altheide & Livermore, 1987; Bazyk, 1989; Epstein, 1987; Humphry, 1989, Lynch & Hanson, 1992; Turnbull & Turnbull, 1986a; Walker, 1989; Warren & Kaiser, 1986).

Systemic Challenges

Effective schools are those that evidence strong instructional leadership, a sense of professional community, empowered decision making, and the collaborative involvement of key stakeholders in supporting school change (Newmann & Wehlage, 1995). A complementary set of descriptors is common to schools evidencing inclusive educational practices (NICHCY, 1995; Villa & Thousand, 1995). Yet, the meaningful incorporation of families in the school context can be thwarted by such policies and practices as procedural barriers (e.g., restrictive visitation and access policies, time-driven meetings); lack of district-level planning and support for the incorporation of families in the school context; the existence of parallel services (e.g., special education versus unified parent–teacher organization); insufficient staff development opportunities for staff to learn how to work more effectively with parents; fragmented coordination (or competition) with agencies that also support the family; rigidly defined structures (e.g., schedules, transportation policies, procedural mazes); and/or site-based governance that marginalizes the family voice (Melaville & Blank, 1994; Roach, 1995; Kysilko, 1995; U.S. Department of Education, 1994b). In order for practices to change and those changes to sustain, the policies that drive those practices must be aligned to support restructuring the instructional and organizational context. It is within this organizational context that teams are created and function. Their ability to work effectively across disciplinary lines, within and outside of the school walls, will be enhanced by a supportive policy foundation and proactive administrative leadership.

Communication

Difficulties often arise when parents and professionals are not able to communicate effectively, either in person or through written correspondence. Two of the most obvious points of difficulty relate to 1) what is communicated and 2) how it is communicated. Communication problems between home and school may arise for one or more of the following reasons.

Communications Are Not in the Parents' Primary Language (Sign or Non-English) Sileo, Sileo, and Prater (1996) note that differences in cultural backgrounds and experiences have an impact on the qual-

ity of family–professional interactions. Differences in when and why the family or their predecessors came to the United States, the nature of their ties to extended family, and the role of education and educators in their native country can influence the norms and concerns of members from culturally diverse communities (Alper, Schloss, & Schloss, 1994; Harry, 1992). These factors, coupled with the manner in which schools respond to unique family circumstances, may hinder parents' abilities to obtain resources that affect their contributions to the school and their community.

Clearly, if professionals do not provide translators or bilingual services for both written and personal communications or recognize the need for and ways to accommodate diverse family needs, the likelihood that parents will participate in their children's education will be significantly reduced. When professionals cannot ensure that parents comprehend the information presented, then parents cannot provide either informed consent or effective support to teachers or their children. It is incumbent on school and community organizations to identify barriers and solutions to access and involvement in the educational process.

Professionals Use Jargon Many professionals use jargon common to their discipline as a shorthand way of communicating with colleagues. Although such practices may be convenient for some, they produce barriers to the participation of others not "in the know." For example, such terms as *ATNR, transdisciplinary, cross-modal,* and *aphasia* may threaten not only parents but also other members of the team. Using plain English and taking the time to define potentially unfamiliar terms enables everyone to be included in the conversation. It should be noted that many literate and well-educated parents find it difficult to understand the jargon-laden letters from school about their rights and protections in the IEP process.

Parents May Have Limitations If parents have intellectual or physical limitations, they may not be able to comprehend the newsletters, notes, and notices from the school or may not be able to respond to inquiries, or both. This point is particularly critical as it relates to the IEP process. In order for consent to be "informed," professionals must ensure that the information in forms and notices associated with the IEP process is fully understood by the parents (Shevin, 1983; Turnbull & Turnbull, 1986b). This may require follow-up telephone calls, face-to-face reviews, and/or alternative versions/modes of imparting important information. It is imperative that administrators demystify both the proceedings and the material to ensure what Shevin (1983) refers to as "informed participation."

Professionals Limit Communication to Administrative Tasks Research in both general and special education indicates that professionals most often communicate with parents to report academic progress, send home school-related information, and report behavior problems. Parents of children in early intervention programs and primary grades report that professionals often share positive information about their child, but that the nature and frequency of this information sharing, as well as the amount of parent involvement, appears to decline sharply as the child moves through the school grades (Epstein, 1987; Salisbury & Evans, 1988). Parents need to hear what their child is doing well just as much as they need to hear about the problems.

Interpersonal Communication Skills May Be Ineffective Turnbull and Turnbull (1986a) provided a cogent description of nonverbal communication skills and their effects on parent–professional interactions. (Readers are referred to this book for more detailed information.) Conceptually, the words professionals use are only one small part of the communication interchange. Nonverbal actions and the paralinguistic features (tone, emphasis, timing) of what is said are equally important in communication with parents and other team members. The sum of both verbal and nonverbal elements of what is being described or discussed can facilitate or hinder contributions from others.

Parents may be ineffective in getting their messages across to professionals for a variety of reasons. For example, parents may be imprecise in their choice of words, making it difficult for others to grasp their meaning; they may be tense and angry if they perceive their contributions are not valued by others in the group; they may be demanding in their tone, actions, or both if their previous experiences with professionals have taught them that such behavior is necessary to get appropriate services for their child; or they may be noncommunicative because they are intimidated by the size and composition of the team. However, it is the professionals', rather than the parents', responsibility to ensure that parents are heard empathetically and that they are afforded meaningful participation.

Perceptions, Attitudes, and Values

How team members perceive themselves and each other, the attitudes they bring to the team meeting, and their own personal and professional value systems all play important roles in interpersonal interactions. Consequently, if we attempt to foster opportunities for meaningful parent and family inclusion in the educational process, it will be important for all members of the team to be aware of how these factors affect both the process and the outcomes of the interactions. The following are some of the major impediments to effective interactions with parents and other family members.

Insensitivity to Differences Among Families It is important for professionals to understand how families differ and what the implications of these unique characteristics are for home–school relationships. Families differ in membership, structure, ideology, culture, beliefs/values, and resources. Recognition of these unique qualities is a necessary prerequisite to effective inclusion of parents as team members. The demographics of America's families are changing, which, in turn, can affect the involvement of parents in the school context (Aronson, 1996; Hanson & Carta, 1996; Vincent & Salisbury, 1988). Professionals can no longer assume that every family is headed by two parents, that English is the primary language, that school is the highest priority for families, or that the child's parents are necessarily the primary decision makers in the family unit. In addition, it is important to recognize that families' resources are different and they will mobilize their resources to address what they perceive to be the most important priorities first (Dunst et al., 1988). Quite often, parents will act to stabilize and meet the family's needs for survival before they will concern themselves with school-valued agendas (Epstein, 1987). Because the structure, resources, and functions within a family change over time, programs must accommodate these changes and create options that are both flexible and responsive to the changing priorities and needs of children and their families.

Cultural Differences Between Families and Professionals The United States is becoming increasingly culturally diverse (Hanson & Carta, 1996), and these differences can and do often influence parent–professional and family–professional relationships. This is increasingly the case when the cultural beliefs, values, and attitudes of families and professionals are different (Lynch & Hanson, 1992). Evidence from any number of studies clearly indicates that cultural heritage shapes and influences parenting beliefs and behaviors, parenting styles, desired or acceptable child behavior, the role parents play in their children's "education," and so on (e.g., Bernstein & Stettner-Eaton, 1994; DeGangi, Wietlisbach, Poisson, Stein, & Royeen, 1994), and that, when these differ from those of professionals, conflict and difficulties in parent–professional and family–professional relationships can occur (Edwards, Gandini, & Giovanni, 1996; Hess, Price, Dickson, & Conroy, 1981; Howes & Matheson, 1992; Weisner, Gallimore, & Jordan, 1988). The fact that more and more families have cultural beliefs, attitudes, and values that differ from those of professionals with whom they interact and work requires increased sensitivity on the part of professionals to be sure that all aspects of involving families in their children's education are culturally relevant and meaningful. Lynch and Hanson's (1992) compilation of the cultural similarities and differences among people having different ethnic and racial origins is especially useful for ensuring that this occurs as part of parent–professional and family–professional partnerships.

Parents Viewed as Adversaries Rather than Partners Our perceptions of others are affected by our experiences, values, and beliefs. When the values and priorities of professionals conflict with those of parents, tensions may surface and effective communication becomes difficult. When the goals of professionals do not match those of parents, some professionals move to judge the parents as somehow less effective or caring. It is counterproductive to the development of a collaborative relationship to assume that, because there is a difference of opinion, parents do not have the best interests of their child at heart. The goals of collaboration are better served by trying to understand what motivates parents to respond as they do and how professionals can work effectively with parents to identify the information necessary to address mutually valued goals and priorities.

Parents Viewed in a Deficits– Versus Strengths–Based Manner The likelihood that parents and professionals are able to communicate positively and productively is influenced by the degree to which professionals view parents in a positive light, recognize family capabilities and competencies, and meaningfully involve parents in their child's education (Dunst et al., 1996). Evidence indicates that parent–professional relationships and transactions produce positive benefits when they are characterized by professional behaviors, attitudes, and beliefs that take a strengths-based, rather than a deficits-based, approach to working with families (Dunst & Trivette, 1996).

Parents Viewed as Less Observant, Perceptive, or Intelligent than Professionals There is a critical need to "elevate" the status of parents in the eyes of professionals to one in which parents are viewed as important sources of knowledge, expertise, and the like concerning their child. Research by Gilliam and Coleman (1981), coupled with observations of professionals in the field (i.e., clinical wisdom), highlights the fact that many administrators and practitioners do not value the input of parents in their child's educational planning process. These findings have been underscored by scholars from the field of general education (e.g., Elam et al., 1994; U.S. Department of Education, 1994b). Actions such as completing the IEP prior to the meeting, failing to provide transportation or child care so that parents can participate in their child's education, making condescending or judgmental statements when parents do make contributions, and displaying an "aura" of preeminent professional knowledge illustrate the concerns of many parents and professionals. In contrast, research by Bricker and others indicates that parents are accurate assessors of their child's abilities and that their contributions can be extremely valuable in the program-planning process (e.g., Bricker & Squires, 1989).

Professional Constraints

Professionals may experience both professional and logistical constraints that affect their ability to be effective team members. They may feel pressured to "have all the answers" when they do not. Because many children with disabilities present complex diagnostic and educational challenges for professionals, it is neither realistic nor appropriate to expect that one discipline will possess all the information necessary to assess and remediate a child's learning difficulties. In addition, to take such a myopic view can convey competitiveness, "turf protection," and/or individualistic agendas. These messages are counterproductive to a cooperative team process and implicitly constrain opportunities for collaboration with other members of the team.

Professionals may also experience time constraints. Some professionals belong to several teams, or they serve on one team that has responsibility for students in many buildings. Consequently, it is difficult to be in several places at one time and relate effectively to individuals in each of those settings in which contact is episodic. Similarly, the ability to organize and manage the scheduling, service delivery, and evaluation elements across teams or sites can make teamwork itself a significant stressor for professionals. Thus, it is important for professionals to be aware that role and time constraints can affect their attitudes, perceptions, and interactions with others.

Process Logistics and Dynamics

Parent attendance at team meetings will be affected by availability of child care and transportation, as well as scheduling of the IEP meeting. For example, if a mother cannot find or afford child care during the day and must bring small children along to a meeting, she may consider the effort too great compared to the meager amount of input she may be given in the decision-making process. However, if she knew that there would be child care provided at the school and that her input is both sought and valued, she might reconsider the amount of time and effort that would be involved to get herself and her young children to the meeting. Such logistical factors are described in greater detail by Turnbull and Turnbull (1986a). Similarly, the extent to which fathers participate will be affected by scheduling and other logistical factors (Vadasy, 1986).

Parent involvement is also affected by the dynamics of the team meeting, that is, how it is conducted and who is in attendance. Specifically, if the meeting is set in a formal conference room with the parents seated opposite a table of professionals, the parents will likely be intimidated and reluctant to contribute. Likewise, if the process at the meeting involves a "round-robin" sharing of formal assessment results rather than an informal discussion of expectations and needed supports, the parents are not likely to contribute actively to the discussion. This process is exacerbated by the number of professionals attending the meeting. Thus, by taking the perspective of the parents, it is easy to understand their reluctance to attend, much less contribute to, a meeting at which they perceive themselves as "outnumbered" by a plethora of professionals. Finally, if the program planning meeting is 1 of 10 for the day, scheduled for 20 minutes each, it is likely that parents will sense that the process is pro forma and that their "participation" is merely required to rubber stamp the planning document. It is important that professionals realize the impact of such factors,

singly or in combination, on the perceptions of parents and their subsequent involvement with district personnel.

PRIMARY IMPORTANCE OF FAMILY CHOICE

The notion of creating an array of program options for parent involvement is not new, but its importance cannot be overemphasized (MacMillan & Turnbull, 1983). Parents, not professionals, must be the ones to choose whether, how often, and in what capacity they will be involved in their child's education program. The fact that legislation requires that parents be afforded the opportunity to be actively involved in the decision-making process does not mean that all parents must be actively involved in the same way or at the same level. Ultimately, parents must make the decision about their degree of involvement. Schools and programs are also responsible for ensuring that the decision is an informed one.

Parents may hold markedly different views about the nature of their involvement in the educational process because of their own experiences as a student, their cultural norms, or their life commitments and priorities. Some may wish only to receive the school newsletter, others may choose to attend occasional meetings at school, and still others may wish to serve as officers in the parent–teacher organization or as members of the school board. Depending on their backgrounds and circumstances, some parents may prefer to support their children's learning at home by working with them on specific activities, whereas others may not actively support, and in some cases may interfere with, efforts of schools to promote particular activities and goals. Parents in this latter group pose particular challenges to school personnel because their actions, whether intentional or not, run counter to effective teaching and learning practices. In such circumstances, schools often reach to their community agency partners for assistance in providing support to students and families who are difficult to reach.

There is growing concern in the field of special education that parent participation is being viewed as an obligation rather than a right (Allen & Hudd, 1987). We must remember that parents have the right to decide what is most important for them, their child, and their family. Parents may decide on minimal levels of involvement. As long as this choice is an informed one, professionals should respect whatever decision parents make. At the same time, professionals must recognize that needs and priorities change over time and parents may elect different levels and types of involvement at different points in their child's life. Schools therefore have an obligation to promote the inclusion of parents and families on a continuing basis by offering a range of flexible involvement options throughout the school years.

How professionals and parents view their respective roles and responsibilities will directly affect the decision-making process and its outcomes for the team. Specifically, if parents see their roles as primarily parents, family providers, and family "stabilizers," whereas professionals see parents primarily as teachers or therapists of their children or more active participants in school-sponsored activities, then there may be a mismatch in the respective "pictures." In such cases teams must then discuss priorities and expectations. Because decisions are needed throughout every phase of the child's education, parents can, and should, be afforded the opportunity for participation at all points throughout the educational process. Other chapters in this book describe specific opportunities and strategies for involving parents in ways they choose or desire.

Finally, although parents and professionals frequently agree on the needs of children with disabilities, they may, from time to time, differ in their goals or expectations for the child. There are at least two types of disagreements that emerge over time. The first involves conflicting time lines. For example, parents may propose a goal that they see as attainable in the short run, one that would promote more positive interactions or reduce caregiving responsibilities (e.g., intelligible communication or independent toileting). Professionals on the team may concur that such goals are desirable but may propose supporting them as long-term, rather than short-term, goals. The reluctance of professionals to identify these goals as short term may reflect 1) a hesitation to commit to something they are not sure they can achieve given the limits of therapeutic or instructional intervention, 2) a different appraisal of the child's capabilities, and/or 3) a different set of instructional priorities for the child. It is important to recognize that abdication of responsibility or concurrence with professional opinion may not necessarily mean that parents approve of the decision. Personal histories, cultural norms, and differing life priorities may all contribute to the appearance of consensus and miscommunications.

A second type of disagreement can emerge when parents place a priority on a goal that professionals see as minimally related to the child's educational program. Such disagreements arise because of discrepant agendas. For example, the family may express an interest in having a child with significant speech and language difficulties learn the family's native language, whereas professionals may place a priority on production of four-word utterances that incorporate proper syntax. Family-valued goals, although perhaps not immediately related to the child's assessed needs, must be given consideration in the development of the IEP/IFSP. "School-valued, school-generated" goals may or may not be important to the family. When they are not, professionals should not be surprised at a lack of commitment or follow-through on the part of families (Dunst et al., 1988). To the extent that parents are provided meaningful vehicles for input into the development of program activities (both instructional and noninstructional), there will be an increased probability that the content will be socially and educationally valid and that implementation will be supported by family members.

BEYOND PARTICIPATION . . . TOWARD INCLUSION AND COLLABORATION

If parents and family members are truly thought of as equals on the IFSP or IEP team, then our actions toward them should be the same as those toward our professional colleagues. But are they? If we use the research literature on parent participation as a source of exemplars and reflect on the way we, as professionals, typically interact with our colleagues (see Table 3.1), our differential treatment of parents as team members becomes graphically apparent. Because these examples are drawn from the literature on preschool- and school-age students, generalization to the birth to 24-month–age range (IFSP team situations) may not be appropriate. For many professionals, however, this exercise helps illustrate areas in which current practices impede the promotion of inclusive team relationships.

Programs based on a belief in broad-based child and family inclusion go beyond the invitation to parents for "participation" in mandated activities such as IFSP or IEP meetings. Rather, inclusive schools and teams commit themselves to the development of collaborative home–school–community partnerships that are longitudi-

nal in nature, allow for fluctuating and flexible interactions across the school years, and respect the unique qualities and abilities of each participant and their contributions to the team process. Such practices lend themselves naturally to the promotion of collaborative teams that include a wide range of constituencies. To the extent that teams function collaboratively, are inclusive in their composition, and strive toward the development of broad-based, supportive relationships, there is a greater likelihood that they will produce positive outcomes for learners, staff, and families.

Based on the literature and constructs described in the preceding sections of this chapter, it is now possible to generate a preliminary list of promising practices to guide the actions of teams as they move toward the development of collaborative partnerships with families and the inclusion of parents as full and equal team members. These principles appear in Table 3.2.

Program planning and policy development are greatly enhanced when professionals have a clear idea of the outcomes or goals they wish to achieve. Program quality is directly affected by the extent to which the program's beliefs, knowledge base, and actions are internally consistent and supportive of the attainment of such outcomes (Salisbury, 1991). This section describes a number of promising practices, strategies, and approaches that are linked to the attainment of positive partnership outcomes. The principles listed in Table 3.2 are used here as a means of organizing the information on strategies for achieving optimal inclusion of parents and family members in the educational context.

Determine Preferences for Parent/Family Involvement

Teams must adopt strategies and procedures for obtaining information from families

Table 3.1.   Differential interactions with colleagues and parents

With my colleagues, I . . .	With parents, I frequently . . .
Take no action without first soliciting their input.	Complete the IEP before they arrive.
Value and respect their comments.	Am skeptical of their motivations and judgmental in my perceptions.
Schedule meetings to fit their commitments.	Notify them about when and where the meeting will be held.
Communicate regularly on progress and problems.	Notify them only when there are problems.
Accept their judgments about how much they need to be involved.	Question their commitment to their child when they do not attend meetings/events.
Collaboratively identify skills and activities to be worked on at school.	Inform them of the tasks they need to follow through on at home.
Suggest activities that are important for school or the community.	Recommend they reinforce skills that are important for school.
Reach consensus when there are differing opinions.	Note their concerns, but then move on.

about their desired involvement. Many programs and schools use checklists, whereas others conduct home visits or conferences. Regardless of the form or process used to gather information, it is important for educational programs to obtain at least the following information:

- Desired frequency of contact with program/school
- Preferred type of contact from school (written, telephone, personal)
- Preferred location of meetings, if necessary, as well as child care and transportation needs
- Preferred type of involvement with school/program

Those programs opting for the checklist approach will find several examples in the literature (e.g., Ford et al., 1989; Turnbull & Turnbull, 1986a). Figures 3.1 and 3.2 provide examples of these kinds of checklists.

Based on our experiences, we recommend sending such inquiries home after staff have determined whether families of the children they serve have any unique needs (e.g., English not primary language; child does not live with parents; parent or guardian has limited reading ability). The information detailed in such a survey will be most useful for long-range planning when it is gathered at the start of the school year. We also recommend that the survey document be in a checklist format and limited to one page. Although there are admittedly drawbacks to forced-choice formats, we find that open-ended questions frequently do not yield information that is specific enough for designing program options.

The wording on checklists is very important because it conveys attitudes about parents. Using a gradient from "prefer not to be involved at this time" to "would like to be directly involved" conveys a more positive array of choices to parents than does

Table 3.2.   Principles of inclusionary practices

1. Each parent or family is given the opportunity to identify how and to what degree he or she wishes or they wish to become involved in the child's educational program.
2. Schools develop a continuum of strategies and options for enhancing the inclusion of parents or families in the educational context.
3. Parents are treated as equal members of teams.
4. Schools support and promote the self-sufficiency and development of families through integrated and normalized resources.
5. Schools employ family-centered principles and practices as a profamily approach to improving child, parent, and family functioning.

"no involvement" to "actively involved." We also recommend that parents be encouraged to send the checklists back in their child's backpack or lunch box as a means of increasing the rate of return.

Programs opting for conference-based information gathering will need to plan for a greater investment of time. That is, although this approach offers a more personal and richer base of information, it also requires considerably more time and energy on the part of staff. For many families, such an approach is more appealing and practical. Consequently, staff must be clear about their objectives prior to initiating contact with the family.

Each approach has advantages and disadvantages that must be balanced against the resources of the program, the needs of the child and family, and the goals toward which all participants are working. Many programs incorporate several methods of information gathering, tailoring each to the outcomes they wish to achieve. Regardless of the method selected, professionals must remain cognizant of how such strategies will be perceived by the family and influence the responses families provide.

Strategies and Options for Including Families in Educational Contexts

It is very important that parent inclusion be defined more broadly than involvement in the IEP or IFSP meeting. Only recently have

we begun to accumulate empirically based information about the scope of parents' involvement outside of the conference situation (e.g., Epstein, 1987; Salisbury & Evans, 1988). This research indicates that parents are "involved" more frequently than professionals previously believed in activities such as reading to their children, checking their children's homework, and discussing events occurring at school.

However, even these "pictures" of parent involvement are traditional and more constrained than they need to be. In reality, the child's educational context encompasses home, school, and community. Such a conceptualization requires that parent, child, and family priorities and interests be explored relative to each environment. Each environment becomes an extension of the school and a viable location for intervention with or on behalf of the child. Regardless of where instruction occurs, children emerge as the prime benefactors when parents and professionals work together during assessment, program design, teaching, and evaluation.

The quality of this partnership will rest, in large part, on the value schools place on parent involvement. One index of such an investment is the nature and frequency of contact between parents and teachers. There is no substitute for personal contact between schools and families. Parents report a preference for more frequent, but informal, con-

What Does Your Family Consider Important About School Contacts?

Parents have different ideas about the kinds and amounts of information they want to get from school about their child. The list below contains different ways you and your child's teacher might communicate with each other. Please circle the number to the right of the phrase to show how important each type of contact is to you.

		NA	not at all					extremely	RANK	COMMENTS
1.	Written notes	0	1	2	3	4	5	(6)	3	
2.	School newsletters	0	1	2	(3)	4	5	6		
3.	Parent/teacher conferences or individualized education program (IEP) meetings	0	1	2	3	4	5	(6)	2	
4.	Open house	0	1	(2)	3	4	5	6		
5.	Informal contacts	0	1	2	3	4	(5)	6	1	Phone call
6.	Parent / Teacher Organization (PTO) meetings	0	1	2	(3)	4	5	6		
7.	Classroom observation	0	1	2	3	(4)	5	6		
8.	Other, please specify: _____	0	1	2	3	4	5	6		

Using the above list, place the numbers 1, 2, or 3 next to the three most important ways of communicating between your family and your child's teacher.

A. How much contact do you want to have with your child's teacher after your child begins public school?
✔Daily   ___Once a week   ___Once a month
___Once a semester   ___Other (specify)

B. Would you prefer
___to initiate most of the contacts with your child's teacher?
___the teacher to initiate contacts with you?
✔or both?

Figure 3.1.   Sample checklist on school communication. (Source unknown.)

tact with professionals (Turnbull & Turnbull, 1986a; U.S. Department of Education, 1994b). We find that having one or two team members cultivate a relationship with parents over a period of time sends a strong message that each partner (parent and professional) cares about the child and the family. We also find, for example, that "shuttle notebooks," weekly newsletters, "minute-a-day" telephone calls, "good news notes,"

What Is Important for Your Child to Learn at School?

Parents want their child to go to a classroom where he or she will make progress. Children can make progress in different areas, and some areas may be more important than others. The list below contains different areas your child may progress in next year. Please circle the number to the right of the phrase to show how important it is for your child to progress in this area next year.

		NA	not at all					extremely	RANK
1.	Learn basic concepts such as colors, numbers, shapes, etc.	0	1	2	③	4	5	6	___
2.	Learn prereading and reading skills such as letters.	0	1	2	3	④	5	6	___
3.	Learn to use a pencil and scissors.	0	1	②	3	4	5	6	___
4.	Learn to listen and follow directions.	0	1	2	3	4	⑤	6	___
5.	Learn to share and play with other children.	0	1	2	3	4	5	⑥	_1_
6.	Learn to be creative.	0	1	2	③	4	5	6	___
7.	Learn more communication skills.	0	1	2	3	4	5	⑥	_3_
8.	Learn confidence and independence.	0	1	2	3	4	⑤	6	___
9.	Learn to work independently.	0	1	2	3	4	⑤	6	___
10.	Learn to climb, run, and jump.	0	①	2	3	4	5	6	___
11.	Learn self-care skills such as toileting, dressing, feeding.	0	1	2	3	4	5	⑥	_2_
12.	Learn to follow classroom rules and routines.	0	1	2	3	④	5	6	___

Using the above list, place the numbers 1, 2, and 3 next to the three most important areas for your child to progress in next year.

Figure 3.2. Sample checklist on child learning. (Source unknown.)

and home and class visits foster an important connectedness between home and school.

Cervone and O'Leary (1982) describe how a matrix of program options can structure parent involvement practices. The unique feature of their model is that both the horizontal and the vertical axes reflect a gradient of opportunities for parent involvement. Each axis moves from greater to lesser degrees of personal time investment on the part of the parents. Their conceptual framework for parent involvement is displayed in Figure 3.3. Although some would take issue with the connotations of their gradient labels, Cervone and O'Leary's matrix is pertinent to a broader definition of school boundaries in that it also includes reference to community and home environments. As an example of involvement options, their

	Progress Reporting	Special Events	Parent Education	Parents Teaching
Parents as Passive Participants	Good News Notes	Open House	Welcoming Committee	
	60 Second Phone Calls	Audiovisual Presentations	Parent Bulletin Board	
	Star of the Week	Potluck Supper	Information on Home & Weekend Activities	
	Newsletter	Father's/Mother's/ Sibling's Day	Information on Community Resources	
		Spring Fling	Lending Library (Book, Toy, Record)	Make and Take Workshop
		End-of-the-Year Picnic	Classroom Observations	Teachable Moments
	Call-in Times	The Gym Show	Workshops on Topics of Interest to Parents	Home Worksheets
	Parent-Teacher Conferences		A Course for Parents	Parents Teaching in the Classroom
	Home-School Notebooks		Parent-to-Parent Meetings	Parent Objectives in the IEP
Parents as Active Participants	(Parent Leaders)	(Parent Leaders)	(Parent Leaders)	(Parent Leaders)

Parents as Passive Participants ————————————→ Parents as Active Participants

Figure 3.3.   Parent involvement continuum. (From Cervone, B.T., & O'Leary, K. [1982]. A conceptual framework for parent involvement. *Educational Leadership, 40*[2], 48–49; reprinted by permission of the Association for Supervision and Curriculum Development. Copyright © 1982 by ASCD. All rights reserved.)

model offers readers a basis for adopting or adapting the content to suit their programs' unique needs.

Professionals often find that parents are more willing to become involved in school-sponsored activities when such events are family oriented rather than exclusively par-ent focused. Specifically, didactic presentations on topics of presumed or expressed interest to parents (e.g., parents' rights, behavior management, advocacy, transition planning) draw smaller, more proactive groups of parents. These activities clearly have merit and should be offered as options for parents and families. In contrast, family-oriented activities such as picnics, open houses, potlucks, holiday craft workshops, and "make-and-take" toy workshops frequently draw more of a cross section of families to the school. Although these latter activities are more labor intensive for staff, the effort necessary to orchestrate the event should be weighed against the potential gains for developing family connectedness to the program. As mentioned previously, programs that offer child care and transportation often see greater levels of parent attendance.

Rainforth and Salisbury (1988) described a practical strategy for assessing each family's typical daily routine as a basis for decision making and intervention in the home. This strategy involves asking a parent(s) to chart the typical flow of family activities during the week, making particular note of what their child with special needs is doing during those times. They are then asked to identify opportunities within that schedule when they normally interact with their child. Finally, they are asked to judge the suitability of these interactions as potential teaching times. Parent-identified times are used as the basis for discussing the feasibility of embedding goals/objectives into naturally occurring family routines. Embedding home programming recommendations into existing family daily routines enables target skills to be taught or reinforced on a consistent basis with minimal inconvenience to the family. The daily routine information can also be used as a basis for parent contributions during the IEP meeting, as well as a tool for identifying appropriate times and situations into which intervention goals can be embedded.

In a related paper, Brinckerhoff and Vincent (1986) described the application of the same "family daily routine" strategy to the IEP context as a vehicle for enhancing meaningful parent contributions. Their data indicate that parent contributions increased significantly during IEP meetings after introduction of the daily routine strategy (see also Bernheimer & Keogh, 1995; Dunst et al., 1987; Helmstetter & Guess, 1987; Kellegrew, 1994; Lubeck & Chandler, 1990; McWilliam, 1996). These various papers describe a highly useful strategy through which parents are afforded equal status as contributing team members.

In addition to the use of home routines as learning contexts and activity settings, an emerging literature indicates that community activity settings are important contexts in which IFSP and IEP activities can be embedded or goals and objectives can be achieved (e.g., Ehrmann, Aeschleman, & Svanum, 1995; Floyd & Gramann, 1993; Gallimore, Goldenberg, & Weisner, 1993; Kretzman & McKnight, 1993; O'Donnel, Tharp, & Wilson, 1993; Trivette, Dunst, & Deal, 1997; Umstead, Boyd, & Dunst, 1995). Expanding IFSPs and IEPs to include community settings as well as home settings as learning contexts is consistent with the ecological systems approach that underscores the approach to education advanced in this chapter.

Early intervention programs, particularly those serving infants and toddlers, are embracing a family-centered and -directed approach to assessment and intervention. Structured interviews described by Bailey and colleagues (1986), Dunst and coworkers (1988), and Mahoney, O'Sullivan, and Dennebaum (1990) are particularly useful for obtaining in-depth information from parents about their family. Although there are conceptual differences among these approaches, each emphasizes the importance of assessing the expectations, resources, and interests of families as the basis of the development of child and family interventions.

There may be times when the expressed or assessed needs of the parents and family are so great that they interfere with the child's school attendance, development, and/or physical well-being. These issues may surface in families in which there is a complex interplay among capabilities, resources, and economic need. Balancing professional roles with responsibilities to the child and the family can be difficult. A number of community collaboration models suggest identifying one member of the team to establish linkages among nonschool agencies, community resources, and the family (e.g., Aronson, 1996; Melaville & Blank, 1994; U.S. Department of Education, 1994b). Such a strategy limits the number of professionals calling on the family and offers greater potential for coordination of potentially competing or limited resources.

Professionals on teams serving school-age students will likely devote the greatest proportion of their time to direct services of the child at school, with indirect assistance provided to the child and family in the home. Infant and preschool teams are more likely to play a more direct role in teaching the child both at home and at school, while providing both direct and indirect support to the family. Interagency, as well as cross-disciplinary, collaboration and coordination will be important in the development of successful services at both age ranges. To the maximum extent possible, teams should invest decision-making responsibilities with the family and provide supportive guidance to parents/families in their efforts to function both adaptively and independently (Dunst et al., 1988; Kaiser & Hemmeter, 1989; Melaville & Blank, 1994).

Treatment of Parents as Equal Team Members

Effective teams are typically those that employ creative problem-solving techniques and cooperative group process skills (e.g., Johnson & Johnson, 1986; Johnson, Johnson, Holubec, & Roy, 1984). There are four elements to cooperative learning (positive interdependence, individual accountability, collaborative skills, and group processing) that have direct implications for how we treat parents as team members. The ability of the team to work effectively (i.e., cooperatively and collaboratively) will require leadership, trust, communication, conflict management, and a commitment to work toward mutually agreed-upon goals.

Johnson and co-workers (1984) suggested that skillful group members are made, not born. It is unrealistic to expect teams to function effectively if they lack knowledge and skills about group processes and collaboration. Teams, as units, and individual members are encouraged to identify their skills in each of the component areas mentioned previously and develop activities to address deficiencies. Mentorships, in-service training, directed reading, continuing education coursework, and in vivo modeling by more experienced colleagues or parents are some of the more popular formal strategies for obtaining both informational and performance competence in this area. Supportive feedback from teammates is an essential, informal strategy that can significantly affect the cohesion of the team.

Clearly group process and collaborative team skills are but two of the elements needed to work effectively as a team. As indicated previously in this chapter, attitudes, values, and beliefs also play an important role in how professionals and parents interact. Kaiser and Hemmeter (1989) provide a valuable framework for examining the relationship of values to educational decision making. In particular, they ask four questions related to interventions with children and families: "Does the intervention enhance community? Does the intervention strengthen the family? Does the intervention enable parents to do their jobs well? Does the intervention enhance individual development and protect the rights of individual family members?" (p. 78). The necessity of including parents in the decision-making process is obvious in light of such questions. In a preliminary attempt to operationalize the four values-based elements, Kaiser and Hemmeter developed an 18-item checklist that addresses intervention plans and how they might affect the family.

Promotion of cross-cultural family involvement in the educational system will require that professionals recognize their own cultural values as a basis for developing sensitivity to the diverse linguistic and cultural backgrounds, attitudes, and customs of the children and youth with whom they work (Alper et al., 1994; Harry, 1992). Sileo and associates (1996) suggest that Western-held values of independence, equity, and efficiency may be differently interpreted by families from other cultures. Such interpretations will likely affect the quality of home–school interactions. Table 3.3 provides a useful comparison of Western and non-Western cultural values and the implications each holds for how we interact with families.

Supporting and Promoting Family, School, and Community Partnerships

Children do not exist in a vacuum; consequently, how a family functions at home will likely affect children's performance at school. If schools expect children to do well, they must act in ways that also promote the well-being of families. Schools and professionals can respond proactively by employing approaches that foster the self-sufficiency and independence of families. Actions that devalue single parents, those whose primary language is not English, those whose child-rearing beliefs are different from the beliefs of the majority, and those whose jobs compete for time with their family are counterproductive to the development of collaborative home–school relationships.

Schools have an obligation to extend their educational expertise to families as well as to children. Membership on the child's team must be broadly defined, taking into account the needs of the family as well as the child. Dryfoos (1994) provides a helpful description of the "full-service school," a one-stop center at which the educational, physical, psychological, and social requirements of students and their families are addressed in a coordinated, collaborative manner using school and community services and supports. For the schools described in her report, the notion of "team" was broadly defined.

Work by Kretzmann and McKnight (1993) and Trivette et al. (1997) finds that recognizing and building on community members' strengths, assets, capabilities, and talents result in experiences and opportunities that promote and enhance child and parent competence in ways that have family-strengthening influence. The extent to which families are supported in meeting basic life needs will determine the strength of their ability to interact in partnership with their children's educational programs and the professionals who support their children.

If schools view their boundaries broadly as encompassing home, school, and community environments, then instruction can and should occur in a variety of settings with or on behalf of the child. When families request support or information concerning their child at home, it is incumbent on educators and therapists to respond with practical, minimally invasive recommendations in a timely manner. Several resources are available for designing effective home- and community-based support activities. For example, McDonald, Kysela, Martin, and Wheaton (1996) provide information on how to improve parent information sessions held at school. Baker and Brightman (1997) offer sound, practical advice for teaching

Table 3.3.   Strategies sensitive to diverse cultures

Western culture/values	Family culture/values	Strategies
Efficiency		
Value/use of time wisely; quality of task may be secondary	Efficient use of time not as important; OK to be late	Avoid scheduling parent–teacher conferences too closely together
Direct approach; get right to the subject; solve problem	Indirect approach: discuss related issues; "talk story"	Avoid "quick fix"; respect quality of the interaction
Tend to rush, fast paced	More slowly paced, need time to think	Slow pace of meetings with parents; allow "thinking time"
Independence		
Prefer to make own decisions	Interdependence, decisions are made as a family; natural family supports in place	Encourage extended family involvement; work with extended family members
Individual right to privacy of feelings	Strong family ties; open sharing of personal feelings; actions of individual reflect on entire family	Respect sense of family; identify cultural attitudes or religious beliefs toward disabilities
Parental responsibility for raising child	Extended family, shared responsibility of child rearing	Identify authority figures; respect deference to authority; allow parents time to take decisions to others
Equity		
Parents are equal partners in team	Perceive professionals as "above" family	Professionals need to be more aware of and "read" parent perceptions; recognize parents as experts
Prefer active parent involvement (e.g., input at meetings, work with child at home)	Accept teachers' opinions; teachers are experts	Decrease control of interaction; involve parents in planning, implementing, and monitoring programs
Information sharing	Passive reception of information	Elicit wants, hopes, and concerns of parents; information sharing versus information giving and question asking; use parent suggestions when possible; provide timely feedback
Democratic family decision making	Matriarchal or patriarchal family structure	Respect lines of authority

From "Parent and professional partnerships in special education: Multicultural considerations" by T.W. Sileo, A.P. Sileo, and M.A. Prater, 1996, *Intervention in School and Clinic, 31*(3), pp. 145–153. Copyright 1996 by PRO-ED, Inc. Reprinted by permission.

specific social and self-help skills to children with disabilities at home, whereas Brand (1996) describes a range of activities for helping teachers develop partnerships with parents. Across each of these resources are unifying themes of reaching parents, validating their priorities and contributions, and designing flexible alternatives for engagement with the school.

Of particular note is Rich's (1988) text, *MegaSkills*, which is based on the premise that parents play a critical role in supporting their child's learning at school and at home. The book is a powerful compendium of concrete, practical strategies for promoting the values, attitudes, and behaviors that determine success in and out of school. "Tips" for integrating important life skills (many of which are "school skills") into activities that naturally occur in the home are provided for children at various age ranges. Other chapters in this book address special issues confronting the home–school partnership. Professionals will find many creative suggestions that should be of value in their work with parents and families.

Family-Centered Practices

School and education reform initiatives of the 1990s include the call for adoption of family-centered principles and practices as one way of promoting increased family–school–community collaboration and partnerships (Andrews, 1995; Melaville, Blank, & Asayesh, 1993; U.S. Department of Education, 1994a). According to Melaville et al. (1993), adoption of family-centered practices leads to profamily schools that "flex and adapt [school] procedures to meet the needs of children and families" (p. 14).

Although the term *family centered* can be traced historically to the 1950s and 1960s, it has only been since the 1980s that the operational features of family-centered practices have been articulated (see Dunst, 1995, in press; Family Resource Coalition, 1996).

A family-centered approach to working with parents, children, and other family members is a philosophy of care characterized by specific principles and elements leading to family-centered practices. These include recognition that families are the primary and principle context for promoting child health and well-being, respect for family choice and decision making, an emphasis on child and family strengths and resources needed for normalized patterns of living, family–professional partnerships as the catalyst for matching resources to desired choices, and mutual respect between families and professionals as they work together to achieve desired outcomes. Comparison of these key features and elements with the content of preceding parts of this chapter finds that a family-centered approach constitutes a viable strategy for promoting and improving parent–school communication.

Table 3.4 lists the core practices of a family-centered approach developed by Dunst (in press) based on an extensive review and integration of the family-centered literature. Several things are noteworthy about these practices in light of what has been described elsewhere in this chapter. First, the practices emphasize positive transactions between parents and professionals as a means for enhancing effective communication and collaboration. Second, the practices place families in pivotal decision-making roles with regard to the focus of intervention practices directed toward the child, his or her parents, and the family. Third, the practices emphasize family–school–community linkages and the use of a broad range of experiences and opportunities as ways of addressing family concerns and desires. Fourth, the practices explicitly detail the kinds of attitudes, beliefs, and behaviors professionals must adopt in order to become family centered.

Dunst and Trivette (1996) described the kinds of helpgiving practices professionals

Table 3.4.   Core practices of a family-centered approach to intervention

- Families and family members are treated with dignity and respect at all times.
- Practitioners are sensitive and responsive to family cultural, ethnic, and socioeconomic diversity.
- Family choice and decision making occur at all levels of family involvement in the intervention process.
- Information necessary for families to make informed choices is shared in a complete and unbiased manner.
- The focus of intervention practices is based on family-identified desires, priorities, and needs.
- The provision/mobilization of supports, resources, and services is done in a flexible, responsive, and individualized manner.
- A broad range of informal, community, and formal supports and resources are used for achieving family-identified outcomes.
- The strengths and capabilities of families and individual family members are used as resources for meeting family-identified needs and as competencies for procuring extrafamily resources.
- Practitioner–family relationships are characterized by partnerships and collaboration based on mutual trust and respect.
- Practitioners employ competency-enhancing and empowering helpgiving styles that promote and enhance family functioning and have family strengthening influences.

must adopt to be family centered. According to these investigations, effective helping comprises three components: technical quality, positive helpgiver traits/attributes, and participatory involvement practices. *Technical quality* is considered the consequence of professional training and experience and includes the knowledge, skills, and competence one possesses as a professional and the expression of this expertise as part of practicing one's craft. *Helpgiver traits* refer to the relational aspects of helping and include such things as active listening, empathy, warmth, compassion, and caring, whereas *helpgiver attributes* include helpgiver beliefs about help receiver competencies and the capacity of help receivers to become capable of dealing effectively with life situations, concerns, and desires. *Participatory involvement* includes practices that provide help receivers with opportunities to discuss intervention options and the benefits and limitations of different choices, provision of information for making such choices, collaboration and shared decision making between help receivers and helpgivers, and

active involvement of the help receiver in carrying out decided-upon options that otherwise involve help receivers actively and meaningfully in the helping relationship. Whereas helpgiver traits/attributes mirror the kinds of "attitude" changes described previously in this chapter, participatory involvement practices constitute precisely the behaviors that promote meaningful inclusion of parents in their children's education. Moreover, the fact that positive helpgiver traits/attributes and participatory practices differentiate family-centered practices from other kinds of helpgiving (Dunst & Trivette, 1996) explains why professional expertise per se is insufficient as a condition for involving families in helping relationships in ways that maximize positive consequences (see Dunst, in press).

SUMMARY

Parent inclusion on teams is necessary for the development of a high-quality educational program for individual students. We must, however, be cautious about narrowly defining the roles and opportunities for parents and family members. There are many ways in which families support the learning needs of children, many of which do not require regular or sustained attendance at school. Because families, as well as children, present diverse needs and capacities, it is essential that professionals recognize and account for these differences in the design, development, and implementation of parent involvement opportunities within the educational context. Efforts to strengthen partnerships among home, school, and community sectors will be aided by the adoption of family-centered practices as a core program value. This point becomes particularly salient when the meaningful inclusion of parents and families on school and community teams is at issue. Strategies exist, but their application must be prescriptive to the families we serve. For many professionals, collaborating with parents and family members will require additional training, altera-tions of historical perceptions, and a commitment to the value of inclusion. Commitment to a collaborative partnership must come first.

TWO SCULPTORS

I dreamed I stood in a studio
And watched two sculptors there,
The clay they used was a young child's mind
And they fashioned it with care.
One was a teacher; the tools she used
Were books, music and art.
One, a parent who worked with a guiding hand
And a gentle, loving heart.
Day after day the teacher toiled
With touch that was deft and sure,
While the parent labored by her side
And polished and smoothed it o'er.
And when at last their task was done,
They were proud of what they had wrought;
For the things they had molded into the child
Could neither be sold nor bought.
And each agreed he would have failed
If he had worked alone,
The parent and the school,
The teacher and the home.

Author Unknown

REFERENCES

Allen, D.A., & Hudd, S. (1987). Are we professionalizing parents? Weighing the benefits and pitfalls. *Mental Retardation, 25*(3), 133–139.

Alper, S.K., Schloss, P.J., & Schloss, C.N. (1994). *Families of students with disabilities.* Newton, MA: Allyn & Bacon.

Altheide, M., & Livermore, J.R. (1987). Supporting families of augmentative communication users. *Physical and Occupational Therapy in Pediatrics, 7*(2), 95–106.

American Occupational Therapy Association. (1989). *Guidelines for occupational therapy services in early intervention and preschool services.* Rockville, MD: Author.

Andrews, A.B. (1995). *Helping families survive and thrive.* Columbia: Alliance for South Carolina's Children.

Aronson, J.Z. (1996). How schools can recruit hard-to-reach parents. *Educational Leadership, 53,* 58–60.

Bailey, D.B., Simeonsson, R.J., Winton, P.J., Huntington, G.S., Comfort, M., Isbell, P., O'Donnell, K.J., & Helm, J.M. (1986). Family-focused intervention: A functional model for planning, implementing, and evaluating individualized family services on early intervention. *Journal of the Division for Early Childhood, 10,* 156–171.

Baker, B.L., & Brightman, A.J. (1997). *Steps to independence: Teaching everyday skills to children with special needs* (3rd ed.). Baltimore: Paul H. Brookes Publishing Co.

Bazyk, S. (1989). Changes in attitudes and beliefs regarding parent participation and home programs: An update. *American Journal of Occupational Therapy, 43*(11), 723–728.

Beckman, P. (1984). Perceptions of young children with handicaps: A comparison of mothers and program staff. *Mental Retardation, 22,* 176–181.

Bernheimer, L.P., & Keogh, B.K. (1995). Weaving interventions into the fabric of everyday life: An approach to family assessment. *Topics in Early Childhood Special Education, 15,* 415–433.

Bernstein, H.K., & Stettner-Eaton, B. (1994). Cultural inclusion in Part H: Systems development. *Infant-Toddler Intervention, 4*(1), 1–10.

Brand, S. (1996). Making parent involvement a reality: Helping teachers develop partnerships with parents. *Young Children, 51*(2), 76–81.

Bricker, D.D., & Cripe, J. (1989). Activity based intervention. In D.D. Bricker (Ed.), *Early intervention for at-risk and handicapped infants, toddlers, and preschool children* (pp. 251–274). Palo Alto, CA: VORT Corp.

Bricker, D.D., & Squires, J. (1989). The effectiveness of parental screening of at-risk infants: The infant monitoring questionnaires. *Topics in Early Childhood Special Education, 9*(3), 67–85.

Brinckerhoff, J.L., & Vincent, L.J. (1986). Increasing parental decision making at the individualized educational program meeting. *Journal of the Division for Early Childhood, 11*(1), 46–50.

Bronfenbrenner, U. (1979). *The ecology of human development: Experiments by nature and design.* Cambridge, MA: Harvard University Press.

Brown, L., Nietupski, J., & Hamre-Nietupski, S. (1976). The criterion of ultimate functioning and public school services for severely handicapped students. In M.A. Thomas (Ed.), *Hey, don't forget about me! Education's investment in the severely, profoundly and multiply handicapped* (pp. 197–209). Reston, VA: Council for Exceptional Children.

Campbell, P.H. (1987). The integrated programming team: An approach for coordinating professionals of various disciplines in programs for students with severe and multiple handicaps. *Journal of The Association for Persons with Severe Handicaps, 12*(2), 107–116.

Cervone, B.T., & O'Leary, K. (1982). A conceptual framework for parent involvement. *Educational Leadership, 40*(2), 48–49.

DeGangi, G., Wietlisbach, S., Poisson, S., Stein, E., & Royeen, C. (1994). The impact of culture and socioeconomic status on family–professional collaboration: Challenges and solutions. *Topics in Early Childhood Special Education, 14*, 503–520.

Dryfoos, J.G. (1994). *Full service schools.* San Francisco: Jossey-Bass.

Dunst, C.J. (1995). Rethinking early intervention. *Analysis and Intervention in Developmental Disabilities, 5*(1/2), 165–201.

Dunst, C.J. (in press). Toward a family-centered approach in psychology practice. In R. Illback,

C. Cobb, & H. Joseph (Eds.), *Integrated services for children and families: Opportunities for psychological practice.* Washington, DC: American Psychological Association.

Dunst, C.J., Lesko, J.J., Holbert, K.A., Wilson, L.L., Sharpe, K.L., & Liles, R.F. (1987). A systemic approach to infant intervention. *Topics in Early Childhood Special Education, 7*(2), 19–37.

Dunst, C.J., & Trivette, C.M. (1996). Empowerment, effective helpgiving practices, and family-centered care. *Pediatric Nursing, 22*, 334–337, 343.

Dunst, C.J., Trivette, C.M., & Deal, A.G. (1988). *Enabling and empowering families: Principles and guidelines for practice.* Cambridge, MA: Brookline Books.

Dunst, C.J., Trivette, C.M., & Deal, A.G. (1994). *Supporting and strengthening families.* Cambridge, MA: Brookline Books.

Dunst, C.J., Trivette, C.M., & Hamby, D. (1996). Measuring the helpgiving practices of human services program practitioners. *Human Relations, 49*, 815–835.

Education for All Handicapped Children Act (EHA) of 1975, PL 94-142, 20 U.S.C. §§ 1400 *et seq.*

Education of the Handicapped Act Amendments of 1986, PL 99-457, 20 U.S.C. §§ 1400 *et seq.*

Edwards, C.P., Gandini, L., & Giovanni, D. (1996). The contrasting developmental timetables of parents and preschool teachers in two cultural communities. In S. Harkness & C.M. Super (Eds.), *Parents' cultural belief systems: Their origins, expressions, and consequences* (pp. 270–288). New York: Guilford Press.

Ehrmann, L., Aeschleman, S.R., & Svanum, S. (1995). Parental reports of community activity patterns: A comparison between young children with disabilities and their nondisabled peers. *Research in Developmental Disabilities, 16*, 331–343.

Elam, S.M., Lowell, C.R., & Gallup, A.M. (1994, September). The 26th annual Phi Delta Kappa/Gallup poll of the public's attitudes toward the public schools. *Phi Delta Kappan.*

Epstein, J. (1987). Parent involvement: What research says to administrators. *Education and Urban Society, 19*(2), 119–136.

Epstein, J. (1993, April). Make parents your partners. *Instructor, 19*, 119–136.

Family Resource Coalition. (1996). *Guidelines for family support practice.* Chicago: Author.

Floyd, M.F., & Gramann, J.H. (1993). Effects of acculturation and structural assimilation in re-source-based recreation: The case of Mexican Americans. *Journal of Leisure Research, 25,* 6–21.

Ford, A., Schnorr, R., Meyer, L., Davern, L., Black, J., & Dempsey, P. (Eds.). (1989). *The Syracuse community-referenced curriculum guide for students with moderate and severe disabilities.* Baltimore: Paul H. Brookes Publishing Co.

Gallimore, R., Goldenberg, C.N., & Weisner, T.S. (1993). The social construction and subjective reality of activity settings: Implications for community psychology. *American Journal of Community Psychology, 21,* 537–559.

Gilliam, J.E., & Coleman, M.C. (1981). Who influences IEP committee decisions? *Exceptional Children, 47,* 642–644.

Goldstein, S., Strickland, B., Turnbull, A.P., & Curry, L. (1980). An observational analysis of the IEP conference. *Exceptional Children, 46,* 278–286.

Gradel, K., Thompson, M.S., & Sheehan, R. (1981). Parental and professional agreement in early childhood assessment. *Topics in Early Childhood Special Education, 1,* 31–39.

Guralnick, M.J. (1989). Recent developments in early intervention efficacy research: Implications for family involvement in P.L. 99-457. *Topics in Early Childhood Special Education, 9*(3), 1–17.

Hanson, J., & Carta, J. (1996). Addressing the challenges of families with multiple risks. *Exceptional Children, 62*(3), 201–212.

Harry, B. (1992). *Cultural diversity, families, and the special education system.* New York: Teachers College Press.

Helmstetter, E., & Guess, D. (1987). Application of the individualized curriculum sequencing model to learners with severe sensory impairments. In L. Goetz, D. Guess, & K. Stremel-Campbell (Eds.), *Innovative program design for individuals with dual sensory impairments* (pp. 255–282). Baltimore: Paul H. Brookes Publishing Co.

Henderson, A.T., & Berla, N. (1994). *A new generation of evidence: The family is critical to student achievements.* Washington, DC: National Committee for Citizens in Education.

Hess, R.D., Price, G.C., Dickson, W.P., & Conroy, M. (1981). Different roles for mothers and teachers: Contrasting styles of child care. In S. Kilmer (Ed.), *Advances in early education and day care* (Vol. 2, pp. 1–28). Greenwich, CT: JAI Press.

Howes, C., & Matheson, C.C. (1992). Contextual constraints on the concordance of mother–child and teacher–child relationships. In R.C. Pianta (Ed.), *Beyond the parent: The role of other adults in children's lives* (New Directions for Child Development, No. 57) (pp. 25–40). San Francisco: Jossey-Bass.

Humphry, R. (1989). Early intervention and the influence of the occupational therapist on the parent–child relationship. *American Journal of Occupational Therapy, 43*(11), 738–742.

Individuals with Disabilities Education Act (IDEA) of 1990, PL 101-476, 20 U.S.C. §§ 1400 *et seq.*

Individuals with Disabilities Education Act Amendments of 1991, PL 102-119, 20 U.S.C. §§ 1400 *et seq.*

Johnson, D.W., & Johnson, R.T. (1986). Mainstreaming and cooperative learning strategies. *Exceptional Children, 52*(6), 553–561.

Johnson, D.W., Johnson, R., Holubec, E., & Roy, P. (1984). *Circles of learning.* Alexandria, VA: Association for Supervision and Curriculum Development.

Kaiser, A.P., & Hemmeter, M.L. (1989). Value-based approaches to family intervention. *Topics in Early Childhood Special Education, 89*(4), 72–86.

Kellegrew, D.H. (1994). *The impact of daily routines and opportunities on the self-care skill performance of young children with disabilities.* Unpublished dissertation, University of California, Santa Barbara.

Kretzmann, J., & McKnight, J. (1993). *Building community from the inside out.* Evanston, IL: Northwestern University, Center for Urban Affairs and Policy Research.

Kysilko, D.A. (Ed.). (1995). *Winning ways: Creating inclusive schools, classrooms, and communities.* Alexandria, VA: National Association of State Boards of Education.

Lubeck, R.C., & Chandler, L.K. (1990). Organizing the home caregiving environment for infants. *Education & Treatment of Children, 13,* 347–363.

Lucca, J.A., & Settles, B.H. (1981). Effects of children's disabilities on parental time use. *Physical Therapy, 61*(2), 196–201.

Lynch, E.W., & Hanson, M.J. (Eds.). (1992). *Developing cross-cultural competence: A guide for working with young children and their fam-*

ilies. Baltimore: Paul H. Brookes Publishing Co.

MacDonald, T.D., & Gillette, Y. (1986). Communicating with persons with severe handicaps: Roles of parents and professionals. *Journal of The Association for Persons with Severe Handicaps, 11*(4), 255–265.

MacMillan, D.L., & Turnbull, A.P. (1983). Parent involvement with special education: Respecting individual preferences. *Education and Training of the Mentally Retarded, 18*(1), 4–9.

Mahoney, G., O'Sullivan, P., & Dennebaum, J. (1990). Maternal perceptions of early intervention services: A scale for assessing family focused intervention. *Topics in Early Childhood Special Education, 10*(1), 1–15.

Mahoney, G., & Powell, A. (1988). Modifying parent-child interactions: Enhancing the development of handicapped infants. *Journal of Special Education, 22,* 82–96.

McDonald, L., Kysela, G., Martin, C., & Wheaton, S. (1996). The Hazeldean Project: Strategies for improving parent information systems. *Teaching Exceptional Children, 29*(2), 28–32.

McWilliam, R.A. (1996). *Family-centered intervention planning: A routines-based approach.* San Antonio, TX: Communication/Therapy Skill Builders.

Melaville, A., & Blank, M. (1994). *What it takes: Structuring interagency partnerships to connect children and families with comprehensive services.* Washington, DC: Education and Human Services Consortium.

Melaville, A., Blank, M., & Asayesh, G. (1993). *Together we can: A guide for crafting a profamily system of education and human services.* Washington, DC: U.S. Government Printing Office.

Minuchin, S. (1974). *Families and family therapy.* Cambridge, MA: Harvard University Press.

Morgan, D.P., & Rhode, G. (1983). Teachers' attitudes toward IEPs: A two year follow-up. *Exceptional Children, 50*(1), 64–67.

Newmann, F.M., & Wehlage, G.C. (1995). *Successful school restructuring.* Madison: University of Wisconsin, Center on Organization and Restructuring of Schools, School of Education.

NICHCY. (1995). *Planning for inclusion, 5*(1).

O'Donnel, C.R., Tharp, R.G., & Wilson, K. (1993). Activity settings as the unit of analysis: A theoretical basis for community intervention and development. *American Journal of Community Psychology, 21,* 501–520.

Powell, D.R. (1989). *Families and early childhood programs* (Research Monograph of the National Association for the Education of Young Children). Washington, DC: National Association for the Education of Young Children.

Rainforth, B., & Salisbury, C. (1988). Functional home programs: A model for therapists. *Topics in Early Childhood Special Education, 7*(4), 33–45.

Rainforth, B., & York, J. (1987). Integrating related services in community instruction. *Journal of The Association for Persons with Severe Handicaps, 12*(3), 190–198.

Rich, D. (1988). *MegaSkills.* Boston: Houghton-Mifflin.

Roach, V. (1995, December). Supporting inclusion: Beyond the rhetoric. *Phi Delta Kappan,* pp. 295–299.

Salisbury, C. (1987). *Parental perceptions of home and school relationships. Binghamton School Partnership Project Technical Report #1.* Binghamton: State University of New York at Binghamton, Center for Education and Social Research.

Salisbury, C. (1991). Mainstreaming during the early childhood years. *Exceptional Children, 58*(2), 146–155.

Salisbury, C., & Evans, J.M. (1988). Comparison of parental involvement in regular and special education. *Journal of The Association for Persons with Severe Handicaps, 13*(4), 268–272.

Salisbury, C., & Vincent, L.J. (1990). "Criterion of the next environment" and "best practices": Mainstreaming and integration 10 years later. *Topics in Early Childhood Special Education, 10*(2), 78–89.

Salisbury, C., Vincent, L.J., & Gorrofa, S. (1987). *Involvement in the educational process: Perceptions of parents and professionals of dual sensory impaired children.* Unpublished manuscript, State University of New York at Binghamton.

Scanlon, C.A., Arick, J., & Phelps, X. (1981). Participation in the development of the IEP: Parents' perspective. *Exceptional Children, 47*(5), 373–374.

Seitz, S., & Provence, S. (1990). Caregiver-focused models of early intervention. In S.J. Meisels & J.P. Shonkoff (Eds.), *Handbook of early intervention* (pp. 400–427). New York: Cambridge University Press.

Shevin, M. (1983). Meaningful parental involvement in long range educational planning for disabled children. *Education and Training of the Mentally Retarded, 18*(1), 17–21.

Sileo, T.W., Sileo, A.P., & Prater, M.A. (1996). Parent and professional partnerships in special education: Multicultural considerations. *Intervention in School and Clinic, 31,* 145–153.

Simeonsson, R.J., & Bailey, D.R. (1990). Family dimensions in early intervention. In S.J. Meisels & J.P. Shonkoff (Eds.), *Handbook of early intervention* (pp. 428–444). New York: Cambridge University Press.

Stone, C.R. (1993). *School–community collaboration: Comparing three initiatives. Brief to policymakers.* Madison: University of Wisconsin, Center on Organization and Restructuring of Schools.

Summers, J.A., Behr, S.K., & Turnbull, A.P. (1989). Positive adaptation and coping strengths of families who have children with disabilities. In G.H.S. Singer & L.K. Irvin (Eds.), *Support for caregiving families: Enabling positive adaptation to disability* (pp. 27–40). Baltimore: Paul H. Brookes Publishing Co.

Trivette, C.M., Dunst, C.J., & Deal, A.G. (1997). Resource-based approach to early intervention. In S.K. Thurman, J.R. Cornwell, & S.R. Gottwald (Eds.), *Contexts of early intervention: Systems and settings* (pp. 73–92). Baltimore: Paul H. Brookes Publishing Co.

Turnbull, A.P., & Turnbull, H.R. (1986a). *Families, professionals, and exceptionalities.* Columbus, OH: Charles E. Merrill.

Turnbull, A.P., & Turnbull, H.R. (1986b). Stepping back from early intervention: An ethical perspective. *Journal of the Division for Early Childhood, 10*(2), 106–117.

Turnbull, A.P., & Winton, P.J. (1984). Parent involvement policy and practice: Current research and implications for families of young, severely handicapped children. In J. Blacher (Ed.), *Severely handicapped young children and their families* (pp. 377–397). Orlando, FL: Academic Press.

Tyler, N., & Kogan, K.L. (1972). The social byproducts of therapy with young children. *Physical Therapy, 52*(5), 508–513.

Umstead, S., Boyd, K., & Dunst, C.J. (1995). Building community resources: Enabling inclusion in community programs and activities. *Exceptional Parent, 25*(7), 36–37.

U.S. Department of Education. (1994a). *Changing education: Resources for systemic reform* (pp. 221–241). Washington, DC: Author.

U.S. Department of Education. (1994b). *Strong families, strong schools: Building community partnerships for learning.* Washington, DC: Author.

Vadasy, P.F. (1986). Single mothers: A social phenomenon and population in need. In R.R. Fewell & P.F. Vadasy (Eds.), *Families of handicapped children* (pp. 221–252). Austin, TX: PRO-ED.

Villa, R.A., & Thousand, J.S. (1995). *Creating an inclusive school.* Alexandria, VA: Association for Supervision and Curriculum Development.

Vincent, L.J., Laten, S., Salisbury, C., Brown, P., & Baumgart, D. (1980). Family involvement in the educational processes of severely handicapped students: State of the art and directions for the future. In B. Wilcox & R. York (Eds.), *Quality education for the severely handicapped: The federal investment* (pp. 164–179). Washington, DC: U.S. Department of Education.

Vincent, L.J., & Salisbury, C. (1988). Changing economic and social influences on family involvement. *Topics in Early Childhood Special Education, 8,* 48–59.

Vincent, L.J., Salisbury, C., Laten, S., & Baumgart, D. (1979). *Designing home programs for families with handicapped children.* Unpublished manuscript, Department of Rehabilitation Psychology and Special Education, University of Wisconsin, Madison.

Vincent, L.J., Salisbury, C., Strain, P., McCormick, C., & Tessier, A. (1990). A behavioral-ecological approach to early intervention: Focus on diversity. In S.J. Meisels & J.P. Shonkoff (Eds.), *Handbook of early intervention* (pp. 173–195). New York: Cambridge University Press.

Vincent, L.J., Salisbury, C., Walter, G., Brown, P., Gruenewald, L.J., & Powers, M. (1980). Program evaluation and curriculum development in early childhood/special education: Criteria of the next environment. In W. Sailor, B. Wilcox, & L. Brown (Eds.), *Methods of instruction for severely handicapped students* (pp. 303–308). Baltimore: Paul H. Brookes Publishing Co.

Walker, B. (1989). Strategies for improving parent–professional cooperation. In G.H.S. Singer & L.K. Irvin (Eds.), *Support for caregiving families: Enabling positive adaptation to disability* (pp. 103–119). Baltimore: Paul H. Brookes Publishing Co.

Walsh, S., Campbell, P.H., & McKenna, P. (1988). First year implementation of the federal program for infants and toddlers with handicaps: A view from the states. *Topics in Early Childhood Special Education, 8*(3), 1–22.

Warren, S.A., & Kaiser, A.P. (1986). Incidental language teaching: A critical review. *Journal of Speech and Hearing Disorders, 51,* 291–299.

Weisner, T.S., Gallimore, R., & Jordan, C. (1988). Unpackaging cultural effects on classroom learning: Native Hawaiian peer assistance and child-generated activity. *Anthropology & Education Quarterly, 19,* 327–353.

Yoshida, R.K., Fenton, K.S., Kaufman, M.J., & Maxwell, J.P. (1978). Parental involvement in the special education pupil planning process: The school's perspective. *Exceptional Children, 44*(7), 531–534.

II

DESIGNING INDIVIDUALIZED EDUCATION PROGRAMS

with contributions
from Cathy Macdonald and Winnie Dunn

The next four chapters, Section II of the book, delineate strategies to design individualized education programs (IEPs) in which related services are integral components. This section of the book focuses on students' programs, including curriculum, assessment, IEPs, and instruction. To help illustrate how the program components evolve, two students with severe disabilities are introduced here and followed throughout Section II.

Kristen is 5 years old. She lives in a suburban community with her parents and her 7-year-old sister, Julie. Kristen has generalized severe developmental delays and cerebral palsy with spastic diplegia. Kristen's family describes her as cute and lovable but a little stubborn. She enjoys all kinds of activities, especially if her dad helps her do them. Currently, she communicates primarily by vocalizations and gestures (desires by reaching, negation by pushing away), which sometimes escalate into tantrums. Kristen is starting to develop speech and has a vocabulary of about 10 words. She seems to prefer playing with people, especially adults, rather than toys. Her ability to manipulate objects is somewhat limited, however, because she uses primarily a palmar grasp. She has just recently started walking. Kristen is graduating from an early childhood special education program, and she will enter a public elementary school in the fall. Her parents have requested that she be placed in a regular kindergarten class at their neighborhood school. The school district has agreed. Although the preschool team knows many of Kristen's needs, the professionals on the kindergarten team do not know Kristen so well, and the kindergarten placement will present new demands and opportunities. Therefore, Kristen's team will be designing a new program.

Jamal is 17 years old and lives in an urban community. He lives in a foster home but spends most weekends with his mother and sister, Keesha. Jamal likes the same kinds of things as other youths his age: Nintendo, MTV, cars and motorcycles, and Coke and french fries. Jamal is labeled as having "profound mental retardation." He has spastic quadriplegia, with slight head control, occasional active movement with his right arm, and many contractures. He communicates preferences with his eyes and facial expressions. After attending segregated programs for many years, Jamal entered an integrated educational program 3 years ago. Currently, he attends the public high school in his community, where he is part of the junior class. Jamal's team, including family, friends, teachers, and therapists, have worked together for some time to develop a comprehensive program composed of activities at school and in the community. Because many components are in place, Jamal's team concentrates on "fine tuning" and preparing Jamal for graduation, with transition to a postsecondary program based largely in the community. The next four chapters describe only two parts of Jamal's program, which illustrate some of the variations and opportunities available at the secondary level. One part of his program builds on learning opportunities in a general education Spanish class, and the other occurs in a community-based worksite.

In summary, Chapters 4–7 present a collaborative team approach to program development and implementation. Program components are illustrated through representative aspects of Kristen's program at home and at school and Jamal's program at school and in the community.

4

An Ecological
Model of Curriculum
A Natural Context for Therapy

Curricula are often construed as commercial packages of activities and materials, used primarily by teachers, with little relevance to other educational service providers. It is more accurate, however, to view a curriculum as a theoretical model that represents beliefs about the content and form of an appropriate education (Eisner, 1994; Kugelmass, 1996). This view suggests several reasons that knowledge of curriculum is important for the entire educational team, including therapists. First, the curriculum guides decision making, particularly about selection of student goals and objectives for the individualized education program (IEP). Because therapists provide related educational services, they are necessarily contributors to the design and content of the IEP. Second, when students have disabilities that affect development of sensorimotor and communication abilities, therapists contrib-

ute to the curriculum by determining whether and how modifications might be made so all students can participate in and learn from that curriculum. Finally, a unifying theoretical model is an important foundation for effective teamwork (Giangreco, 1996; Thousand, Villa, & Nevin, 1994). Educational teams often encounter problems because they have not consciously addressed curriculum in a collaborative manner. Without a curricular framework, teams may resort to prescribed activities and isolated interventions, spend excessive time inventing program content, or provide programs with little relevance or consistency. Without agreement about theoretical curricular models, teams lack a consistent basis for making decisions, and members are more likely to experience ambivalence and conflict. A curriculum provides the framework and direction—a road map of sorts—so that all members of the educational team have a clear understanding of the educational program.

APPROACHES TO CURRICULUM

Three common approaches to curriculum in special education programs for students with severe disabilities are the developmental approach, the functional approach, and the ecological approach. Each approach is discussed in this section.

Developmental Curriculum Approach

The traditional model for both special education curricula and pediatric habilitation has been a developmental approach, based on the scope and sequence of typical development of young children (see Ayres, 1972; Bloom & Lahey, 1978; Bobath & Bobath, 1972; Bricker & Bricker, 1974; Chapman & Miller, 1980; Frostig & Horne, 1973; Gesell & Amatruda, 1947; Miller, 1977). The theory underlying this model is that typical development of children progresses in a predictable sequence, which should be taught to students with disabilities. Teaching the normal sequence is expected to remediate delays and prevent deviations that would lead to greater delays and disability. A thorough understanding of typical child development is considered a fundamental competency in teacher and therapist training programs and is valuable for planning effective instructional strategies (see, e.g., Alexander, Boehme, & Cupps, 1993). Numerous weaknesses have been identified in the developmental model, however, especially if it is used as the only or the primary approach to curriculum for students with severe disabilities (Brown, Nietupski, & Hamre-Nietupski, 1976; Orelove & Sobsey, 1996; Reichle & Karlan, 1985; Reichle & Keogh, 1986).

First, typical development presents the very sequences through which students with severe disabilities have failed to progress.

Rigid adherence to achieving normalcy can become a barrier to learning achievable functional skills. Some teachers and therapists have focused for years on the next skill in a usual developmental sequence (e.g., prereading skills, babbling, rolling segmentally) and have discouraged working on more meaningful skills because they are considered to be at a higher developmental level. Attention is focused on form rather than function, and alternative forms or adaptations to achieve desired functions (e.g., wheelchair or tricycle rather than walking) are not part of the model. Second, typical development does not actually prescribe a clear and valid teaching sequence. Although the presence or absence of "normal" behaviors may be significant, some behaviors are neither necessary nor desirable to teach, particularly for older students with disabilities (e.g., cry when separated from parent, gaze at mirror image). Research has demonstrated that typical children form skills in a variety of sequences and patterns, which often differ from traditional norms (Alexander et al., 1993; Loria, 1980; Van Sant, 1988). Even if traditional sequences did prove valid, few developmental assessments or curricula present clear linear progressions of skill development, much less the "lattices" (Bricker & Iacino, 1977), interrelated horizontal and vertical development (Stremel & Schutz, 1995), or "circular loops" (Alexander et al., 1993) that lead to more complex skills. Third, using developmental curricula encourages teachers and therapists to view students with severe disabilities as "developmentally young" and to use educational activities and materials that are more appropriate to infants than to older children, adolescents, or adults. This limits opportunities to acquire more age-appropriate skills, creates a perpetual cycle of incompetence, and negatively affects others' perceptions of and expectations for students with severe disabilities (Bates, Morrow, Pancsofar, & Sedlak, 1984), promoting the attitudes of paternalism and pity against which disability rights advocates fight (Shapiro, 1994). Finally, curricula referenced only to typical development fail to provide information about the contexts and functions that are most important for an individual student to participate more fully in everyday life.

Functional Curriculum Approach

Having recognized the shortcomings of a pure developmental approach, many teams serving children and adults with severe disabilities have adopted a functional approach to curriculum. The philosophy of this approach is that students with severe disabilities need to acquire age-appropriate and functional skills. Two general strategies have been used to operationalize this philosophy. The first strategy is still referenced to typical child development, but items in developmental assessments (or curricula) are analyzed to identify the significant component behaviors. For example, shaking a rattle for several seconds demonstrates beginning abilities to maintain a palmar grasp, to dissociate arm movement from the rest of the body, to use an object for a particular purpose, and to sustain intentional activity. If the team determined that any or all of these behaviors were deficient but needed by the student, it would identify functional contexts and age-appropriate materials for teaching the component behaviors. For a 10-year-old boy with severe disabilities, the same component behaviors might be taught as he learns to feed himself, brush his teeth, erase the chalkboard at school, or assist with snack preparation (e.g., shake chips from their box into a bowl). This approach is acceptable to many teachers and therapists because it both acknowledges typical sequences of skill development and, by having identified activities that appear more

functional and age appropriate, enables the student to achieve greater independence and social acceptance.

The second strategy to establish functional curricula is based on criterion-referenced assessment of independent living skills. This approach is especially familiar to occupational therapists because it is the basis for much of their work in adult rehabilitation (see, e.g., Breines, 1984; Harvey & Jellinek, 1981; Klein & Bell, 1982). In special education, numerous packaged curricula have been developed to teach skills deemed necessary for participation in adult environments (e.g., activities of daily living and vocational curricula). The scope and sequence of skills and the task analyses that comprise these curricula are typically identified and deemed "functional" because they contain activities performed 1) by people without disabilities or 2) in programs or environments that serve only people with disabilities.

The functional approach to curriculum has one major advantage over a strictly developmental approach: It reflects higher expectations for students with severe disabilities and promotes opportunities to acquire age-appropriate skills. The major weakness of the functional approach is that there is no clear organizational framework. Although there is an underlying presumption of functionality and age appropriateness, the content of the curriculum is largely idiosyncratic, and there are no established criteria for determining what is actually functional and relevant for an individual student. Many functional curricula have been field tested and formally validated with children and adults with disabilities. "Validation" can be defined in numerous ways, however, and it may only mean that users found the package usable and the content achievable. Validation does not necessarily mean a curriculum leads to successful participation in integrated environments (see, e.g., Brown, Rogan, et al., 1987). Furthermore, validation for a specific population of students does not ensure that the skills are relevant, important, or properly sequenced for an individual. As a result, the functional approach may produce programs that are as inappropriate and nonfunctional for individual students as those devised using the developmental approach.

Ecological Curriculum Approach

In an effort to ensure a more appropriate and relevant curriculum for individual students, Brown and colleagues (1979) delineated a strategy known as an ecological approach (also referred to as an environment-referenced or community-referenced approach). With many years of use and refinement, the ecological approach to curriculum has been considered a "recommended practice" in educating students with severe disabilities (see, e.g., Williams, Fox, Thousand, & Fox, 1990).

Ecology refers to the study of relationships between people and their environments (*Merriam-Webster's Collegiate Dictionary,* 1993). Therefore, an ecological approach to curriculum reflects characteristics of both the individual student and the environments in which his or her participation is desired. The team for each student generates an individualized curriculum that encompasses the environments, activities, and skills that are most relevant and important for that student. The specific content evolves continually as the student's needs, goals, and opportunities change, as described in the next section.

The ecological approach respects the strengths of other curriculum models but also has several advantages. It promotes teaching skills that are age appropriate and relevant to an individual's daily life, while it respects the need to teach skills in order of progressive refinement and complexity. It

also encourages use of adaptations to accommodate disability or simplify task demands. Many teams find that an ecological curriculum expands the options for their students, including options for participation in more inclusive environments. For collaborative teams, an advantage of the ecological curriculum model is that it tends to unify, rather than fragment, team member efforts because the environments and activities identified as priorities for each student are "discipline free" and provide a natural context for integrating occupational, physical, and speech-language therapy services (Giangreco, Cloninger, & Iverson, 1993). A potential disadvantage of an ecological approach is that teams will generate curricula that look so different from general education curricula that classroom teachers will think that students with severe disabilities cannot be educated appropriately in inclusive classes (Ford, Davern, & Schnorr, 1992). The curriculum for students with severe disabilities can be both relevant and well aligned with the general education curriculum, as is discussed further in this and later chapters.

Much has been written for teachers about an ecological approach to curriculum. This chapter outlines steps and strategies to develop an ecological curriculum, with particular reference to the contributions of occupational and physical therapists and speech-language pathologists. Readers who desire a more thorough examination and guide to developing an ecological curriculum are referred to Falvey (1989) and Ford et al. (1989).

DEVELOPING THE ECOLOGICAL CURRICULUM

Brown et al. (1979) conceptualized an ecological curriculum organized around four life domains: domestic, vocational, community, and recreation/leisure. Initially, school was not identified as a domain because, for students with severe disabilities, "school" was designed to address the other four domains. As increasing numbers of students with severe disabilities have gained access to education in typical school settings, however, the importance of the school domain has emerged as a substantial element of the lives of all children and youth (York & Vandercook, 1991). These domains provide the framework for the ecological curriculum.

An ecological curriculum is designed by conducting ecological inventories, in which team members identify 1) the home and community environments that are important for an individual, 2) the priority activities that occur in those environments, and 3) the skills the individual needs to participate in those activities (Brown et al., 1979). As teams have used this analytical process, often they have also used a more intuitive process to identify some skills as priorities for individual students. Such skills might be important for a student to participate in many relevant activities (e.g., hand use) or to expand and enrich participation in many environments (e.g., making choices). In recognition of these priorities, the Brown et al. (1979) process has been modified over time to include a parallel step to identify important embedded skills, which are used in a variety of contexts (Ford et al., 1989; York & Vandercook, 1991).

The ecological curriculum process has also been influenced by two innovations in how education and human services agencies plan for people with disabilities (Vandercook, York, & Forest, 1989). First, family members, friends, and neighbors are assuming important roles in educational planning, not because of legal mandates but because of growing self-advocacy and self-determination movements and because growing numbers of professionals recognize the crit-

ical value of their input. Second, many educational teams now start their planning by envisioning a desirable future for the student with disabilities and then focusing on ways to achieve or approximate the vision as they design the educational program (Falvey, Forest, Pearpoint, & Rosenberg, 1994; Vandercook et al., 1989; York & Vandercook, 1991).

The major steps in designing an individualized ecological curriculum are described below and depicted in Figure 4.1. Although clarity necessitates describing the process as linear, with a sequence of discrete steps, it is more accurate to characterize the components as interwoven and the process as flexible and evolving. Teams are urged to conceptualize and use the process with that understanding. The results of this process are presented at the end of this chapter for two students, Kristen and Jamal, who were introduced at the beginning of Section II.

Establish the Planning Team

The first and most important member of the planning team is the student with severe disabilities, who is encouraged to participate in planning to the greatest extent possible. The student's parents, general education teacher(s), special education teacher, and related services professionals typically form the core of the educational planning team. Although parent and professional perspectives are essential to plan an appropriate program, their views can be complemented and expanded by including friends, other family members, and even neighbors or other significant people. Additional team members are included as appropriate for a student's educational priorities. For example, a job coach, employer, and co-workers may be included in planning for an older student who receives the majority of his or her instruction in a community vocational site. Classmates and co-workers without disabilities offer

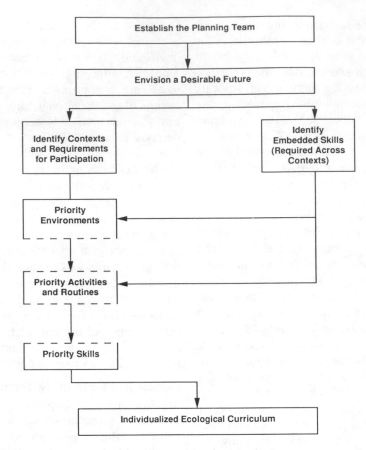

Figure 4.1. Steps in designing an individualized ecological curriculum.

great insights about actual (versus hypothesized) opportunities, requisites, and supports to participate in school, work, and community environments. When students with severe disabilities first enter new program settings, team members from the new setting initially may feel less comfortable with planning. Input from general education teachers and employers is essential to understand the opportunities and demands of their domains, and input from students and co-workers enriches the team's perspective. Given opportunities to get acquainted with the student and given support and encouragement to participate in the planning process, these "novices" can become active and insightful

members of planning teams for students with severe disabilities. When selecting planning team members, it is important to ensure involvement by people who know the student and who have a sincere interest in designing and implementing a program that produces successful life outcomes. Their success in implementing the plan later is greatly enhanced by active involvement in the design process (Kruger, 1988).

Envision a Desirable Future

Several strategies have been used to generate visions of desirable futures for people with disabilities (Falvey et al., 1994; Mount & Zwernik, 1988; O'Brien, Forest, Snow, &

Hasbury, 1989; Vandercook et al., 1989). A common theme in these strategies is that a desirable future is one in which a person with disabilities is a participating member of a family and an integrated community. In an educational program, the team's vision of where and with whom a student will live, go to school, work, spend leisure time, and use other community facilities sets the context for deciding what to teach. Until this vision or context is established, the team has no clear direction and cannot ensure relevance of the curriculum for the individual student.

Envisioning a desirable future requires knowledge of individual student characteristics, in a holistic sense: interests, assets, challenges, and needs. The student is not defined by test scores or by the skills and deficits revealed through formal assessment. Although addressing relevant challenges is important, building on capacities and interests is central to designing an educational program. At the same time, a vision becomes reality only if the team also has a plan and takes action. One strategy to both envision a desirable future and start planning to achieve it is the McGill Action Planning System (MAPS), or Making Action Plans, in which teams discuss the following questions together (Falvey et al., 1994; Vandercook et al., 1989):

What is _____'s history?
What is your dream for _____?
What is your nightmare?
Who is _____?
What are _____'s strengths, gifts, and abilities?
What does _____ need to make the dream come true and to avoid the nightmare?
What would _____'s ideal day at school look like and what must be done to make it happen?
What is our plan of action?

Kristen's team and Jamal's team each held a MAPS meeting to create a vision of a desirable future and to start planning for it. The results are presented in Figure 4.2 and Figure 4.3, respectively.

A shared vision for a student helps team members maintain a holistic view of the student as a person rather than a collection of deficits. Furthermore, MAPS establishes a unified view and purpose to guide the team as it delves into design of a meaningful educational program.

Identify Environments for Participation
Within the domestic, school, vocational, community, and leisure domains, the educational team identifies the specific environments in which it is most desirable for the student with severe disabilities to participate. The student's current home, school, and community environments are considered, and particular attention is placed on integrated or "typical" environments used by peers without disabilities, even if the integrated environments are not currently used by or available to the student. Before a student begins using integrated environments, the team can analyze future settings but can only speculate about exactly how the particular student will participate. Some team members will speculate that the student will fail in integrated settings, but program philosophy, team planning, and student support have proven to be better predictors of successful inclusion than student characteristics (see, e.g., Hunt et al., 1993). As the student enters these new environments, the opportunities for participation, the demands on the student, and the supports that are available there become more clear to the team. As students develop friendships in integrated environments, typical peers become invaluable team members who provide more relevant and accurate information about environmental demands and strategies for inclusion.

What is Kristen's history?

- Premature; stayed in hospital 8 weeks
- Sick and irritable for first year; in hospital three times
- Diagnosed with cerebral palsy at 6 months
- Early intervention, preschool, and therapies at Children's Center
- Walked independently at 4 years; still clumsy
- Doesn't talk yet, gets frustrated (tantrums)
- Needs help with lots of things Julie could do by this age

What is your dream for Kristen?

- Go to the same school as her sister, and ride the same bus
- Have friends—invitations to play and to birthday parties; take care of her, teach her things; they'll know how sweet she is
- Could run, swing, laugh, play like other kids
- She'll do some of the things important to our family—read or listen to stories, make Christmas cookies, learn to cook
- When she grows up, be able to take care of herself (probably can't live alone, but Julie shouldn't have to take care of her)
- Be able to talk and tell what she's thinking
- Go everyplace with the family (church, museums)
- She'll have her own interests

What is your nightmare?

- She'll end up in an institution
- Her tantrums will get worse and she'll be uncontrollable
- When her parents are gone, no one will watch over her
- She'll remain dependent on others for self-care
- She won't have any friends
- She'll never learn to explain what she wants

Who is Kristen?

- Our little girl
- Julie's younger sister [Julie is 7]
- A 5-year-old, almost a kindergartner
- Cute, but stubborn
- Happy and sad
- A little bit slow
- An important member of our family

What are Kristen's strengths, gifts, and abilities?

- Loving, especially loves her dad and dog (Duke)
- A wonderful smile that attracts people
- Follows some short simple directions, especially in routines
- Plays with adults several minutes, sometimes initiates play, especially with soccer ball (her favorite toy)
- Says a few words—Mom, Dad, Julie (Doo-wee), pop, ball (ba)
- Good appetite, eats by herself; favorite food is pizza
- Learned to walk—gives us hope she can learn a lot more
- Usually well-behaved (except when frustrated)
- Loves music and cartoon videos (Pocahontas)

What does Kristen need to make the dream come true and to avoid the nightmare?

- Learn to communicate to express herself (vs. tantrum)
- Have friends, be more interested in kids her own age, learn to play with other kids

(continued)

Figure 4.2. (continued)

- Learn to take care of herself (dress, use toilet, take bath)
- Get around better (walking)
- Be part of kindergarten, do what the other kids do

What would Kristen's ideal day look like and what must be done to make it happen?

- Go to and from school on regular bus—Mom will put her on, get her off at home. Who will get her off/on at school? Paraeducator?
- Follow the regular kindergarten class routine—need to figure out exactly what she can do in the routine, what has to be adapted
- Leave class as little as possible—special ed support and therapies part of class routine (not in corner of class). But how?
- Involve other children as soon as possible
- Notebook for communication with home

What is our plan of action?

- Coordinate paraeducator schedule with bus schedule
- By end of September, ask friends to bring Kristen to classroom
- Kindergarten teacher will outline class routines for rest of team
- Team will assess Kristen in class routines during September—figure out specific abilities, needs, and adaptations
- Mom and school team list topics for regular communication; teacher will make journal
- Meet at end of September to check our progress

Figure 4.2.   Profile of Kristen. Kristen's profile was compiled by Kristen's parents, her older sister, and teachers and therapists from the elementary program she will enter in the fall. It is expected that Kristen will make friends in kindergarten, and the friends will help expand Kristen's profile next spring. (Questions adapted from Falvey et al. [1994] and Vandercook et al. [1989].)

Each of the life domains, including a range of environments for elementary, middle, and high school–age students, is described in more detail in the remainder of this section. Readers interested in a more comprehensive discussion of the scope and sequence of activities comprising each domain are referred to Ford et al. (1989).

Domestic Environments   In this domain, the team considers the student's life in and around his or her actual home. If a family is considering an alternative community living setting, such as a supported home or supervised apartment, the team would inventory that environment also. If a child or adolescent currently lives in a residential facility, the student's family home (with better supports for the family), an adoptive home, or a foster home would be the future, more desirable, and less restrictive environment (Shoultz, O'Connor, Hulgin, & Newman, 1994). Team members identify specific areas within and around the home (e.g., bedroom, bathroom, yard) where greater student participation is desired.

School Environments   For students between the ages of 5 and 18, general education classrooms and other inclusive school environments are the most relevant current or future educational environments (Falvey, 1995; Vandercook et al., 1989; York & Vandercook, 1991). The grade level and classroom environments that are appropriate for the student's chronological age are identified in the inventory process. Figure 4.4 identifies the routines and activities of a general education kindergarten class. Kristen's team used this inventory to identify the activities and skills that are age appropriate for and important to teach to Kristen and the oppor-

What is Jamal's history?
- 17 years old
- Lives in foster home, at home on weekends whenever possible
- Sister Keesha (age 10); cousins Michael (14) and Jiles (17); foster brothers MC (15), Andrew (14), and James (12)
- Programs at developmental center since a baby
- Placed at developmental center when 5 years old
- No real support to keep him at home—Mom always worked
- 3 years ago, moved to foster home close to home, started special class at Central High
- 2 years ago, started regular classes at Central High

What is your dream for Jamal?
- Live with his own family again; have his own place when he grows up; he'll always need someone to take care of him
- Always have family and friends around to watch after him
- Have a job, for pay, where people know him and care about him (e.g., "read" stories for child care or library; run errands in wheelchair)
- A good social life—belong to groups or clubs

What is your nightmare?
- He'll be alone, no one will care about him
- He won't have any way to communicate
- He'll just stay home, won't be able to go any place for fun
- Someone will hurt him; he's vulnerable because he can't talk and depends on others for everything
- His physical condition will get worse; he'll be sick more, have pain, or lose his abilities

Who is Jamal?
- A young man
- Older brother, a favorite family member, good friend
- Easygoing, good sense of humor
- Stubborn (about food)
- A junior in high school
- A pioneer

What are Jamal's strengths, gifts, and abilities?
- Likes to do things with other people (not by himself)
- Sense of humor, his smile
- Friends at high school, especially David and foster brother MC
- Flexible about changes as long as he's with people he likes
- Eye gaze (when his head is secure) to greet people, make choices
- Same interests as others his age—rap music (MTV best, radio OK), french fries, Coke, Nintendo (likes to play with help), motorcycle and car magazines, sports (cheers), rides at amusement park (watches)
- Handsome, good muscles, sharp clothes
- Likes young children, and they seem to like him
- Likes to get out of his chair to stretch; helps stand for transfers
- Works hard

What does Jamal need to make the dream come true and to avoid the nightmare?
- A good social life, with lots of friends
- Expanded communication system

(continued)

Figure 4.3. (continued)

- Ability to direct others (friends, caregivers)
- More independent mobility; learn to drive his power chair and use city bus
- Career education—job sampling and training
- Male paraeducator, well trained, involved in team

What would Jamal's ideal day look like and what must be done to make it happen?

- Keep going to regular classes (to build social circle and explore interests)—continue Homeroom, Horticulture, Home Economics, Media Center (Library, Computer Lab), Choir; try Spanish, Literature
- Work–study program 2–3 times a week (with paraeducator at first)
- Alternate between lunch at school and off campus (coordinate with work–study schedule)
- After-school activities—a club or sports?
- Accommodate physical needs (positioning, movement, eating, rest room) without infringing on social interactions and class schedules

What is our plan of action?

- Investigate more low-tech communication, and high-tech systems: switch controls, scanning methods and devices (Ann)
- Investigate head, arm controls for power wheelchair (Lisa)
- Contact work–study coordinator about possible sites (John)
- Inventory Spanish, Home Economics, worksite (John)
- Investigate after-school clubs and sports (John, in September)
- See which paraeducators will be available in fall (John)

Figure 4.3.   Profile of Jamal. (Questions adapted from Falvey et al. [1994] and Vandercook et al. [1989].)

tunities that are already available to her to address priority motor and communication needs in the classroom. At the secondary level, whether students change classes every 45–50 minutes or participate in longer (2- to 3-hour) blocks of instruction, the team selects a variety of specific classes to inventory, based on individual interests and needs. There are additional school environments besides regular classes that also may be priorities for individual students of all ages. These include the library, office, nurse's room, hallways, playground, and bus area. Ford et al. (1992) caution against focusing too narrowly on the "explicit" curriculum of the school and advise identifying the "implicit" curriculum, which teaches societal and interpersonal relationships. Mendler (1992) further advises that, for many students, these may be the most important and

difficult lessons to be learned and should be a priority for teachers.

For children younger than 5 years, integrated preschools and child care settings would be among the age-appropriate school environments (Vincent, 1995). For young adults between 18 and 21 years of age who are still entitled to educational services, classrooms and other facilities at a community college, university, or other integrated adult setting would be included in the inventory (Frank & Uditsky, 1988; Panitch, 1988; Smith & Puccini, 1995). When determining priority environments in which to provide instruction, an important guideline is to identify the environments used by same-age peers who do not have disabilities. Segregated schools or special classes in regular public schools would not be identified as priority environments because neither of-

---

8:30   Arrival and Free Play
Children walk from their bus and find their classroom. They hang their coats and bags in their cubbies. The aide checks to see who needs to use the bathroom. (Many kindergarten children need help with dressing, using toilet paper, flushing the toilet, and washing their hands.) The room has several areas where the children can play (blocks, house, etc.) or they can choose from the toy shelves. Children check the job board.

9:00   Opening Group (at tables)
Children sit at tables for attendance, calendar, weather, and review of the schedule for the day. (Activities each day follow a unit theme.) Job   assignments for the day are reviewed.

9:20   Story (on rug)
Children listen to a story and participate in a discussion.

9:45   Gross Motor / Perceptual Activity (on rug) [a]
Activities teach body awareness, concepts of size and space.

10:15   Fine Motor / Perceptual Activity (at tables) [a]
Hands-on activities involving size, shape, color, number, and use of senses and leading to reading, writing, and counting.

10:45   Snack
Children wash hands and then try a variety of healthy snacks, help make their snack, work on sharing and manners, and help clean up.

11:10   Free Play
Children have their choice of activities (see 8:30). The group goes outside sometimes, weather permitting. This is also a time to finish class jobs or projects from small group. Children use the bathroom, wash up, collect their things, and get dressed to go home.

11:25   Dismissal
Children line up and walk to the bus.

Figure 4.4.   Kindergarten routine and activities. ([a]Or art, music, library, gym [on a rotating basis 2–3 times weekly]. Children walk in line to other areas of the school and work with other teachers.)

fer opportunities to learn to participate in integrated settings. Rather, teams should focus on building and expanding opportunities for inclusion.

Vocational Environments A community-based vocational training model (as opposed to a segregated prevocational model) provides the greatest opportunity for secondary school–age students with severe disabilities to perform real work and to achieve social integration (Brown, Rogan et al., 1987). Using this model, the team identifies environments in which people of the same age without disabilities work. For children in elementary and middle school, the voca-

tional domain usually is subsumed in the home and school environments, where children have chores and class or school jobs. Students with severe disabilities would also participate in the career development components of elementary and middle school curricula. During high school, opportunities available to same-age peers who do not have disabilities influence decisions about vocational education for students with severe disabilities. One option is to provide vocational instruction after school, on weekends, and during school breaks, when peers are also learning to work (Tashie & Schuh, 1993). Service learning, career education, work study, and school–community business alliance programs offer other options for integrated, community-based vocational education for high school students. Finally, vocational education is usually among the highest priorities for 18- to 21-year-old students with severe disabilities. Wehman and Kregel (1995) recommend that secondary and postsecondary educational programs for students with severe disabilities provide career development, to include career exploration and community-based work experience, rather than narrow job training. Sampling several types of jobs provides information about preferences and aptitudes and allows students and their families to make informed choices about careers.

When vocational preparation becomes a curriculum priority, the team identifies jobsites and, within them, the actual work area, as well as other areas the student would need to use successfully in the course of the workday, such as the cafeteria or breakroom, rest rooms, storage rooms, main office, and hallways. Co-workers may join the student's team to help create the vision and a specific plan for how the student can participate as a member of the work force. Individual decisions about when and how to emphasize vocational preparation reflect student interests, family preferences, educational opportunities, and existing or potential support systems. The Individuals with Disabilities Education Act (IDEA) of 1990 (PL 101-476) requires that the IEP include an individualized transition plan for each student with disabilities "beginning no later than age 16 . . . and beginning at age 14 or younger" for students with greater needs (20 U.S.C. §§ 1401(20)(D)). Extensive guidance is available to develop integrated vocational education programs for students with severe disabilities (see, e.g., Simon & Halloran, 1994; Sowers & Powers, 1991).

Figure 4.5 shows a weekly schedule for Jamal, a high school student with severe disabilities. Jamal's schedule was designed to include regular instruction at a community vocational site, in addition to instruction in several environments at his high school and in other community settings. (More information about Jamal's activities in these settings is presented later in this chapter.)

Community Environments Community environments include transportation systems, streets and sidewalks, and all businesses, services, and facilities in the community. Because of the number of possible instructional environments, priorities are clearly needed. For children at the elementary school age, public school environments have priority over other community environments. Therefore, children might receive instruction related to riding the bus and crossing streets, but other community training would occur only if a family identified particular needs that could not be addressed in typical school environments. At the middle school level, priority environments might include fast-food restaurants, grocery stores, department stores, community recreation facilities, and bus systems. Specific environments would be identified according to student interests and preferences, peer preferences (e.g., age-appropriate community hangouts, preferred activities), family preferences, opportunities for social interaction, and proximity to home or school. During the high school years, environments would be selected to reflect the solidifying vision of postsecondary community participation for the individual student. In addition to environments identified previously, these might include a bank, express teller stations, laundromat, barber or hairdresser, more formal restaurants, and other environments used by adults who live and work in the community. As with the vocational domain, decisions about whether to provide community-based instruction during the school day must be individualized, but with a high preference

	Monday	Tuesday	Wednesday	Thursday	Friday
Before school 7:00–7:45	Regular bus (Restroom 7:30)	Regular bus (Restroom 7:30)	Regular bus (Restroom 7:30)	Regular bus (Restroom 7:30)	Regular bus (Restroom 7:30)
Homeroom 7:45–8:00	HOMEROOM	HOMEROOM	HOMEROOM	HOMEROOM	HOMEROOM
Period 1 8:05–8:55	SPANISH	SPANISH	SPANISH	SPANISH	SPANISH
Period 2 9:00–9:50	COMMUNITY: TRAVEL & WORK	HOME ECONOMICS	COMMUNITY: TRAVEL & WORK	HOME ECONOMICS	COMMUNITY: TRAVEL & WORK
Period 3 9:55–10:45	WORK (Restroom 10:30)	HOME ECONOMICS (Restroom 10:30)	WORK (Restroom 10:30)	HOME ECONOMICS (Restroom 10:30)	WORK (Restroom 10:30)
Period 4 10:50–11:40	WORK	CHOIR OR HORTICULTURE	WORK	CHOIR OR HORTICULTURE	WORK
Period 5 11:45–12:35	WORK & LUNCH (at school or in community)	LUNCH	WORK & LUNCH (at school or in community)	LUNCH	WORK & LUNCH (at school or in community)
Period 6 12:40–1:30	LUNCH (cont.) (Restroom 1:15)	MEDIA CENTER* (Restroom 1:15)	LUNCH (cont.) (Restroom 1:15)	MEDIA CENTER* (Restroom 1:15)	LUNCH (cont.) (Restroom 1:15)
Period 7 1:35–2:25	EARTH SCIENCE	EARTH SCIENCE	EARTH SCIENCE	EARTH SCIENCE	EARTH SCIENCE
After school				Swim Team Manager	

Figure 4.5. Jamal's weekly schedule. (*Media Center, including Library and Computer Lab, is available throughout the day.)

for providing instruction when and where students without disabilities use the community. For example, Jamal's high school has an "open campus," so students use surrounding stores and restaurants at lunch and when they are not scheduled for classes, offering options for Jamal to use the community with friends during the school day.

Leisure Environments   Some leisure environments will overlap with environments identified previously because leisure activities occur at home, school, and work and in many locations in the community. At home, leisure environments may be the bedroom, den, and yard, with homes of friends and relatives also considered. School areas such as the playground, cafeteria, student lounge, hallways, rest rooms, club areas, and athletic areas might be included. At work, the cafeteria or employees' lounge, or an area outside the jobsite, may be an important leisure environment. The community offers many leisure opportunities, including parks, public organizations such as a community center, private health and country clubs, churches, museums, libraries, theaters, arcades, and malls. Selection of leisure environments would reflect interests and preferences of each student with severe disabilities. Selection may also be highly dependent on interests and priorities of family members and typical peers because they ultimately enable the student to gain access to the environments.

Factors in Selecting Priority Instructional Environments   When considering the range of current and potentially least restrictive environments for a student, teams frequently identify more environments than can be addressed instructionally in any given school year. Therefore, it becomes necessary to set priorities. One strategy for prioritization is to project a time frame for each identified environment: 1) high priority for this year, 2) will become a priority within the

next 3 years, and 3) will not be a priority until 3 or more years from now. In ranking priorities, teams are cautioned about assigning low priority to environments simply because students do not use them yet. This becomes a self-fulfilling prophecy. Frequently students are provided access to new environments only when the environments are given high priority.

Another strategy for setting priorities evolves naturally from involving peers without disabilities as "experts" on the team. Children from kindergarten through high school and adult co-workers are far more knowledgeable about participation in their respective spheres than most parents or professionals. When they participate in personal futures planning for their friend with a disability, typical peers often identify the most relevant needs and help teams determine workable strategies to address priorities. Implied in the previous discussions are that high priority will be given to environments that are appropriate to the student's chronological age and that promote social integration.

Identify Priority Activities and Routines
Once priority instructional environments have been identified, the team identifies the activities and routines that typically occur in those environments. At first, team members will need to visit the actual environments and observe, participate, and interview others who use the environment. Conducting this part of the environmental inventory is expedited as information is compiled about a widening assortment of integrated environments used by various students on a regular basis. The team identifies the activities and routines that are priorities for an individual student by considering the student's chronological age, preferences, and abilities; the family's preferences; the activities that offer the greatest opportunity for active inclusion

in integrated environments now; and the possibilities for the future. (Criteria for selecting priorities are discussed in greater depth in Chapter 6.)

Identify Priority Skills

As priority activities and routines are identified, the team also identifies the skills that are typically required for participation. Designated team members go to the actual environment and perform an activity analysis (much like an extensive task analysis). This delineation of tasks and skills serves as the guide for assessing student performance in the environments (described in detail in Chapter 5). Included in the activity analysis is identification of common components of routines, as well as specific skills.

Common Components of Activities and Routines When conducting environmental inventories, it is important to consider the range of components that comprise functional activities and routines, rather than focusing narrowly on only the core components. For example, ordering a meal at a fast-food restaurant involves more than just saying, "I'd like a hamburger, small fries, and a chocolate shake." Students must appropriately initiate, prepare for, and terminate the ordering sequence. Similarly, activities in general education classrooms are defined more broadly than completing core academic tasks (e.g., math problems) while sitting at a desk. Students need to receive instructions, get materials, form work groups, perform core academic tasks, ask for assistance, check and turn in work, clean up, and prepare for the next class or activity. Considering only the core reading, writing, or computing tasks would limit options for participation and learning.

Brown, Evans, Weed, and Owen (1987) conducted a component analysis of functional routines, which provides a framework for examining complete activities. Brown et al. differentiated components as core skills (which typically define participation in an activity/routine), extension skills (required to perform a task independently), and enrichment skills (not required for independence, but desirable for social acceptance and pleasure). For our purposes, it is useful to designate components as either sequential or interwoven, as delineated in Table 4.1.

As an example of the process, consider the activity of using a bank to deposit or withdraw money, as performed by an adolescent or young adult who does not have a disability. *Initiation* of the activity might occur through the natural cues of receiving an allowance or paycheck or participating in a discussion about an event for which money is needed (e.g., taking a trip, buying a birthday gift). The person might announce plans, ask permission, or respond to questions or suggestions to go to the bank. *Preparation* might include collecting money (if making a deposit), bankbook, and bus pass; putting on outerwear; walking to the bus stop; boarding the correct bus; riding the bus; buzzing the driver at the correct stop; exiting the bus; walking to the bank; and entering. The *core component* of the activity would include getting a deposit or withdrawal slip; filling it out and signing it; standing in line until called; giving the deposit/withdrawal slip, bankbook, and money to the teller; waiting for a receipt or money; and leaving the window. *Termination* of the activity would include telling companion(s) of plans to leave the bank and returning to work, school, or home.

The interwoven components would occur throughout the activity. *Movement* might include the mobility for traveling to the bus, entering and exiting the bus, and continuing on to the bank, and the manipulation necessary for opening doors, writing, and handling money. (Movement was not one of the components identified by Brown, Evans, et

Table 4.1.   A component analysis of functional routines

Sequential Components

Initiation
communicate need, desire, intent to engage in activity
ask permission for activity
respond to natural cues to perform activity

Preparation
gather materials, go to location for activity

Core
perform central part of activity
(tasks that are the usual focus of instruction)

Termination
signal the end of the activity
put away material, clean area

Interwoven Components
Movement
for postural control, mobility, and manipulation of materials

Preferences
regarding activities, materials, other participants

Communication
about activity, participants, other events

Social Interactions
sharing, taking turns, helping

Problem solving
incidental opportunities as they arise
intentional or arranged opportunities

Monitor quality of performance
completeness, accuracy, need for assistance

Monitor tempo of performance
latency, duration, rate

Adapted from Brown, F., Evans, I., Weed, K., & Owen, V. (1987). Delineating functional competencies: A component model. *Journal of The Association for Persons with Severe Handicaps, 12*(2), 117–124.

al. [1987]. It was added by the authors of this book.) *Preferences* might include making choices about how much money to deposit or withdraw; whether a companion would go to the bank and, if so, who that would be; where to sit on the bus; and whether to make any other stops during the trip. *Communication* could be directly re- lated to other components of the activity, such as asking the bus driver at which stop to get off, requesting assistance to access the deposit or withdrawal slips, or asking for a particular denomination of money. *Social interactions* might include greeting the bus driver, offering a seat to another passenger, talking with others about upcoming events or about scenery during the bus ride, and thanking the teller. *Problem solving* could occur as incidents arise naturally (e.g., missing the bus, deciding in which line to stand, finding no deposit slips) or could be arranged (e.g., student is not reminded to take his jacket). *Monitor quality* could refer to clothing being coordinated and fastened appropriately, legibility of handwriting on the deposit slip, agreement between cash and amount on the deposit slip, or intelligibility of speech to strangers. *Monitor tempo* could refer to the amount of time it takes to walk to the bus stop, an acceptable rate to fill out forms or move in line, or the duration of waiting in line before tiring or becoming impatient.

The component analysis strategy illustrates that the opportunities for participation and instruction extend far beyond the core of an activity or routine. In fact, components other than the core may comprise the most important and generalizable targets for instruction throughout a student's public education. As teams conduct environmental inventories, the components they include are likely to be influenced by both a typical person's routine, the abilities and needs of the particular student for whom they are planning, and the discipline perspectives of the team members who conduct the analyses. Participation by occupational and physical therapists and speech-language pathologists increases attention to the range of sensorimotor and communication demands and opportunities presented by various activities. After the team members identify priority activities and analyze the activity routines, they will conduct a discrepancy analysis, in which they compare the actual performance of the student with the desired or typical performance. (This step is part of the assessment process and is discussed further in Chapter 5.) For students with severe disabilities, the discrepancy analysis is important not so much to show what they cannot do,

but more to discover ways that students can actively participate in the routine. All steps in the activity and discrepancy analyses will not translate into IEP objectives, but the steps do suggest normalized routines to follow in various settings, and they identify natural opportunities for distributed practice and generalization of priority skills (Mulligan, Lacy, & Guess, 1982).

Priority Skills within Activities In addition to identifying common components in the activity analysis, the team identifies skills that are required within the context of those activities. The skill areas considered by the team are similar to those addressed in developmental curricula: sensorimotor, communication, social, self-care, and cognitive or academic. The distinction is that, in a developmental curriculum, skills are considered priorities because they are next in the developmental sequence. In the ecological curriculum, skills are considered priorities because they are components of functional routines and because acquiring or improving the skills would enhance the student's participation in priority activities and environments. Following this logic, sensorimotor and communication skills are viewed as embedded within daily activities, with both assessment and instruction being more meaningful and valid than when these skills are approached as isolated entities (see, e.g., Falvey, 1995; Ford et al., 1989; Giangreco et al., 1993).

Individual teachers and therapists are each likely to take more responsibility for some skill areas than others because professional education, training, and experience promote knowledge and skills in specific areas. This does not sanction team members to assign or assume sole responsibility or authority for particular skill areas. All team members offer important perspectives, and the student needs comprehensive integrated services to acquire the clusters of skills embedded within activity routines. With this precaution in mind, the areas of sensorimotor skills and communication skills are discussed, with the perspective that these are the areas in which occupational and physical therapists and speech-language pathologists bring considerable expertise. Because students with severe disabilities are so frequently excluded from meaningful instruction, the discussion of embedded skills includes numerous examples to illustrate the feasibility of teaching sensorimotor and communication skills within activity routines.

Sensorimotor Skills Occupational and physical therapists are concerned with quantitative and qualitative aspects of motor performance and the sensory processing that influences performance. In relation to activity routines, it is useful to look first at the quantifiable, functional outcomes of sensorimotor skills for transitions, positioning, hand use, eating, vision, and activity-specific motor participation (Rainforth, Giangreco, & Dennis, 1989; York, Giangreco, Vandercook, & Macdonald, 1992; York, Rainforth, & Wiemann, 1988; York-Barr, Rainforth, & Locke, 1996).

Transitions refer to the mobility skills that students use when traveling from one area to another within the home, classroom, school, workplace, or community. Although many students with severe disabilities lack independent mobility, providing students with a means to move themselves increases their control over the environment and decreases "learned helplessness" (Seligman, 1975). Hulme, Poor, Schulein, and Pezzino (1983) found that young children with physical disabilities became more active and interested participants in environmental events when they achieved a means of independent mobility. York (1989) found that adults with physical disabilities typically used two or more types of mobility (e.g., walking, wheeling a chair, crawling/scooting on the floor), and were selective about where they used the various forms. Robinett and Von-

dran (1988) found that actual environmental demands for independent mobility varied tremendously among people, and that physical therapists needed to look beyond the rates and distances on "independent living scales" if they were to be successful in rehabilitation of adults with disabilities. These findings emphasize the importance of looking at mobility within the context of the student's daily environments and teaching a variety of types of mobility.

Options for independent mobility include walking, pushing or driving a wheelchair, riding a bicycle or tricycle (with adaptations if needed), creeping on hands and knees, crawling on the stomach, and rolling. Most teachers and therapists are familiar with the practice of whisking students from one area of the school building to another—from the classroom to the therapy room, for example—and then creating artificial situations to assess and teach mobility skills. An inventory of the school day reveals many opportunities to address transition and mobility skills in functional contexts. Arrival from the bus, transitions between classrooms, transitions from one area to another within a classroom, and departure are natural situations in which mobility skills increase options for participation and in which students may be most motivated to use their skills. Expectations can be individualized in numerous ways. Students who walk or wheel without assistance can increase their rate or endurance by systematically increasing the distance or decreasing the time for transitions.

> Brian was extremely motivated to go outside after lunch, so he was expected to wheel his chair the full 100 feet from the cafeteria to the door. (Brian's friends understood that he was to do this himself but that, once he reached the door, they could push his chair.) During transitions between other activities and classes, Brian was pushed to within 25 feet of the classroom, with 3 minutes to reach

the door before the other students began to change classes.

Within his classroom, David was learning to creep reciprocally (rather than bunny hop) and rise to stand/lower to kneel reciprocally during free play time. He also worked on rising from a chair and cruising during transitions in the classroom. During transitions between classrooms, he worked on walking with a walker and ascending/descending stairs.

Even students with the most severe disabilities can "partially participate" (Baumgart et al., 1982; York et al., 1988) in transitions.

Missy has severe spastic quadriplegia and poor head control. In order to get to the table for a snack, a teacher or aide facilitated Missy through four cycles of segmental rolling, ending at her chair. Missy's objectives during this transition were to maintain normalized tone, to rotate her head actively in the direction she was rolling, and to reach to touch her chair. To transfer out of her wheelchair, Missy was expected to stay relaxed, keep her neck flexed forward, and move her head in the direction of the transfer. When Missy was carried with total support at the trunk and shoulders, she was to maintain her head in an upright position with minimal support.

These examples reflect typical sequences of motor development, where those sequences represent logical progressions of movement control and complexity for the individuals. The examples also reflect adaptations in sequence and mode to maximize current functional participation while facilitating a quality of movement that will improve functional participation in the future.

Positioning refers both to the postural control a student uses to assume and maintain upright positions and to the positions used during various activities. The functional outcome of both supported and independent positioning is that students with severe disabilities are able to participate most efficiently in some activity. Appropriate positions are selected by considering the student's current postural control, typical positions for each activity, and the demands of participation in the activity. Although the typical position for many school and work activities is sitting, typical children and adults also move continually from sitting upright to leaning and reaching to kneeling and standing, interspersed with walking, running, and even jumping, in the course of a school or work day. In contrast, students with severe disabilities are often dependent on others to change positions. When students sit or maintain any particular position for several hours each day, they have a high risk for developing irreversible deformities and decubitus ulcers (Rainforth & York-Barr, 1996). An effective strategy to avoid these problems is to develop a positioning plan for each student with severe physical disabilities. The plan would include at least two different positions and provisions to change positions at least once per hour. Because contractures at the hip and knee are common, it is beneficial for the selected positions to incorporate changes between hips and knees being flexed (e.g., sitting) and extended (e.g., standing, lying). When students have poor head and trunk control, it is advantageous to alternate between upright and reclined positions to avoid scoliosis secondary to fatigue.

Typical positions for activities reflect a combination of social norms and activity demands. For example, people usually stand to cook and wash dishes.

When Ricardo stood at the counter to prepare food, hip and knee flexion contractures and poor coordination caused him to slowly droop toward the floor. Sitting at a table gave him insufficient mechanical advantage to cut or stir food. A parapodium stander in the home arts classroom enabled Ricardo to stand with his legs properly aligned and to use his hands for food preparation.

Rosemary might have washed dishes sitting in a wheelchair at an accessible sink or with dishpans on a table, but a prone stander allowed her to reach the basin and faucets easily, practice standing, and take a break from her usual position of sitting.

In Todd's middle school art class, typical students sat at long tables. Todd could hold a marker and draw most successfully when sidelying, however, so his team proposed that Todd be positioned sidelying at the end of an art table where typical students also sat. With a rationale provided, the typical students were quite comfortable with this arrangement, which they understood as merely another accommodation to facilitate Todd's inclusion and participation.

Like mobility, postural control reflects typical sequences of skill acquisition and refinement, in the context of functional participation.

Tracy was developing head and trunk control. During storytime, she was expected to sit on the rug leaning on her arms. When positioned in her adapted wheelchair, Tracy was expected to maintain her head in an upright position without the aid of a headrest. When Tracy ate, used her hands, or rode over uneven surfaces, however, she was provided with external trunk and head support because the movement demands of the situations exceeded her current abilities. Many of Tracy's classmates learned when she needed her headrest put in place and when she could stabilize her head independently. Quite unobtrusively, they were the ones who most often assisted with removal and replacement of her headrest. Tracy's activities and abilities were reassessed regularly to ensure that she was challenged to use and improve her postural control and to ensure that positioning enabled her to participate successfully in a variety of activity routines.

Hand use refers to the patterns of reach, grasp, manipulation, and release required for participation in activities. Once again, a developmental sequence serves as a useful guide, particularly when the sensorimotor components of tasks are identified and applied to age-appropriate tasks with age-appropriate materials. Putting pegs in a

board is not inherently important, but the ability to use a fingertip grasp, precise placement, and controlled release are important. The student's ability to perform these movements separately or in combination can be assessed and taught within a variety of functional activities. Grooming, for example, requires similar hand use in the course of face washing, teethbrushing, hair brushing, shaving, and applying makeup. Figure 4.6 presents a task analysis of shaving with an electric shaver, with a corresponding movement analysis to illustrate both the requirements and the teaching possibilities within any task.

Although hand use is an appropriate focus for functional outcomes, the movement analysis denotes the student's need for a foundation of control and movement at the shoulder and trunk. The student may provide this foundation internally, or it can be augmented externally through positioning equipment or dynamic support and facilitation.

During hair brushing, Sandra needed trunk support, assistance to grasp the brush, and assistance to bring the brush to her head. A standard wheelchair provided adequate trunk support. The teacher facilitated grasp by holding Sandra's wrist in a neutral or slightly extended position and facilitated her upward reach by facilitation at Sandra's wrist and just above her elbow. When Sandra's tone increased, strokes with the brush were interspersed with relaxation techniques, consisting of rhythmic movement alternating between reach away from the body (shoulder horizontal abduction with elbow extension) and reach overhead (shoulder flexion–external rotation with slight elbow flexion).

Antonio used an immature palmar grasp when using his fingers to eat and would not allow an adult to physically prompt a fingertip grasp throughout his meal. A better alternative was to fabricate a small splint to cross the web space of Antonio's hand, which was sufficient to facilitate the more mature grasp.

Adaptations are an important consideration when analyzing how a student with se-

Position: Sitting in wheelchair in front of mirror, electric razor on counter

Task Analysis	Trunk	Shoulder	Elbow	Forearm	Wrist	Fingers/Thumb
1. Reach to pick up electric razor	Slight forward flexion	60° flexion neutral rotation	Full extension	Pronation	Neutral	Extension Abduction
2. Grasp electric razor	Same	Same	Same	Same	20° extension	Flexion Adduction
3. Bring razor to right cheek	Extension	45° flexion 60° external rotation 30° abduction	140° flexion	Neutral	20° extension Ulnar deviation	Same
4. Shave right cheek	Same	Alternate +/- 10° from above	Same	Same	Same	Same
5. Move razor to neck	Same	45° flexion 30° external rotation 75° horizontal abduction	Same	Same	Same	Same
6. Shave neck	Same	Same	Same	Same	Alternate ulnar and radial deviation	Same
7. Move razor to chin/upper lip	Same	45° flexion 30° external rotation 30° horizontal abduction	130° flexion	Supination	Ulnar deviation	Same
8. Shave chin/upper lip	Same	Alternate +/- 5° from above	Same	Same	Same	Same
9. Transfer razor to other hand	Same	0° flexion 15° external rotation	90° flexion	Neutral	Neutral	Same
10. Repeat 3 - 8 to shave left cheek with other hand						
11. Put razor on counter	Slight forward flexion	60° flexion neutral rotation	Full extension	Pronation	20° extension	Same

Figure 4.6. Task analysis and movement analysis of shaving with an electric razor. *Note:* Joint angles are approximations to illustrate position changes.

vere disabilities might participate in an activity. Some students may be unable to achieve controlled grasp and release as a generalized skill, but they might learn to reach in specified planes and positions to increase participation in specified activities. Some students may need adaptations to substitute for hand use. Bruce, Paul, and Sara are students for whom such adaptations were needed (York-Barr et al., 1996).

Bruce learned to press a switch with the back of his hand to activate a variety of leisure materials when he was positioned side-lying. Although he could maintain a prone standing position with moderate ease, effort, and control, attempts at directed reach in this position exceeded his current abilities.

Paul, who had only limited use of one arm, learned to collate papers while lying on his back. He activated a switch to move collating trays and "picked up" papers by putting his splinted hand, with Plasti-Tac adhesive on the tip, in the appropriate trays.

Sara has congenital anomalies that prevented her from holding her own finger foods. Her team devised a sandwich holder from a butterfly hairclip mounted on a stand and secured to the table, which enabled Sara to feed herself without using her hands. Sara also offers an excellent example of a student with severe disabilities who, having acquired the means to participate in a meaningful activity, surpassed the professionals' expectations. After some months of feeding herself with the sandwich holder, Sara surprised her team by picking up the sandwich, apparently preferring the independence and efficiency of holding the sandwich in her own hands. Given Sara's new ability at mealtime, her team quickly reassessed her hand use in several other activities to maximize her participation.

Vision refers to the use of orientation, gaze, scanning, and tracking as needed to participate in priority activities. As with other motor skills, students with severe disabilities often are required to practice vision skills in isolated contexts before teams iden-

tify or offer instruction in naturally occurring situations in which students actually need to use vision skills.

Rather than have Jacques orient to and track a flashlight, Jacques's team involved him in leisure activities by using a Light-Bright flashlight and battery-operated cars with sirens and flashing lights, which motivated him to use his limited vision. During leisure and other activities, Jacques was taught to focus on an object at mid-line and track it to the table, focus on and track a second object, scan the two, and gaze at his preference.

Goetz and Gee (1987) cautioned teams to carefully analyze tasks to ascertain that vision is actually needed for accurate and efficient performance.

Luana would not scan the school bathroom to find the soap dispenser, paper towels, and garbage can. When team members observed Luana, they realized she (and most other students) found these items easily without looking. The team determined that visual scanning was required for participation in other environments that were not so familiar or predictable.

Eating refers to the oral-motor aspects of consuming liquid and solid foods, including sucking, sipping, biting, chewing, and swallowing, which are often considered pre-speech skills as well. Self-feeding requires the skills of both eating and hand use. Most people recognize the functional contexts for eating; the precaution here is to avoid overloading mealtime with instruction. One team decided to stress oral-motor skill development during a snacktime in the classroom. During the integrated lunch period in the elementary school cafeteria, they used good but unobtrusive feeding facilitation techniques and stressed the social aspects of mealtime. These alternatives are even more important for a family of a child with severe disabilities. A harried mother once warned a therapist to pare down the hour of prefeeding and feeding instruction to something manageable, that is, something she could do while preparing dinner, handling two other young children, greeting her husband, and having a pleasant meal with her family. With the support of other team members, therapists are encouraged to carefully weigh the numerous needs related to eating and mealtime, and evaluate the cost–benefit ratio of all intervention strategies. For example, if proper spoon placement is as effective alone as when combined with jaw control and facilitation to the lips, the former is preferable because it is simpler. If systematic guided teethbrushing and face washing are as effective to reduce oral sensitivity as 10 minutes of brushing and icing techniques, the former would be preferable because it is a natural part of the daily routine and addresses other needs simultaneously.

Activity-defined motor participation refers to the unique sets or combinations of motor skills used in activities such as swimming, dancing, or horseback riding, in which movement characterizes the activity core. Because they are so unique, the cores of these particular activities often are approached as therapeutic programs. As with other activities, teams are reminded to analyze the entire activity routine, however, to identify other sequential and interwoven components and to determine which skills are priorities for instruction. Another example of activity-specific motor participation is found in the task of putting chairs on desks each afternoon and on the floor the next morning.

When Juan was assigned this class job, it appeared that motor planning problems interfered with his performance. Juan was physically guided through lifting, turning, and placing approximately 100 chairs over several days, after which he spontaneously devised his own strategy to perform the task. Although Juan was still considered to have mo-

tor planning problems, he had learned to plan and execute the motor skills for this particular job.

Qualitative aspects of motor task performance, such as sensory processing, normalized tone, pelvic stabilization, and glenohumeral dissociation, are the focus of much therapeutic intervention. Many occupational and physical therapists have extensive training in assessing the presence and effects of sensory and perceptual motor dysfunction, and this information is invaluable to educational teams. Although quality is always an important consideration, it becomes an intervention priority only when specifically referenced to participation in current and future activities and integrated environments. This does not devalue attention to sensorimotor quality; it challenges all members of the educational team to examine how quality affects performance in integrated settings now and how it might do so in the future.

When a team determines that quality is an intervention priority, it is compelled to design and use interventions in the activities and environments where participation has been compromised.

Alan has severe spastic diplegia, and by the age of 5 he had already had hip adductor releases. Despite aggressive intervention, Alan continued to use bunny-hopping as his primary mobility, he used his arms rather than his legs to hoist himself to standing, and his hips were becoming tighter. Rather than provide intervention for circumscribed portions of the day, Alan's team decided on a more comprehensive approach. In addition to intensive relaxation and elongation each morning, the team physically intervened whenever Alan started pulling to stand, guiding his legs through a reciprocal kneel to half-kneel to stand pattern. To provide additional opportunities for pelvic–femoral dissociation, the team also arranged for Alan to ascend and descend a flight of stairs at least once daily to do errands or travel to other activities. The team reasoned that these motor skills were both a means and an end for maintaining hip joint flexibility.

Saleh's team started a "sensory stimulation" program to decrease his tactile defensiveness. After several weeks he was more tolerant of the stimulation session, yet still resisted physical assistance during dressing, grooming, and eating. Saleh's team reviewed its intervention, considering all areas of sensory processing as well as how his sensory needs were addressed during routine tasks. The team found that Saleh's defensiveness decreased dramatically when, rather than performing tasks on him, the members engaged his attention, told him what was about to happen, and assisted him to participate. The team also infused opportunities to make choices during each routine (e.g., with which item to start, which position to use), increasing Saleh's ability to predict and control these challenging situations. Finally, the team learned that Saleh was more tolerant of certain textures (e.g., rubbery rather than soft or hard) and used these textures (e.g., rubber grip on pencil, fork, toothbrush) when performance was enhanced.

Considerations for assessment and intervention related to sensory processing are discussed further in Chapters 5 and 7.

Communication Skills Some traditional models of communication development and instruction have emphasized discrete components (e.g., phonology, syntax, semantics) as the basis for assessment and intervention. Such abstract approaches have been unsuccessful for many students with severe disabilities, especially when programs occurred in isolation from everyday contexts for communication. Other communication models have emphasized behavioral prerequisites (e.g., visual attending, discrimination, compliance) or cognitive prerequisites (e.g., object permanence, means–ends relationships), and have relegated many students with severe disabilities to years of "getting ready" to communicate. Strict program entry criteria (e.g., reliable yes/no responding) and

service eligibility criteria (e.g., significant discrepancy between mental and language developmental ages) have completely excluded other students from speech and language services.

Fortunately, speech-language pathologists now recognize the integral relationship of communication with cognitive and social behaviors, the importance of the environment as a context for meaningful communication, and the roles of other team members as well as children without disabilities in facilitating communication development (Beukelman & Mirenda, 1992; Norris & Hoffman, 1990; Reichle, York, & Sigafoos, 1991; Stremel & Schutz, 1995). The resulting models of communication development and intervention have positively influenced how speech-language pathologists serve students with the most severe disabilities.

Pragmatics, the study of language usage and its relationship to the structure of language (Prutting & Kirchner, 1987), has emerged as a useful model for communication development and instruction. In the applied pragmatics model, assessment and intervention are most concerned with three areas: context, function, and form for communication. *Context* refers to the situations (e.g., people, daily routines, places) the student uses for communication now or the situations that could be used to expand the number and quality of communicative interactions. Pragmatic *functions* refer to how the student wants to affect the environment (e.g., requests for attention, refusal to participate, greeting). *Form* refers to how the student expresses each function (e.g., tap shoulder to request attention, say "no" to refuse participation, vocalize to greet). Closely related to form are the *modes* students use to communicate, which may include speech, sign language, gestures, pictograms, objects, and behaviors. Halle (1988) asserts that, within the pragmatics model, "all learners possess a communicative repertoire" (p. 158). It is the responsibility of the educational team to ensure that every student has something motivating to communicate about, someone to communicate with, and means to communicate.

Pragmatic approaches do not set the "prerequisites" for communication instruction that previously excluded many students. Emphasis on prerequisites for communication development has waned because empirical evidence does not support the need for cognitive prerequisites, and such approaches cannot meet immediate communication needs. The only prerequisite to communication development is the availability of opportunities to communicate (Mirenda, Iacono, & Williams, 1990). Even intent to communicate is viewed as a result of, rather than exclusively a prerequisite to, communicative interactions.

Infant development research shows that caregivers routinely assign communicative intent to their infants' behavior, although they do not believe such intent actually exists. For example, a caregiver interprets an infant's flailing reach to mean "I want the toy you are holding." The caregiver responds by presenting the toy and saying, "Here it is." Repeating such interactions exposes the infant to routines with social, cognitive, and language components that will eventually be differentiated and understood. The quality and quantity of these interactions seems to influence language learning in infants (Norris & Hoffman, 1990). For students with severe disabilities who demonstrate limited communication skills, Siegel-Causey and Guess (1989) advised educators to observe, interpret, and respond to student behaviors as expressive and meaningful, whether or not the behavior seems intentional. The listener's response

teaches the student that the behavior has an effect and thereby teaches meaning.

Use of formal symbols (e.g., signs, pictograms) is no longer considered necessary for communication to occur. Instead, intervention often focuses on teaching others in the student's environment to recognize, acknowledge, reinforce, and expand both nonsymbolic and symbolic communication functions and forms.

> Dante had fewer than 10 words in his symbolic communication repertoire. Dante's teacher was taught to recognize and record additional, less complex communication forms and functions. In one day of intermittent observations, the teacher saw Dante express five functions (greeting, farewell, emotions, comments, requests) by using eight specific forms, and vocal, verbal, tactile, and gestural modes. Dante's teacher was surprised by the extent of his nonsymbolic communication repertoire, which previously had been dismissed as meaningless or annoying behaviors. With this new perspective, Dante's teacher worked with the speech-language pathologist to reinforce and expand Dante's communication forms and functions, and to move him toward more spontaneous and complex means of communication.

As shown in this example, communication intervention can build upon a well-identified nonsymbolic communication repertoire, rather than focus on remediation of deficits, when students lack formal symbol systems (Mirenda et al., 1990).

Within a pragmatic theoretical framework for language development and instruction, it is useful to organize the embedded communication targets around three general communication outcomes: social interaction, comprehension, and expressing wants and needs (Mirenda & Smith-Lewis, 1989; Reichle & Keogh, 1986; Siegel-Causey & Guess, 1989).

Social interaction refers to a broad range of communicative functions, including attention to people and activities in the environment, reciprocal interactions, and social conversation. Social aspects of communication may also include matching communication style and content with people, activities, and environments.

Initially, it may seem that some students with severe disabilities give little or no attention to their environment. Usually, however, careful observation reveals some reactions to people, activities, and living conditions. Crying, quieting, and even "tuning out" are very basic responses to the environment, which can become the basis for communication instruction. Participation with a communication partner in reciprocal interactions, such as taking turns in early social games, moves beyond these basic responses to environmental conditions. Van Dijk (1986) recognized that reciprocal interactions were an early form of intentional communication by infants, and he applied this principle to his work with children classified as deaf-blind. Curricula based on van Dijk's work have been developed to teach reciprocal interactions to students with profound and multiple disabilities (see, e.g., Feiber, 1975; Robinson, 1975; Sternberg, Ritchey, Pegnatore, Wills, & Hill, 1986). More recently, application of van Dijk's strategies has been extended from instruction in isolated contexts to communication instruction throughout daily routines (Gee, Graham, Oshima, Yoshioka, & Goetz, 1991; Siegel-Causey & Guess, 1989; Writer, 1987). Siegel-Causey and Guess (1989) provide extensive guidelines and examples for how to recognize, support, and teach nonsymbolic communicative interactions in the context of daily routines.

As students acquire more formal modes of communication, they establish and maintain social interactions by labeling objects, people, and events, which develops into social conversation. Teaching labeling for purposes of commenting, describing, or transferring information may be a high priority when it fulfills student needs for social closeness (Beukelman & Mirenda, 1992); this is not to be confused with the once prevalent practice of teaching labeling as an isolated exercise. Reichle and Keogh (1986) also emphasized the need to differentiate between the social functions of labeling and the requesting function. In one situation, a student may point to a friend to share thoughts about the friend. In another situation, pointing to a friend may be a request for a partner. Team members must consider the context to interpret the intent of students' spontaneous communications properly and to determine which function to teach.

Other social aspects of communication include etiquette, such as saying "please" and "thank you," and using different types of greetings with friends, familiar adults, and strangers. In secondary school programs, teams often find it important to teach students with severe disabilities to use certain vocabulary and nonverbal communication skills, so the students can "hang out" in ways consistent with the culture of the school.

Comprehension refers to understanding situations and language, which is inferred from some type of student response. Consistent demonstration of comprehension, or receptive communication, often is considered the prerequisite for teaching formal modes of expressive communication. Traditionally, comprehension has been assessed and taught to students with severe disabilities through series of adult-directed command–response and question–answer tasks. Although this format is convenient for instructors, it is inherently problematic.

Martha consistently followed directions and answered questions. When Martha reached the age of 17, her team realized that she rarely engaged in any communications or activities unless she was verbally directed to do so. The team established the priority of teaching Martha to make requests and initiate activities in response to natural cues.

Henry had no recognized mode of communication, so he could not answer questions. He rarely followed directions, and he became violent when adults tried to control his actions. When adults began to watch Henry more closely, they realized that he clearly understood many things in his environment, and he responded to natural cues in appropriate ways.

Because of cerebral palsy and deaf-blindness, Atif's repertoire of behavior was severely limited. Adults typically did things for him and, although they talked to him, they did not expect him to respond or to participate actively in routines. When Atif's team established consistent routines, guided his participation, and then interrupted those routines in systematic ways, Atif made slight hand movements as attempts to continue his part, thereby demonstrating both comprehension of the routine and expression of his wish to continue (see Gee et al., 1991).

For students like Henry and Atif, who lack formal means to communicate their wants and needs, traditional interventions to "improve comprehension" do not produce functional outcomes. Teams now recognize that emphasis on following verbal directions as the primary approach to receptive communication skills encourages student dependence on artificial cues, limits student outcomes, sometimes reduces motivation to communicate, encourages students to use undesirable behavior to communicate, and unnecessarily delays instruction in expressive communication. These disadvantages do not minimize the need to teach receptive communication; more intentional instruction in receptive communication is essential for students with severe and multiple disabilities (Stremel & Schutz, 1995). One strategy to address these issues is to focus on expressive communication needs first and then assess and teach receptive communication skills as

integral to expressive communication interactions. Several examples are presented next.

Expressing wants and needs refers to conveying desires, needs, and protests. Even when students demonstrate no reliable receptive communication skills, opportunities can be arranged for students to learn to control their environment by conveying preferences (Siegel-Causey & Guess, 1989).

George seemed oblivious to his surroundings and cried or slept for much of the school day. His team suspected that he was often uncomfortable and devised an object communication system in which objects signified lying down, drinking water, and being changed. When George began fussing, team members interpreted his needs, guided him to touch the corresponding item, and immediately addressed the need. Not only did George begin to express these needs himself but, because his basic needs were being addressed, he started attending to other activities in his daily routine.

Henry presented serious behavior problems, as described previously. Henry's team learned to interpret his behaviors from an ecological perspective and then taught him to express his needs with pictograms and sign language. Henry's acquisition of new, expressive communication skills had the added benefits of reducing his use of inappropriate behavior for communication and staff describing him as "more manageable."

The team for Atif, also described previously, often missed the slight body movements he used to try to communicate. The team taught him to activate a tape that said, "Come here, please," which amplified his nonverbal attempts to initiate communication.

Jawana, a first grader with severe disabilities, had no formal way to communicate with her teachers or peers at school. When she continually refused to eat at lunchtime, her team tried to make Jawana's food more appetizing and arranged for her to eat in a calm, quiet area. Jawana still refused lunch. The team then hypothesized that her rejection of food was one of the few means she had to control her environment at school. Team members from school talked with Jawana's parents and found that she used her eyes in regular and reliable ways to communicate with family members. Although this was a rudimentary form of communication and she needed careful positioning for success, Jawana's communicative intents were clear. When the team consistently gave Jawana similar ways to control routine events throughout the day at school, she began eating her lunch.

Jawana and the other students discussed previously were trying to communicate through their behaviors. One way to improve the success of their efforts is to increase awareness and responsiveness of others in the environment to each student's patterns of behavior. When teams identify and amplify subtle but intentional behaviors, students with multiple disabilities are recognized as communicators. When teams identify the communicative intent of "problem" behaviors and provide (or recognize) more appropriate forms of communication, many "problem" behaviors can be eliminated (Carr et al., 1994).

A complementary way to improve success of students' efforts to communicate is to address *qualitative aspects of their communication,* including mode, form, content, and rate. As with motor skills, the importance of qualitative features such as clear articulation, appropriate grammatical structure, and vocabulary size is determined through analysis of the function and context for communication (Browder, 1991; Stremel & Schutz, 1995).

Nick could point to and clearly name scores of objects when asked, but only began using his vocabulary for meaningful communication when the team arranged for Nick to request materials when needed in daily routines.

Maria had no verbal language but demonstrated her receptive language skills by following directions throughout the school day. In the context of daily routines, there were many indications that she could recognize pictures of people, actions, and objects. Her team was anxious to develop a formal communication system for her, but when "prerequisite" training tasks of pointing to pictures were presented, Maria did not seem to attend visually and randomly touched any picture. Nevertheless, Maria's immediate needs to communicate in daily routines were examined, and on this basis a communication board was designed. When meaningful opportunities for daily use were introduced, Maria was successful immediately. Her knowledge of language and pictures had no impact on her expressive communication development until a purpose or function for communication was evident to her.

It is also important to use all available modes of communication (Orelove & Sobsey, 1996), to match modes with functions and to recognize that social interaction is a vital communicative function (Beukelman & Mirenda, 1992; Stremel & Schutz, 1995).

Yolanda learned 20 manual signs at school to communicate her wants and needs. Her team then struggled with the fact that few people outside of Yolanda's school and home environments understood her signs. Furthermore, she tended to sign inappropriately, repeating signs over and over while refusing to accept what she had just requested. Although Yolanda displayed some ability to master this mode of communication, its function for her in a wide range of contexts was questionable. Her team initiated a multimodal approach to communication, including sign language to convey basic needs to close acquaintances, pictograms to remind herself of schedules and routines, pictograms to express wants and needs, and recognition of gestures and physical contact Yolanda already used as legitimate communication (e.g., pointing at or leading to something she wanted). Finally, the team realized that Yolanda's "inappropriate" use of signs was her only option for social closeness, so they provided pictograms and small objects representing past, ongoing, and upcoming activities, as well as jokes and riddles, along with instruction to initiate, maintain, and terminate social conversations (Beukelman & Mirenda, 1992; Reichle et al., 1991; Stremel & Schutz, 1995).

Joe has a severe physical disability and a strong desire to communicate. He was learning to produce two distinct sounds: "hi" to greet people, and "hey" to gain attention. Once Joe initiated interactions with these verbalizations, he communicated needs and preferences with pictures and symbols. Because he had poor control of his head and both arms, Joe's team engaged in ongoing evaluation of the optimal means for him to convey his selection of symbols (e.g., gaze versus direct touch versus scanner).

Just as with sensorimotor skills, communication skills for students with severe disabilities can be addressed in the context of the ecological curriculum. The task of all team members, including related services providers, is the integration of their expertise for development of meaningful learning experiences within prioritized environments, activities, and daily routines.

AN INDIVIDUALIZED CURRICULUM

As the team identifies priority environments, activities, and skills for each student, an individualized curriculum begins to take shape. Kristen's and Jamal's teams used an IEP worksheet to begin identifying and organizing priorities for their respective curricula (Figures 4.7 and 4.8), following the steps outlined in this chapter. The format is intentionally called a "worksheet" because each team member receives a copy and is free to write and revise his or her own thoughts about priorities as the team discussion takes place (York & Vandercook, 1991). The worksheet is divided into two sections. The top section provides space to list environments, activities, and routines corresponding with life domains in which the student's participation is desired. Skills or other targets that are anticipated as important in a specific situation can be included in parentheses. The domains are not mutually exclusive, and many items could be written in more than one column. The

bottom of the worksheet also lists skills the student needs to acquire, but these skills may apply to many activities and environments. The term *embedded skills* reflects the fact that these skills are important not in isolation, but rather within the context of various activities and routines. The worksheet format presented here is one of many ways a team can organize the individualized ecological curriculum content. Perhaps the most important function of the worksheet is to focus all team members' attention on the same curricular content and process. Therefore, format adaptations are encouraged to meet varying team and student needs.

Initially, teams may fear that the curriculum for each student will be so diverse that it will be impractical to implement for one student and impossible for more than one student. In reality, there is overlap and meshing of priority environments and activities for many students, with the greatest diversity occurring in selection of skills to teach. Another concern is that establishing an ecological curriculum is a process that occurs over a period of time and that gradually replaces existing approaches to curriculum development. Although there have been published versions of ecological curricula and assessments that may serve as models (see Freagon, Wheeler, McDaniel, Brankin, & Costello, 1983; Renzaglia & Aveno, 1986), these tend to reflect local circumstances. A variation is an "activity catalogue" that provides an extensive list of domain-referenced activities, which users abstract and expand to reflect local opportunities and student priorities (Kleinert & Hudson, 1989; Wilcox & Bellamy, 1987).

Whether working from an existing ecological curriculum model or starting from scratch, early curriculum development provides the foundation for later work. When a team identifies priority school or community environments and achieves access for one

Life Domains: Environments, Activities, and Routines

Home	School	School (continued)	General Community

Bedroom
•choose clothing
•ask for help
•dressing
  -raise/lower pants
  -hold out arms/legs
•select story
•listen to story
 	
Bathroom
•raise/lower pants
•use toilet
•wash hands
•take a bath
 	
Kitchen
•hold cup without handle
•express preferences
•use "more" and "all done"
 	
Family room/backyard
•play alone
•more interest in objects/toys
•play with sister
•develop social routines
  (e.g., soccer ball)
	Bus
	•travel without parents
	
	Hallways
	•walk in halls (mobility)
	•find gym
	•find lunchroom
	
	Classroom
	•transitions
	•follow directions
	•follow routines
	•communicate with others
	
	Play Areas
	•select play materials
	•play with toys
	•interact with peers
	
	Restroom
	•raise/lower pants
	•use toilet
	•wash hands
		Art, Music, Library
		•transitions
		•follow routines
		•cooperate with other teachers
		•listen to story
		•follow directions
		•get/put away materials
		•clean up
		
		Gym
		•follow group directions
		•work with peers
		•perform specified actions
			Doctor, Dentist, Hairstylist
			•cooperate
			
			Church
			•interact with other children
			•participate in Sunday school activities
			
			Restroom
			•raise/lower pants
			•use toilet
			•wash hands
			
			Fast Food Restaurant
			•express preferences
			•use "more" and "all done"
			
			Library
			•select story
			•follow routines
			
			Grocery Store
			•select favorite cereal
			•follow routines
			•walking
			
			YMCA
			•follow routines
			•swim with adult
			•dressing
			  -raise/lower pants
			  -hold out arms/legs

Embedded Skills

Motor	Communication	Social	Other
•walk without falling •climb stairs •pincer grasp •reciprocal rise to stand	•express wants and needs (alternative to tantrums) •make choices	•take turns in play and other social routines	•play with toys •functional use of objects

Figure 4.7. IEP worksheet for Kristen. (Adapted from York & Vandercook [1991].)

Life Domains: Environments, Activities, and Routines

School	School (continued)	Community	Recreation/leisure	Domestic	Vocational (work experience >12 mos)
Homeroom •greetings •choice of magazines •choice of partner •head control •signal to turn page (vocalize) **Horticulture (T,Th)** •identify materials •plant watering (adaptation) •choice of partner **Home economics (M,W,F)** •identify materials •select recipe cards •operate appliances (with switch) •choice of correct partner •head control •eating •push recipe items away on tray to signal use **Lunchroom** •identify materials •select location •head control •eye gaze/scan for next bite	**Hallways** •choice of peer partner •mobility training with peer and walkman •transport materials on wheelchair **Media center (T,Th)** •explore computers, library use •choice of partner •games with peer **Choir (T, Th)** •identify materials •relaxation •music appreciation (taped to replay at home) **Spanish** •locate partners/group •activate prerecorded messages •participate in all cooperative learning group activities •team scorekeeper	**Bus stop** •greetings **Fast food** •identify materials •greet waitperson •select seat •picture request **Sidewalk & mall** •mobility training •select store (health/beauty aides vs. clothing) •select direction **Church** •relaxation •greetings •select location	**After school sports** •appreciation, enjoyment •greetings •swim team manager **Movie rental/MTV** •indicate desire •select snacks •operate appliance (milkshakes) **Community center/pool hall (VFW)** •select beverage •select activity •select partner/group **Mall wheeling** •mobility •greetings	**Kitchen (home)** •choice of drink, food •operate appliances •forward head position for spoon/cup •eye gaze/scan for next bite •indicate "done" **Bedroom** •choice of clothes •scan/eye gaze •call for attention upon waking (radio alarm) **Bathroom** •indicate order of grooming activities	**Inclusion specialist** •co-present slide series about school and community inclusion to high school students **Nursing home** •deliver mail •book cart •visit •escort residents to game room •carry items for residents **Insurance agency** •greetings •mobility practice during mail delivery •date stamping

Embedded Skills

Communication	Motor	Other
•give directions (eye gaze) •direct attention to identifying information •self-determination: indicate wants, needs, and choices throughout daily routines (using eye gaze) to choose actual objects, people, locations	•explore power mobility using control switch adapted for head turning or gross arm movement •head or hand movement to deflect switches for activating simple electronic devices, communication •maintain/increase functional upper extremity use for specific tasks using adaptations •improve/maintain head and neck control during transitional movement sequences in selected positions and when eating/drinking •increase/maintain range of motion during transfers and in selected positions after relaxation and facilitation •explore use of switch to indicate choices when objects are manually scanned (1 situation initially) •initial exposure to pictures for communication in the context of daily activities (no choice making) •vocalize to get attention (drop head, open mouth, vocalize)	•extend arm to press name stamp adaptation •transport materials on wheelchair

Figure 4.8. IEP worksheet for Jamal. (Adapted from York & Vandercook [1991].)

student, the process is established for the future. As the team delineates components of an activity routine for one student, its task is simplified for subsequent students. As new students enter the program, they participate in typical activities until assessments and IEPs are completed, just as they would with any other curriculum. In our experience, teams that adopt an ecological curriculum consider the benefits to outweigh the costs. Students receive more relevant and successful instruction and, as a result, team members find their own work more meaningful, enriching, and rewarding. More positive and extensive collaboration often occurs between school personnel and families because design and implementation of

an individualized ecological curriculum requires significant family input. As to our purposes here, the ecological curriculum offers teams a unifying focus for their work. The curriculum encourages team members to view sensorimotor and communication skills as components of educational activities and thereby facilitates implementation of an integrated therapy approach.

Given the legal requirement to develop an IEP prior to placement, initial goals and objectives may be projected as teams identify priorities for the curriculum. Prior to finalizing goals and objectives for the IEP, however, teams must assess student performance in the environments and activities they identified as priorities. The next chapter describes such an assessment process.

REFERENCES

Alexander, R., Boehme, R., & Cupps, B. (1993). *Normal development of functional motor skills: The first year of life.* San Antonio, TX: Therapy Skill Builders.

Ayres, A.J. (1972). *Sensory integration and learning disorders.* Los Angeles: Western Psychological Services.

Bates, P., Morrow, S.A., Pancsofar, E., & Sedlak, R. (1984). The effect of functional vs. nonfunctional activities on attitudes of nonhandicapped college students: What they see is what we get. *Journal of The Association for Persons with Severe Handicaps, 9*(2), 73–78.

Baumgart, D., Brown, L., Pumpian, I., Nisbet, J., Ford, A., Sweet, M., Messina, R., & Schroeder, J. (1982). The principle of partial participation and individualized adaptations in educational programs for severely handicapped students. *Journal of The Association for Persons with Severe Handicaps, 7*(2), 17–27.

Beukelman, D.R., & Mirenda, P. (1992). *Augmentative and alternative communication: Management of severe communication disorders in children and adults.* Baltimore: Paul H. Brookes Publishing Co.

Bloom, L., & Lahey, M. (1978). *Language development and language disorders.* New York: John Wiley & Sons.

Bobath, K., & Bobath, B. (1972). Cerebral palsy. In P.H. Pearson & C.E. Williams (Eds.), *Phys-*

ical therapy services in the developmental disabilities (pp. 31–185). Springfield, IL: Charles C Thomas.

Breines, E. (1984). The issue is . . . : An attempt to define purposeful activity. *American Journal of Occupational Therapy, 38*(8), 543–544.

Bricker, D., & Iacino, R. (1977). Early intervention with severely/profoundly handicapped children. In E. Sontag, J. Smith, & N. Certo (Eds.), *Educational programming for the severely and profoundly handicapped* (pp. 166–176). Reston, VA: Council for Exceptional Children.

Bricker, W., & Bricker, D. (1974). An early language strategy. In R.L. Schiefelbusch & L. Lloyd (Eds.), *Language perspectives: Acquisition, retardation, and intervention* (pp. 431–468). Baltimore: University Park Press.

Browder, D.M. (1991). *Assessment of individuals with severe disabilities: An applied behavior approach to life skills assessment* (2nd ed.). Baltimore: Paul H. Brookes Publishing Co.

Brown, F., Evans, I., Weed, K., & Owen, V. (1987). Delineating functional competencies: A component model. *Journal of The Association for Persons with Severe Handicaps, 12*(2), 117–124.

Brown, L., Branston-McLean, M.B., Baumgart, D., Vincent, L., Falvey, M., & Schroeder, J. (1979). Using the characteristics of current and future least restrictive environments in the development of curricular content for severely handicapped students. *AAESPH Review, 4*(4), 407–424,

Brown, L., Nietupski, J., & Hamre-Nietupski, S. (1976). Criterion of ultimate functioning. In M.A. Thomas (Ed.), *Hey, don't forget about me! Education's investment in the severely, profoundly and multiply handicapped* (pp. 2–15). Reston, VA: Council for Exceptional Children.

Brown, L., Rogan, P., Shiraga, B., Zanella Albright, K., Kessler, K., Bryson, F., Van Deventer, P., & Loomis, R. (1987). *A vocational follow-up evaluation of the 1984 to 1986 Madison Metropolitan School District graduates with severe intellectual disabilities.* Seattle, WA: The Association for Persons with Severe Handicaps.

Carr, E.G., Levin, L., McConnachie, G., Carlson, J.I., Kemp, D.C., & Smith, C.E. (1994). *Communication-based intervention for problem behavior: A user's guide for producing positive change.* Baltimore: Paul H. Brookes Publishing Co.

Chapman, R.S., & Miller, J.F. (1980). Analyzing language and communication in the child. In R.L. Schiefelbusch (Ed.), *Nonspeech language and communication: Analysis and intervention* (pp. 159–196). Baltimore: University Park Press.

Eisner, E.W. (1994). *Cognition and curriculum reconsidered.* New York: Macmillan.

Falvey, M.A. (1989). *Community-based curriculum: Instructional strategies for students with severe handicaps* (2nd ed.). Baltimore: Paul H. Brookes Publishing Co.

Falvey, M.A. (Ed.). (1995). *Inclusive and heterogeneous schooling: Assessment, curriculum, and instruction.* Baltimore: Paul H. Brookes Publishing Co.

Falvey, M.A., Forest, M., Pearpoint, J., & Rosenberg, R.L. (1994). Building connections. In J.S. Thousand, R.A. Villa, & A.I. Nevin (Eds.), *Creativity and collaborative learning: A practical guide to empowering students and teachers* (pp. 347–368). Baltimore: Paul H. Brookes Publishing Co.

Feiber, N.M. (1975). *Movement in communication and language development of deaf-blind children.* Unpublished paper, Southwest Regional Center for Deaf-Blind Children, Sacramento, CA.

Ford, A., Davern, L., & Schnorr, R. (1992). Inclusive education: Making sense of the curriculum. In S. Stainback & W. Stainback (Eds.), *Curriculum considerations in inclusive classrooms: Facilitating learning for all students* (pp. 37–61). Baltimore: Paul H. Brookes Publishing Co.

Ford, A., Schnorr, R., Meyer, L., Davern, L., Black, J., & Dempsey, P. (Eds.). (1989). *The Syracuse community-referenced curriculum guide for students with moderate and severe disabilities.* Baltimore: Paul H. Brookes Publishing Co.

Frank, S., & Uditsky, B. (1988). On campus: Integration at university. *Entourage, 3*(3), 33–40.

Freagon, S., Wheeler, J., McDaniel, K., Brankin, G., & Costello, D. (1983). *Individual student community life skill profile system for severely handicapped students.* DeKalb, IL: DeKalb County Special Education Association.

Frostig, M., & Horne, D. (1973). *The Frostig program for the development of visual perception* (Rev. ed.). Chicago: Follett.

Gee, K., Graham, N., Oshima, G., Yoshioka, K., & Goetz, L. (1991). Teaching students to request the continuation of routine activities by using time delay and decreasing physical assistance in the context of chain interruption. *Journal of The Association for Persons with Severe Handicaps, 16*(3), 154–167.

Gesell, A., & Amatruda, C.S. (1947). *Developmental diagnosis.* New York: Harper & Row.

Giangreco, M.F. (1996). *Vermont interdependent services team approach (VISTA): A guide to coordinating educational support services.* Baltimore: Paul H. Brookes Publishing Co.

Giangreco, M.F., Cloninger, C.J., & Iverson, V.S. (1993). *Choosing options and accommodations for children (COACH): A guide to planning inclusive education.* Baltimore: Paul H. Brookes Publishing Co.

Goetz, L., & Gee, K. (1987). Functional vision programming: A model for teaching visual behavior in natural contexts. In L. Goetz, D. Guess, & K. Stremel-Campbell (Eds.), *Innovative program design for individuals with dual sensory impairments* (pp. 77–98). Baltimore: Paul H. Brookes Publishing Co.

Halle, J.W. (1988). Adopting the natural environment as the context of training. In S. Calculator & J. Bedrosian (Eds.), *Communication assessment and intervention for adults with mental retardation* (pp. 155–185). Boston: College-Hill Press.

Harvey, R.F., & Jellinek, H.M. (1981). Functional performance assessment: A program approach. *Archives of Physical Medicine and Rehabilitation, 62*(9), 456–460.

Hulme, J.B., Poor, R., Schulein, M., & Pezzino, J. (1983). Perceived behavioral changes observed with adapted seating devices and training programs for multihandicapped, developmentally disabled individuals. *Physical Therapy, 63*(2), 204–208.

Hunt, P., Haring, K., Farron-Davis, F., Staub, D., Rogers, J., Beckstead, S.P., Karasoff, P., Goetz, L., & Sailor, W. (1993). Factors associated with integrated educational placement of students with severe disabilities. *Journal of The Association for Persons with Severe Handicaps, 18*(1), 6–15.

Individuals with Disabilities Education Act (IDEA) of 1990, PL 101-476, 20 U.S.C. §§ 1400 *et seq.*

Klein, R.M., & Bell, B. (1982). Self-care skills: Behavioral measurement with Klein-Bell ADL scale. *Archives of Physical Medicine and Rehabilitation, 63*(7), 335–338.

Kleinert, H., & Hudson, N. (Eds.). (1989). *Model local catalogue and curriculum process for students with moderate and severe handicaps.* Lexington: University of Kentucky, Kentucky Systems Change Project, Interdisciplinary Human Development Institute.

Kruger, L. (1988). Programmatic change strategies at the building level. In J.L. Graden, J.E. Zins, & M.J. Curtis (Eds.), *Alternative educational delivery systems: Enhancing instructional options for all students* (pp. 491–512). Washington, DC: National Association of School Psychologists.

Kugelmass, J.W. (1996). Reconstructing curriculum for systemic inclusion. In M. Berris, D. Ferguson, P. Knoblock, & C. Woods (Eds.), *Creating tomorrow's schools today: Stories of inclusion, change, and renewal.* New York: Teachers College Press.

Loria, C. (1980). Relationship of proximal and distal function in motor development. *Physical Therapy, 60*(2), 167–172.

Mendler, A.N. (1992). *What do I do when . . . ? How to achieve discipline with dignity in the classroom.* Bloomington, IN: National Educational Service.

Merriam-Webster's Collegiate Dictionary (10th ed.). (1993). Springfield, MA: Merriam-Webster.

Miller, J. (1977). On specifying what to teach: The movement from structure, to structure and meaning, to structure and meaning and knowing. In E. Sontag, J. Smith, & N. Certo (Eds.), *Educational programming for the severely and profoundly handicapped* (pp. 378–388). Reston, VA: Council for Exceptional Children.

Mirenda, P., Iacono, T., & Williams, R. (1990). Communication options for persons with severe and profound disabilities: State of the art and future directions. *Journal of The Association for Persons with Severe Handicaps, 15*(1), 3–21.

Mirenda, P., & Smith-Lewis, M. (1989). Communication skills. In A. Ford, R. Schnorr, L. Meyer, L. Davern, J. Black, & P. Dempsey (Eds.), *The Syracuse community-referenced curriculum guide for students with moderate and severe disabilities* (pp. 189–209). Baltimore: Paul H. Brookes Publishing Co.

Mount, B., & Zwernik, K. (1988). *It's never too early, it's never too late: A booklet about personal futures planning.* St. Paul, MN: Metropolitan Council.

Mulligan, M., Lacy, L., & Guess, D. (1982). Effects of massed, distributed, and spaced trial sequencing on severely handicapped students' performance. *Journal of The Association for the Severely Handicapped, 7*(2), 48–61.

Norris, J., & Hoffman, P. (1990). Language intervention in naturalistic environments. *Language, Speech, and Hearing Services in Schools, 21*(2), 72–84.

O'Brien, J., Forest, M., Snow, J., & Hasbury, D. (1989). *Action for inclusion.* Toronto, Ontario: Frontier College Press.

Orelove, F.P., & Sobsey, D. (1996). *Educating children with multiple disabilities: A transdisciplinary approach* (3rd ed.). Baltimore: Paul H. Brookes Publishing Co.

Panitch, M. (1988). Community college integration: More than just an education. *Entourage, 3*(3), 26–32.

Prutting, C., & Kirchner, D. (1987). A clinical appraisal of the pragmatic aspects of language. *Journal of Speech and Hearing Disorders, 52*(2), 105–119.

Rainforth, B., Giangreco, M., & Dennis, R. (1989). Motor skills. In A. Ford, R. Schnorr, L. Meyer, L. Davern, J. Black, & P. Dempsey (Eds.), *The Syracuse community-referenced curriculum guide for students with moderate and severe disabilities* (pp. 211–230). Baltimore: Paul H. Brookes Publishing Co.

Rainforth, B., & York-Barr, J. (1996). Handling and positioning. In F.P. Orelove & D. Sobsey, *Educating children with multiple disabilities: A transdisciplinary approach* (3rd ed., pp. 79–118). Baltimore: Paul H. Brookes Publishing Co.

Reichle, J., & Karlan, G. (1985). The selection of an augmentative system of communication intervention: A critique of decision rules. *Journal of The Association for Persons with Severe Handicaps, 10*(3), 146–156.

Reichle, J., & Keogh, W.J. (1986). Communication instruction for learners with severe handicaps: Some unresolved issues. In R.H. Horner, L.H. Meyer, & H.D.B. Fredericks (Eds.), *Education of learners with severe handicaps: Exemplary service strategies* (pp. 189–219). Baltimore: Paul H. Brookes Publishing Co.

Reichle, J., York, J., & Sigafoos, J. (1991). *Implementing augmentative and alternative communication: Strategies for learners with severe disabilities.* Baltimore: Paul H. Brookes Publishing Co.

Renzaglia, A., & Aveno, A. (1986). *Manual for administration of an individualized functional curriculum assessment procedure for students with moderate to severe handicaps.* Charlottesville: University of Virginia.

Robinett, C.S., & Vondran, M.A. (1988). Functional ambulation velocity and distance requirements in rural and urban communities. *Physical Therapy, 68*(9), 1371–1373.

Robinson, P. (1975). *An educational approach utilizing developmental sequencing and the coactive movement theory.* Unpublished paper, Northern Regional Service Center, South Bend, IN.

Seligman, M. (1975). *Helplessness: On depression, development, and death.* San Francisco: W.H. Freeman.

Shapiro, J.P. (1994). *No pity: People with disabilities forging a new civil rights movement.* New York: Times Books.

Shoultz, B., O'Connor, S., Hulgin, K., & Newman, P. (1994). *Permanency planning in Michigan: From philosophy to reality.* Syracuse, NY: Syracuse University, Center on Human Policy.

Siegel-Causey, E., & Guess, D. (1989). *Enhancing nonsymbolic communication interactions among learners with severe disabilities.* Baltimore: Paul H. Brookes Publishing Co.

Simon, M., & Halloran, W. (1994). Community-based vocational education: Guidelines for complying with the Fair Labor Standards Act. *Journal of The Association for Persons with Severe Handicaps, 19*(1), 52–60.

Smith, T.E.C., & Puccini, I.K. (1995). Position statement: Secondary curricula and policy issues for students with mental retardation. *Education and Training in Mental Retardation and Developmental Disabilities, 30*(4), 275–282.

Sowers, J., & Powers, L. (1991). *Vocational preparation and employment of students with physical and multiple disabilities.* Baltimore: Paul H. Brookes Publishing Co.

Sternberg, L., Ritchey, H., Pegnatore, L., Wills, L., & Hill, C. (1986). *A curriculum for profoundly handicapped students.* Rockville, MD: Aspen Publishers, Inc.

Stremel, K., & Schutz, R. (1995). Functional communication in inclusive settings for students who are deaf-blind. In N.G. Haring & L.T. Romer (Eds.), *Welcoming students who are deaf-blind into typical classrooms: Facilitating school participation, learning, and friendships* (pp. 197–229). Baltimore: Paul H. Brookes Publishing Co.

Tashie, C., & Schuh, M. (1993, Spring). Why not community based instruction? *Equity and Excellence,* pp. 15–17.

Thousand, J.S., Villa, R.A., & Nevin, A.I. (1994). *Creativity and collaborative learning: A practical guide to empowering students and teachers.* Baltimore: Paul H. Brookes Publishing Co.

Vandercook, T., York, J., & Forest, M. (1989). The McGill action planning system (MAPS): A strategy for building the vision. *Journal of The Association for Persons with Severe Handicaps, 14*(3), 205–215.

van Dijk, J. (1986). An educational curriculum for deaf-blind multi-handicapped persons. In D. Ellis (Ed.), *Sensory impairments in mentally handicapped people* (pp. 375–382). London: Croom-Helm.

Van Sant, A.F. (1988). Age differences in movement patterns used by children to rise from supine position to erect stance. *Physical Therapy, 68*(9), 1330–1338.

Vincent, L.J. (1995). Preschool curriculum and instruction. In M.A. Falvey (Ed.), *Inclusive and heterogeneous schooling: Assessment, curriculum, and instruction* (pp. 285–318). Baltimore: Paul H. Brookes Publishing Co.

Wehman, P., & Kregel, J. (1995). At the crossroads: Supported employment a decade later.

Journal of The Association for Persons with Severe Handicaps, 20(4), 286–299.

Wilcox, B., & Bellamy, G.T. (1987). *The activities catalogue: An alternative curriculum for youth and adults with severe disabilities.* Baltimore: Paul H. Brookes Publishing Co.

Williams, W., Fox, T., Thousand, J., & Fox, W. (1990). Level of acceptance and implementation of best practices in the education of students with severe handicaps in Vermont. *Education and Training in Mental Retardation, 25*(2), 120–131.

Writer, J. (1987). A movement-based approach to the education of students who are sensory impaired/multihandicapped. In L. Goetz, D. Guess, & K. Stremel-Campbell (Eds.), *Innovative program design for individuals with dual sensory impairments* (pp. 191–224). Baltimore: Paul H. Brookes Publishing Co.

York, J. (1989). Mobility methods selected for use in home and community environments. *Physical Therapy, 69*(9), 736–747.

York, J., Giangreco, M.F., Vandercook, T., & Macdonald, C. (1992). Integrating support personnel in the inclusive classroom. In S. Stainback & W. Stainback (Eds.), *Curriculum considerations in inclusive classrooms: Facilitating learning for all students* (pp. 101–116). Baltimore: Paul H. Brookes Publishing Co.

York, J., Rainforth, B., & Wiemann, G. (1988). An integrated approach to therapy for school-aged learners with developmental disabilities. *Totline, 14*(3), 36–40.

York, J., & Vandercook, T. (1991). Designing an integrated education for learners with severe disabilities through the IEP process. *Teaching Exceptional Children, 23*(2), 22–28.

York-Barr, J., Rainforth, B., & Locke, P. (1996). Developing instructional adaptations. In F.P. Orelove & D. Sobsey, *Educating children with multiple disabilities: A transdisciplinary approach* (3rd ed., pp. 119–159). Baltimore: Paul H. Brookes Publishing Co.

5

Collaborative Assessment

Students with severe disabilities are evaluated for numerous purposes, including determination of service needs, identification of program content, and evaluation of program effectiveness (Browder, 1991). The Individuals with Disabilities Education Act (IDEA) of 1990 (PL 101-476) requires that a multidisciplinary team conduct a comprehensive evaluation to determine whether a child has exceptional educational needs that warrant special services. If special education is warranted, a comprehensive evaluation must be conducted at least once every 3 years for the duration of services. The student also must be assessed at least annually to determine his or her present level of educational performance, to ascertain progress on the current individualized education program (IEP), and to establish IEP goals and objectives for the next year. In addition, effective instructional practices require frequent and ongoing assessment of student performance on IEP and individualized family service plan (IFSP) objectives, as the basis for instructional decision making and responsive program modification (Browder, 1991).

Eligibility for special education services has not been an issue for students with severe disabilities, and assessment to ascertain eligibility is not discussed here. This chapter presents assessment strategies related to the triennial evaluation, the annual review, and ongoing assessment as integral to daily instruction. The strategies described here presume that 1) an ecological curriculum model has been (or is being) adopted and 2) educational team members collaborate in the assessment process. The assessment process includes four main steps: 1) planning, 2) assessing student performance in natural environments, 3) analyzing performance discrepancies and generating hypotheses, and 4) conducting diagnostic assessment.

Because the steps in the process are nominally familiar to most teachers and therapists, it is important to note some distinctions. In traditional approaches, individual team members conduct independent assessments using a variety of formal and informal instruments. Often a disability in one area (e.g., movement) limits performance in another area (e.g., communication) without professionals from the respective disciplines recognizing or adjusting for this interaction effect. Also, different professionals may collect information about similar skills (e.g., teacher, occupational therapist, and physical therapist all assess sensorimotor skills). Although varied perspectives are important for collaborative planning, parallel efforts tend to result in duplicated efforts. In traditional approaches, each discipline completes a separate report, so overall results might be redundant, conflicting, irrelevant, or incomplete. Furthermore, multidisciplinary assessment is very costly and does not necessarily lead to effective program planning. Bricker and Campbell (1980) analyzed recommendations made by multidisciplinary teams who conducted educational assessments of 17 students with multiple disabilities. Although 397 recommendations were made, only 30% were directly related to educational programming, appropriate for the designated student, and specific enough to be implemented. Only 11% of the recommendations were ever implemented. This means that, from an average of 23 recommendations per student, only 7 were educationally relevant and only 2 or 3 may have benefited the student. This is especially disappointing when one considers that the conservative cost estimate for these assessments was $1,500 per student in 1980. Similar assessments cost far more today.

Some of the shortcomings of traditional multidisciplinary and interdisciplinary assessment were addressed by the "arena" approach, in which the entire team assembled to observe the student's performance (Connor, Williamson, & Siepp, 1978). The assessment process was planned, team member participation was coordinated, and observations and conclusions were integrated. In a pilot study of arena assessment, parents reported increased satisfaction with this approach, which they considered more thorough and more likely to produce an accurate picture of their child (Wolery & Dyk, 1984). Staff found that arena assessment increased parent participation, produced more accurate pictures of preschool-age children with severe disabilities, and resulted in more positive interactions, fewer miscommunications, and more team consensus than the interdisciplinary assessment process they had used previously.

Although the arena approach addressed many weaknesses of traditional assessments, it still established artificial settings and contrived tasks, which did not promote accurate assessment of students with severe disabilities. More recently, Linder (1993) described a "transdisciplinary play-based assessment" (TPBA) for young children. This variation on arena assessment recognizes play as a normal activity for young children that provides a natural context for assessment. A comparison of traditional multidisciplinary assessment and TPBA showed that TPBA was more timely, was a positive experience for parents and staff, and yielded valid and useful assessment reports (Myers, McBride, & Peterson, 1996). Because some aspects of the formal TPBA might be artificial for some children, Linder (1993) encouraged teams to apply the same strategies to children's natural routines and environments. A study of ecological assessment combined with more traditional assessment in an inclusive preschool showed that the model promoted skill instruction in the context of developmentally appropriate preschool activities, enhancing both social and instructional inclusion (Haney & Cavallaro, 1996).

In the collaborative assessment process described in this chapter, observation of students performing typical activities in natural environments precedes more formal assessment by specific disciplines for several reasons. Aside from the problems discussed previously, starting with formal and discipline-specific assessment leads to pre-conceived notions about what a student cannot do and tends to deny opportunities for participation in normalized activities and environments. Many students with severe disabilities have surpassed professionals' expectations when presented with real-life tasks in natural situations. Furthermore, it is performance in natural environments that is most significant. If a student points to the pictures of preferred food items at a fast-food restaurant but will not point to the same pictures in the speech therapy room or in the formal assessment arena, an instructional need has not been identified. If a student can rotate and retrieve toys from the floor while sitting on a therapy ball but does not reach down to get materials from a shelf in the classroom, a need exists. This need exists within the context of the typical activity in the classroom, however, and cannot be assessed accurately in another situation.

Finally, the disciplinary expertise of each team member can be used to the greatest advantage when it focuses on determining why a student has specific performance problems and how that performance can be improved. In traditional assessment, individual team members often perform this diagnostic assessment intuitively and fail to articulate conclusions or their bases for other team members. When team members see performance problems only from their own disciplinary perspective and plan interventions accordingly, conflict, confusion, and clumsy use of resources are likely (Bundy, 1995). Therefore, it is essential that team members discuss their respective hypotheses prior to drawing conclusions. It is during the processes of assessment and program development that team members draw upon their stores of scientific, theoretical, and practical knowledge to analyze situations and hypothesize solutions. Because it would be impractical and impossible to share all of this knowledge, *we do not advocate role release to the extent that any relevant discipline would be eliminated from the assessment team.* We do advocate that team members share information during the process, however, because this enables everyone to perform more effective assessment. The extensive information sharing, coordination, and cooperation among team members throughout the assessment process lays the groundwork for designing comprehensive and integrated programs for students with severe disabilities.

THE ASSESSMENT PROCESS

The assessment process consists of four main steps: 1) planning the assessment, 2) assessing student performance in natural environments, 3) analyzing performance discrepancies and generating hypotheses, and 4) conducting diagnostic assessment. Although each step in the process is described in this chapter as a separate entity, an actual assessment proceeds at varied rates, and steps may overlap. For example, priorities or logistical constraints may result in a team completing almost all steps of an assessment at school before beginning assessment in community settings. As team members become skilled in the process, they are also likely to start collecting some diagnostic information while observing the student in routine activities. Examples of the process for an initial or triennial evaluation and for ongoing program development are presented for Kristen and Jamal, who were introduced in Chapter 4. The flow chart in Figure 5.1 provides an overview of steps in the assessment process.

Planning the Assessment

When using a collaborative team approach and an ecological curriculum model, coordination of assessment is challenging. It is desirable for all team members to assess stu-

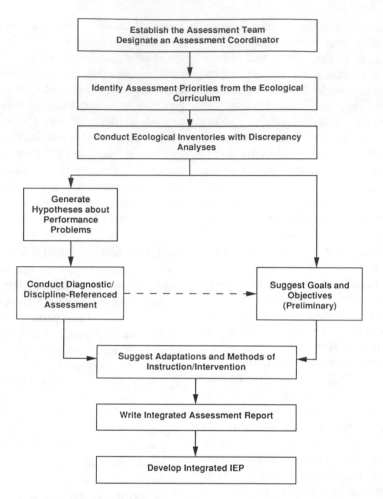

Figure 5.1.   Steps in collaborative assessment to design an educational program.

dent performance in every priority environment, but, logistically, it usually is not possible to arrange this before instruction begins. Therefore, parent and professional members of the educational team must set priorities regarding the order of environments and activities in which the student will be assessed, and they must determine which team members will participate in each stage of the assessment.

The first step in planning is to establish the assessment team. As with any other assessment, the student's known and presumed needs determine team composition, and other members are added as new needs are identified. (Considerations for selecting specific team members are discussed in Chapter 8.) Once established, the team designates an assessment coordinator. Typically this is the teacher because he or she has the most frequent contact with the student, family, and other school personnel. The teacher also manages the student schedule and knows the support staff schedules, which expedites coordination. The assessment coordinator develops a chart to organize and document the assessment process for each student. Examples of ecological assessment planning charts for Kristen and Jamal are presented later in this chapter (see Figures 5.6 and 5.10 on pp. 160–161 and 171, respectively). Across the top of the chart are listed all the disciplines on the student's team. Down the left side are listed the environments and activities or routines in which ecological assessment will occur. Using this chart as a guide, the team meets to identify the initial environments for assessment. The highest priorities are identified, and the team decides which team member(s) will assess the student's performance in these environments first. Dates are entered in the corresponding spaces to indicate when the assessments will be conducted. As reflected in Kristen's and Jamal's planning charts, it may take several days to complete ecological assessments in the limited number of environments that are designated highest priority. Because assessment in all environments is a long-term venture, it is better to think of ecological assessment as a process rather than an event.

The environments and activities in which the assessment will occur are derived from the IEP worksheets and individualized ecological curriculum, as described in Chapter 4. Decisions about initial priorities will depend on where the student currently participates and where participation is desired, both immediately and in the future. Family members often identify home or community environments where needs exist, and they may also have definite ideas about priority school environments. Family members are encouraged to identify their priorities first, after which professionals might add environments and activities they believe are priorities. At school, students are usually assessed first in environments and activities that comprise typical routines. As additional environments and activities are identified to meet individual needs, the team expands its assessment to those areas. When students reach middle and high school age, community environments assume increasing impor-

tance. Considerations in scheduling the assessment include choosing the time when priority activities occur most naturally and when the child's performance will be most representative. Staff scheduling strategies that allow flexibility for team members to work with students in a variety of environments are presented in Chapter 8.

Teams are urged to recognize that all members cannot conduct meaningful assessment of student performance in all environments and activities during the first month of school. Priorities must be set. For example, a team may decide that the occupational therapist and speech-language pathologist should be the first ones to assess a student at his or her jobsite. The special educator will assess the student there eventually, but that team member's first priority may be to assess the student in two inclusive high school classes. Deciding which team members will be involved in initial assessments will depend on student needs, family priorities, and staff schedules. All team members might not need to observe the student in all activities, but they do need to observe representative performance in priority areas. For example, it may be important that the speech-language pathologist assess the student's communication in individual, small-group, and large-group activities, or where the student has particular success or difficulty. It is also highly desirable for two or more team members to observe the student together, for more reliable and multifaceted interpretations of performance. For therapists to participate in this way, block scheduling is recommended (see Chapter 8). Teams are cautioned to limit the number of observers at any one time, however, to minimize the confusion, congestion, and artificial effects produced when too many adults are present.

There are special considerations for planning an assessment when a new student is entering a program. It is most appropriate for the assessment to start with observation in a familiar environment such as the home, the child care center, or another education program. Observation in familiar environments and routines yields more valid information on performance, provides a general baseline for measuring growth, introduces the student to school personnel in a less stressful way, and offers bases for understanding or assessing the student's behavior at school. A team usually identifies one or two members to perform the ecological assessment at home. Considerations in selecting assessors include family preference, perceived needs, and staff schedules.

Many students demonstrate different abilities and personalities at home, and most perform under different expectations and limits than they do at school. Therefore, periodic reassessment at home or in a child care setting can also be helpful. Factors such as geography, staffing, and program policies and procedures influence each team's ability to make home visits and preplacement visits. In some cases, alternative strategies, such as videotaping, can provide useful baseline information.

Assessing Student Performance in Natural Environments

The student's daily schedule and participation in priority environments provide the context for assessment of abilities and needs relevant to the educational program. Prior to the assessment, team members conduct inventories of priority environments and activities. An ecological inventory delineates the performance expected by a person of about the same age who does not have a disability. Depending on the abilities and needs of the student being assessed, the steps in the inventory may be expanded or condensed (Black & Ford, 1989). For example, Kristen's team considered her age, her prior educational experiences, and the nature of her

disabilities when it based her inventories on performance of typically developing 5-year-olds, with steps added to emphasize sensorimotor and communication skills. For Jamal, a high school student with severe disabilities, some of the motor skill sequences were shortened for his assessment at work. The team had previously made systematic and concerted efforts to increase Jamal's motor participation in removing his jacket, yet he continued to need full assistance. Team members agreed that this performance probably would not improve significantly, so they did not break down this task. They carefully analyzed other motor skill sequences relevant to Jamal's job, however.

As inventories are developed, the student is observed during naturally occurring activities to determine how he or she performs without assistance. Assistance is given, of course, when failure to do so would endanger the student or completely preclude performance. An important aspect of assessment when students are not able to demonstrate a necessary skill is an initial attempt at intervention. Team members engage the student in designated activities, using a variety of teaching and intervention strategies to elicit optimal performance. Otherwise the assessment results would indicate whether or not the student performed the task but would provide no information about possible interventions. Using the environmental inventory as the guide for assessment, team members record whether the student performed designated activities independently, how the student participated, and what type of assistance elicited optimal performance. Examples of ecological inventories and corresponding assessments of Kristen and Jamal are presented later in this chapter (see Figures 5.6, 5.12, and 5.14 on pp. 160–161, 173–174, and 176–177, respectively).

Part of Jamal's ecological assessment was conducted in the general education classes in which he was included. Some students with severe disabilities develop a strong interest in a particular secondary curriculum area (e.g., biology) but require modifications in scope and quality of performance. As students with severe disabilities grow older, however, their learning priorities tend to become more discrepant from the priorities for students without disabilities. For example, in the Spanish or Home Economics classes in which Jamal was enrolled, his learning priorities had little to do with the core curricular content, so it was inappropriate to design ecological assessments that focused exclusively on the core curriculum. Routines in general education classes present many other types of demands and learning opportunities that are priorities for students with severe disabilities, and it is important to conduct ecological assessments of these opportunities (York & Vandercook, 1990). Based on strategies to analyze general education classroom environments (see, e.g., Browder, 1991; Brown, Evans, Weed, & Owen, 1987; Meyer et al., 1985; Thousand et al., 1986; Williams, Hamre-Nietupski, Pumpian, McDaniel-Marx, & Wheeler, 1978), the Assessment of Student Participation in General Education Classes (Macdonald & York, 1989) was developed to assess student participation in two major areas: classroom routines and activities, and social and communication skills (see Figure 5.2). Jamal's ecological assessment for Spanish class, presented later in this chapter, reflects this approach.

When multiple team members participate in an assessment, it is helpful to designate roles. The facilitator engages students in routine activities, eliciting both typical and optimal performance. Observers watch and suggest alternative strategies to the facilitator. Recorders take notes on what the student does, how the student does it, and what he or she does not do. A complete assessment usually takes several sessions, and, in the course of the assessment, each team member would alternate among the roles of facilitator, observer, and recorder. Parents participate in each of these roles as they feel comfortable and as the team (including the parents) deems appropriate. Experienced teaching assistants often have an active role in assessment.

Even within one assessment session, a team member may assume all three roles. For example, during snacktime at school, a teaching assistant worked with Kristen on finger feeding. When the occupational therapist observed difficulties, he asked the assistant to seat Kristen on a higher chair, support her feet with a large block, and prompt at the elbow. Kristen responded well to each change. Then the occupational therapist stepped in as facilitator to see how he could prompt a fingertip grasp. He modeled one method for the assistant, who then resumed working with Kristen. The occupational therapist made notes about the situation as he continued to observe.

Analyzing Discrepancies and Generating Hypotheses

After performance information is recorded and the assessment is completed for a specific environment, discrepancies are identified between the way in which designated activities are performed by the student and the way in which they are performed by a person without disabilities. For each discrepancy, team members begin to hypothesize about factors that may contribute to the student's performance difficulties. As individual team members accumulate information about what the student does and does not do in a variety of situations, each begins to categorize his or her observations and draw conclusions about the student's abilities, disabilities, and needs. The processes of analyzing discrepancies and generating

Assessment of Student Participation in General Education Classes

Student: _____
Classroom Teacher: _____
Assessment Completed by: _____

Grade, Subject, and Class Period: _____
Prep Periods: _____ Room Number: _____ # of Students in Class: _____
Date: _____

Instructions:
1. After the student attends the specific general education class for approximately one week, the team reviews all the skills identified in Sections I and II of this assessment tool.

Score.	+	for items that student consistently performs;
	+/-	for items that student does some of the time but not consistently;
	-	for items that student never or very rarely performs; and
	NA	for items that are not appropriate for the student/class

2. Circle about 5 items that the team identifies as priorities for instructional emphasis for the individual student.
3. Write objectives for each of the circled items, then design related instructional programs.
4. Review student progress on all items at least 2 more times during the school year. Revise as needed.

I. CLASSROOM ROUTINES AND ACTIVITIES

Date: _____

1. Gets to class on time.					
2. Gets seated in class on time.					
3. Performs transitional activities during class in response to situational cues (e.g., changes in seating, activity)					
4. Begins tasks.					
5. Stays on task.					
6. Participates in some regular class activities without adaptations.					
7. Terminates tasks.					
8. Tolerates out-of-the-ordinary changes in classroom routine					
9. Follows class rules.					
10. Locates / brings materials to class as needed.					

Date: _____

11. Shares materials with peers when appropriate.					
12. Uses materials for their intended purpose.					
13. Puts materials away after use.					
14. Uses classroom materials and equipment safely.					
15. Works cooperatively with a partner.					
16. Works cooperatively with a small group.					
17. Performs competitive learning tasks.					
18. Readily accepts assistance.					
19. Evaluates quality of own work (given a model).					
20. Copes with criticism / correction without incident and tries an alternative behavior.					

136

II. SOCIAL AND COMMUNICATION SKILLS

Date: _____ Date: _____

21. Interacts with peers:
    a. responds to others
    b. initiates

22. Interacts with the classroom teacher:
    a. responds to the teacher
    b. initiates

23. Uses social greetings:
    a. responds to others
    b. initiates

24. Uses farewells:
    a. responds to others
    b. initiates

25. Uses expressions of politeness
    (e.g., please, thank you, excuse me):
    a. responds to others
    b. initiates

26. Participates in joking or teasing:
    a. responds to others
    b. initiates

27. Makes choices and indicates preferences:
    a. responds to others (cue or question)
    b. initiates

28. Asks questions:
    a. asks for help
    b. asks for information (e.g., clarification, feedback)

29. Follows directions:
    a. for curricular tasks
    b. for helping tasks/errands
    c. given to the student individually
    d. given to students as a group

30. States or indicates:
    a. don't know / don't understand
    b. when finished with an activity

31. Orients toward the speaker or other source of input.

32. Secures listener attention before communicating.

33. Maintains eye contact with the listener when speaking.

34. Takes turns communicating in conversation with others.

35. Gives feedback:
    a. gives positive feedback
    b. gives negative feedback

36. Uses appropriate gestures and body movements when interacting with others.

37. Uses appropriate language / vocabulary / topic of conversation.

38. Uses intelligible speech (volume, rate, articulation, etc.)

Comments:

Figure 5.2. Classroom assessment tool. (From Macdonald, C., & York, J. [1989]. Regular class integration: Assessment, objectives, instructional programs. In J. York, T. Vandercook, C. Macdonald, & S. Wolff [Eds.], *Strategies for full inclusion* [pp. 83–116]. Minneapolis: University of Minnesota, Institute on Community Integration; reprinted by permission of authors.)

137

hypotheses have tremendous influence on how teams design instructional programs, but rarely are these processes conducted in a collaborative manner. Although each team member's experience and discipline perspective is an important contribution to the process, it can also constrain or negatively bias the analysis. Conflict may arise when different team members ascribe different causes to the same behavior and then recommend different types of intervention. Consider, for example, a student with severe disabilities who starts crying soon after starting lunch in the cafeteria. Different observers might attribute this to various factors, such as sensory overload in the loud and busy cafeteria, fear or discomfort with ineffective feeding techniques, frustration with inability to communicate likes and dislikes, or underlying emotional disorders.

It is essential that team members identify and discuss the bases for their interpretations. An effective strategy to resolve differences among professional views is for the team to identify one or more performance problems, observe the student together, and brainstorm possible explanations and contributing factors. Observing the student together increases the likelihood that team members will agree on what they saw and, therefore, that they will understand and respect the perspective of other disciplines. During brainstorming, team members generate as many ideas as possible and refrain from judgments, which limit creative thinking. After considering a variety of possibilities, the team eliminates those that are not supported by many other aspects of the student's performance. In the situation of the student crying in the school cafeteria, for example, the team might rule out an underlying emotional disorder because the student is happy and cooperative in almost all other situations. The team might also note that the student is not distressed in other busy, noisy

routines, such as when several classes are changing classrooms, during the beginning of a school assembly, or during the school's afternoon dismissal. The team will still be left with several possibilities, however, which the members formulate into questions. They then devise systematic strategies to test the various hypotheses. Examples of how this process was used with Kristen and Jamal are presented later in this chapter.

Parents or special education programs sometimes refer students with severe disabilities to other agencies for independent or specialized assessments to complement those conducted by the educational program staff. Educational teams are often disappointed that the resulting assessment reports tell them little more than what they already knew. Frequently, school-based teams can elicit more satisfactory and enlightening results if they go through the process of hypothesis generation, formulate specific questions, and send their written questions to the outside assessment team. Given the high cost and poor outcomes from the multidisciplinary assessments discussed previously, referring teams must provide a framework to improve the benefits of outside assessments.

Conducting Diagnostic/ Discipline-Referenced Assessment

It is after performance discrepancies in educational environments are identified and initial discrepancy analyses are performed that assessment by individual disciplines can produce the most useful information. This step in the assessment process has been termed "diagnostic assessment" (Hupp & Donofrio, 1983) because it analyzes the nature of and relationship among specific aspects of performance. The first purpose of the diagnostic assessment is to answer the questions raised during hypothesis generation, using a variety of informal and formal strategies. Informal diagnostic assessment consists of systematically testing the influence of various factors on the student's performance. In the case of the student crying in the cafeteria, the team might learn that the student also cries when eating at home and during teethbrushing at both home and school. Then team members try a variety of strategies, one at a time, to see if the student accepts the food more easily if given different prompts around the mouth, if told more about what is going to happen, if given time to smell the food before eating, if given choices between foods, if given foods of more consistent flavor or temperature, and so on. Because testing multiple factors at the same time tends to mask the positive, negative, and neutral effects of each factor, only one possibility is tested at a time.

For formal diagnostic assessment, Hupp and Donofrio (1983) recommended the identification and use of numerous assessment instruments, or portions of instruments, each with slightly different applications. Commercial tools that are useful for analyzing sensorimotor and communication performance are described later in this section. It is emphasized that the tools listed here offer diagnostic guidance; they need not be administered in totality. Furthermore, the information needed to complete most items can be obtained in routine school and community activities, rather than through isolated testing. Finally, commercial assessment tools provide only one piece of information for the team to consider when designing instruction.

The second purpose of diagnostic/discipline-referenced assessment is to gather additional information that any team member considers important but that was not available or appropriate for assessment during routine home, school, and community activities. This can also be done using formal or informal assessment strategies. For example, a speech-language pathologist may formally assess receptive language using a standardized instrument to establish a baseline for later comparison or to fulfill school district requirements. After informally gathering information about functional range of motion during routine activities, a physical therapist might want to assess range of motion formally and record exact measurements for a student who has spasticity. When collaborative teams adopt an ecological curriculum, the diagnostic/discipline-referenced assessment focuses on performance difficulties that have already been identified as educational priorities by the team. This differs significantly from traditional, isolated assessments that serve as the initial and primary basis for determining program content.

Sensorimotor Assessment The areas considered here for sensorimotor assessment parallel the functional outcomes of sensorimotor skills identified in Chapter 4. Several tools that might support formal assessment of sensorimotor skills for students with severe disabilities are described in this section.

Postural Control and Mobility The Assessment of Behavioral Components (ABC) (Hardy, Kudar, & Macdonald, 1988) is a criterion-referenced assessment for children with severe motor disabilities related to cerebral palsy. The assessment has three sections: Tone and Range of Motion (17 items), Reflexes (10 items), and Gross Motor Development (65 items). The Gross Motor Development section has six subdivisions: Head and Trunk Control, Prone Position, Supine Position, Rolling, Sitting, and Standing. Organization of gross motor items by position is particularly useful to assess students whose development is uneven or who use only certain positions. An instructional manual describes important considerations for assessment of children with cerebral palsy and uses a self-study format to prepare professionals, parents, and paraprofessionals to administer the assessment accurately. Each of the 92 items has jargon-free directions for testing, a description and illustration of the normal response, and descriptions and illustrations of other responses that might be observed when a child has cerebral palsy. Many items have separate descriptions of performance associated with high or low tone. Scores from 1 (normal) to 4 (severely abnormal), defined behaviorally for each item, correspond with small increments of change. A self-graphing score sheet has space for results of 12 test administrations to show trends over time.

The ABC has been field-tested with professionals, parents, and paraprofessionals with high levels of interobserver and test–retest reliability. The ABC has not been normed and does not yield a total motor performance score, which limits its utility for program evaluation or research (Campbell, 1989), but this does not affect its use for diagnostic assessment. Because the ABC is based primarily on infant development, it should be used cautiously with older children. The large number of items for fundamental gross motor skills, the organization of gross motor items by position, and the unique scoring system make the ABC particularly useful for assessment of students with severe motor disabilities. Although not used widely yet, the ABC offers several advantages over other available assessment tools.

The T.I.M.E. Toddler and Infant Motor Evaluation (Miller & Roid, 1994) is a norm-referenced, standardized assessment intended to be sensitive to subtleties of typical motor development, to patterns of movement that suggest delays or deviations, and to small increments of change resulting from treatment. Although full-scale standardization research has not been completed, preliminary research (with a heterogeneous population of 731 children) produced high levels of internal consistency and test–retest and interrater reliability, as well as high content, construct, and discriminant validity. With a strong underlying set of values regarding the role of the family in assessment and programs for their child, the T.I.M.E. is designed so the parent elicits the child's optimal performance through play, while a therapist or teacher facilitates, observes, and records performance.

The T.I.M.E. has eight subtests, most with illustrations of the motor abilities being assessed. Parts of the Social-Emotional Abilities subtest, administered at the start of the evaluation, indicate if the child is well and composed enough for testing to be valid and to proceed. The Mobility subtest involves placing the child in each of five basic positions (supine, prone, sit, quadruped, stand), and recording the child's subsequent positions and movement on a pictorial rating form. The Stability subtest identifies the most mature positions the child can maintain, based on performance in the Mobility subtest. The Motor Organization subtest examines postural control, movement, and use of the arms and hands to reach, grasp, release, and stabilize the body. This subtest is most like the "hand function" section of traditional developmental assessments but with particular attention to the patterns of movement used to perform the tasks. The Functional Performance subtest screens the child's abilities in daily living activities, to see if they are affected by motor difficulties and to help team members recognize relationships between abstract motor abilities (e.g., trunk rotation) and functional performance (e.g., dressing). This subtest is scored from parent report rather than direct observation.

The last three subtests are scored from observations during the Mobility subtest and free play. The Atypical Positions subtest screens for postures and movements associated with high or low muscle tone. Each atypical position can be studied more carefully in the Quality Rating subtest, focusing on four sections of the body (head/neck, trunk/pelvis, shoulder/arm, leg). The Component Analysis subtest provides for a similar study of the postures and movements typically observed in the development of young children. Standardization research has not been completed for the last three subtests, so they are included as clinical observation scales.

The T.I.M.E. offers a unique combination of the validity and reliability benefits of standardized assessment with strategies to record detailed information about posture and movement. Previously, information of this sort could be recorded only in a narrative format that, being subjective and idiosyncratic, prevented valid comparisons over time or across children. Although the T.I.M.E. holds great promise for assessment of students with severe disabilities, it has disadvantages. One disadvantage is that, like most other standardized developmental assessments, it was developed for use with young children (ages 4 months to 3½ years), so it is inappropriate to assign or attempt to interpret scores for older children. This relatively new assessment has not been used widely, and no information is available about use with older children with severe disabilities. Therefore, it must be used with caution. An advantage of the T.I.M.E. is that it reflects the subtleties, complexities, and interrelationships among many aspects of posture, movement, and functional performance, rather than a simplified linear sequence of development. The corresponding disadvantage is that the observer must have a strong foundation in motor development to recognize the details to be recorded, with "advanced training and comprehensive knowledge about the motor development of children" required to score the last three subtests (Miller & Roid, 1994, p. 69). The procedures for administering and scoring the T.I.M.E. are also quite complex, so qualified examiners are advised to seek training. Because the context for "testing" with the T.I.M.E. is the parent playing with the child, teams considering this assessment for older children in public school settings will need to deliberate about what constitutes the appropriate context for each of their students.

The Peabody Developmental Motor Scales (Folio & Fewell, 1983) is one of the very few traditional assessments that examines early stages of gross motor development extensively (with 70 items up through the initial stage of walking) and is standardized. According to the examiner's manual, the scales have high levels of interrater and test–retest reliability and good ethnic, concurrent, construct, and predictive validity. Others have raised concerns about test construction, content, administration, and scoring, however (see Hinderer, Richardson, & Atwater, 1989). Although the scales are normed, the authors also discuss their use as a criterion-referenced assessment and item adaptations for children with known disabilities. A recent study of the Gross Motor Scale with 12 children with mild or moderate cerebral palsy produced high scores for test–retest, intrarater, and interrater reliability (Boulton et al., 1995). The Gross Motor scale has five subscales: Reflexes, Balance, Nonlocomotor, Locomotor, and Receipt and Propulsion (of a ball). The authors recommend that interpretation of results include comparison of performance on the various subscales. Although this has appeal, especially from a diagnostic perspective, the construct examined by each subscale is not defined by the authors. Users might define the scope of each subscale for themselves, but occupational and physical therapists may be troubled by some item placements (e.g., righting reactions included with primitive reflexes rather than balance). Hinderer et al. (1989) raised concerns about clarity of directions and criteria for scoring but found these problems surmountable. Activity cards, intended to promote development of deficient skills, offer some useful suggestions but need to be referenced to activities in natural environments. Because the scales and activity cards were developed with children under 7 years of age with no known disabilities, users are cautioned about use with children who are older or present severe disabilities, or both. In spite of the limitations, the Peabody Developmental Motor Scales offer a comprehensive scope and sequence of typical gross motor development that may be useful for diagnostic purposes.

The BRIGANCE® Diagnostic Inventory of Early Development (Brigance, 1978) is a criterion-referenced assessment with a unique organization of motor skills. The Pre-Ambulatory Motor Skills and Behaviors section delineates sequences separately for the supine, prone, sitting, and standing positions. This facilitates more careful assessment within positions and is particularly useful for students who display uneven development or predominant use of certain positions. The Gross Motor Skills and Behaviors section delineates separate sequences for 13 different areas, including walking, climbing, and running. This organization can help teams focus on skill areas deemed important for individual students. The BRIGANCE is not standardized, and performance criteria are not always defined clearly. Because the BRIGANCE is referenced to the typical development of children from birth to 7 years, it should be used cautiously with older students with severe disabilities.

Hand Function The Erhardt Developmental Prehension Assessment (EDPA) (Erhardt, 1982) is a 100-item scale designed to assess prehension of children with develop-

mental delays or motor disabilities. The items were derived from integration of typical child development literature and field testing with children with disabilities, and the EDPA is not considered a standardized tool (Erhardt, 1982). Despite this limitation, the EDPA seems to have advantages for use with students with severe disabilities. Items focus on posture of the hand, arm, and body rather than infant tasks. Illustrations and behavioral descriptions are provided for all items in the scale. The specified materials are not inherently functional (e.g., dowels), but they neither encourage use of infant materials nor seem to preclude substitution of materials deemed age appropriate and functional for an individual student. A videotape on administration and a book including case studies are also available from the publisher.

The T.I.M.E. (Miller & Roid, 1994), discussed thoroughly under Postural Control and Mobility, is important to mention here because it is a unique standardized assessment of movement. The Motor Organization subtest includes use of the arms and hands to reach, grasp, release, and stabilize the body, more like the "hand function" section of traditional developmental assessments. This subtest is standardized using toys and activities intended for young children, however, which would not be appropriate for use with older children with severe disabilities.

The Peabody Developmental Motor Scales (Folio & Fewell, 1983) are also important to mention here because they offer a standardized measure of fine motor development. (Standardization of the Peabody Scales was discussed in the section on Postural Control and Mobility.) The Fine Motor Scale is divided into four subscales: Grasping, Hand Use, Eye–Hand Coordination, and Manual Dexterity. Unfortunately, the construct for each subscale is neither defined nor evident from examining the items, with similar items sometimes appearing in two or more subscales. The scales focus on tasks and materials for infants and preschoolers, further limiting utility for diagnostic assessment of older students with severe disabilities.

The *Assessment, Evaluation, and Programming System (AEPS) for Infants and Children: Vol. 1, AEPS Measurement for Birth to Three Years* (Bricker, 1993) is designed for use with children up to 6 years of age who function at a developmental age of between 1 month and 3 years. Studies indicate that the AEPS is reliable and valid, but it is more useful for assessing children with mild and moderate disabilities than for children with severe disabilities (Bricker, Baily, & Slentz, 1990). As a criterion-referenced assessment, it includes "only skills that may enhance the child's ability to cope with and adapt to the demands of the social and physical environment" (Bricker, Gentry, & Bailey, 1985, p. 10). The assessment is not intended as a diagnostic tool, however, and the limited number of items in the Fine Motor domain is a shortcoming. Advantages of the Fine Motor domain are that instructions encourage use of optimal positioning, a context of functional tasks, and attention to generalization; therefore, teams just starting ecological assessment may find it helpful. Cautions about performance using abnormal movement patterns are included with several items, which can assist occupational and physical therapists to communicate with other team members. The Family Report is also available to assist families to participate in the assessment and evaluation of their children's skills and abilities.

Vision   The Erhardt Developmental Vision Assessment (EDVA) (Erhardt, 1986) is a unique test of vision in that it examines visual-motor development rather than acuity. The EDVA is based on development of normal vision patterns through the age of 6 months, the age at which fairly mature functional components are achieved. The EDVA is designed to assess reflexive visual patterns (i.e., pupillary, doll's eyes, and eyelid reflexes) and voluntary eye movements of children with motor disabilities. Each item has both an illustration and a behavioral description of the motor performance. Initial field testing indicates that the content of the EDVA is useful and the instructions are clear, with high levels of interrater reliability (Erhardt, Beatty, & Hertsgaard, 1988). A videotape on administration and a book including case studies are also available from the publisher.

Informal Assessment of Sensorimotor Skills   When students have severe disabilities, informal assessment strategies often yield more meaningful information than formal assessment tools. Therapists can devise a task analysis of virtually any motor task, similar to the task analysis in Chapter 4 (see Figure 4.6), as the basis for assessment of priority skills. In this type of assessment, emphasis is on whether and how the student performs the component movements, rather than where the student's performance is in relation to a typical developmental sequence.

Another important consideration in assessment is how the student's sensory systems receive, transmit, and interpret stimuli, both from the environment (e.g., touch, temperature, light, sounds, smells) and from the student's own body (e.g., head position in space, joint position, muscle tension). Dunn (1996) outlined characteristics of the six sensory systems, describing the kinds of stimulation to each system that help arouse or alert a person to receive information and the kinds that help organize the person to make adaptive responses (see Table 5.1). Dunn also provided many examples of how difficulty with sensory processing can interfere with performance of tasks in typical daily routines (see Table 5.2). She recommended analyzing the sensory characteristics of routine tasks and determining task

Table 5.1. Arousal/alerting and discriminating/mapping descriptors of the sensory system

Sensory system	Arousal/alerting descriptors[a]	Discriminating/mapping descriptors[b]
For all systems	*Unpredictability:* The task is unfamiliar; the child cannot anticipate the sensory experiences that will occur in the task	*Predictability:* Sensory pattern in the task is routine for the child, such as with diaper changing—the child knows what is occurring and what will come next
Somatosensory	*Light touch:* Gentle tapping on skin; tickling (e.g., loose clothing making contact with skin)	*Touch pressure:* Firm contact on skin (e.g., hugging, patting, grasping); occurs both when touching objects or people, or when they touch you
	Pain: Brisk pinching; contact with sharp objects; skin pressed in small surface (e.g., when skin is caught between chair arm and seat)	*Long duration stimuli:* Holding, grasping (e.g., carrying a child in your arms)
	Temperature: Hot or cold stimuli (e.g., iced drinks, hot foods, cold hands, cold metal chairs)	*Large body surface contact:* Includes holding, hugging; also holding a cup with the entire palmar surface of hand
	Variability: Changing characteristics during the task (e.g., putting clothing on requires a combination of tactile experiences)	
	Short duration stimuli: Tapping, touching briefly (e.g., splashing water)	
	Small body surface contact: Using only fingertips to touch something	
Vestibular	*Head position change:* The child's head orientation is altered (e.g., pulling the child up from lying on the back to sitting)	*Linear head movement:* Head moving in a straight line (e.g., bouncing up and down, going down the hall in a wheelchair)
	Speed change: Movements change velocity (e.g., the teacher stops to talk to another teacher when pushing the child to the bathroom in a wheelchair)	*Repetitive head movement:* Movements that repeat in a simple sequence (e.g., rocking in a rocker)
	Direction change: Movements change planes (e.g., bending down to pick up something from the floor while carrying the child down the hall)	
	Rotary head movement: Head moving in an arc (e.g., spinning in a circle, turning head side to side)	

Category	Descriptions
Proprioceptive	*Quick stretch:* Movements that pull on the muscles (e.g., briskly tapping on a belly muscle)
	Sustained tension: Steady, constant action on the muscles, pressing on or holding the muscle (e.g., using heavy objects during play)
	Shifting muscle tension: Activities that demand constant changes in the muscles (e.g., walking, lifting and moving objects)
Visual	*High intensity:* Visual stimulus is bright (e.g., looking out the window on a bright day)
	Low intensity: Visual stimulus is subdued (e.g., finding objects in the dark closet)
	High contrast: Great difference between the visual stimulus and its surrounding environment (e.g., cranberry juice in a white cup)
	High similarity: Small difference between the visual stimulus and its surrounding environment (e.g., oatmeal in a beige bowl)
	Variability: Changing characteristics during the task (e.g., a television program is variable visual stimulus)
	Competitive: The background is interesting or busy (e.g., the junk drawer, a bulletin board)
Auditory	*Variability:* Changing characteristics during the task (e.g., a person's voice with intonation)
	Rhythmic: Sounds repeat in a simple sequence/beat (e.g., humming, singing nursery songs)
	High intensity: The auditory stimulus is loud (e.g., siren, high volume radio)
	Constant: The stimulus is always present (e.g., a fan noise)
	Competitive: The environment has a variety of recurring sounds (e.g., the classroom, a party)
	Noncompetitive: The environment is quiet (e.g., the bedroom when all is ready for bedtime)
	Low intensity: The auditory stimulus is subdued (e.g., whispering)
Olfactory/gustatory	*Strong intensity:* The taste/smell has distinct qualities (e.g., spinach)
	Mild intensity: The taste/smell has nondistinct or familiar qualities (e.g., cream of wheat)

From Dunn, W. (1996). The sensorimotor systems: A framework for assessment and intervention. In F.P. Orelove & D. Sobsey, *Educating children with multiple disabilities: A transdisciplinary approach* (3rd ed., pp. 40–41). Baltimore: Paul H. Brookes Publishing Co.; reprinted by permission.

[a]Tend to generate "noticing" behaviors; the individual's attention is momentarily drawn toward the stimulus and away from ongoing behavior; can become part of a functional behavior sequence. (See text for example.)

[b]Create temporal and spatial qualities of body and environments (maps created) that can be used to create goal-directed movement. (See text for example.)

Table 5.2. Examples of observable behaviors that indicate difficulty with sensory processing during daily life tasks

Sensory system	Personal hygiene	Dressing	Eating	Homemaking	School/work	Play
Somatosensory	Withdraws from splashing water; Pushes washcloth/towel away; Cries when hair is washed and dried; Makes face when toothpaste gets on lips, tongue; Tenses when bottom is wiped after toileting	Tolerates a narrow range of clothing items; Prefers tight clothing; Is more irritable with loose textured clothing; Cries during dressing; Pulls at hats, head gear, accessories	Tolerates food at only one temperature; Gags with textured food or utensils in mouth; Winces when face is wiped; Hand extends and avoids objects and surfaces (finger food, utensils)	Avoids participation in tasks that are wet, dirty; Seeks to remove batter that falls on arms	Cries when tape or glue gets on skin; Overreacts to pats, hugs; avoids these actions; Tolerates only one pencil, one type of paper, only wooden objects; Hands extend when attempting to type	Selects a narrow range of toys, textures similar; Cannot hold on to toys/objects; Rubs toys on face, arms; Mouths objects
Proprioceptive	Cannot lift objects that are heavier (a new bar of soap); Cannot change head position to use sink and mirror in same task	Cannot support heavier items (belt with buckle, shoes); Fatigues prior to task completion; Misses when placing arm or leg in clothing	Uses external support to eat (propping); Tires before completing meal; Cannot provide force to cut meat; Tires before completely eating foods that need to be chewed	Drops equipment (broom); Uses external support (leaning on counter to stir batter); Difficulty pouring a glass of milk	Drops books; Becomes uncomfortable in a particular position; Hooks limbs on furniture to obtain support; Moves arm, hand in repetitive patterns (self-stimulatory)	Unable to sustain movements during play; Tires before game is complete; Drops heavy parts of a toy/game

Vestibular	Becomes disoriented when bending over the sink Falls when trying to participate in washing lower extremities	Gets overly excited/distracted after bending down to assist in putting on socks Cries when moved around a lot during dressing	Holds head stiffly in one position during mealtime Gets distracted from meal after several head position changes	Avoids leaning to obtain cooking utensil Becomes overly excited after moving around the room to dust	Avoids turning head to look at people; to find source of a sound After being transported in a wheelchair, more difficult to get on task Moves head in repetitive pattern (self-stimulatory)	Avoids play that includes movement Becomes overly excited or anxious when moving during play Rocks excessively Craves movement activities
Visual	Cannot find utensils on the sink Difficulty spotting desired item in drawer Misses when applying paste to toothbrush	Cannot find buttons on patterned or solid clothing Overlooks desired shirt in closet or drawer Misses armhole when donning shirt	Misses utensils on the table Has trouble getting foods onto spoon when they are a similar color to the plate	Cannot locate correct canned item in the pantry Has difficulty finding cooking utensils in the drawer	Cannot keep place on the page Cannot locate desired item on communication board Attends excessively to bright or flashing objects	Has trouble with matching, sorting activities Has trouble locating desired toy on cluttered shelf

(continued)

Table 5.2. (continued)

Sensory system	Personal hygiene	Dressing	Eating	Homemaking	School/work	Play
Auditory	Cries when hair dryer is turned on Becomes upset by running water Jerks when toilet flushes	Distracted by clothing that makes noise (crisp cloth, accessories)	Distracted by noise of utensils against each other (spoon in bowl, knife on plate) Cannot keep eating when someone talks	Distracted by vacuum cleaner sound Distracted by television or radio during tasks	Distracted by squeaky wheelchair Intolerant of noise others make in the room Overreacts to door closing Notices toilet flushing down the hall	Play is disrupted by sounds Makes sounds constantly
Olfactory/ gustatory	Gags at taste of toothpaste Jerks away at smell of soap	Overreacts to clothing when it has been washed in a new detergent	Tolerates a narrow range of foods Becomes upset when certain foods are cooking	Becomes upset when house is being cleaned (odors of cleaners)	Overreacts to new person (new smells) Intolerant of scratch-n-sniff stickers Smells everything	Tastes or smells all objects before playing

From Dunn, W. (1996). The sensorimotor systems: A framework for assessment and intervention. In F.P. Orelove & D. Sobsey, *Educating children with multiple disabilities: A transdisciplinary approach* (3rd ed., pp. 64–66). Baltimore: Paul H. Brookes Publishing Co.; reprinted by permission.

adaptations that might increase successful performance by a student who has difficulty processing sensory stimuli. Later in this chapter, Figure 5.8 on pages 165–166 shows a worksheet in which these sensory characteristics are analyzed and adaptations suggested for Kristen during her arrival and free play routine in kindergarten. This type of informal assessment adds information that is vital for effective program planning and cannot be obtained through more formal approaches to sensorimotor assessment.

Communication Assessment Assessment of communication abilities has valuable prescriptive functions whether or not a student communicates with symbolic language such as speech or sign language. Typical areas for communication assessment, regardless of student ability, are expression, comprehension, and opportunities to communicate in social and physical contexts of the environment. Whereas the first two areas focus on student abilities, the third examines the extent to which the environment supports and promotes student efforts to communicate. The range of assessment considerations related to each of these three areas is outlined in Table 5.3. This table shows that specific considerations in communication assessment are much the same, whether the student uses nonsymbolic or symbolic communication.

Limitations of Formal Assessment Tools Many commercial tests are available for assessment of communication abilities, although most are designed for individuals who use some symbolic language. Table 5.4 provides a list of assessment tools that can be used to assess students with severe communication disabilities. The tools are classified for use in assessing nonsymbolic, emerging symbolic, and symbolic communication. The Placement Checklist (Waryas & Stremel-Campbell, 1982) and Program for the Ac-

quisition of Language with the Severely Impaired (Owens, 1982b) are actually components of communication intervention programs that can be adapted for use as criterion-referenced assessments. Of the seven tools listed in Table 5.4, only three have been standardized: the Communication and Symbolic Behavior Scales (Wetherby & Prizant, 1990), the Nonspeech Test for Receptive/Expressive Language (Huer, 1983), and the Sequenced Inventory of Communication Development (Hendrick, Prather, & Tobin, 1984). Standardization was conducted with typically developing children, but the first two tools were also field-tested with children with disabilities, adding to their value when formal assessment of such children is required.

Unfortunately, few formal communication assessment tools yield relevant or functional information about students with severe disabilities. Available tests are generally inadequate for evaluation of students with limited symbolic language in that they are oriented toward speech for communication, are deficient in providing representative information about communication usage in natural environments, and are unrelated to ultimate communication interventions (Browder, 1991; Orelove & Sobsey, 1996). Because of these limitations, informal assessment methods using structured observations of the student during routine activities frequently are more applicable to answering the questions raised in the hypothesis generation phase of program development.

Prescriptive Informal Assessment Blau, Lahey, and Oleksiuk-Velez (1984) found that more communication goals could be developed from a communication sample than from a formal test. Communication sampling procedures have been utilized for many years by speech-language pathologists, and there are standard methods to analyze samples of symbolic communication.

Table 5.3.   Range of considerations for communication assessment

Nonsymbolic Focus	Symbolic Focus	
Student:		
Expressive Communication	**Expressive Language**	
Pragmatics	Pragmatics	
•function	•function	Syntax
•social rules	•social rules	Semantics
•relationship between communication and behavior	•relationship between communication and behavior	Articulation
		Rate
		Fluency
Form	Form	Volume
Quantity	Quantity	Vocal quality
Mode	Mode	
Intelligibility	Intelligibility	
Spontaneity	Spontaneity	
Comprehension	**Comprehension**	
For nonsymbolic language	For symbolic language	
For symbolic language	For nonsymbolic language	
Environment:		
Context	**Context**	
Social	Social	
Physical	Physical	

Symbolic language samples are evaluated for utterance length, syntax usage, pragmatic functions, semantic usage, articulation, and other quantitative and qualitative characteristics. Samples of communication for nonsymbolic communicators are usually analyzed from a pragmatic perspective, which emphasizes form, function, and context of communication. Assessment of form includes understanding and use of a variety of communication modes, including touch, objects, photographs, pictograms, gestures, and signs, as well as speech. Functions that might be assessed include protesting or rejecting, requesting more, requesting objects or actions, requesting attention, directing attention elsewhere, sharing information, and social etiquette (Beukelman & Mirenda, 1992; Orelove & Sobsey, 1996; Stremel & Schutz, 1995). Kristen's and Jamal's assessments later in this chapter illustrate procedures for recording and analyzing samples of nonsymbolic and emerging symbolic communication use (see Figures 5.7 and 5.15 on pp. 163–164 and 180–182, respectively). Excerpts from their assessment reports, also presented later in this chapter, provide examples of conclusions derived from pragmatic assessments.

When a student presents undesirable behaviors (e.g., aggression, self-injurious behavior, tantrums), the relationship between the student's lack of communication skills and undesirable behavior must be explored in the course of assessment. This involves formulating hypotheses about the communicative functions that undesirable behaviors serve for the student and designing interventions to teach new, more acceptable communication forms that will serve the same

Table 5.4.   Communication assessment tools for students with severe disabilities

Tool	Use
Communication and Symbolic Behavior Scales (Wetherby & Prizant, 1990)	Nonsymbolic, emerging symbolic
Environmental Language Inventory (J. MacDonald & Nickols, 1974)	Emerging symbolic
Environmental Pre-Language Battery (Horstmeier & J. MacDonald, 1975)	Nonsymbolic, emerging symbolic
The Nonspeech Test for Receptive/Expressive Language (Huer, 1983)	Nonsymbolic, emerging symbolic, symbolic
Sequenced Inventory of Communication Development (Hendrick, Prather, & Tobin, 1984)	Nonsymbolic, emerging symbolic, symbolic
- -	- - - - - - - - - - - - -
Placement Checklist: Communication Training Program (Waryas & Stremel-Campbell, 1982)	Nonsymbolic, emerging symbolic, symbolic
Program for the Acquisition of Language with the Severely Impaired (PALS) (Owens, 1982b)	Nonsymbolic, emerging symbolic, symbolic

functions. Excellent descriptions of this process can be found in Baumgart, Johnson, and Helmstetter (1990), Carr et al. (1994), and Donnellan, Mirenda, Mesaros, and Fassbender (1984).

Assessment of communication comprehension typically involves making verbal requests of students to perform a movement, act on an object, or interact with another person (Baumgart et al., 1990). During assessment, it is important to note what contextual cues (e.g., supporting gestural, temporal, and spatial cues) are present for future use in instruction. For example, as part of assessment, a student may demonstrate understanding of the suggestion, "Let's get a drink," when it is given after physical education class and near the drinking fountain but not when the same words are used at a different time or in a different environment. This would indicate the probability that the student's understanding of the words "Let's get a drink" is limited to

a specific time and place. Language learners are thought to acquire comprehension skills through a process of "progressive decontextualization" (Bates, Benigni, Bretherton, Camaioni, & Volterra, 1979), gradually becoming less dependent on specific nonverbal and verbal contexts for comprehension. At the most basic level, students can be assessed in their understanding of the natural cues that comprise routines (Gee, Graham, Oshima, Yoshioka, & Goetz, 1991). Further development of representation is seen as students are able to communicate at increasing distance from the people, objects, contexts, and times that are the subject of communication, and with less familiar communication partners (Stremel & Schutz, 1995).

Informal assessment of basic comprehension skills for students with severe disabilities can be accomplished within daily routines through two strategies. The first is to use criterion-referenced measures, including requests for the student to look at, act on, or interact with people and things. The second is to observe the student's responses to communications from or among others in the same environment. Assessment for comprehension of both verbal language and nonverbal communication can be done this way. During assessment, contextual cues, supporting gestures, and appropriate receptive modes are varied systematically and carefully recorded with performance data. The results of assessment consist of information about verbal and nonverbal communications understood by the student and the contextual cues needed for support. This approach enables the team to systematically enhance the student's communication comprehension throughout the day.

Communication is an interactive activity; that is, successful communication requires that at least two people participate, with one sending and the other receiving a message. Maintaining or extending the communicative relationship requires that the partners also take turns, exchanging the roles of sender and receiver. For students with severe disabilities, communication development depends on the participation of communication partners and the presence of other environmental conditions that support and encourage communication. Because essential conditions for successful communication extend beyond student abilities, meaningful assessment must include examination of representative communication environments. This type of assessment involves analysis of existing social and physical contexts that support communication and of changes in the environment that would better facilitate communication development. For example, assessment may show that an environment provides too few predictable routines for the student to learn to develop anticipatory responses, but slight modifications would provide ample opportunities. Alternatively, assessment might show that potential com-

munication partners do not recognize or reinforce student attempts to communicate, but the situation could be corrected by providing information about nonsymbolic communication.

Some formal tests have subsections to evaluate environmental contexts for communication (see, e.g., Owens, 1982a). The Communication Environment Checklist (see Figure 5.3) was designed for informal assessment of communication opportunities in the environment. Another inventory, Analyzing the Communicative Environment (the ACE), has been validated for use with students who communicate through presymbolic and emerging symbolic behaviors (Rowland & Schweigert, 1993). The ACE was developed to assess specific activities or routines through 52 statements about six sets of variables: the activity, the communication system, adult interaction, group dynamics, materials, and specific opportunities to communicate. Environmental assessment is an important complement to assessment of student abilities.

During informal assessment, the student is observed across priority environments and routines to obtain communication samples to determine how he or she communicates through speech, vocalization, gestures, or other behavioral means. Assessment also includes observations made about comprehension and about who and what in the environment support or impede communication efforts. Results of the informal assessment can be applied directly to program development, to expand communication forms and functions, and to increase participation in priority activities and environments.

WRITING A TEAM ASSESSMENT REPORT

The natural outcome of a collaborative educational assessment process is one compre-

Communication Environment Checklist

Student _____

Environment _____

Rating Scale: 1 = Not provided in current environment; needs intensive intervention
2 = Provided on a limited basis; needs expansion and refinement
3 = Generally provided; needs some refinement
4 = Provided consistently; needs no intervention

Dates

I. OPPORTUNITIES: Something To Communicate About

1. Consistent routines are present to allow students to learn natural cues.
2. Communication opportunities are integrated into daily routines.
3. Multiple opportunities to communicate are provided within activities that have multiple or repetitive parts (e.g.,turntaking).
4. Natural opportunities to communicate are not eliminated by others in the environment (i.e., by guessing the student's wants and needs before they can be expressed).
5. Additional opportunities to communicate are created by delaying action on wants/needs and by interrupting daily routines.

II. MOTIVATION: The Desire To Communicate

6. Instructional routines and activities utilized have a high reinforcer value for the student, especially at first.
7. Instruction ensures the student is reinforced by natural consequences of communication acts.
8. Reinforcement is of high frequency and/or duration in order to provide success.

III. MEANS: Partners and Tools for Conveying Messages

9. Communication partners who are familiar with the student's means of communication are accessible at all times as listeners, conversation partners, and models.
10. There are many opportunities for communication with same-age peers in the environment.
11. Others in the environment recognize and respond to/reinforce alternate forms of communication used by the student (especially nonverbal).
12. If an augmentative means of communication is used by the student, it is accessible at all times.

IV. MAINTENANCE, GENERALIZATION, AND SPONTANEITY: Varying Contexts and Fading Cues

13. Spontaneous, initiated communication is agreed upon as the ultimate goal of communication.
14. Opportunities for practice of specific communication skills continue to be available even after skills are "mastered."
15. Cues and prompts are individualized and faded to "natural" cues as soon as possible.
16. Communication partners are familiar with the hierarchy of cues and prompts for an individual student and know the student's current level.
17. Partners use directives and questions sparingly to increase initiation, independence, and problem-solving.
18. Opportunities are available for practicing communication skills in a variety of environments and with a variety of people.

Figure 5.3. Assessment of the communication environment.

hensive and integrated assessment report, rather than separate reports from each team member. There are two approaches to writing a team report. In the first approach, the team describes each area of skill development and then relates it to performance in activity routines. This approach is more like the interdisciplinary approach with which most professionals are familiar and may be easier for teams when they first adopt a collaborative assessment process. The first approach is illustrated in an excerpt from Kristen's assessment report later in this chapter. In the second approach, the team describes the student's overall performance in activity routines, with corresponding discussions of embedded sensorimotor, communication, and other skills. This approach focuses on the activities as the unifying and functional application for a variety of skills, and thus it is consistent with the ecological curriculum design. The second approach is illustrated later in this chapter in an excerpt from Jamal's assessment report. The authors strongly recommend that teams move toward the second approach because it is more consistent with an ecological curriculum design. Furthermore, the process of writing the integrated report reinforces adoption of a common curriculum as a unifying framework and helps team members clarify their roles within the curriculum.

Whichever approach a team uses, considerable coordination is required. One strategy for writing the report is for team members to discuss their observations and diagnostic findings at a team meeting. Afterward, one person drafts a report, which is circulated for additions and corrections. Another strategy is for each person to draft portions of the report, which one person integrates. Personal preference of the team and logistical considerations guide this decision.

The team report includes a brief description of the student, a brief description of the assessment process, a description of data-gathering techniques (e.g., interviews, ecological inventories, directed observations), and a list of formal assessment instruments used. The team describes the student's independent performance, as well as the conditions that facilitated and limited performance. The report is written in language that can be understood by all team members, including parents. When unfamiliar technical terms are needed, they are accompanied by a brief explanation or diagram. The report is signed by all participating team members.

ONGOING ASSESSMENT

When the IEP is developed, it must include "objective criteria and evaluation procedures and schedules for determining . . . whether instructional objectives are being achieved" (IDEA, 1990, 20 U.S.C. §§1400 et seq.). Thus, in addition to annual assessment for program planning, the team must conduct ongoing assessment of student performance on IEP objectives. The purpose of ongoing assessment is to determine effectiveness of intervention strategies and to guide timely program revision, both when intermediate objectives are achieved and when satisfactory progress does not occur. A good rule of thumb is to collect data on student performance at least once weekly. This yields sufficient data to make decisions without being unmanageable. A weekly interval also approximates the schedule of data collection for students without disabilities (i.e., grades on homework, quizzes).

Therapists traditionally have recorded progress and concerns through "running notes." Although anecdotal data are useful, they do not fulfill the need for objective measures of performance to evaluate student change and intervention effectiveness (Miller & Roid, 1994; Ottenbacher, 1986).

Therefore the team must determine the type(s) of data that will reflect the most relevant aspects of performance for each IEP objective and then devise strategies to collect, analyze, and make decisions based on these data. When therapists have difficulty measuring performance, it is often because the target skill is too broad or vague (e.g., cope with frustration). It is helpful for therapists to remember that behaviors selected for measurement are intended to represent salient performance parameters (e.g., request assistance with difficult tasks), rather than to show all possible occurrences of all related skill development (e.g., improve social skills).

Educational programs often record performance in terms of frequency, duration, latency, rate, portion correct, and performance scoring (reflecting the prompts needed to elicit desired performance). Permanent products, including written work and videotapes, are valuable to capture quantitative and qualitative aspects of performance that can be analyzed retrospectively (see, e.g., Guidry, van den Pol, Keeley, & Neilsen, 1996). Student portfolios, including quantitative and qualitative data on past and current performance, can be particularly valuable to give a complete picture of a student and to facilitate transition to a new school, employment, or community residence (Wesson & King, 1996). Examples of data collection strategies are infused in the instructional programs presented in Chapter 7. Readers are also referred to Browder (1991), DeGangi (1994), and Ottenbacher (1986) for guidance on strategies for data collection and analysis and responsive decision making.

EXAMPLES OF ASSESSMENT PROCESS

Two examples of the assessment process described in this chapter are presented in the following pages. Both examples include ecological assessment, diagnostic/discipline-referenced assessment, and a team assessment report. Representative aspects of each stage have been included for each student. Kristen's team is working on a comprehensive assessment, as conducted for an initial evaluation or triennial review. The team also is working to move from a developmental to an ecological orientation for curriculum and assessment. Jamal's team has used an ecological approach for some time. Because a comprehensive assessment was completed within the last 3 years, Jamal's assessment this year updates his performance in areas continued from last year's program and conducts in-depth analysis of opportunities and performance in new program areas.

Initial Assessment: Kristen

Planning the Assessment For Kristen, planning began in the spring, when her school district held her annual planning and placement meeting. Kristen's team decided she would be placed in a regular kindergarten in September and that her parents, a special education teacher, kindergarten teacher, speech-language pathologist, and physical therapist (as primary sensorimotor therapist) would comprise her core educational team. An occupational therapist, nurse, psychologist, and social worker would be available for consultation but would not serve on the core team. Shortly after the meeting, the special education teacher contacted Kristen's parents to start identifying their priorities. Home and school were quickly identified as priority environments, and the school team agreed to observe Kristen at her early childhood special education program (the program she was leaving) in the spring, at home during the summer, and in kindergarten (the program she was entering) in September. Kristen's ecological assessment planning chart reflects priorities for each of the three phases (see Figure 5.4). The chart also illustrates the fact that ecological assessment is a *process* rather than an *event*.

The kindergarten teacher and physical therapist observed Kristen at the early childhood special education program. They noted abilities and difficulties in Kristen's performance, and they generated numerous questions about Kristen's communication skills. Because of these questions and because the special education teacher had not yet observed Kristen, the team agreed that the speech-language pathologist and special education teacher would assess Kristen at home. Kristen's parents identified mealtimes, using the toilet, grooming, playing alone, and playing with her sister as priority and representative activities for assessment that could be observed during the early afternoon at home.

Ecological Assessment at Home   The speech-language pathologist and special education teacher observed Kristen at home and recorded her performance anecdotally for each activity. Although Kristen demonstrated many abilities, her mother expressed frustration with what typically occurred in the bathroom after meals. The two observers noted the following:

> Kristen finished lunch. Mrs. F. [Kristen's mother] told Kristen, "Time to go clean up." Mrs. F. led Kristen to the bathroom, seated Kristen on the toilet (lid down), pulled off Kristen's shirt, and wiped her face and hands with a wet washcloth. Kristen whined more each minute, rocked back and forth with her hands near her face, and finally fell back and hit her head. Mrs. F. dried Kristen's face and hands. Kristen cried, held her hands near her face, and tried to push her mother's hands away. Mrs. F. talked to Kristen throughout (but not to prepare Kristen or to ask for participation). [Mrs. F. says this is actually better than usual, but she is frustrated and embarrassed.] Mrs. F. slid Kristen off the toilet, then saw that Kristen's pants were wet. Kristen's legs seemed stiff. Mrs. F. held Kristen by her shoulders

> (previously she just held one hand). Mrs. F. sighed and pulled down Kristen's pants and seated Kristen on the toilet (with seat adapter for size). Kristen sat with her trunk and arms flexed, legs extended, and head forward. Mrs. F. reported some successes on the toilet but lots of accidents and no consistent pattern.

> After finishing in the bathroom, Mrs. F. took Kristen to the bedroom to get dressed. Kristen sat in a small armchair with her feet on the floor. Her trunk, arms, and legs appeared relaxed. As Mrs. F. got clothes from the dresser, Kristen began singing and "dancing" in her chair. Mrs. F. smiled and explained that she and Kristen sing a variation of "Pop Goes the Weasel" while dressing. Mrs. F. sang as she positioned a T-shirt on Kristen's head and helped Kristen grasp the hem of the shirt. Kristen sang a clear "pop" as she quickly pulled the shirt down over her head and again as she pushed each hand through the sleeve. The routine was repeated with underpants, shorts, and sneakers. When finished, Kristen reached toward her mother. Mrs. F. sang a little more and snatched Kristen from her chair as they sang "POP goes Kristie." (Kristen sang "Pop o e-o.") Mrs. F. and Kristen both laughed. Mrs. F. lowered Kristen to stand and told Kristen to go find her ball. Kristen walked toward the family room. She walked with her arms flexed with hands near her waist, her hips and knees bent slightly and turned inward, and her feet pronated (inner side turned down).

Hypothesis Generation   The team noted the following strengths in Kristen's performance:

- When her trunk and feet are supported in a sitting position, she seems to have normal posture and movement.
- In the context of an enjoyable routine, she maintains near-normal muscle tone and relaxes quickly after episodes of excitement.
- She uses her hands and arms functionally when gross movements are required.
- She walks independently.
- She initiates and sustains a play routine for several minutes.

Priority Environments and Routines Where Assessment Is Conducted	Team Members Conducting Assessment				
	Parents	Kinder-garten Teacher	Special Education Teacher	Physical Therapist	Speech-Language Therapist
Special Education Preschool		5/29 (done)		5/29 (done)	
Home Mealtime, Toileting, Grooming, Dressing, Play with sister	6/26 (done) ↓		6/26 (done) ↓		6/26 (done) ↓
School - Kindergarten Bus				9/14	
Hallways			9/14	9/14	
Classrooms (transitions)					
Bathroom					
Play area	9/11	9/11		9/21	9/21
Tables (opening)					
Rug (story)					
Rug (gross motor)					
Tables (fine motor)					
Tables (snack)					
Nurse's office					

Figure 5.4. Ecological assessment planning chart for Kristen.

- In the context of a known routine, she takes turns and participates actively, anticipating the next step in the sequence.
- She is nearly independent in putting on pull-on clothing.
- She has some articulate and appropriate speech.
- She follows simple verbal directions.

The team suggested the following possible explanations for Kristen's performance problems during the toileting routine:

- She experienced tactile defensiveness and was irritated by having the shirt, washcloth, and towel touch her face and hands.
- She was frightened because she was unsteady sitting on the toilet.
- She wanted to use the toilet and cried in an attempt to communicate that need.
- She was frustrated because she wanted to participate in the routine more actively.
- She did not anticipate events in the routine and cried out of confusion.

The teacher, speech-language pathologist, and Kristen's mother discussed Kristen's strengths, with special attention to the interactive nature of Kristen's participation in the dressing routine. They also discussed possible reasons for Kristen's difficulties in the toileting routine and suggested some strategies to improve the situation. Before drawing conclusions about Kristen's needs, however, the team would conduct an ecological assessment at school.

Ecological Assessment at School
Kristen was assessed in her new program after she began school in the fall. The kindergarten schedule, outlined in Figure 5.5, is composed of many routines. The team delineated the typical participation of children without disabilities for each of these routines, creating ecological inventories that would be used to assess Kristen and other children with disabilities who joined the kindergarten class. The special education teacher and therapists also served two other children with disabilities in the kindergarten, which enabled them to schedule blocks of time with the class (see Chapter 8 for scheduling strategies). During the course of the assessment, team members would observe Kristen during all scheduled activities. During the first month of school, the physical therapist, speech-language pathologist, and teachers assessed Kristen during arrival and the free play routine, using the ecological inventory format. The planning chart shows that Kristen's assessment occurred over several days and that all team members did not participate in all parts of the assessment. Kristen's performance is summarized in Figure 5.6.

Hypothesis Generation Although Kristen had steadily increased her participation in the arrival and play routine, she had persistent difficulties, as indicated in the Student Inventory with Discrepancy Analysis column of the ecological assessment. The team considered the following as possible reasons for Kristen's performance difficulties during arrival and the play routine in the classroom:

- She does not really understand routines.
- She prefers the attention of adult assistance over playing with other children.
- She knows adults will help her if she waits long enough.
- She does not enjoy social interactions and prefers to be by herself.
- She is distracted by the visual and auditory stimuli from the other children's activities.
- She cannot "motor plan" transitions with so many children, toys, and pieces of furniture as obstacles.
- She cannot carry objects while walking.

8:30	Arrival Bathroom Job assignments Free play at tables, gross motor area, or playhouse
9:00	Opening group at tables
9:20	Storytime on rug [a]
9:45	Gross motor / perceptual activity on rug [a]
10:15	Fine motor / perceptual activity at tables [a]
10:45	Snack
11:10	Free play at tables, gross motor area, playhouse, or outside Bathroom, cleanup, and gather belongings
11:25	Departure

Figure 5.5.   Kindergarten schedule. ([a]Or art, music, library, gym, or special activities.)

- She is too unsteady to walk through the play area alone with the obstacles and activity of the other children.
- She does not hear the verbal directions in the noisy room.
- She does not understand the verbal directions.
- She does not use other children as models.
- She does not know how to initiate interaction with her classmates.

Diagnostic/Discipline-Referenced Assessment   Based on the observation at home and many observations at school, team members eliminated some of their hypotheses by identifying circumstances and performance that did not support the hypotheses (e.g., they identified several instances when Kristen appeared to have good motor planning abilities). Other hypotheses seemed to be supported (e.g., there were many instances when Kristen watched but did not participate in busy environments). The Teaching and Adaptation Hypotheses column of the ecological assessment shows

that the team was already testing a variety of hypotheses through informal strategies. The team was still left with the following questions regarding Kristen's performance and effective instructional strategies:

- To what extent does Kristen understand and anticipate task sequences in routines?
- How quickly does she learn new routines?
- Should task sequences be more predictable?
- To what extent does Kristen attend to and imitate other children as models?
- What is Kristen's understanding of oral language?
- How well does Kristen hear verbal directions under different background noise conditions?
- To what extent is Kristen distracted by visual and auditory stimuli?
- What types and sequences of prompts are most effective to improve Kristen's responding?

Student: Kristen F.
Date: 9/11, 9/14, & 9/21
Team Members: Jill M. (Kdg), Cathy
R. (SpEd), Lisa S. (PT), Jan M. (Sp/Lang)

Scoring Key:
+   performs consistently
+/- performs sometimes or in other environments, but not consistently
-    performs rarely or never

Inventory for Person without Disabilities		Student Inventory with Discrepancy Analysis	Teaching and Adaptation Hypotheses
SUBENVIRONMENT: OUTSIDE SCHOOL BUILDING			
Skills:			
Say goodbye to bus driver	-	No, and does not acknowledge bus driver's goodbye	•Teach to respond to bus driver's goodbye with eye contact and wave •Train bus driver to reinforce or respond appropriately
Exit bus	-	Carried down steps and lifted up curb	•Teach to descend steps holding rail •Step up on curb holding hand
Walk to building entrance	+	Follows other students with gestural and verbal cues from teaching assistant	
SUBENVIRONMENT: SCHOOL HALLWAY			
Skills:			
Walk to classroom	+	Walks independently	
Carry tote bag	-	Tries to carry bag, but falls	•Wear backpack
Locate classroom	+/-	Gets lost, but recognizes classroom	•Backward chain
SUBENVIRONMENT: KINDERGARTEN CLASSROOM			
Skills:			
Greet teacher at doorway	-	No, and does not acknowledge the teacher's greeting	•Teacher add physical component to her greeting routine •After establish routine, gradually add delays to teacher initiation of greeting and use sequence of prompts for Kristen to initiate
Locate cubby	-	Goes to cubbies, doesn't find name	•Match name from card •Photo cue of Kristen next to name at first
Put bag in cubby	-	Leaves on base	•Assist to remove backpack and place in cubby

(continued)

Figure 5.6.   Ecological assessment: kindergarten arrival and play routine.

Figure 5.6.   *(continued)*

Inventory for Person without Disabilities		Student Inventory with Discrepancy Analysis	Teaching and Adaptation Hypotheses
Remove coat	-	Full assist with zipper and first sleeve, independent with second sleeve	•Teach to ask for help by touching a picture mounted in her cubby •Prompt to unzip and take off
Hang coat in cubby	-	Full assist to hang	•Prompt to grasp and lift
Go to play area	-	Stands and looks, must be led, did not follow general or direct verbal instructions	•Clear path to area •Use prompt sequence •Teach to follow peer •Instruct partner on least congested route
Select materials from shelves	-	Watches others, did not stoop and retrieve; prefers social games to toys	•Prompt to kneel •Begin with daily observations recording object preferences •Give two choices for play by holding objects out to her in two hands •Assist to put on counter
Take materials to proper area	-	Full assist to carry and find space	•Ask peer for assistance by giving object to peer •Have peer carry material •Teach to follow peer to play space
Play (solitary, parallel, or cooperative)	-	Watches others	•Teach to use various materials near and with other children •Start with simple social games (e.g., ring-around-the-rosey), gradually add the functional use of objects (e.g., find the ball and throw to peer)
Clean-up time	-	Full assist	•Backward chain
Transition to tables for opening group	-	Won't walk during the commotion of clean-up time	•Leave before clean-up starts or after finished •Choose a peer partner to follow during transition •Instruct partner on least congested route •Hold partner's hand

- What expressive communication behaviors does Kristen demonstrate?
- When and how can more intentional communication be elicited?

- What mode(s) of expressive communication should be taught?
- To what extent does poor coordination/spasticity interfere with Kristen's abili-

ties to walk, change position, and use her hands?

- Are there new motor skills that Kristen needs to learn to increase participation?
- What handling and facilitation strategies are effective to improve Kristen's motor participation?
- In which routine tasks could Kristen use peers for assistance?

Team members determined that they could gather the information needed to answer most questions during routine activities, using more focused behavioral observation strategies. The speech-language pathologist, for example, conducted an informal pragmatic communication assessment (see excerpt in Figure 5.7). She conducted informal hearing assessment under a variety of environmental conditions and arranged for formal hearing tests. She also thought it appropriate to conduct an Environmental Pre-Language Battery (Horstmeier & MacDonald, 1975) to learn more about Kristen's receptive and presymbolic expressive language and an informal assessment to learn more about her expressive communication use. The physical therapist chose to record some observations about motor skills on the ABC (Hardy et al., 1988). As part of the ABC, she also measured the range of motion at Kristen's hips, knees, and ankles, areas at which she was at risk for developing contractures. In consultation with the occupational therapist, the physical therapist completed the EDPA (Erhardt, 1982) and analyzed the sensory characteristics of the morning arrival and play routines (see Figure 5.8). More formal testing (Environmental Pre-Language Battery, range of motion) was performed in the classroom, usually when the class went to an outside activity.

Assessment Report   The team chose to organize the report around skill areas but made sure to relate findings to performance in routine activities. The following are excerpts from the team's report.

INITIAL ASSESSMENT

STUDENT: Kristen F.
DATE OF BIRTH: 4/29/91
DATE OF REPORT: 10/1/96
TEAM MEMBERS: Mr. & Mrs. F. (parents), Jill M. (Kindergarten), Cathy R. (SpEd), Jan M. (Sp/Lang), Lisa S. (PT), Jim D. (OT)

Kristen is a 5-year, 5-month-old girl with generalized developmental delays and spastic cerebral palsy. She entered the kindergarten at Richmond Elementary School in September 1996. Kristen's team observed her participating in routine activities at the Special Preschool Program (May 29, 1996), at home (June 26, 1996), and at the Richmond kindergarten (September 9–28, 1996). Ecological inventories were completed in kindergarten during arrival and free play routines. The following assessment tools were also used:

Assessment of Behavioral Components (9/14/96)
Erhardt Developmental Prehension Assessment (9/28/96)
Environmental Pre-Language Battery (9/21/96)

Gross Motor Skills

Kristen's gross motor development is delayed, and flexor tone in her legs and trunk interferes with normal movement patterns. Kristen sits on a stool or chair with relatively normal posture as long as her feet are supported but with increased tone and poor posture when her feet are not supported. For table activities, she needs a large chair with added back and foot supports so she can sit at a proper height relative to the table. When playing on the floor, she tends to W-sit, which carries over to a persistent pattern of hip flexion–adduction–internal rotation in tall kneeling and standing. Her range of motion is within normal limits at all joints. She rises to stand and lowers to kneel in a symmetrical pattern, by straightening or bending both knees while rolling over the insides of her ankles as she pulls up/lowers on furniture. The more normal reciprocal pattern (one foot at a time) can be facilitated easily by holding one ankle and tapping her opposite

Date & Time	Context	Form	Message Expressed (intent)	Pragmatic Function	Consequence	# Times Observed
9-21	KINDERGARTEN CLASSROOM: SNACK					
10:45 AM	Students were excused from previous activity to wash hands one table at a time. Kristen and Leah sat together waiting. Leah tried to get Kristen to play pat-a-cake (Kristen passively let Leah prompt motion, but was attentive.) A friend started to talk to Leah; Leah turned away from Kristen and terminated hand play.	Kristen reached toward Leah and pulled at her hand.	More pat-a-cake.	Request continuation of event	Leah said, "Oh, you want to play more. Wait just a second, Kristen."	II
10:48 AM	Kristen followed others from her table to the sink without cues. She stood near the sink watching the others. Teacher asked, "Kristen, are you going to wash, too?"	Looked at teacher when heard her name and then said "No" clearly.	"No" (verbal).	Comment/ response to question	Teacher approached and provided physical guidance for handwashing.	I
10:52 AM	Teacher took Kristen to the snack table and asked, "What kind of cookie do you want? Choose one," while holding a cookie out in each hand.	Reached and took the cookie to her right.	That one.	Comment/ response to question	Teacher said, "That one looks good."	I
10:54 AM	After Kristen picked her cookie, the teacher said, "Now, get some juice."	Kristen looked toward the 15 or so cups filled with juice and began to whine.	Help me get my juice.	Feeling / frustration, request for assistance	Teacher carried Kristen's cup of juice to her table for her. Kristen followed.	I
11:00 AM	A classmate (Joe) at Kristen's table began to make faces while eating. Other children at the table laughed.	Kristen giggled with others.	Funny.	Feeling / happy	None observed.	II

(continued)

Figure 5.7. Kristen: pragmatic communication assessment (excerpts).

163

Figure 5.7. (continued)

Date & Time	Context	Form	Message Expressed (intent)	Pragmatic Function	Consequence	# Times Observed
11:02 AM	Joe chewed his snack with his mouth open saying, "Yum, yum."	Verbalization: "um-um."	Yum, yum.	Comment/ social interaction with others	Classmates continued to laugh and giggle.	II
11:10 AM	Teacher had just announced that it was time for free play. Classmates started to transition to play area.	Kristen headed in the opposite direction from the rest of the class and stood by the cubbies, then looked back at class.	I want to go outside. or I'm ready to go home.	Request for attention	Teacher walked over to Kristen and said, "No, we're going to play inside now."	I
11:12 AM	Teacher attempted to guide Kristen back to the play area.	Kristen slipped down to the floor, whining.	No, I want to go now.	Reject event	Teacher left the cubbie area to let Kristen "cool down."	I
11:17 AM	Teacher returned to cubbie area (Kristen still on floor) and said, "Kristen, come see the new toy with me," and tried to assist her to stand.	Kristen's body stiffened and she whined again.	No.	Reject event	Teacher said, "Ok, but you'll miss play time."	I
11:25 AM	Teacher returned again to Kristen and said, "Kristen, it's time to go home now."	Kristen sat up and reached out her arms for support to stand.	OK, I'm ready. Help me get up.	Comment, request for assistance	Teacher helped Kristen get up, saying, "Let's go get your bag."	I

Sensory Characteristics of Task Performance

Routine/Task: *Arrival, Free play*

Sensory Characteristics		What does the Task or Routine hold? A	B	C	What does the specific environment hold?	What adaptations are likely to improve functional outcomes?
Somatosensory	light touch (tap, tickle)	X	X			
	pain					
	temperature (hot, cold)				Room temp. fluctuates	
	touch-pressure (hug, pat, grasp)	X	X			Use tactile cues more than auditory
	variable	X	X			Doesn't seem to interfere
	duration of stimulus (short/long)	S	S/L			
	body surface contact(small/large)	S/L	S/L			
	predictable	X	X			A - keep predictable, good cues
	unpredictable		X			B - doesn't seem to interfere
Vestibular	head position change	X	X			
	speed change		X			
	direction change		X			
	rotary head movement					
	linear head movement					
	rhythmic head movement		X			
	predictable	X	X			A - can novel mvmt regain attention??
	unpredictable		X			B - seems to enjoy some novelty, surprises
Proprioceptive	quick stretch					
	sustained tension					Use firm pressure on shoulders +
	shifting muscle tension					arms to calm when overloaded

(continued)

Figure 5.8. Worksheet for analysis of task sensory components. (Adapted from Dunn, W. [1996]. The sensorimotor systems: A framework for assessment and intervention. In F. Orelove & D. Sobsey, *Educating children with multiple disabilities: A transdisciplinary approach* [3rd ed., pp. 35–78]. Baltimore: Paul H. Brookes Publishing Co.)

Figure 5.8. (continued)

	Component	A	B	C		Strategy
Visual	high intensity		X		Play area bright, movement	
	low intensity	X	X		Cubby - dark	Use neon for name tag inside cubby
	high contrast		X			
	high similarity (low contrast)	X			Cubby - plain	Screen cubby from play area; make choice of where to play from 2-3 objects
	competitive		X		Cubby vs Play area	or photos before leaving cubby.
	variable		X			Give time to accommodate to room
	predictable	X	X			before trying to elicit performance.
	unpredictable	X	X		Peers arriving in play area	
Auditory	rhythmic					Use clapping patterns to refocus attention
	variable	X	X			at cubby, as used during class.
	constant		X			
	competitive	X	X		Cubby vs Play area	Screen cubby - ask for sound-absorbing partition units
	noncompetitive					
	loud		X		Peers in play area	Minimize adult talk to reduce
	soft	X	X		Teacher's voice	over load - Use touch cues to
	predictable	X	X			prompt, use deep pressure to calm
	unpredictable		X		Peers arriving in play area	
Olfactory	mild	X	X			
	strong					
	predictable	X	X			
	unpredictable					

Task Components   A = Arrival   B = Free play   C =

166

knee. She walks with a "scissor" pattern (one knee crosses in front of the other). She can step over objects or climb stairs only with both hands held.

Kristen's tone increases when she is excited or upset or when there are high levels of visual and auditory stimulation. As a result, Kristen seems reluctant to move in some school situations. For example, she walks freely through the classroom and hallways when there are few children present or when they are engaged in quiet activity. During transitions and noisy activities, however, Kristen sits or stands in one place, and she moves only when led by an adult. On three occasions, another child was asked to hold Kristen's hand during a transition; Kristen and her friend both seemed to like this alternative. Although Kristen tends to W-sit on the floor during free play, she responds positively to tone reduction (brief rocking while seated straddling adult's lap) followed by physical prompts to sidesit, kneel, half-kneel, and rise to stand. After prompting to change position several times during free play, Kristen will walk approximately 10 feet unassisted in transition to the next activity. This strategy can be generalized to other transitions in the classroom. For transitions to other areas of the school, it seems appropriate to give Kristen a head start until she is more adept at classroom transitions.

Fine Motor Skills

Kristen's fine motor development also is delayed, with posture and movement of her arms and hands influenced by flexor tone. She typically holds her elbows close to her sides with all joints flexed and her hands held near her waist or the upper part of her chest. When walking, she often holds her hands up near her shoulders (high guard position), especially when excited. During arrival and play, she holds her bag and large toys with two hands, but she carries them only four or five steps before dropping the object or falling. When performing routine tasks in familiar situations (e.g., put arm in shirt/coat sleeves), she is able to extend her elbows and wrists completely. When playing with a ball, she extends her elbows, wrists, and fingers to hold the ball, but alternates between extremes of flexion and extension when she tries to throw and catch. Although flexor tone (including shoulder internal

rotation and forearm pronation) tends to interfere with reach and grasp, physical prompts just above the elbow (to flex the shoulder) are effective to elicit reach and grasp in several contexts (e.g., take paper towel from dispenser, take toys off shelf).

Kristen uses a palmar grasp to hold most objects (e.g., crayons, spoon, sandwiches, paper), but can use a lateral pinch or thumb–fingertip grasp to hold small objects when given physical prompts to hold her wrist in extension and to hold the space between her thumb and first finger open. Kristen can release only against resistance (e.g., hang coat on hook), with her wrist stabilized (e.g., heel of hand pressed on table), or when her fingers are stabilized so she can pull them into extension. Although she can eat finger foods independently, Kristen tends to hold food in her palm and then press her hand against her face to open her fingers—a messy strategy. Kristen's oral-motor skills appear satisfactory for eating a variety of whole foods. Kristen does not yet isolate her index finger, but she does use her arm to point to people/objects in the distance and the thumb–index finger portion of her hand to point to objects in her reach. Although Kristen is cooperative and seems willing to try almost any motor task once, she tends to give up or has a tantrum when unsuccessful.

Social Skills

Kristen does not play with toys, except balls. She uses a limited number of objects, such as a spoon, cup, ball, and brush (to help brush her dog), in functional, rather than symbolic, acts. She shows little interest in using blocks, cars, dolls, or other toys found at home or in the kindergarten classroom, although she watches other children play. Kristen seems to prefer simple social games and routines with adults; she will initiate games, sustain interaction for several minutes, take turns, and anticipate events in a play routine. Kristen's mother reported that Kristen is more likely to play with her older sister if an adult is involved (e.g., roughhousing with Dad), but the two girls do chase the dog around together and laugh. At school Kristen has not initiated interactions with other children, but she is starting to respond to and sustain interactions that they initiate.

Communication Skills

Kristen appears to prefer predictable routines. When predictable routines are changed or have not been established, she participates much less, sometimes refusing to participate or even having tantrums. Informal and formal testing suggested that Kristen is dependent on contextual cues in routine activities for language comprehension. During classroom observation, Kristen responded appropriately, given contextual and gestural cues, to the following directions: "give me," "come here," "stand up," "go get," and "let's go to the bathroom now." Formal testing of receptive language abilities did not yield additional useful information. Kristen's mother reported that she follows simple directions for some routines at home. Kristen's hearing is within normal limits for awareness of environmental sounds. The influence of background noise on Kristen's hearing could not be assessed. Given her current language comprehension abilities, however, it is most appropriate for adults to work in close proximity to Kristen and to shield her from auditory and visual distractions, using the same strategies as if background noise interference were confirmed.

Information gathered about Kristen's understanding of pictures was inconclusive. Kristen reportedly enjoys a particular children's videotape and the "Sesame Street" TV show, but representational images may not be the salient feature; Kristen may be attracted to other features such as color, movement, and/or music. At home, Kristen likes to look at a set of cards depicting "Sesame Street" characters, but she has no interest in a magazine depicting the same characters. Her mother reported that Kristen enjoys looking at the family photo album and points to pictures of immediate family members and the dog when asked "Where is . . .?" In formal testing, she identified a picture of a baby (from a choice of two images) but was unsuccessful on other items.

Kristen did not respond to formal expressive language assessment items requiring verbal production. She did imitate some gestures accompanied by verbal cues (e.g., waves when adult waves and says "bye"). During informal pragmatic communication assessment, Kristen used communication 18 times (during 1 hour) with functions for greetings, feelings, requests, rejections, and comments. Use was evenly distributed among functions, except for greetings,

for which there were fewer opportunities. Classroom observation suggested a connection between behaviors defined as tantrums and Kristen's lack of communication skills. Kristen's mother and teachers all reported that she has tantrums to reject activities and when she cannot get what she wants. This strategy is successful for her at least part of the time, because adults are making appropriate efforts to interpret and respond to Kristen's nonsymbolic communication.

Expressive communication included a variety of forms, such as smiling, reaching for another person, whining, going to the location of an activity, laughing, alternating gaze, reaching for food, and two verbalizations: "no" and "um-um" (for "yum-yum"). She was observed to imitate peers' communication twice, once laughing and once approximating "yum-yum." Kristen's spoken vocabulary includes the following words and approximations: Mom, Dad, Doowee (Julie), Doot (Duke, the dog), pop, no, ba (ball), and Nana.

CONCLUSIONS AND RECOMMENDATIONS

1. The quality of Kristen's gross and fine motor skills needs improvement to enable her to participate more successfully in daily routines at home and at school. Kristen also needs to develop more advanced patterns of grasp, manipulation, and release for play, academic, and self-care activities.

2. Kristen is distracted from task performance when sights and sounds are intense or unpredicted. Strategies are needed to help her modulate background visual and auditory stimuli (e.g., environmental adaptations, calming sensory input) and to refocus her attention.

3. Kristen expresses herself through a few spoken words and a variety of nonverbal forms and functions, but she needs to expand these, particularly to direct the behavior of others. With consistent communication opportunities and appropriate prompting sequences, routines at home and school offer excellent contexts for this type of instruction. Additional opportunities should be created to use and expand existing single-word verbalizations. Use of pictures for communication in actual contexts also should be explored.

4. Kristen's tantrums seem to reflect frustration with inabilities to perform motor tasks,

to filter environmental stimuli, to direct the behavior of others, and to understand changes in routines. At this time, tantrums should be addressed only through positive means, by interpreting her wishes, providing assistance, and guiding more appropriate ways to express requests and rejections. The team will need to devise a strategy to help Kristen understand changes in routines and to deal with her spontaneous requests and rejections when they conflict with home/school goals.

5. Although Kristen's social development is delayed, this is undoubtedly influenced by her motor disability, which previously would have limited her success with toys and typical children's play routines. Instruction in play needs to include attention to sensorimotor, communicative, and social abilities.

Annual Assessment: Jamal

Planning the Assessment   During Jamal's spring IEP conference, his team discussed his interests and needs and identified priority environments, activities, and skills, as discussed in Chapter 4. On this basis, they outlined a weekly schedule of activities for the next school year (see Figure 5.9). Since entering high school, Jamal's schedule had reflected increasing participation in general education classes and community environments. The fall schedule included two new opportunities: a high school Spanish class and a work experience program. The Spanish class was chosen for Jamal because he frequently heard Spanish in his own home, especially when his grandmother visited; the structure of the class offered many opportunities for Jamal to participate; and the Spanish teacher had expressed interest in opening his classroom to students with diverse abilities and interests. In addition, a student who had just finished Spanish I was interested in providing daily peer support for Jamal (with guidance from Jamal's team) as part of the course Disability and Society (see Fisher & Rodifer, 1996). The work experience at the Metro Insurance Agency was part of the plan to prepare Jamal for his transition to adulthood and would require him

to spend increasing amounts of time away from school. Although the team projected goals and objectives related to these new environments, the members knew they would need to modify those goals and objectives in the fall after ecological assessments were conducted in actual learning environments.

Early in the fall, Jamal's core team met to plan his assessment. The core team included Jamal and those individuals with whom he would have the most contact across learning environments: his mother, foster parents, special education teacher, occupational therapist, speech-language pathologist, special education teaching assistant, and transition specialist. Because Jamal would be enrolled in general education classes, his homeroom teacher was selected as the representative for general education. His other teachers indicated that they wanted to provide information relevant to assessment and to learn strategies to support Jamal in their classes, but they preferred not to participate directly in the actual assessment. A nurse, psychologist, physical therapist, and county case manager (social worker) were available for consultation but were not part of the core team. After considering the highest priorities for assessment, Jamal's core team completed an ecological assessment planning chart (see Figure 5.10).

Ecological Assessment   Ecological assessment was planned for each environment that was part of Jamal's school day. Because Jamal had not previously participated in Spanish class or work at the Metro Insurance Agency, the team gave high priority to assessing him in these two environments so appropriate objectives and instructional routines could be established as soon as possible. These two environments have been selected as representative examples for Jamal's assessment. Both inventories include a discrepancy analysis describing Jamal's actual performance. Jamal's participation in the two learning environments was observed

	Monday	Tuesday	Wednesday	Thursday	Friday
Before school 7:00–7:45	Regular bus (Restroom 7:30)	Regular bus (Restroom 7:30)	Regular bus (Restroom 7:30)	Regular bus (Restroom 7:30)	Regular bus (Restroom 7:30)
Homeroom 7:45–8:00	HOMEROOM	HOMEROOM	HOMEROOM	HOMEROOM	HOMEROOM
Period 1 8:05–8:55	SPANISH	SPANISH	SPANISH	SPANISH	SPANISH
Period 2 9:00–9:50	COMMUNITY: TRAVEL & WORK	HOME ECONOMICS	COMMUNITY: TRAVEL & WORK	HOME ECONOMICS	COMMUNITY: TRAVEL & WORK
Period 3 9:55–10:45	WORK (Restroom 10:30)	HOME ECONOMICS (Restroom 10:30)	WORK (Restroom 10:30)	HOME ECONOMICS (Restroom 10:30)	WORK (Restroom 10:30)
Period 4 10:50–11:40	WORK	CHOIR OR HORTICULTURE	WORK	CHOIR OR HORTICULTURE	WORK
Period 5 11:45–12:35	WORK & LUNCH (at school or in community)	LUNCH	WORK & LUNCH (at school or in community)	LUNCH	WORK & LUNCH (at school or in community)
Period 6 12:40–1:30	LUNCH (cont.) (Restroom 1:15)	MEDIA CENTER* (Restroom 1:15)	LUNCH (cont.) (Restroom 1:15)	MEDIA CENTER* (Restroom 1:15)	LUNCH (cont.) (Restroom 1:15)
Period 7 1:35–2:25	EARTH SCIENCE	EARTH SCIENCE	EARTH SCIENCE	EARTH SCIENCE	EARTH SCIENCE
After school				Swim Team Manager	

Figure 5.9. Jamal's weekly schedule. (*Media Center, including Library and Computer Lab, is available throughout the day.)

170

Priority Environments and Routines Where Assessment Is Conducted	Team Members Conducting Assessment			
	Parents	Special Education Teacher	Occupational Therapist	Speech-Language Therapist
Home				
Kitchen	9/10	9/10		
School				
Arrival				
Hallways		9/18		
Rest room				
Homeroom				
Spanish class		9/18	9/25	9/25
Choir				
Lunchroom				
Media center				
Home economics				
Horticulture				
Locker room				
Pool area				
Community				
Work experience (Metro Insurance Agency)		9/18	9/25	9/25
Shopping mall				
Fast food restaurant				

Figure 5.10. Ecological assessment planning chart for Jamal.

and recorded in order to clarify and validate instructional needs, priorities, and necessary supports.

Spanish Class The Spanish teacher followed a fairly regular routine of tasks, which served as the inventory for people without disabilities for the ecological assessment (see Figure 5.11). Jamal's team did not expect him to master Spanish core curriculum objectives (i.e., learn Spanish), but the class was an excellent setting to address other individualized learning priorities. The team se-

8:05 - 8:15	**Class opens with greeting exercise** •choose partners •introduce selves (Hola, Señor John!) •teacher indicates a context for conversation using specific vocabulary from a previous lesson listed on blackboard daily (e.g., One student is a baker and the other a customer. The customer asks, "Do you have any fresh bread?") •required to write up the greeting conversation in Spanish and turn in at the end of class; usually 2-3 sentences
8:15 - 8:25	**Jokes of the day** •different student is assigned to tell an English joke in Spanish each day •teacher usually comments on the joke's translation and if it would be considered funny in Spanish •teacher tells a Spanish joke after the student and the English translation is discussed

8:25 - 8:45	**Daily lesson and oral practice** [a]
	•whole group instruction
	•use of scripts in textbook or a worksheet
	•teacher first introduces new vocabulary, word forms, etc.
	•choral responses to teacher with new words, forms, etc.
	•conversational practice
	      -teacher provides situational context and vocabulary list
	      -teacher circulates in the classroom to comment and answer questions
	      -pre-recorded lesson on a tape recorder sometimes used

8:45 - 8:55	**Closing and competency measures** [a] •group game with teams; keeps pressure off individuals •score kept for teams •beanbag thrown for responses •crossword puzzles •fill-in-the-blank poetry (rhyming words omitted) •poem and story writing •other word games

Figure 5.11. Spanish class routine. ([a]With daily variation.)

lected items from the Assessment of Student Participation in General Education Classes, presented earlier in this chapter (see Figure 5.2), for an ecological inventory of the Spanish class that corresponded with priorities the team had previously identified. The resulting assessment focused on Jamal's participation in classroom routines and activities and in social and communication interactions. The completed ecological assessment is presented in Figure 5.12.

Community Work Experience Jamal's work–study experience at Metro Insurance Agency was scheduled for three mornings per week. Immediately after Spanish class, Jamal rode the city bus with other work–study students from his school and a special education teaching assistant. Jamal worked alongside clerical staff for the insurance agency, which had about 30 employees. Another student with moderate disabilities opened, stapled, and stacked incoming mail. Jamal stamped the date on the mail, and the first student sorted the mail for delivery around the office. The sequence of events in the community work experience routine of-

Student: Jamal W.
Date: 9/18 & 9/25
Team Members: Trish G. (Spanish), John K. (SpEd), Jake S. (teaching assistant), Ann E. (Sp/Lang), Lisa W. (OT)

Scoring Key:
+   performs consistently
+/-   performs sometimes or in other environments, but not consistently
-    performs rarely or never

Inventory for Person without Disabilities	Student Inventory with Discrepancy Analysis		Teaching and Adaptation Hypotheses
SUBENVIRONMENT: SPANISH CLASS			
I. CLASSROOM ROUTINES AND ACTIVITIES			
3. **Performs transitional activities during class in response to situational cues (e.g., changes in setting, activity)**	-	J cannot maneuver his w/c due to lack of space, movement required within the classroom for activities daily. Follows situational cues to change activities in other environments.	•Peer assistance to move within the classroom •Teach to request peer assistance to move during transition times •Request that teacher use consistent daily routine when possible •Learn situational cues to change activities
7. **Terminates task without extra direction**	+	Keeps giggling after "joke of the day"; usually not a problem for other activities.	•A competing task built into the routine may help terminate
9. **Follows class rules**	+/-	Needs to quiet down after "joke of the day"; gets silly; quiet conversation is encouraged and teacher reports he is usually fine.	•See above (#7)
15. **Works cooperatively with a partner**	+	Repeatedly chooses his friend David as a partner. Attends to group activities.	•Greeting exercise - could be a 3rd partner in groups of 2 •Choose what group he will be in and request •Encourage J to join a group that doesn't include David
16. **Works cooperatively with a small group**	+	Attends to group activities.	•Flip score card for competitive games •Classmates write one response/day for J to give w/cues •Switch on/off tape recorder when used
19. **Copes with criticism / correction without incident and tries an alternative behavior**	+/-	Usually OK, but after "joke of the day" did not quiet down to three requests by teacher.	•See above (#7)

(continued)

Figure 5.12.   Ecological assessment: Spanish class. (The items for this assessment were prioritized from the Assessment of Student Participation in General Education Classes [Figure 5.2].) (W/C, wheelchair.)

Figure 5.12. (continued)

Inventory for Person without Disabilities		Student Inventory with Discrepancy Analysis	Teaching and Adaptation Hypotheses
II. SOCIAL AND COMMUNICATION SKILLS			
21. Interacts with peers			
a. responds	+	a. Uses facial expressions/ vocalizations, body posture.	•New augmentative system being developed
			•Instruct teacher and classmates on best ways to communicate with J
b. initiates	+	b. Usually vocalizes for attention or greeting.	•Initiate Spanish greetings
			•Initiate requests for assistance
23. Uses social greetings			
a. responds to others	+	a. Uses facial expressions/ vocalizations, body posture.	•Initiate Spanish greetings
b. initiates	+	b. Same as above.	
26. Participates in joking or teasing			
a. responds to others	+	a. Loves "joke of the day."	•Use peer support and a written joke when it is his turn to present a joke
b. initiates	+/-	b. Limited motor and communication, sometimes pretends is asleep to joke.	•Carry over "joke of the day" to the work setting with coworkers
27. Makes choices or indicates preferences			
a. responds (cue or ?)	+/-	a. With objects, but new augmentative system being developed.	•Choose a friend to greet
			•Choose a partner
b. initiates	+/-	b. Sometimes, can be facilitated within class routines.	
28. Asks questions			
a. asks for help	-	a. No, can be facilitated within class routines.	•Ask for help to move w/c around classroom for activities
b. asks for information (clarification, feedback)	-	b. Not a priority.	•Needs to initiate request for help when uncomfortable
29. Follows directions			
a. for curricular tasks	+/-	a-d. Needs routine or situational cues, but can do if short, direct, and in close proximity (but consider physical capabilities).	•Instruct teacher and classmates on needs for following directions
b. for helping tasks/errands			
c. given to the student individually			
d. given to the students as a group			

fered many opportunities for Jamal and the other students to learn skills (see Figure 5.13).

Prior to the ecological assessment, Jamal had made several short visits to the worksite to become familiar with the environment. He did not spend the entire morning at the worksite because he was unable to perform his work tasks without adaptive devices and/or personal assistance. Thus, the primary purpose of the assessment was to determine opportunities for participation and instruction and strategies for teaching and adaptation. The completed ecological assessment is presented in Figure 5.14.

Hypothesis Generation The completed assessments show that both Spanish class and the work experience offered many opportunities for Jamal to participate in routine activities and to work on embedded social, communication, and sensorimotor skills. Although the Student Inventory with Discrepancy Analysis column of the assessment in Spanish class shows that Jamal already participates in the routine, the Teaching and

Adaptation Hypotheses column shows that new skills would increase the amount and quality of his participation. The assessment at work shows that Jamal currently is unable to perform many of the skills required for participation and will need instruction, adaptations, and personal assistance. Unlike the hypotheses generated for Kristen earlier in this chapter, the team knew Jamal very well and spent less time on conjecture about why he performed a certain way and more on how he performed and what adaptations could be made to facilitate increased participation. Generally this will be true for older students with whom team members have had extensive experience. Teams are cautioned about becoming complacent, however, and encouraged to use the triennial review as an opportunity to take a fresh look at their students.

After completing its ecological assessments, Jamal's team developed a long list of ideas for teaching and adaptations but still had questions that would be best addressed through diagnostic assessment. The follow-

9:05	Catch bus in front of school
9:15	Arrive at Metro Insurance bus stop
9:27	Greet co-workers
9:35	Go to coat rack and store belongings
9:40	Go to work station
9:42	Do work tasks
10:15	Go to rest room and use facilities
10:30	Go to break room and take a break
10:43	Finish break and go back to work
10:48	Do work tasks
11:35	Prepare to leave work area
11:42	Go to coat rack and get belongings
11:48	Go to front office area and say good-bye to co-workers
11:53	Go to bus stop
12:00	Catch bus

Figure 5.13. Community work experience routine. (Times vary slightly from day to day.)

Student: Jamal W.
Date: 9/18 & 9/25
Team Members: John K. (SpEd), Jake
S. (teaching assistant), Ann E. (Sp/Lang),
Lisa W. (OT)

Scoring Key:
+   performs consistently
+/- performs sometimes or in other environments, but not consistently
-    performs rarely or never

Inventory for Person without Disabilities		Student Inventory with Discrepancy Analyses	Teaching and Adaptation Hypotheses
SUBENVIRONMENT: BUILDING ARCADE (FIRST FLOOR)			
Activity: Arriving at work			
Skills:			
Scan store fronts	+	Yes	
Locate insurance agency	+/-	Sometimes vocalizes at destination	Use of vocalization and eye gaze to indicate entrance
Walk to entrance and enter through archway	-	Power w/c with assistance	Develop power w/c skills to cruise arcade and enter open arch
SUBENVIRONMENT: METRO INSURANCE AGENCY FRONT OFFICE AREA			
Activity: Greeting coworkers			
Skills:			
Walk to/by coworkers' desks	-	Space too small to maneuver given present w/c mobility skills	Teaching assistant wheels to agency coworkers
Establish eye contact	+	Yes	
Smile and say "hi"	-	Vocal approximation	
Initiates appropriate conversation	-	Initates requests for attention with vocal, but can't initiate topics	•Develop augmentative communication skills •Bring joke to tell from Spanish class
Respond to questions and comments	+/-	Uses facial expression	•Needs more augmentative communication skills for conversation •Instruct coworkers on best ways to communicate with Jamal
Depart after greetings	-	Needs assistance with w/c	Develop augmentative means to ask to go to coat rack
Scan for coat rack	+	Looks in direction	
Walk between desks to coat rack	-	Space too small to maneuver given present w/c mobility skills	Teaching assistant wheels to coatrack
Remove jacket	-	Full physical assistance	Teach to drop head as a way to remain relaxed

(continued)

Figure 5.14. Ecological assessment: community work experience (excerpts). (W/C, wheelchair.)

Figure 5.14. *(continued)*

Inventory for Person without Disabilities	Student Inventory with Discrepancy Analyses	Teaching and Adaptation Hypotheses
Hang up jacket	- Full physical assistance	Relaxation and facilitation for full range of motion reach
Scan for work area	+ Looks in direction	
Walk between desks to work area	- Space too small for present mobility skills	Teaching assistant wheel to edge of work area

SUBENVIRONMENT: WORK AREA

Activity: Stamping and stacking mail

Skills:		
Walk to counter	- Power w/c with assistance	Develop power w/c skills for work area
Request date stamp	- Unable to communicate	Request date stamp by vocalizing and looking at photo
Walk to work station	- Power w/c with assistance	Develop power w/c skills for work area
Get opened mail from coworker	- Unable to communicate	Develop augmentative means to request work
Set stamp to correct date	- Full physical assistance	Usually already set by coworker
Walk to chair	- Power w/c with assistance	Develop power w/c skills to maneuver in work area
Get seated	+ Already seated	
Stamp top piece of mail	- Full physical assistance	Develop adaptation for stamping
Move stamped piece to finished work stack	- No, but can push the entire stack	Develop adaptation to allow for use of a sliding movement
Stamp next piece	- Full physical assistance	Adaptation for stamping
[repeat previous steps]		
Get up from chair and take finished work stack to coworker	- Unable to use hands to move paper stack	•Develop augmentative means to request that coworker pick up finished work and put on w/c tray •Drive power w/c to recipient of stamped mail
Get more opened mail from coworker	- Unable to use hands to get more work	Develop augmentative means to request more work from coworker
[repeat previous steps]		

Activity: Preparing for break

Skills:		
Decide it is break time (10:15AM)	- Does not tell time	Set kitchen timer to ring at 10:15AM (J will go to break before others to allow for extra time in rest room)
Place work materials on counter in work area	- Full physical assistance	Develop augmentative means to ask for help

177

ing needs, identified in Spanish class and at Metro Insurance Agency, require further investigation by the team.

In Spanish class, Jamal continued giggling long after the "joke of the day" was over, detracting from the next task for all students in the class. Some team members thought Jamal might not be able to control his giggling once initiated. Others thought giggling may have been one of the few means Jamal had to participate in Spanish class and that it might become less important to him if he had more ways to communicate.

At Metro Insurance Agency, Jamal's participation was also severely limited by his lack of communication abilities. Assessments indicated that he initiated interactions frequently, but he communicated primarily by facial expressions and vocalizations. The lack of progress in communication by Jamal and other students with severe disabilities had frustrated the speech-language pathologist for a long time, so she took a short course on assessment and facilitation of communication for students who, like Jamal, had no symbolic means of communication. The speech-language pathologist learned strategies to conduct a more thorough diagnostic assessment of Jamal's communication abilities and needs.

Another priority for Jamal was to learn to use his motor capabilities to maximize participation in all activity routines. This included learning to use his new power wheelchair, assuming responsibilities in Spanish class (e.g., turn tape recorder on and off, keep score), and performing work tasks at Metro Insurance Agency. Routines in Spanish class and at work required movement around the room, but the classroom and parts of Metro Insurance were too congested for him to drive his chair. Other tasks requiring motor performance seemed beyond Jamal's current abilities. Therefore, the occupational therapist would investigate the feasibility of the ideas noted in the Teaching and Adaptation Hypotheses column of the ecological assessments.

The team quickly reached agreement regarding one aspect of Jamal's motor performance. For several tasks in Jamal's assessment at Metro, team members wrote "personal assistance" in the Teaching and Adaptation Hypotheses column. After years of professional efforts to teach Jamal tasks such as putting on and removing his coat, Jamal's team was satisfied that certain motor tasks were simply too difficult for Jamal to perform independently, with or without adaptations. Therefore the assistance and adaptations previously provided for these tasks would continue. Team members agreed that instructional time would be used more productively by focusing on participation in other components of work activities. Team members also recognized that Jamal would always need assistance with personal care, so teaching him to express specific interests, wants, and needs was a high priority as he approached adulthood. It is emphasized that legitimate decisions to abandon long-term efforts are made only on an individual basis, after concerted efforts with a variety of instructional strategies, after thorough consideration by the entire team, and when more appropriate priorities or strategies have been identified.

Diagnostic/Discipline-Referenced Assessment Ecological assessments for the Spanish class and community work experience environments were representative of assessments done for other environments Jamal used during his school day. After considering this information along with additional observations, the team still had the following questions regarding Jamal's performance and instructional strategies for Spanish class and work environments:

- What communication forms and functions and what augmentative system(s) are the most appropriate learning priorities for Jamal at this time?
- What specifically is important to communicate in Spanish class?
- How can interactions be facilitated between Jamal and his classmates in Spanish class?
- Can Jamal control his giggling behavior voluntarily? Has similar behavior been a problem in other environments in the past?
- How can Jamal's giggling be addressed in a positive, nonpunitive manner without discouraging social interactions with his peers?
- What specifically is important to communicate in the workplace?
- How can interactions be facilitated between Jamal and insurance agency co-workers?
- Which workplace subenvironments would provide realistic practice for Jamal to maneuver his power wheelchair?
- What adaptations should be made to capitalize on Jamal's strengths and enable him to perform his job tasks?

The team determined that the occupational therapist and speech-language pathologist would conduct the needed diagnostic assessments because the questions listed above were most related to their areas of expertise. Both therapists decided that the information the team was seeking could best be obtained through observation of Jamal's performance in the context of routine activities and that formal tests would reveal few useful data for instructional purposes for a student like Jamal.

The occupational therapist focused her observations on how Jamal used his power wheelchair in various subenvironments, what positions allowed Jamal to participate most fully in motor tasks (e.g., using gross arm movements) in instructional environments, and how to maximize Jamal's motor participation in instructional tasks, especially for his job at the insurance agency. She gave particular consideration to simple adaptations to maximize outcomes from Jamal's limited arm movements.

The speech-language pathologist conducted observations in various subenvironments to collect a nonsymbolic communication sample, which revealed communicative forms and functions already in Jamal's repertoire (see Figure 5.15). From this information, communication forms and functions for instruction were selected to fit the needs of Jamal's specific learning environments. The Communication Environment Checklist, presented previously in this chapter, was used as an informal assessment of conditions in instructional settings that either facilitated or hindered communication (see Figure 5.3).

Assessment Report The following excerpts from Jamal's assessment report are consistent with the ecological curriculum design. Jamal's overall performance for activity routines is described, along with a discussion of embedded motor, communication, and other broad skill areas for each priority environment. This arrangement of assessment information better accommodates variations in student performance related to the assortment of environments and people typically found in students' schedules, especially at the secondary level, where instructional environments change every 45–50 minutes.

ANNUAL ASSESSMENT

STUDENT: Jamal W.
DATE OF BIRTH: 6/1/79
DATE OF REPORT: 10/1/96
TEAM MEMBERS: Mrs. W. (Parent), Mr. M. (Foster Parent), John K. (SpEd), Ben G.

Date & Time	Context	Form	Message Expressed (Intent)	Pragmatic Function	Consequence	# Times Observed
9-18	**SPANISH CLASS (8:05 - 8:55 AM)**					
8:00 AM	Friend David greeted with "Hey Jamal!" as he entered class.	Arm moved away from body, vocalization.	Hi.	Greeting	David looked at Jamal and put a hand on his shoulder.	I
8:05 AM	Teacher instructed students to find partners.	Looked toward David, then teacher, then David.	I choose David.	Request social event	David said, "Ok, Jamal, we can be partners again."	I
8:20 AM	Teacher told joke about red shoes.	Looked at Kelly and then his feet, moved his leg.	I have red shoes, too (red high tops).	Request for attention	Kelly said, "What are you so excited about, Jamal?"	I
8:21 AM	Jamal responded to Kelly.	Vocalization and continued leg movement.	I have red shoes, too.	Comment in response to question	Kelly said, "Oh, you have red shoes."	I
8:30 AM	Teacher said, "I wonder if Jamal can help us out today." Jamal didn't respond, so Kelly said, "Look at the tape recorder, Jamal."	Looked from teacher to tape recorder and back to teacher.	Wanted teacher to know he'd help switch on the tape recorder.	Comment	Teacher directs classmate to set up tape recorder on Jamal's tray.	I
8:35 AM	Students practicing oral lesson for whole group instruction.	Repeated neck extension, throwing head back.	Seems to do this when bored or unable to do task.	Feeling / boredom	Nobody commented?	Many (3 min.)
8:45 AM	Leon asked, "Hey Jamal, are you ready to play the game?" (Not as active participant.) Students moving about.	Blank facial expression, no movement.	No.	Reject event	Ignored. Jamal was wheeled to group.	I
8:46 AM	When moved to group, foot got entangled in foot rest.	Vocalization, body stiffened.	Ouch, help.	Requests for attention and help	Leon approached to figure out what was wrong.	III
8:55 AM	Kelly said, "See you at the swim meet, Jamal."	Vocalization, looked at Kelly.	Yeah, goodbye.	Farewell	None.	I

180

9-18	METRO INSURANCE AGENCY (Observation 9:15 AM)					
9:15 AM	Jamal was assisted in moving his w/c off the van lift. Teaching assistant (Jake) asked, "OK, Jamal, now where do we go?"	Looked at Jake and then toward building entrance and back at Jake.	Go over there to the door.	Comment/giving information in response to question	Jake assisted Jamal in directing his power w/c to the building entrance.	I
9:17 AM	Jake was helping man the w/c controls with Jamal. Arcade hallway empty.	Pushed Jake's hand away from w/c controls and looked at his face.	I want to do it by myself.	Reject assistance	Jake said, "Sorry Jamal, I have to help until we get around this corner."	II
9:25 AM	Jamal stopped w/c near entrance to Metro Insurance Agency.	Looked back to Jake as he approached and vocalized.	Signaled arrival at destination.	Comment/giving information	Jake acknowledged.	II
9:27 AM	Jake wheeled Jamal to office coworkers.	Vocalization.	Hi.	Greeting	Two coworkers greeted Jamal.	II
9:28 AM	Coworkers asked Jamal if it was still raining outside.	Looked at Jake and vocalized.	Yes (?).	Comment in response to a question	Coworker acknowledged by talking about weather some more.	I
9:57 AM	Finished his first tray of work (with assistance). Jake asked, "What do we need now?"	Vocalized and looked toward student coworker.	Signaled done with worktray and needed more work from student coworker.	Request object	Jake cued student coworker to bring Jamal more work.	I
10:15 AM	Timer went off for Jamal's break time.	Vocalized and got excited (body stiffened).	Signaled break time.	Comment on event	"Oh, it's break time for Jamal."	I

(continued)

Figure 5.15. Jamal-pragmatic communication assessment.

Figure 5.15. *(continued)*

Date & Time	Context	Form	Message Expressed (Intent)	Pragmatic Function	Consequence	# Times Observed
10:20 AM	In restroom. Jake gave urinal/ toilet for choices (as reported by Jake).	Looked at urinal.	I need the urinal.	Request object	Jake assisted with urinal.	I
10:31 AM	In break room with coworkers and Jake. Jake asked, "Do you want a drink today, Jamal?"	Smiled and looked at vending machine with juice.	Yes, juice.	Request object	Jake assisted Jamal to vending machine to make choice of juice.	I
10:32 AM	Jamal and Jake at vending machine. Jake pointed to juice boxes behind Plexiglas in the machine one at a time, saying, "Which one?"	Vocalized (when Jake was pointing to apple juice).	I want apple juice.	Request object	Jake pressed button for apple juice.	I
11:00 AM	Jamal was doing the stamping task with physical assistance, and the rubber was coming loose from the handle of the stamp.	Vocalized and banged on his tray, tried to get free of Jake's assistance.	Look, the stamp needs to be fixed.	Request for attention and help	Jake told Jamal to stop fooling around and get back to work. Jamal whined and Jake took a closer look and discovered the problem.	II

(GenEd), Ann E. (Sp/Lang), Lisa W. (OT), Jake S. (SpEd Teaching Assistant), Sandy B. (Transition)

Jamal is a 17-year-old junior at Central High School who enjoys school and friends and participates in school activities with determination and a sense of humor. He has developmental disabilities, including spastic quadriplegic cerebral palsy and communication skills limited to the use of eye movements, facial expressions, and vocalizations. An augmentative communication system using scanning for objects, symbols, or both is being considered. Anecdotal data about Jamal's communication behaviors have always suggested that his comprehension skills for language far surpass his expressive communication abilities. Jamal has received special education services since the age of 2, primarily at the Developmental Center. He entered a special class at Central High School 3 years ago when he moved to his foster home in the city. During Jamal's past 2 years at Central, the time he has participated in general class and community environments has increased steadily. For this assessment, team members observed Jamal in the context of daily routines at school, at a work–study site, and in other relevant community environments.

Spanish Class

Jamal travels to Spanish class in his power wheelchair. He is learning to operate his wheelchair by using a joystick. He needs assistance to relax his right arm and to secure his right hand to the joystick by using a glove adaptation. Jamal is developing greater control pushing the joystick in forward directions when he is positioned correctly and his peer partner provides stability by holding firmly around Jamal's right shoulder. His accuracy for travel in a straight line has increased dramatically since the start of school; he now drives up to 20 feet before hitting walls in hallways. He still requires full assistance to turn and to drive in reverse.

Jamal typically greets classmates spontaneously on entry into the classroom. Classmates appear to enjoy Jamal and include him in a series of small-group activities throughout the period. A communication sample indicates Jamal uses only nonsymbolic communication, with the majority of his expressive communication in Spanish class serving the functions of commenting (20%), and requesting assistance, objects, or activities (50%). Additional communication functions noted were greeting, rejecting, and expressing emotions. Jamal uses vocalizations, body posture, eye gaze, and limb movement in various combinations to get the attention of others. About one third of the time, he used his nonsymbolic communication to specifically direct the behavior of others.

Students who are most familiar with Jamal are better at interpreting his nonsymbolic communications and responding to them. Other students do not provide Jamal with enough response time to interact and tend to provide assistance before he signals for it. More opportunities for communication could be facilitated by informing classmates about how to recognize Jamal's nonsymbolic communications, how to provide appropriate levels of assistance and time delays, and how to take advantage of natural opportunities for Jamal to communicate.

The Spanish teacher reported that Jamal continues to giggle after the "joke of the day" activity, often disrupting the next scheduled activity for class. Thus far, observations have not provided clear information about why Jamal continues to giggle. The therapists conducting the assessment both recommended that initial intervention strategies emphasize teaching and/or eliciting alternative behaviors that might fulfill the same communication function as giggling (e.g., commenting). At the same time, the team should monitor for signs that Jamal has difficulty regulating the level of his arousal.

Community Work Experience

Jamal travels to a community worksite three times per week (MWF) in the work–study program. He displays the same skills for power wheelchair use as in other environments (e.g., hallways and classrooms at school). The location of his work experience program in an office building with power doors and long halls provides many excellent opportunities to practice wheelchair mobility skills. He does not currently receive instruction on driving his power wheelchair in outside environments.

At the time of the assessment, Jamal was not spending the projected 2½ hours on site because of his inability to complete work tasks without task adaptations. (Adaptations are now being developed based on results of this assessment. Jamal's use of the adaptations will be assessed as soon as they are available.) Jamal was dependent on the special education teaching assistant for communication interactions and motor assistance during the observation. Co-workers appeared friendly but needed instruction to recognize Jamal's nonsymbolic communications, to provide appropriate assistance, and to identify natural opportunities for Jamal to communicate within work routines.

Jamal's nonsymbolic communication at the worksite was similar to that found for Spanish class. The communication sample revealed the communication functions of requesting (40%) and commenting (33%), with the remaining 27% of the sample distributed between greeting, rejecting, and expressing emotions.

SUMMARY

Communication intervention is needed to increase Jamal's use of the five communication functions presently in his repertoire, expanding his use of communication forms that direct the behaviors of others. Intervention will also focus on the introduction of an augmentative communication system that uses scanning to select objects/symbols on a display board. The new system will be designed to meet specific communication needs in a variety of environments. In the environments sampled for assessment, the number of recognized and successful communication attempts was up to 50% greater in settings in which a person familiar with Jamal's nonsymbolic communication forms was present. This indicates a clear need to instruct communication partners as an integral part of Jamal's communication intervention, to ensure sufficient learning opportunities.

Maintaining and improving Jamal's motor abilities is important to ensure maximal involvement in priority daily environments and activities. Specific motor targets to be addressed across his day are 1) developing mobility with a power wheelchair; 2) positioning to provide optimal alignment and stability for active participation, and to prevent contractures and deformities; and 3) active and assisted movement, especially of the head/neck and arms, to promote participation and control in daily routines. Handling procedures to achieve appropriate alignment will be instituted immediately prior to 1) positioning changes to achieve/maintain optimal alignment in new positions (e.g., prior to positioning in standing, kneeling, and sidelying equipment); 2) facilitating active use of arms/hands, such as when reaching to obtain his coat, deflecting microswitches, indicating choices, or driving his power wheelchair; and 3) facilitating active head/neck movement during position/equipment changes, such as during transfers in/out of his wheelchair.

REFERENCES

Bates, E., Benigni, L., Bretherton, I., Camaioni, L., & Volterra, V. (1979). *The emergence of symbols: Cognition and communication in infancy.* New York: Academic Press.

Baumgart, D., Johnson, J., & Helmstetter, E. (1990). *Augmentative and alternative communication systems for persons with moderate and severe disabilities.* Baltimore: Paul H. Brookes Publishing Co.

Beukelman, D.R., & Mirenda, P. (1992). *Augmentative and alternative communication: Management of severe communication disorders in children and adults.* Baltimore: Paul H. Brookes Publishing Co.

Black, J., & Ford, A. (1989). Planning and implementing activity-based lessons. In A. Ford, R. Schnorr, L. Meyer, L. Davern, J. Black, & P. Dempsey (Eds.), *The Syracuse community-referenced curriculum guide for students with moderate and severe disabilities* (pp. 295–311). Baltimore: Paul H. Brookes Publishing Co.

Blau, A., Lahey, M., & Oleksiuk-Velez, A. (1984). Planning goals for intervention: Can a language test serve as an alternative to a language sample? *Journal of Childhood Communication Disorders, 7*(1), 27–37.

Boulton, J.E., Kirsch, S.E., Chipman, M., Etele, E., White, A.M., & Pape, K.E. (1995). Reliability of the Peabody Developmental Motor Scale in children with cerebral palsy. *Physical and Occupational Therapy in Pediatrics, 15*(1), 35–51.

Bricker, D. (Ed.). (1993). *Assessment, evaluation, and programming system for infants and children: Vol. 1. AEPS measurement for birth to three years.* Baltimore: Paul H. Brookes Publishing Co.

Bricker, D., Bailey, E.J., & Slentz, K. (1990). Reliability, validity, and utility of the "Evaluation and Programming System for Infants and Young Children" (EPS-1). *Journal of Early Intervention, 14*(2), 147–148.

Bricker, D., Gentry, D., & Bailey, E.J. (1985). *Evaluation and programming system for infants and young children (EPS-1).* Eugene: University of Oregon, Center on Human Development.

Bricker, W.A., & Campbell, P.H. (1980). Interdisciplinary assessment and programming for multihandicapped students. In W. Sailor, B. Wilcox, & L. Brown (Eds.), *Methods of instruction for severely handicapped students* (pp. 3–45). Baltimore: Paul H. Brookes Publishing Co.

Brigance, A.H. (1978). *Brigance diagnostic inventory of early development.* North Billerica, MA: Curriculum Associates.

Browder, D.M. (1991). *Assessment of individuals with severe disabilities: An applied behavior approach to life skills assessment* (2nd ed.). Baltimore: Paul H. Brookes Publishing Co.

Brown, F., Evans, I., Weed, K., & Owen, V. (1987). Delineating functional competencies: A component model. *Journal of The Association for Persons with Severe Handicaps, 12*(2), 117–124.

Bundy, A.C. (1995). Assessment and intervention in school-based practice: Answering questions and minimizing discrepancies. *Physical and Occupational Therapy in Pediatrics, 15*(2), 69–88.

Campbell, S. (1989). Review of Assessment of Behavioral Components. *Physical and Occupational Therapy in Pediatrics, 9*(2), 155–156.

Carr, E.G., Levin, L., McConnachie, G., Carlson, J.I., Kemp, D.C., & Smith, C.E. (1994). *Communication-based intervention for problem behavior: A user's guide for producing positive change.* Baltimore: Paul H. Brookes Publishing Co.

Connor, F.P., Williamson, G.G., & Siepp, J.M. (1978). *Program guide for infants and toddlers with neuromotor and developmental disabilities.* New York: Teachers College Press.

DeGangi, G. (1994). *Documenting sensorimotor progress: A therapist's guide.* Tucson, AZ: Therapy Skill Builders.

Donnellan, A.M., Mirenda, P., Mesaros, R.A., & Fassbender, L.L. (1984). Analyzing the communicative functions of aberrant behavior. *Journal of The Association for Persons with Severe Handicaps, 9*(3), 201–212.

Dunn, W. (1996). The sensorimotor systems: A framework for assessment and intervention. In F.P. Orelove & D. Sobsey, *Educating children with multiple disabilities: A transdisciplinary approach* (3rd ed., pp. 35–78). Baltimore: Paul H. Brookes Publishing Co.

Erhardt, R.P. (1982). *Developmental hand dysfunction: Theory, assessment, treatment.* Laurel, MD: RAMSCO Publishing Co.

Erhardt, R.P. (1986). *Erhardt developmental vision assessment.* Laurel, MD: RAMSCO Publishing Co.

Erhardt, R.P., Beatty, P.A., & Hertsgaard, D.M. (1988). A developmental visual assessment for children with multiple handicaps. *Topics in Early Childhood Special Education, 7*(4), 84–101.

Fisher, D., & Rodifer, K. (1996). *Peer support strategies for students with severe disabilities in an inclusive high school.* Unpublished manuscript, Interwork Institute, San Diego State University.

Folio, M.R., & Fewell, R.R. (1983). *Peabody Developmental Motor Scales.* Allen, TX: DLM Teaching Resources.

Gee, K., Graham, N., Oshima, G., Yoshioka, K., & Goetz, L. (1991). Teaching students to request the continuation of routine activities by using time delay and decreasing physical assistance in the context of chain interruption. *Journal of The Association for Persons with Severe Handicaps, 16*(3), 154–167.

Guidry, J., van den Pol, R., Keeley, E., & Neilsen, S. (1996). Augmenting traditional assessment information: The videoshare model. *Topics in Early Childhood Special Education, 16*(1), 51–65.

Haney, M., & Cavallaro, C.C. (1996). Using ecological assessment in daily program planning for children with disabilities in typical preschool settings. *Topics in Early Childhood Special Education, 16*(1), 66–81.

Hardy, M., Kudar, S., & Macdonald, J.A. (1988). *Assessment of behavioral components: Anal-*

ysis of severely disordered posture and movement in children with cerebral palsy. Springfield, IL: Charles C Thomas.

Hendrick, D., Prather, E., & Tobin, A. (1984). *Sequenced Inventory of Communication Development* (2nd ed.). Los Angeles: Western Psychological Services.

Hinderer, K.A., Richardson, P.K., & Atwater, S.W. (1989). Clinical implications of the Peabody Developmental Motor Scales: A constructive review. *Physical and Occupational Therapy in Pediatrics, 9*(2), 81–106.

Horstmeier, D., & MacDonald, J. (1975). *Environmental Pre-language Battery.* Columbus, OH: Charles E. Merrill.

Huer, M.B. (1983). *The Nonspeech Test for Receptive/Expressive Language.* Wauconda, IL: Don Johnston Developmental Equipment, Inc.

Hupp, S., & Donofrio, M. (1983). Assessment of multiply and severely handicapped learners for the development of cross-referenced objectives. *Journal of The Association for Persons with Severe Handicaps, 8*(3), 17–28.

Individuals with Disabilities Education Act (IDEA) of 1990, PL 101-476, 20 U.S.C. §§1400 *et seq.*

Linder, T.W. (1993). *Transdisciplinary play-based assessment: A functional approach to working with young children* (Rev. ed.). Baltimore: Paul H. Brookes Publishing Co.

Macdonald, C., & York, J. (1989). Regular class integration: Assessment, objectives, instructional programs. In J. York, T. Vandercook, C. Macdonald, & S. Wolff (Eds.), *Strategies for full inclusion* (pp. 83–116). Minneapolis: University of Minnesota, Institute on Community Integration.

MacDonald, J., & Nickols, M. (1974). *Environmental Language Inventory.* Columbus, OH: Charles E. Merrill.

Meyer, L., Reichle, J., McQuarter, R., Cole, D., Vandercook, T., Evans, I., Neel, R., & Kishi, G. (1985). *Assessment of Social Competence (ASC): A scale of social competence functions.* Minneapolis: University of Minnesota Consortium Institute for the Education of Severely Handicapped Learners.

Miller, L.J., & Roid, G.H. (1994). *The T.I.M.E. Toddler and Infant Motor Evaluation.* Tucson, AZ: Therapy Skill Builders.

Myers, C.L., McBride, S.L., & Peterson, C.A. (1996). Transdisciplinary, play-based assessment in early childhood special education: An examination of social validity. *Topics in Early Childhood Special Education, 16*(1), 102–126.

Orelove, F.P., & Sobsey, D. (1996). *Educating children with multiple disabilities: A transdisciplinary approach* (3rd ed.). Baltimore: Paul H. Brookes Publishing Co.

Ottenbacher, K.J. (1986). *Evaluating clinical change: Strategies for occupational and physical therapists.* Baltimore: Williams & Wilkins.

Owens, R. (1982a). Caregiver interview and environmental observation. In *Program for the acquisition of language in the severely impaired.* San Antonio, TX: Psychological Corporation.

Owens, R. (1982b). *Program for the acquisition of language with the severely impaired.* Columbus, OH: Charles E. Merrill.

Rowland, C., & Schweigert, P. (1993). Analyzing the communication environment to increase functional communication. *Journal of The Association for Persons with Severe Handicaps, 18*(3), 161–176.

Stremel, K., & Schutz, R. (1995). Functional communication in inclusive settings for students who are deaf-blind. In N.G. Haring & L.T. Romer (Eds.), *Welcoming students who are deaf-blind into typical classrooms: Facilitating school participation, learning, and friendships* (pp. 197–229). Baltimore: Paul H. Brookes Publishing Co.

Thousand, J., Fox, T., Reid, R., Godek, J., Williams, W., & Fox, W. (1986). *The homecoming model: Educating students who present intensive educational challenges within regular education environments.* Burlington: University of Vermont, Center for Developmental Disabilities.

Waryas, C., & Stremel-Campbell, K. (1982). *Placement checklist: Communication training program.* Hingham, MA: Teaching Resources Corporation.

Wesson, C.L., & King, R.P. (1996). Portfolio assessment and special education students. *Teaching Exceptional Children, 28*(2), 44–48.

Wetherby, A., & Prizant, B. (1990). *Communication and Symbolic Behavior Scales* (Research ed.). San Antonio: Special Press.

Williams, W., Hamre-Nietupski, S., Pumpian, I., McDaniel-Marx, J., & Wheeler, J. (1978). Teaching social skills. In M. Snell (Ed.), *Systematic instruction of the severely handicapped* (pp. 281–300). Columbus, OH: Charles E. Merrill.

Wolery, M., & Dyk, L. (1984). Arena assessment: Description and preliminary social validity data. *Journal of The Association for Persons with Severe Handicaps, 9*(3), 231–235.

York, J., & Vandercook, T. (1990). Strategies for achieving an integrated education for middle school students with severe disabilities. *Remedial and Special Education, 11*(5), 6–15.

6

Collaborative Individualized Education Programs

The individualized education program (IEP) is the written document that outlines a child's abilities and needs and defines the educational program designed to meet those needs. It is intended to be a planning document that shapes and guides day-to-day provision of special education and related services. The IEP document is most useful to the student and team when it reflects the integrated approach to curriculum and instruction that emanates from the collaborative team process.

Initial guidelines for developing IEPs were established in the late 1970s and reflected the educational procedures of that time. Unfortunately, many educational teams have adhered to older models of curriculum, instruction, and teamwork, which are no longer considered good practice. As a result, many IEPs still contain separate lists of strengths and needs for discrete areas of skill development (e.g., fine motor, language), recommendations for episodic and isolated related services (e.g., 30 minutes three times

a week), and goals that are too general to define the scope or priorities of the educational program (e.g., improve communication skills). Frequently each discipline submits a separate list of objectives, which are stapled together under the misconception that this creates a "team IEP" (Giangreco, 1986). When team members generate an IEP through this type of isolated, discipline-focused process, it is understandable that they will have difficulty in organizing and delivering integrated transdisciplinary services. Individual service providers may assume that they are not responsible for integrating the disparate pieces into a comprehensive, coordinated program or that someone with a greater interest will assume the responsibility. When service providers fail to design and implement integrated and coordinated educational programs, however, they unwittingly delegate to others their responsibility to students with severe disabilities and decrease the likelihood of student success. If the planners cannot integrate and coordinate the program, the recipient of the program certainly will experience difficulty. When teams design collaborative IEPs, they lay the foundation for effective service provision.

Collaborative assessment, as described in Chapter 5, is the first step in developing a team IEP. The assessment provides team members with information about student performance in priority activities in inclusive environments, including the student's specific strengths and needs for participation. From this information, the team can more easily reach consensus on educational program content, priority goals and objectives, and the type and amount of special education and related services required to address these priorities. This chapter presents strategies for 1) identifying a single, comprehensive set of educational priorities; 2) writing goals and objectives that support transdisciplinary instruction and a curriculum referenced to routines and activities in least restrictive environments; and 3) making service recommendations that promote efficient use of personnel and provision of integrated therapy services. The relationship among these three components is depicted in Figure 6.1.

The Individuals with Disabilities Education Act (IDEA) of 1990 (PL 101-476) mandates that the IEP be developed by a team.

The process will be more productive and the resulting document more meaningful when teams adopt principles of effective group decision making (e.g., Fisher, Ury, & Patton, 1991; Giangreco, Cloninger, Dennis, & Edelman, 1994; Johnson & Johnson, 1987). The first principle is that the group must have enough members to provide the necessary information but few enough so that all members participate (usually between four and eight). For students who need input from more members, it is advisable to identify a core team that assumes primary responsibility for the IEP process, including day-to-day planning and instruction. The core team also assumes responsibility for seeking needed input from members of the extended team (Giangreco, 1996b). Second, team members need to believe they have the power to make decisions about an individual student and that their decisions will not be overridden by an authority above the group. Third, members need to feel safe in discussions with their team, knowing that their input will not be negated or devalued by others. An open exchange of ideas will lead to a more inclusive and representative outcome when the group regards its diverse views as vital and negotiates resolutions, rather than suppresses conflict. Finally, the group needs sufficient time to work through the decision-making process. Adopting any new ap-

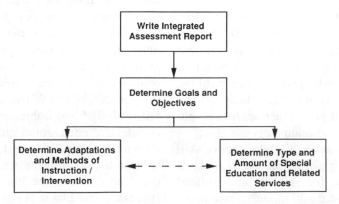

Figure 6.1.   Relationship among components of an integrated IEP.

proach initially takes more time than using familiar methods. It is also understandable that school personnel may want to work out some of their differences before meeting with parents, especially when staff are first adopting new roles, processes, and procedures. For all of these reasons, it may be appropriate and necessary for teams to have planning meetings before the formal IEP conference.

It is emphasized that the purpose of such planning meetings is not to develop the IEP. Furthermore, it is essential that parents be involved in informal planning and that they feel as influential in decision making as any other member of the team. Parents can be encouraged to participate in planning through ongoing written, telephone, and face-to-face communications with staff. Then parents meet with the core team to finalize planning. Prior to the IEP meeting, staff "suggestions" are not written onto forms or typed because this conveys finalization and lessens the parents' perception of their own power to influence team decisions.

When parents and staff develop an IEP, use of creative problem solving (Giangreco, Cloninger, et al., 1994) and consensual decision-making (Johnson & Johnson, 1987) strategies can produce a better IEP. The process includes the following steps:

- Identify the problem or need.
- Gather information.
- Brainstorm options without clarification or evaluation of ideas.
- Establish criteria to choose among options.
- Apply criteria.
- Act on decisions.
- Evaluate outcomes.

The process is consensual when all team members contribute ideas and negotiate agreement on decisions (reach consensus), rather than vote or defer to an authority fig-

ure. This process is discussed in relation to group problem solving in Chapter 8. The steps in the consensual decision-making process are discussed here with specific application to the major decisions that shape the IEP.

SELECTING PRIORITIES FOR THE IEP

As discussed in previous chapters, identifying educational priorities begins long before the team meets to develop the IEP. Through the processes of completing the IEP worksheet and the assessment planning chart, the educational team works with the family to identify the integrated environments and activities in which the student's participation is most important. During the assessment, the team identifies the student's abilities and needs in specific educational activities and gains information about how specific disabilities (e.g., cerebral palsy, visual impairment) may influence the student's overall performance. When the team engages in a collaborative assessment process and writes an integrated assessment report, a natural extension is a single, integrated list of the student's needs. Although this list is highly individualized, the team usually must make further determinations about which needs have the highest priority for the current year's IEP. Although this discussion focuses on making final decisions about what to include in the IEP, many considerations apply to the processes for determining priorities described in Chapters 4 and 5.

Students with severe disabilities often have several significant needs in the areas of posture and mobility, hand use, receptive and expressive communication, functional academics, socialization, self-care and independent living, use of leisure time, community participation, work, and related areas. Even with a collaborative team approach, it is necessary to set priorities to ensure relevance of the IEP and balance in the student's life. Although students with severe disabilities have extensive needs, they also have finite time and energy to participate in education. Furthermore, each student is first and foremost a child and family member and second a student with disabilities (Benson & Turnbull, 1986; Giangreco, 1996a). Every child needs opportunities for unstructured and self-directed activities in addition to adult-directed activities and instruction, both at home and at school. Finally, each child with severe disabilities has unique needs related to his or her individual disabilities. Rather than competing for student time and energy, seeking consensus on priorities enables teams to maximize student outcomes.

When first adopting a team approach, it is natural for service providers to see priorities from the vantage of their own discipline. A collaborative and consensual approach to determining priorities may be the most difficult aspect of designing the IEP because it frequently requires one or more team members to let go of what they view as important from their discipline's perspective. As team members observe and work with students in inclusive environments, consensus about priorities is usually achieved more easily because each team member sees the student in a functional context working to meet daily demands. Instead of asking questions such as "How can we improve gross motor skills?", team members start asking, "What is most important for this student to participate in this educational situation?" The context of the student's performance, rather than an isolated skill orientation, starts driving decisions about priorities.

The consensual decision-making process is used to establish priorities through the following steps. First, at the conclusion of the student's assessment, the team generates a list of specific needs without evaluating the appropriateness or relative importance of individual items. Evaluation at this point tends

to limit contributions. Next, the team establishes criteria to select the highest priorities from the list. It is not necessary for the team to generate new criteria for each student, but the relative importance of each criterion will vary from student to student, especially given variations in family values and perspectives. Numerous authors (Bricker & Campbell, 1980; Browder, 1991; Brown et al., 1988; Giangreco, Cloninger, & Iverson, 1993; Meyer & Evans, 1989) have identified criteria for selecting educational priorities, which include the following:

- Maintains health and vitality
- Enhances participation in current and future inclusive environments
- Increases social integration, including interactions with peers
- Has frequent or multiple applications across environments and activities
- Is essential for further development
- Is a student priority, including individual preferences or interests
- Is a family priority
- Is a priority of a significant person in a target environment

Needs meeting more than one of these criteria would be high priorities for translation into goals and objectives. Some programs use a weighting system in which needs are given points for meeting various criteria and are ranked according to their total number of points (e.g., Renzaglia & Aveno, 1986). When needs meet the previously listed criteria, final selection or ranking might reflect the following considerations:

- A majority of the team considers the need a priority.
- People, materials, and time are available to address the need.
- Real or simulated environments are available for instruction.

- Real environments are available for validation of learning.
- The student can achieve the goal relatively easily.

When needs are selected as priorities because they meet one or more of the previous criteria, it is important that the resulting goals and objectives reflect the same criteria. For example, if independent mobility is a priority for a child with muscular dystrophy, different objectives might be written depending on whether the determining criterion was "maintain vitality" or "participate in inclusive environments" or both. Illustrative criteria are discussed in this section, with examples of goals and objectives.

Maintains Health and Vitality

For students with health impairments, this criterion usually determines the highest priorities because it reflects the minimum conditions necessary for those students to participate in education. Increasing fluid and caloric intake would be a high priority for a child with inadequate nutrition and hydration. Regular changes in position would be a high priority for a student who is at risk for decubitus ulcers, contractures, and constipation. These needs might be translated into the following goals:

David will improve oral-motor patterns for eating and drinking.
Ming-Wah will communicate discomfort and request position changes.

These student goals should not be confused with "passive" or "management" goals and objectives, such as

David will receive a high-calorie dietary supplement.
Ming-Wah's position will be changed every half hour.

Downing (1988) found that students with the most severe disabilities had a high proportion of passive objectives on their IEPs. When students have significant care and management needs, it may be important to record recommendations of this type on the IEP. It is most appropriate to record them as student supports or service objectives for the team, however, because they do not address student learning (Giangreco et al., 1993).

Occasionally this health criterion has the effect of limiting educational opportunities. Because most learning presents some element of risk, teams must weigh the potential benefits against the potential risks and recall that there is dignity in risk (Perske, 1988). It is certainly appropriate to ensure safety, but adults often discover that their fears were disproportionate with reality. One mother, who had been warned not to let her daughter participate in community activities, found that her daughter actually had fewer and less severe respiratory infections when she left the "protective" environment of the special school. Another mother was relieved to see that her child could eat solid foods fairly easily, with no more risk of choking than any other child. For a child with poorly controlled seizures, the team was concerned that inclusion in general education classes would increase the likelihood of warning signs being missed. Instead, the student's close proximity to classmates resulted in ongoing, albeit inadvertent, monitoring of signs. Parents often desire a higher quality of life for their child and understand that risks accompany such opportunities. Involving parents in the discussion of risks and benefits is essential; it increases the likelihood that students will be allowed to take reasonable risks, that safeguards will be adequate, and that individuals charged with implementation will feel sufficient support during new ventures.

Enhances Participation in Current and Future Inclusive Environments

This criterion assists with selection of appropriate activities and materials, as well as specific skills and behaviors. It may be reflected in IEP goals such as

Kristen will increase her participation in kindergarten activities.

Tomas will participate in work routines in the middle school cafeteria.

Brian will select books and listen to stories in the school library.

Meg will play with her third-grade friends for 15 minutes.

Jodi will partially participate in planning and cooking a meal.

Goals and objectives that meet this criterion are also likely to meet one or more of the other criteria discussed here.

Increases Social Integration, Including Interactions with Peers

Related aspects of this criterion are that improved performance would both enhance the student's social status and increase social interactions with other students. When considering this criterion, it is often useful to include chronological-age peers without disabilities in the decision-making process. Friends are generally pleased to offer social validation (Kazdin, 1977; Wolf, 1978)—that is, to evaluate whether proposed activities and materials are socially acceptable and desirable. For example, Meg's team agreed that a priority was for Meg to play with third-grade friends. They considered the following objective:

Meg will dress and undress large dolls as a preferred leisure activity.

When Meg's friends explained that only Barbie Dolls are acceptable at their age, the team needed to consider whether Meg could readily develop the dexterity to manage Barbie Dolls or whether another leisure task would better meet the criterion of increasing social integration.

Friends of Eric, a 7-year-old boy with severe intellectual and physical disabilities, identified two specific pieces of playground equipment on which Eric should play. Their recommendation was made not because Eric could play on the equipment independently, nor even because he might like it, but because all the 7-year-olds used those two pieces of equipment.

Has Frequent or Multiple Applications Across Environments and Activities

Tracy's need to improve communication skills was previously addressed through objectives to name objects when asked "What is this?" When the team members considered the criterion of frequent/multiple applications, they modified the objective:

Tracy will request the following by pointing to and then naming
a. Preferred foods and drinks
b. Preferred leisure materials
c. Materials needed to complete assigned tasks (e.g., household chores, functional academics, clerical work)

Thus, the skill has application to mealtimes, leisure activities, and a variety of other tasks at home, school, and work. Tracy also needs to improve her ability to manipulate small objects, which has frequent and multiple applications. The team specified the important manipulation skills and materials in an objective:

Tracy will improve fine motor skills to perform the following tasks in her daily living routine:

a. Button/unbutton her coat, fasten her shoes, fasten her belt
b. Remove/replace toothpaste/shampoo cap, open soap/toothpaste cartons
c. Open milk carton, straw, and utensil packs in the cafeteria
d. Dial and touch numbers accurately on telephones to call home

When priority skills can be taught frequently in naturally occurring situations, there is little justification for removing students from integrated learning environments for isolated instruction.

Is Essential for Further Development

Some behaviors and skills are desirable primarily because they form the foundation for other skills or learning. Teams are cautioned about this criterion, however, because many people with severe disabilities have spent their lifetimes working on "prerequisites" without opportunities to learn meaningful and useful skills. Furthermore, many skills in typical developmental sequences have proven not to be valid as "prerequisites" to further development or participation. Therefore, teams must examine whether skills proposed to meet this criterion are really essential and whether teaching them would really provide greater opportunities for participation than alternative approaches, such as task adaptations. Although such skills may be legitimate prerequisites, this does not suggest they should be taught in an isolated fashion. Essential skills can be taught in the context of meaningful activities and often meet the criterion of having frequent/multiple applications.

Kim's physical therapist identified the need to improve Kim's head and trunk control. Some team members questioned this priority because Kim already used her vision and hands functionally in a variety of tasks and used good oral-motor skills during mealtime when positioned in her adapted wheelchair. After discussion, the team agreed that Kim might still achieve better control, which would increase her options for positioning, mobility, and task participation. They also agreed that objectives for improved head and trunk control could be incorporated into activities throughout the day.

Before Jamal's speech-language pathologist attended a workshop on presymbolic communication, she assumed that students must display clear communicative intent (i.e., desire to communicate) before moving toward use of an augmentative system. As a consequence, she did not facilitate use of objects or pictures as symbols before a student established intent in a wide variety of daily events. From her new information on presymbolic communication, she realized that instruction to develop communicative intent could take place within the context of existing daily routines and simultaneously with instruction to use objects, pictures, or both as communication symbols. For example, she could teach a student to signal primitive intent (e.g., hold out a cup for more juice) and to signal more complex intent with symbols (e.g., touch a picture to get a snack) at the same time. The speech-language pathologist learned that adhering to a strict progression from primitive to symbolic intent may just make it more difficult for students with severe disabilities to make the transition to more symbolic communication (Reichle, York, & Sigafoos, 1991). Furthermore, lack of demonstrated intent does not necessarily mean that students cannot learn other types of communication skills. Students with severe disabilities often lack opportunities to display intent, such as when unresponsive listeners extinguish intent or caregivers provide so much assistance during daily routines that the student does not need to display intent (Johnson, Baumgart, Helmstetter, & Curry, 1996).

Is a Student Priority, Including Individual Preferences or Interests/Is a Family Priority

Some programs use student/family priority as their primary criterion, reaffirming that the child and family are the central focus of the IEP.

> A priority for Chrissandra's mother was for Chrissandra to crawl up and down stairs because the only bathroom at home was on the second floor and Chrissandra was hard to carry. The team arranged situations at school to teach Chrissandra to climb stairs and worked with her mother on designing a home program.

> Ricardo had poor articulation because of athetoid cerebral palsy but wanted to communicate via speech, rather than a communication board. Although some team members doubted that Ricardo would ever speak intelligibly, the speech-language pathologist agreed to provide intensive training on articulation.

> Jeremy's mother wanted the team to focus on toilet training. For 2 years, team members disagreed about this priority and failed to put it on the IEP because some members considered it unrealistic. Finally, in the third year, toilet training was made a priority. After a couple of months, Jeremy's mother reported that she saw no progress and thought they should move on to other needs.

Some readers may conclude that the professionals finally "beat" this unrealistic parent, but another view is that the team might have achieved a unified effort 3 years earlier if it had started by honoring the mother's priority. Controversies often can be resolved with less conflict if the team agrees to implement an intervention, records objective data, and then evaluates results of the actual intervention, rather than continuing to speculate about possible outcomes.

Is a Priority of a Significant Person in a Target Environment

Many students with severe disabilities are being educated in inclusive school and community settings. General education teachers, employers, and others may express priorities for student performance while in inclusive environments. Some teachers place great importance on students working cooperatively and assisting each other; others want students to raise their hands and wait for assistance. Similarly, some work environments are arranged to require solitary work, whereas others promote regular opportunities for co-workers to interact for work tasks and social events. Successful placements in integrated settings require identification of these preferences, responsive instructional priorities, and thoughtful placement decisions.

WRITING GOALS AND OBJECTIVES

The IDEA specifies that an IEP "shall include . . . a statement of annual goals, including short-term instructional objectives, . . . and appropriate criteria and evaluation procedures and schedules for determining, on at least an annual basis, whether instructional objectives are being achieved" (1990, 20 U.S.C. §§ 1400 *et seq.*). Within these specifications, there are numerous variations on how to write goals and objectives for an IEP. Typically, goals describe general performance, whereas objectives outline either a scope or a sequence of skills that comprise the goal. Frequently, goals and objectives are written in ways that make it difficult to determine exactly what performance is desired, how performance is to be evaluated, and whether progress is being made (e.g., improve gross motor development as judged by therapist) (Giangreco, Dennis, Edelman, & Cloninger, 1994). Mager (1984) recommended that objectives include 1) the target behavior(s) defined in observable and measurable terms, 2) conditions under which the behaviors are performed, and 3) objective criteria to evaluate achievement. Behavioral objectives improve communication among team members and facilitate systematic and responsive instruction.

Therapists often struggle with behavioral objectives because they are concerned with qualitative aspects of performance. Although it is sometimes difficult to conceive of quality components in behavioral terms, the desired outcomes of improved quality usually can be defined. The following objectives address quality first by defining the desired performance as clearly as possible and then by specifying conditions or criteria under which the desired quality occurs. The first two objectives define quality by using social validation as an evaluation strategy (Kazdin, 1977; Van Houten, 1979; Wolf, 1978):

Ricardo will make verbal requests that can be understood by five of five friends.
Ricardo will make verbal requests that can be understood by three of five people unfamiliar with his speech.

The next two objectives address quality, partly by defining what the desired performance will look like and partly by specifying the performance conditions, that is, the type, location, and amount of prompting (or facilitation) necessary to achieve the desired performance:

After 1 minute of tone reduction and while given physical guidance at the elbow and wrist, Sonja will reach to her communication board five times without pulling back for 3 consecutive days.
With a verbal cue to relax and with support maintained at the shoulder, Sonja will reach for and grasp her electric toothbrush without pulling her shoulder up and back, for the first 2 minutes of teethbrushing on 3 consecutive days.

When writing behavioral objectives, team members' diverse perspectives are helpful to determine whether desired performance is defined clearly and to identify considerations most relevant to performance quality.

The criterion for any objective contains two components. The first reflects the standard of accuracy or fluency in any given day or evaluation period, such as "80% correct on a weekly quiz," "for 5 minutes," or "during the first two of three opportunities each day." The second component reflects the consistency of performance over time to confirm that performance is typical, rather than chance, such as "on 3 of 5 days" or "for 4 consecutive days." Unfortunately, some computer-generated IEPs have predetermined that one criterion (e.g., "80% correct for 4 of 5 days") is proper for all students and tasks. Like all other aspects of an IEP, the standards for both accuracy and consistency must be determined individually based on the student's current level of performance, the time frame for achievement, and social validity considerations (Browder, 1991; Giangreco, Dennis, et al., 1994).

Incorporating the Ecological Curriculum

The importance of an ecological curriculum as a "recommended practice" and context for integrated therapy services was discussed in Chapter 4. Because an ecological curriculum is the basis for educational priorities, the corresponding goals and objectives must maintain an ecological orientation. Therefore, IEP goals and objectives should identify the priority environments and activities in which priority skills will be used. There are two general approaches to writing such goals and objectives on the IEP.

Approach 1: Goals Specify Priority Skills; Objectives Specify Contexts for Performance Some teams find this approach easier when first moving from a developmental or functional skills curriculum to an ecological curriculum. Each goal identifies a skill or skill area; the corresponding objectives identify the educational contexts (activities and environments) in which the skill must be performed. The contexts must be derived from an ecological analysis of actual demands in priority environments, rather than from guesses or presumptions about functional activities. Goals and objectives organized in this way tend to remain discipline referenced; that is, each team member can easily write and locate the sets of goals and objectives most relevant to his or her discipline. Because the priorities of each discipline are easier to identify, so is each discipline's role in the educational program. The familiarity of this approach can be reassuring for educational team members as they adopt other changes in their model of service provision.

Examples of this approach include the following:

GOAL
Brian will improve positioning of his posterior walker to perform functional activities.
OBJECTIVES
1. When given visual cues and verbal reminders, Brian will align his walker next to the cafeteria counter and walk through the line for 3 consecutive days.
2. When given visual cues and verbal reminders in Homeroom, Brian will position his walker behind his chair and pivot into his seat, using his seat back for support, for 3 of 4 days.
3. When given visual cues and verbal reminders, Brian will position his walker to the left of his locker, open the door, and remove and hang his coat for 3 of 4 days.

GOAL
Ming-Wah will improve visual scanning and focusing to make and convey choices in daily routines.
OBJECTIVE
When positioned in her chair with her head stabilized and presented with two objects at eye level, Ming-Wah will look at each object for 1 second and focus on her preference for 5 seconds in three of four trials, on 3 consecutive days, and in each of the following situations:
1. Mealtime (choose between food and drink)

2. Free time (choose between toys for microswitch)
3. Grooming (choose sequence from washcloth, toothbrush, hairbrush)

Kristen's IEP, presented at the end of this chapter, is written using this format for goals and objectives. Kristen's mother and other team members were most familiar with a developmental approach, and they felt most comfortable when the IEP goals outlined priorities for skill development.

Although this is a vast improvement over traditional approaches that do not specify contexts for performance at all, there is danger of remaining in a discipline context rather than adopting an environmental context. If the starting point for generating priorities varies among team members, the resulting program will still be fragmented. There is also danger of contriving "functional" contexts and losing sight of those environments and activities in which performance was originally desired. Thus, opportunities to address skills might determine the activities in which students participate and limit attention to skills that support participation in inclusive school and community environments and activities. For these reasons, we encourage teams to move on to the approach decribed next.

Approach 2: Goals Specify Priority Environments and Activities; Objectives Specify Component Skills Many team members find this format difficult at first, especially for young children and children with profound/multiple disabilities. Teams become more comfortable with this approach as they focus on the team goal of teaching students to participate in inclusive community environments and as they become more versed in using an ecological approach to assessment. In the following examples, goals specify priority environments and activities, and objectives outline a cluster of skills required to reach the goal.

Goals and objectives organized in this way are the natural extension of an ecological curriculum and assessment.

GOAL
Becky will water plants at home.
OBJECTIVES
1. After being assisted once with facilitation at the pelvis, Becky will push to stand from half-kneeling, with controlled weight shift while using support from the sink edge.
2. Becky will maintain symmetrical upright trunk alignment without reminders while standing at the sink to fill the watering can.
3. Becky will use two hands to support the watering can while kneewalking from the sink to the family room.
4. Becky will follow a left-to-right sequence to water plants, with visual cues, and pour for a count of 3.
Criteria for all objectives: 8 of 10 opportunities in 1 week

This goal–objective format also matches well with the organization of secondary-level programs, when students typically change classes every 45–50 minutes. Goals reflect the various learning environments (classes), and objectives reflect the priority skills relevant for class participation.

GOAL
Tess will participate in a sixth-grade science class.
OBJECTIVES
1. Tess will read "science" from her schedule and print "science" next to the model, without overlapping letters, for 1 week.
2. When given a verbal reminder, Tess will tell other students in her science group, "I can do this, thanks," or "I need help, please" on 80% of opportunities for 1 week.
3. At the end of class, Tess will converse with a friend in a turn-taking routine by answering the friend's question and then asking a question about the preceding science activity daily for 1 week.

Jamal's IEP, presented at the end of this chapter, is written using this format. His team has fully adopted an ecological curriculum and assessment strategy and finds that this is the logical model for IEP development. It might be noted that each goal on Jamal's IEP has some objectives unique to the learning environment identified in the goal, as well as some objectives that are similar across learning environments.

MAKING SERVICE RECOMMENDATIONS

A major challenge for teams adopting a transdisciplinary and integrated therapy model is how to determine which services are necessary, how frequently, and for how long. One difficulty is that traditional service recommendations, such as "30 minutes of occupational therapy three times a week," lock therapists into rigid schedules that prevent effective integration of related services into educational programs. Many students who need occupational or physical therapy or speech-language services have been referred from early intervention or medical rehabilitation programs in which therapy is a primary service, rather than a related service. Through these primary services, the "30 times 3" approach may inadvertently be established as the only "correct" model. An analysis of variables influencing service recommendations showed that therapists recommend direct services for many reasons, but, despite rhetoric to the contrary, characteristics of the individual child proved to be the least influential factor (McWilliam & Bailey, 1994). In addition, in a primary service model, children typically receive physical therapy if they demonstrate any gross motor disabilities, occupational therapy for any fine motor or perceptual difficulties, and speech-language services for any communication problems. In educational programs, children receive these as related services, if deemed necessary to achieve IEP goals and objectives. When children move from early intervention and rehabilitation systems into educational systems, parents may view digression from the primary/direct service model as decreasing the intensity of their child's services.

Giangreco (1996b) noted that decisions about the type and amount of related services are guided by assumptions and values, although they may not be openly stated. The "more is better" approach may guide parents and benevolent professionals to advocate for extensive direct services but confuses quantity with value. In fact, providing too much service may have negative effects for students, families, and other team members. The "return on investment" approach suggests that students who are most deserving of specialized services are those with the greatest potential to improve, signaling parents and children that related services are a privilege reserved for children who might overcome their disabilities (Giangreco, 1996a). Some states and school districts have criteria for eligibility for related services, which may be used to disqualify students with severe or multiple disabilities on the basis that they are "too disabled" to benefit or will not derive sufficient benefit from the professional investment (see Rainforth & Giangreco, 1996). Such criteria are clearly contradictory to the intent of the Education for All Handicapped Children Act of 1975 (PL 94-142), the forerunner of IDEA, which gave highest priority to services for students with the most severe disabilities. This priority was reaffirmed in the case of *Timothy W. v. Rochester, NH, School District* (1989).

The third value that guides related services decision making is "only as special as necessary." Giangreco (1996b) encourages teams to consciously adopt this value, committing themselves to provide the resources that are adequate to meet each student's needs and to work together in ways that maximize the benefit of those resources.

Therefore, the challenge to educational teams is to make related services recom-

mendations that ensure 1) the desired scope, intensity, and coordination of services; 2) the flexibility for therapists to work in a variety of school, home, and community settings; and 3) accountability to students and fellow team members. Strategies to determine and document the type, amount, and form of related services are examined in the following sections. In Chapter 8, broader considerations in scheduling to meet the needs of multiple students are discussed.

Types of Related Services

In general, teams will determine which related services to recommend by matching the student's priority needs with the personnel who can meet those needs. If a student needs to improve oral-motor skills for eating, for example, a team member with expertise in feeding facilitaton must be identified. It cannot be assumed that every speech-language pathologist and occupational therapist will have the necessary skills, or that a physical therapist, teacher, or nurse does not possess the skills to address this need (Giangreco, 1996b; Rainforth & Roberts, 1996). If no one on the team has the required expertise, the team must collaborate with outside resources to expand the skills of one or more team members.

When therapists have similar skills, program coordination and efficient resource allocation can be maximized if the team agrees to use an occupational therapist or a physical therapist as the primary sensorimotor therapist. For example, Kristen needs to learn normalized movement patterns for posture, mobility, and manipulation of materials. Both the occupational therapist and the physical therapist available to support Kristen reported that they could address most of those needs. After discussing the interrelationship and relative importance of Kristen's needs, the therapists' overlapping and separate skills, and considerations such as program coordination and therapist scheduling, the team determined that the physical therapist would be the primary therapist for Kristen. In addition, the occupational therapist would consult with the physical therapist for specific needs related to hand use and sensory processing. By arranging for the occupational therapist to offer consultation, rather than a separate service, the physical therapist can integrate the occupational therapist's recommendations, devise comprehensive strategies, coordinate priorities across daily routines, and ensure more consistent program implementation.

The decision to use a primary therapist is based on similarity or overlap of therapist skills and the need to coordinate strategies to achieve priority objectives. Personnel resources and student time are not used well when team members use different strategies to achieve the same outcome, use similar strategies to achieve different outcomes, or merely duplicate services. This does not mean that there is no time when the team draws on every available resource. A high priority for Jamal is to use a communication system, but his team has not achieved much success on this goal. As the team makes decisions about types of communication systems, selection modes, positioning, prompting strategies, contexts for use, and vocabulary, input will be needed from many team members. Although they will address overlapping questions, each team member will bring unique perspectives and skills to the process. The need for input from a particular discipline during decision making does not necessarily mean the discipline will be needed to provide ongoing services, however.

This does not suggest that teachers who are highly skilled in addressing sensorimotor and communication needs should be encouraged to work without the support of therapists. Few teachers receive the same scope or intensity of training in these specialized areas as therapists. Even when teachers do have great expertise, it is inappropriate to place full responsibility for educating children with the most challenging needs on one staff member. The importance of teamwork in effective education for students with severe disabilities cannot be overemphasized.

Models of Related Services

A variety of terminology has been used to delineate the various models of service provision (see, e.g., Dunn, 1988). The choice of terms is not so important as making sure they are clearly defined and communicated to all members of the educational team. In this book, the terms *integrated therapy*, *direct therapy*, and *consultation* are used. Collaborative teamwork is necessary for any of these models to be truly effective.

Integrated Therapy   The key feature of the integrated therapy model is that therapy services are provided and then strategies associated with the disciplines providing therapy are used within the activities and environments the team deems a priority for a given student. Implementing this model requires hands-on, indirect, and transdisciplinary service components. Hands-on services by the therapist are necessary while assessing the student, determining intervention strategies, training others to use specific strategies, solving implementation problems, and modifying programs. The therapist also provides indirect services, such as providing general training, observing program implementation, monitoring performance data, and developing equipment and materials. The transdisciplinary component occurs as therapists release parts of their roles to other team members so students can receive frequent and ongoing instruction on sensorimotor, communication, and other skills in priority educational contexts in the absence of the therapist. All components of integrated therapy are ongoing processes that clearly require collaborative teamwork.

Implementing an integrated therapy approach requires therapists to break away from the traditional "30 times 3" approach to scheduling services. One approach is to add up the time typically recommended for therapy sessions over the course of a month, so as to create a large block of therapy time that could be used in more flexible time allocations during the month. Another approach is for a related services provider to co-teach with a classroom teacher for certain subjects every day. This is most likely to occur when the class has a relatively high need for that service, such as when a speech-language pathologist supports a primary class in which many children need speech, language, and/or communication development. These approaches to scheduling are discussed more thoroughly in Chapter 8.

Service recommendations specify the amount of time the therapist is needed to provide the direct and indirect services outlined previously. The recommendation for each related service is in proportion to the priorities outlined in the IEP and with consideration of which team member can competently address each priority. For example, the goals and objectives on Jamal's IEP (excerpts are provided at the end of this chapter) all reflect sensorimotor and communication needs and require input from a speech-language pathologist and an occupational or physical therapist or both. Sensorimotor and communication needs seem equal, but the team thought additional speech-language pathologist time would be needed at the start of the year to develop Jamal's new communication system. The occupational therapist was selected as the primary sensorimotor therapist because this individual had more expertise than the available physical therapist to meet Jamal's greatest needs (adaptations, use of hands/arms). The therapists, special education teacher, and special education teaching as-

sistant had worked as a collaborative team with Jamal and his family for some time, but Jamal would be working in new environments with new general education teachers and new co-workers who would need education about Jamal's needs. Based on all these considerations, the team recommended 4 hours per month of integrated speech-language services, 4 hours per month of integrated occupational therapy, and 1 hour per month of physical therapy consultation. Rather than state time recommendations in minutes per day or week, block schedules were recommended to increase the therapists' flexibility to work with Jamal and other students in their routine activities.

When first changing from direct therapy to integrated therapy, the team may want to recommend the same amount of time but state it in terms of time per month. For example, Kristen had received speech-language services for 30 minutes three times a week, occupational therapy for 30 minutes twice a week, and physical therapy for 30 minutes twice a week in her previous program. This would translate to 6 hours per month for speech-language services and 4 hours per month each for occupational and physical therapy. Kristen's parents had fought hard to get the services they thought she needed, so they were apprehensive about an unfamiliar service provision model. With explanation of the rationale for integrated therapy, assurance that therapists would be accountable for their services, and agreement that Kristen would receive the equivalent amount of therapist time, Kristen's parents agreed to try integrated therapy with 7 hours per month of integrated physical therapy and 1 hour per month of occupational therapy consultation. (The physical therapist was selected as the primary sensorimotor therapist.) The team went on to recommend 6 hours per month of integrated speech-language services for Kristen, extensive classroom support from a special education teacher, and possible support from a paraeducator, although they had growing concerns about the possibility of too much service from too many adults.

About the same time, the entire school was engaged in discussion about how to support the growing numbers of students who were eligible for speech-language, special education, and/or Title I services. After many configurations of support were considered, it was agreed that the school would try co-teaching as the principal model of classroom support (see, e.g., Rainforth & England, 1997). In this framework, Kristen's team reconsidered its recommendations and proposed that the speech-language pathologist co-teach with the kindergarten teacher 7½ hours per week (8:30 A.M.–10:00 A.M. daily), with consultation from the special education teacher if needed. This would allow the speech-language pathologist to help create a language-rich environment from which all kindergarten students would benefit, address specific speech-language needs of certain students, address Kristen's intensive communication needs throughout the week, and engage in all the components of integrated therapy described previously. Kristen's parents were satisfied that having the speech-language pathologist co-teach in kindergarten would meet Kristen's "therapy" needs, and school personnel thought it would help meet the needs of the school as a learning community. Because Kristen still needed support available all morning, a paraeducator was assigned to the class for 7½ hours per week (10:00 A.M.–11:30 A.M. daily), supervised by the kindergarten teacher with opportunities for guidance from the speech-language pathologist and physical therapist.

It might be noted that more block-scheduled time was recommended for Kristen's services than for Jamal's. Several

factors entered into these decisions. Jamal's mother was more comfortable with the concept of integrated therapy and block time recommendations because she had seen the benefits for her son in the past. Jamal's core team had worked together longer than Kristen's, so the members of Jamal's team were more skilled at collaborating with one another, infusing motor and communication instruction into educational routines, and educating others about Jamal's needs. Jamal's therapists had had more time to establish good rapport with his family. Over time, Jamal's core team also had become more familiar with Jamal's abilities and needs and knew that he would not change as quickly as when he was younger. For all of these reasons, Jamal's team was comfortable with recommending less therapist time than Kristen's team. Jamal's team did not consider Jamal less able to benefit from related services; his core team had become more efficient in the way it developed and provided services.

Integrated therapy is considered the primary model of service for most students with severe disabilities because it provides the most educationally relevant services in the least restrictive environments (Giangreco, York, & Rainforth, 1989). When teams recommend direct therapy for students with severe disabilities, it is as a support and supplement to integrated therapy.

Direct Therapy Direct therapy generally refers to hands-on treatment that is episodic and provided in isolation. Services are considered "isolated" when they occur outside the context of meaningful daily routines and activities, whether the location of those services is a therapy room, the back of a classroom, or in the midst of children without disabilities. Because synthesis and generalization of new skills cannot be assumed under these circumstances, direct services must be justified carefully and reevaluated frequently. Some common reasons for considering direct services are discussed here. Note that some of the justifications initially seem appropriate because they reflect familiar thinking about use of therapist time. When analyzed further, however, appropriateness must be questioned.

"Lizzie is changing so quickly right now that I must address new needs each time I see her." In this situation, the therapist uses treatment time most efficiently to work directly with the child, rather than teach teammates new strategies that will be outdated immediately. Even in this situation, however, the therapist regularly works with other team members in applied contexts to ensure that student needs are being addressed effectively. The therapist also works to identify a set of strategies that teammates can begin to learn, with the goal of returning to transdisciplinary and integrated services as soon as feasible.

"I haven't figured out how to handle this need." Some students present particularly challenging needs, so it may take longer to complete assessment and program planning. In addition, a therapist may be learning a new strategy to address a certain type of need, such as when Jamal's speech-language pathologist first applied her new knowledge about nonsymbolic communication to develop a communication system for Jamal. Although these may be legitimate concerns on a short-term basis, parameters must be established to avoid prolonged indecision or experimentation, which does not benefit the student.

"This needs to be done privately to maintain dignity." It may be preferable to perform procedures such as postural drainage in a private area, such as a nurse's office. Privacy, typical activities, and acceptance of disability as an individual difference are all considered when making decisions, however.

Michael has a severe tongue thrust and loses a lot of food when eating. The speech-language pathologist has established oral-motor procedures, and the team considered feeding Michael in the classroom until his eating improved. When they considered that it might be several years before Michael ate "neatly" and that he already ate in a variety of public settings, they decided he would eat lunch in the cafeteria. Michael seemed to enjoy being there, and most other students seemed to be unaffected by his eating habits. The teacher did overhear remarks about Michael's appearance and talked with those students (and teachers!) about Michael's needs and their discomforts.

"Chang is too distractible to work with in the classroom." Some students are highly distractible, but retreating to an isolated environment often addresses adults' short-term needs more than students' long-term needs. Because stimuli in the community resemble those of inclusive school settings more than a quiet therapy room, the team as a whole faces the challenge of teaching students to participate and work in distracting settings. Teachers and therapists need to engage in joint planning to ensure that they coordinate with and complement one another, rather than compete for the student's attention in the classroom. If the team decides that there is a compelling reason to address a need in an isolated setting, criteria and strategies for bringing the student back to natural settings are established at the outset.

"Yolanda isn't ready to use this skill in her daily routine yet." Many students with severe disabilities have spent months and years "getting ready" for some unspecified application of prerequisite or component skills. In most cases, the student has not had the opportunity to learn the skill in the context of routine activities but engages in those activities without good instruction on the target skill. If the team does determine a legitimate need to teach a skill out of context first, it is essential that members also set objective, attainable, and valid criteria to initiate generalization and to discontinue isolated skill instruction and then collect, analyze, and respond to data on effectiveness of the approach.

"I need to use special equipment and materials, which are only in the therapy room" or **"I use specialized techniques, which are not appropriate to teach to others"** or **"There is no meaningful context."** In all of these situations, a compelling justification is needed to remove a student from priority educational activities and environments to receive services that cannot be applied to these priorities. By refocusing on the student's needs, the team can often determine alternative strategies that can be incorporated into the student's routine activities.

"I have extra time." It is difficult to imagine that therapists might make this claim, but if therapists find that they do have extra time, they might provide additional services. Occasional opportunities can be used to conduct a specialized assessment, fit a piece of equipment, or address some other circumscribed need. Therapists must keep their services in perspective, however, and recall that direct services pull students away from classroom activities with diverse learning opportunities. Any extra services must be provided in the context of priorities identified by the team.

In summary, long-term direct therapy services are difficult to justify for students with severe disabilities, and the rationales for even short-term direct services must be examined carefully. When making decisions about service models, teams must remember that related services are provided to enable students to perform clusters of important skills with a variety of people in a variety of inclusive activities and environments. Although direct services may be appropriate

for some students for short periods, exclusive use of a direct therapy model limits students' opportunities for generalized learning. Furthermore, the rigid scheduling usually associated with the direct therapy model limits therapist flexibility to work with students in multiple contexts. Collaborative teams work together to ensure that, when direct services are recommended, services are well integrated in the student's overall program.

Consultation Consultation refers to a variety of services that are infrequent and of short duration. For a student who does not receive a related service, on request a therapist might confer with a parent, teacher, or another therapist; observe the student; make general suggestions; and/or recommend referral for evaluation. A therapist may check at specified intervals (e.g., once per marking period) on students who previously received related services and students who are considered at risk but not currently in need of services. Therapists may also be "on call" for students who do not need related services but have adapted equipment that needs periodic adjustment or repair. To ensure that IEPs provide access, rather than barriers, to needed services, some programs include a statement on all IEPs that consultation from other services may be arranged as needed. School districts have widely varying policies and procedures on consultation, however, and teams may want to influence the type and amount of support available through consultation. As with the other models of service provision, collaborative teamwork increases the relevance of consultation as a related educational service.

Documenting Therapist Responsibilities

In traditional service provision models, each team member submits the goals and objectives for which he or she is responsible, and therapists address their respective objectives during an episodic schedule of therapy. Because responsibilities are circumscribed, accountability seems clear. Actually, this system provides little accountability for achieving the ultimate goal of skill synthesis, generalization, and maintenance in applied contexts. Other systems have been devised that both increase accountability for outcomes and provide clear documentation for the IEP. Two ways to document the need for related services and to document therapist responsibilities for the IEP are suggested here. Strategies to document day-to-day service provision are described in Chapters 7 and 8.

Goals State Required Services   When IEPs are written so that goals specify priority skills, a statement of the services required to teach those skills is included. For example,

> Brian will improve positioning of his posterior walker to perform functional activities, through general education, special education, and integrated physical therapy services.

> Ming-Wah will improve visual scanning and focusing to make and convey choices in daily routines, through general education, special education, integrated occupational therapy, and integrated speech-language services.

The disciplines identified in the goal are responsible for all of the corresponding objectives because the objectives specify the contexts in which the student will perform the skill. Kristen's IEP (presented in the next section) is written in this format.

Objectives Are Followed by Required Services   When IEPs are written so that objectives specify skills that are components of priority activities, each objective is followed by a notation of services required to teach the skill. If the IEP includes a space for "Methods and Materials," the services can be listed in that space. Separate columns

can be added for each related service, with a check mark placed in the appropriate column(s) after each objective. A third option is to list the services at the end of each objective. For example,

> Tess will read "science" from her schedule and print "science" next to the model, without overlapping letters, for 1 week. (SpEd, OT)

> When given a verbal reminder, Tess will tell other students in her science group, "I can do this, thanks," or "I need help, please" on 80% of opportunities for 1 week. (GenEd, SpEd, SLP)

Jamal's IEP (presented in the next section) is written in this format.

EXAMPLES OF IEP DEVELOPMENT

The IEPs for Kristen and Jamal include service recommendations, goals, and objectives. Kristen's IEP contains a complete list of goals and objectives, whereas Jamal's includes only the goals and objectives established for Spanish class and work at Metro Insurance Agency. For brevity, neither IEP includes statements of current levels of performance, which would repeat the assessment results presented in Chapter 5.

INDIVIDUALIZED EDUCATION PROGRAM

STUDENT: Kristen F.
SCHOOL: Richmond Elementary
AGE: 5.2 years
MEETING DATE: 10/5/96
CORE EDUCATIONAL TEAM: Mr. & Mrs. F. (Parents), Jill M. (Kindergarten Teacher), Cathy R. (Special Education Teacher), Jan M. (Speech-Language Pathologist), Lisa S. (Physical Therapist), Jim D. (Occupational Therapist)
PLACEMENT: Kindergarten, 15 hours per week (8:30 A.M.–11:30 A.M.)
SUPPORT SERVICES: Speech-language pathologist as co-teacher, 7.5 hours per week (8:30 A.M.–10:00 A.M. daily); integrated physical therapy, 7 hours per month; occu-

pational therapy consultation, 1 hour per month; special education consultation, 0–1 hour per month, as needed; paraeducator, assigned to classroom 7.5 hours per week (10:00 A.M.–11:30 A.M.)

Goals and Objectives

A. Kristen will increase her independence in dressing and using the toilet through kindergarten, integrated physical therapy services, special education consultation, and a home program (developed in collaboration with family).
   1. After assisted to put her thumbs inside her waistband, Kristen will push down and pull up her pants independently.
      a. For two of four trips to the bathroom at home, on 4 of 5 days
      b. For three of three trips to the bathroom at school, on 4 of 5 days
   2. When taken to the toilet on a regular schedule at home and at school, Kristen will have no accidents for 10 consecutive days.
   3. When seated on a chair with feet and trunk supported, Kristen will remove and put on pullover tops, with prompts only at the upper arm, for 8 of 10 opportunities during 1 week.
      a. To wear sweatshirt outside at home and school
      b. To change dirty shirt after lunch at home and school
      c. At bathtime at home, 5 of 7 days
B. Kristen will improve social, receptive language, and expressive language skills through kindergarten and integrated speech-language services.
   1. When the teacher delays an already-established greeting routine, Kristen will say "hi" within 10 seconds for three of three opportunities daily, for 3 consecutive days.
      a. At the doorway on arrival
      b. Just prior to morning circle
      c. On approaching the snack table
   2. When given a verbal reminder, Kristen will say "all done" calmly and push her materials (or adult hands) away gently on each occasion when she demonstrates frustration for 4 of 5 days.
      a. In kindergarten
      b. At home

3. When given a verbal cue during routine social games, Kristen will maintain a turn-taking interaction using a toy/daily living materials with an adult, classmate, or her sister by requesting "more" for four of six turns on 3 consecutive days.
      a. Free play time at school (three opportunities)
      b. Play or other daily routines at home (three opportunities)
   4. Given a gestural cue and pictures placed in natural contexts in the classroom, Kristen will make requests by touching pictures representing her wants/needs 10 times per day for 4 of 5 days. (Vocabulary: cookie, cracker, cheese, drink, help with coat, help wash, ball, Ernie doll, paint)
   5. Kristen will choose one of two items held out to her by reaching for one item four of six times daily for 3 consecutive days.
      a. Toys during free play (four opportunities)
      b. Snack/drink (one opportunity)
      c. Materials for fine motor activity (one opportunity)
C. Kristen will improve her fine motor skills from using a palmar grasp for all objects to using palmar, lateral pinch, and thumb–fingertip grasps appropriate for the object, through kindergarten, integrated physical therapy services, occupational therapy and special education consultation, and a home program (designed with family).
   1. When cylinders are presented in a vertical position, Kristen will use a palmar grasp and neutral forearm position 8 of 10 times daily for 3 consecutive days.
      a. Crayon, marker, or pencil during small group
      b. Cup during snack/mealtime
      c. Toothbrush, brush, and lotion during grooming
   2. When reminded before presentation, Kristen will grasp cards/papers using a lateral pinch or thumb–fingertip grasp during circle and small-group work four of five times daily for 3 consecutive days.
   3. After wearing her splint for the first 10 minutes of snack time, Kristen will use a pincer grasp (one or two fingers) for finger foods for 3 consecutive days.
      a. At school, four of five bites

b. At home, four of five bites

D. Kristen will improve postural stability, trunk and lower limb mobility, and reciprocal patterns through kindergarten, integrated physical therapy, and a home program (designed with family).
  1. When reminded before activities, Kristen will assume a sidesitting position on the floor and maintain the position for a minimum of 3 minutes without additional cues for three of three activities daily for 5 consecutive days.
     a. Playtime at arrival
     b. Morning circle
     c. Playtime at departure
  2. When holding stable objects and given tactile cues at the hip, knee, and ankle, Kristen will use a reciprocal pattern to ascend from and descend to the floor for three of three activities daily for 5 consecutive days.
     a. Playtime (five opportunities)
     b. Storytime on rug (one opportunity)
     c. Gross motor activity (two opportunities)
  3. When physically assisted to position forearms in neutral with hands open and when stabilized at the shoulders, Kristen will hold large objects with two hands and carry them at least 10 feet four of five times daily for 5 consecutive days.
     a. Carry bag to cubby from classroom door
     b. Carry toys (in bins) to play area
     c. Carry materials for class job
     d. Carry materials for snack
     e. Carry book, shoes, ball, and so forth during special activities

Service Goals

A. Kristen's team will adopt co-teaching and integrated therapy models for education and related services.
  1. The core team will plan and teach collaborative lessons, integrating education and related services goals, objectives, and methods.
  2. The special educator and occupational therapist will provide consultation to the core team on a regular basis.
B. Kristen's team will investigate strategies to help her modulate background visual and auditory stimulation, with effective strategies in use by November 1.

INDIVIDUALIZED EDUCATION PROGRAM

STUDENT: Jamal W.
SCHOOL: Central High School
AGE: 17 years
MEETING DATE: 10/08/96
CORE EDUCATIONAL TEAM: Mrs. W. (Parent), Mr. M. (Foster Parent), John K. (Special Education Teacher), Lisa W. (Occupational Therapist), Ann E. (Speech-Language Pathologist), Jake S. (Special Education Teaching Assistant), Sandy B. (Transition Coordinator), Ben G. (General Education Teacher)
PLACEMENT: General education, 18 periods per week (Spanish, Earth Science, Home Economics, Choir/Horticulture, Media Center, plus Homeroom and Lunch); community-based instruction, 12 periods per week (work–study)
SUPPORT SERVICES: Special education, 35 hours per week (from teacher, teacher assistant, and teacher-supervised peer support); integrated speech-language services, 6 hours per month (decreasing to 4 hours per month on November 1); integrated occupational therapy, 4 hours per month; physical therapy consultation, 1 hour per month

Goals and Objectives
[Excerpts for Spanish and Community Work Experience]

A. Jamal will participate in Spanish I class.
  1. Jamal will vocalize to get the attention of others when he wants to communicate for at least three of four planned communication opportunities daily for 5 consecutive days. (GenEd, SpEd, SLP)
  2. In response to a question, Jamal will choose a partner for group by maintaining gaze toward a selected classmate nearby for 10 seconds for two of two opportunities daily for 3 consecutive days. (GenEd, SpEd, SLP)
  3. Jamal will make requests by scanning a communication display and selecting the desired object/symbol for four of

four opportunities on 5 consecutive days. (GenEd, SpEd, SLP)

   a. To request assistance moving his supine stander during group transitions (two opportunities)

   b. To request the tape recorder to tape the joke of the day (one opportunity)

   c. To request assistance placing the joke cassette tape in his bag (one opportunity)

4. Jamal will turn on/off the tape recorder with a light touch switch for 100% of two or more opportunities per day for 3 consecutive days. (GenEd, SpEd, OT)

B. Jamal will participate in his community work experience at Metro Insurance Agency using work and work-related skills.

1. When provided with stability around his right shoulder, Jamal will operate an adapted joystick with his hand to drive his wheelchair down the hallway to/from the insurance agency within 3 minutes for two of two opportunities for 3 consecutive workdays. (SpEd, OT)

2. Jamal will drop his head to remain relaxed while his jacket is put on/taken off for two of two opportunities on 3 consecutive workdays. (SpEd, OT)

3. Jamal will vocalize to get the attention of others when he wants to communicate for 100% of at least 10 planned communication opportunities daily for 3 consecutive workdays. (SpEd, SLP)

4. Jamal will make requests by scanning a communication display and selecting the desired object/symbol at least 10 times daily for 3 consecutive workdays. (SpEd, SLP)

   a. To request the tape recorder to play the joke of the day from Spanish class (two opportunities)

   b. To request assistance to initiate/maintain/terminate various work tasks (at least eight opportunities)

5. Jamal will turn on/off the tape recorder to tell a joke by deflecting a paddle switch for 100% of at least two opportunities per day for 3 consecutive workdays. (SpEd, OT)

6. When given stabilization around his right shoulder, Jamal will raise and lower his forearm to depress an adaptive device to date-stamp mail, stamping mail at a rate of two pieces per minute for 2 of 3 workdays. (SpEd, OT)

Service Goals

A. Jamal's team will develop an augmentative communication system that will enable him to socialize as well as express wants and needs, with the basic system set up by November 1.

B. Jamal's team will establish a positioning schedule to use positions other than sitting whenever possible, by October 1.

REFERENCES

Benson, H.A., & Turnbull, A.P. (1986). Approaching families from an individualized perspective. In R.H. Horner, L.H. Meyer, & H.D.B. Fredericks (Eds.), *Education of learners with severe handicaps: Exemplary service strategies* (pp. 127–157). Baltimore: Paul H. Brookes Publishing Co.

Bricker, W.A., & Campbell, P.H. (1980). Interdisciplinary assessment and programming for multihandicapped students. In W. Sailor, B. Wilcox, & L. Brown (Eds.), *Methods of instruction for severely handicapped students* (pp. 3–45). Baltimore: Paul H. Brookes Publishing Co.

Browder, D.M. (1991). *Assessment of individuals with severe disabilities: An applied behavior approach to life skills assessment* (2nd ed.). Baltimore: Paul H. Brookes Publishing Co.

Brown, L., Shiraga, B., Rogan, P., York, J., Zanella Albright, K., McCarthy, E., Loomis, R., & VanDeventer, P. (1988). The "why" question in programs for people who are severely intellectually disabled. In S.N. Calculator & J.L. Bedrosian (Eds.), *Communication assessment and intervention for adults with mental retardation* (pp. 139–153). Boston: Little, Brown.

Downing, J. (1988). Active versus passive programming: A critique of IEP objectives for students with the most severe disabilities. *Journal of The Association for Persons with Severe Handicaps, 13*(3), 197–201.

Dunn, W. (1988). Models of occupational therapy service provision in the school system. *American Journal of Occupational Therapy, 42*(11), 718–723.

Education for All Handicapped Children Act of 1975, PL 94-142, 20 U.S.C. §§ 1400 *et seq.*

Fisher, R., Ury, W., & Patton B. (1991). *Getting to yes: Negotiating agreement without giving in.* New York: Penguin Books.

Giangreco, M.F. (1986). Delivery of therapeutic services in special education programs for learners with severe handicaps. *Physical and Occupational Therapy in Pediatrics, 6*(2), 5–15.

Giangreco, M.F. (1996a). "The stairs didn't go anywhere!" A self-advocate's reflections on specialized services and their impact on people with disabilities. *Physical Disabilities: Education and Related Services, 14*(2), 1–12.

Giangreco, M.F. (1996b). *Vermont interdependent services team approach (VISTA): A guide to coordinating educational support services.* Baltimore: Paul H. Brookes Publishing Co.

Giangreco, M.F., Cloninger, C.J., Dennis, R.E., & Edelman, S.W. (1994). Problem-solving methods to facilitate inclusive education. In J.S. Thousand, R.A. Villa, & A.I. Nevin (Eds.), *Creativity and collaborative learning: A practical guide to empowering students and teachers* (pp. 321–346). Baltimore: Paul H. Brookes Publishing Co.

Giangreco, M.F., Cloninger, C.J., & Iverson, V.S. (1993). *Choosing options and accommodations for children (COACH): A guide to planning inclusive education.* Baltimore: Paul H. Brookes Publishing Co.

Giangreco, M.F., Dennis, R.E., Edelman, S.W., & Cloninger, C.J. (1994). Dressing up your IEPs for the general education climate: Analysis of IEP goals and objectives for students with multiple disabilities. *Remedial and Special Education, 15*(5), 288–296.

Giangreco, M.F., York, J., & Rainforth, B. (1989). Providing related services to learners with severe handicaps in educational settings: Pursuing the least restrictive option. *Pediatric Physical Therapy, 1*(2), 55–63.

Individuals with Disabilities Education Act (IDEA) of 1990, PL 101-476, 20 U.S.C. §§ 1400 *et seq.*

Johnson, D.W., & Johnson, F. (1987). *Joining together: Group theory and group skills* (2nd ed.). Englewood Cliffs, NJ: Prentice Hall.

Johnson, J.M., Baumgart, D., Helmstetter, E., & Curry, C.A. (1996). *Augmenting basic communication in natural contexts.* Baltimore: Paul H. Brookes Publishing Co.

Kazdin, A.E. (1977). Assessing the clinical or applied importance of behavior change through social validation. *Behavior Modification, 1*(4), 427–451.

Mager, R. (1984). *Preparing instructional objectives* (2nd ed.). Belmont, CA: Lake Publishing Co.

McWilliam, R.A., & Bailey, D.B. (1994). Predictors of service delivery models in center based early intervention. *Exceptional Children, 61*(1), 56–71.

Meyer, L.H., & Evans, I.M. (1989). *Nonaversive intervention for behavior problems: A manual for home and community.* Baltimore: Paul H. Brookes Publishing Co.

Perske, R. (1988). *Circles of friends: People with disabilities and their friends enrich the lives of one another.* Nashville, TN: Abingdon Press.

Rainforth, B., & England, J. (1997). Collaborations for inclusion. *Education and Treatment of Children, 20*(1).

Rainforth, B., & Giangreco, M.F. (1996). Limitations to degree of involvement: A reply to Parette, Hourcade, and Brimer. *Physical Disabilities: Education and Related Services, 15*(1), 1–6.

Rainforth, B., & Roberts, P. (1996). Physical therapy. In R.A. McWilliam (Ed.), *Rethinking pullout services in early intervention: A professional resource* (pp. 243–265). Baltimore: Paul H. Brookes Publishing Co.

Reichle, J., York, J., & Sigafoos, J. (1991). *Implementing augmentative and alternative communication: Strategies for learners with severe disabilities.* Baltimore: Paul H. Brookes Publishing Co.

Renzaglia, A., & Aveno, A. (1986). *Manual for administration of an individualized, functional curriculum assessment procedure for students with moderate to severe handicaps.* Charlottesville: University of Virginia.

Timothy W. v. Rochester, NH, School District, 875 F.2d 954 (1st. Cir. 1989).

Van Houten, R. (1979). Social validation: The evolution of standards of competency for target behaviors. *Journal of Applied Behavior Analysis, 12*(4), 581–592.

Wolf, M.M. (1978). Social validity: The case for subjective measurement or how applied behavior analysis is finding its heart. *Journal of Applied Behavior Analysis, 11*(2), 203–214.

7

Collaborative Instructional Design

The previous chapters in this section have addressed team tasks that lay the foundation for the team's ultimate responsibility: providing instruction. As used in this chapter, the term *instruction* refers to the intervention methods associated with each of the various disciplines, as well as the more multifaceted interventions designed by an educational team collectively. In educational settings, the instructional strategies associated with each discipline are among the most significant contributions team members make in the collaborative teamwork process. Because integration of multiple and varied perspectives increases the magnitude of instructional effectiveness, a team's diversity truly is its strength. The collaboration and interdependence required for intentional planning, systematic decision making, role release, and ongoing role support are challenging, particularly for new teams. Professionals who previously worked autonomously must reach consensus with others from varied personal and professional backgrounds representing different philosophies and experiences. As discussed in other chapters, the ultimate goal of education for students with severe disabilities is to enable them to participate in a variety of home, school, and community routines, with a variety of people, using the supports and responding to the cues that occur naturally in those settings. Therefore, the benefits of professional contributions are maximized when a team assumes responsibility for integrating instructional strategies from the component disciplines into a coordinated approach that can be applied in a variety of natural environments and activities.

As more and more students with severe disabilities become members of inclusive educational communities, the scope of domains represented in the team increases, thereby increasing the number of domains with which team members must familiarize themselves. In addition to the methods used by special educators and related services providers, team members must learn the philosophy, curriculum, and methods for the schools, grades, and general education classes in which students with disabilities are enrolled. Most of us have some idea of what occurs in general education classrooms, from working in schools, having our own children who attend schools, and going through 12 years of school ourselves. Often those ideas are vague or skewed, however, and may not represent current recommended practice in general education. For example, many special educators infer that classroom teachers rely heavily on "seatwork" and adult-centered expository approaches. Although elementary school teachers may use worksheets to drill academic skills and secondary teachers may lecture while students take notes, few educational leaders would advocate these as the only or primary approaches to instruction. In fact, the general education reform literature advocates instruction designed to reach children and youth of diverse cultures, abilities, and learning styles; actively involve them through hands-on and exploratory activities, interdisciplinary and thematic instruction, and community-referenced instruction; and guide them to work individually, with partners, and in small groups to learn the academic curriculum as well as the social curriculum of peacemaking and social responsibility (Falvey, 1995; Fisher, Sax, Pumpian, Rodifer, & Kreikemeirer, in press; Udvari-Solner & Thousand, 1996). Schools and classrooms reflecting these practices are ideal for educating students with severe disabilities.

Despite these positive developments, differences between general education and special education may still arise regarding issues of who directs learning experiences, who is the source of knowledge, and how the learning environment is structured. In reformed classrooms, teachers play subtle roles while students discover principles and construct meaning for themselves. In traditional special education programs, adults are more likely to direct children to learn specific information or skills, often before application in real-life contexts. This disparity is a challenge to teams, partly because the traditional separation of disciplines has

> resulted in such different approaches to teaching and learning that communication is awkward at best, and completely blocked at worst. It is as if these teachers are operating on different spheres of discourse, often using the same words only to misunderstand each other—dampening, even extinguishing the respect, trust, and exchange so necessary to real collaboration. (Ferguson, Meyer, Jeanchild, Juniper, & Zingo, 1992, p. 223)

Failure to identify and address these issues will have a negative impact on not only the professionals on the team, but also the students with disabilities, their families, and the paraeducators who support them ("Inclusive Education," 1994).

One strategy recommended to address differences in professional cultures is to use the value of "only as special as necessary" to guide instructional planning (Giangreco, 1996b; Taylor, 1988). This means that Kristen will participate in the same activities and receive the same instruction as other children in kindergarten *as long as that meets her needs*. Kristen's team will provide the specialized services, materials, and instructional strategies that she needs to succeed and achieve, *but not more than necessary* because that would actually interfere with her education and be a poor use of resources (Giangreco, 1996b). Jamal's high school classes and work–study program were selected because of opportunities they provided, and he will participate as typical students do whenever possible. His team will provide physical adaptations, curriculum modifications, more intentional teaching strategies, and direct support from special education and related services personnel as needed to improve his participation and achievement. Although several frameworks for making adaptations to include students with severe disabilities in general education have been suggested (see, e.g., Ryndak, 1996; Salisbury, Mangino, Petrigala, Rainforth, & Syryca, 1994; Udvari-Solner, 1994), all start by asking whether the student could participate and learn without adaptations. Only when this cannot occur does the team consider small increments of change in specific aspects of instruction. This is not an all-or-nothing decision; it varies with the student's abilities and the features of typical classroom activities, along with stage of collaboration among the classroom teacher and other team members.

The Individuals with Disabilities Education Act (IDEA) of 1990 (PL 101-476) defines related services in terms of assisting children to benefit from special education, defines special education as "specially designed instruction," and defines both special education and related services in terms of services and supports, rather than places (20 U.S.C. §§ 1400 *et seq.*). Most students with severe disabilities do require "specially designed instruction" to develop new abilities. Therefore, it is important to consider instructional strategies that will assist students with severe disabilities to participate and learn more than if they did not receive special education and related services, still guided by the value of "only as special as necessary."

Systematic instruction is considered a recommended practice in special education. In early forms, adults controlled most aspects of the learning situation, including task selection, preparation of materials, use of direct prompts, determination of acceptable performance, and schedules of rewards (see, e.g., Snell, 1978). Difficulties inherent in this approach have been identified, however, and more effective alternatives validated.

For example, after intensive use of direct instruction, students with severe disabilities often needed additional instruction to respond to natural cues and correction procedures (Ford & Mirenda, 1984). When programs for young children with mild to severe disabilities used less structure and more incidental teaching procedures, the children spent more time engaged in learning activities, which translated to greater achievement (McWilliam, Trivette, & Dunst, 1985). Young children with disabilities developed more language in classrooms by using more natural consequences, more opportunities for peer interaction, more shared control of topics, more contingent access to materials, more nonverbal prompts, and less teacher descriptive talk (Schwartz, Carta, & Grant, 1996). When paraeducators in inclusive classrooms used fewer verbal, gestural, and physical prompts and directed students with severe disabilities to use photo activity schedules, the students worked more independently on priority activities (Hall, McClannahan, & Krantz, 1995). Making life arrangements that are enriched and support self-determination has proven to effect as much change as, but require less sophistication than, "contingency management" for children and adults with highly challenging behavior (Meyer & Evans, 1989; Risley, 1996). Although systematic instruction has proven necessary and effective for teaching children and adults who were once considered "ineducable" (Kauffman, 1981), a combination of environmental, incidental, and systematic strategies that are neither intrusive nor stigmatizing can be the most effective and least restrictive alternatives. It is only through continually questioning the appropriateness and effectiveness of instructional strategies, considering new alternatives, and collecting and analyzing data on outcomes of implementation that teams can make good decisions about instruction.

Systematic instruction and data-based decision making represent a quantitative and analytical approach, sometimes characterized as the "science" of education. In contrast, the "art" is evident when a master practitioner acts intuitively, sometimes leaving observers awestruck at the master's apparently magical abilities (Watts, 1983; Yonemura, 1986). The artist is highly creative, easily devising new strategies, making decisions about what strategy will be effective under which circumstances, and solving problems before a problem is even evident to others. Whereas analytical approaches to instruction have been criticized as too rigid and technocratic, intuitive approaches have been criticized as too idiosyncratic. After working with and observing scores of practitioners, we have concluded that the most effective members of educational teams use a combination of intuitive and analytical approaches. Analytical approaches enable practitioners to define needs and possible solutions and to evaluate the effectiveness of those instructional solutions; intuitive approaches are necessary when solutions are not predictable, when traditional solutions are not effective, and to alert the team that something does not seem right and needs attention. The combination enables team members to expand their current practice and discover more effective strategies but also enables them to analyze what did or did not work and why. This is particularly important when a team of people is responsible for supporting students. In contrast with autonomous practitioners, individuals working as members of a collaborative team must be able to identify and communicate the reasoning and subtle cues that influenced their decisions, the specific steps that elicited the desired participation from a student with learning difficulties, and the precise distinctions between the strategy that worked and

the ones that did not. Only when this occurs can a collection of people operate as a team that consistently guides students with disabilities, rather than confuses them.

As child-centered experiential approaches to education have evolved, qualitative and systemic (i.e., holistic, context-based) approaches to assessment have gained popularity. This approach to assessment differs from the running records kept by many teachers and the treatment notes traditionally written by therapists because it entails systematic documentation of socially significant changes in children's behavior in natural settings (Schwartz & Olswang, 1996). Together, analytical and systemic data tell how much a child's performance has changed, what factors did or did not influence the change, and how the change affects the quality of life for the child and others (i.e., family, friends, staff). Without the qualitative aspect of assessment, teams may inadvertently teach important skills in ways that do not improve, or actually interfere with, quality of life (Giangreco, 1996a). Using a blend of analytical and systemic data to evaluate student performance and program efficacy is discussed later in this chapter.

Just as a blend of analytical and systemic data is useful for instructional decision making, a blend of teaching strategies is useful to ensure that instruction is both normalizing and effective. This chapter provides an overview of principles and strategies of systematic instruction and illustrates how they can be combined with strategies associated with the disciplines of occupational therapy, physical therapy, and speech-language pathology. Examples also incorporate strategies rooted in general education instructional design, such as self-direction, incidental teaching, and cooperative learning, which promote academic and social inclusion of students with severe disabilities. Figure 7.1 shows the steps that collaborative teams follow in designing instructional programs.

PRINCIPLES OF SYSTEMATIC INSTRUCTION

Considerations in design of systematic instruction include how often and where instruction will occur, how the student will be prepared for instruction, what system and type of cues and prompts will be used to elicit the desired performance, what adaptations will be used to enhance performance, and how performance will be assessed. Each of these questions is addressed here. Albano (1983) found that written instructional procedures and student performance data were essential tools for communication among members of educational teams. As programs for students with disabilities become more decentralized, team members experience even greater need for efficient alternatives to face-to-face meetings. To facilitate such communication, this chapter includes a variety

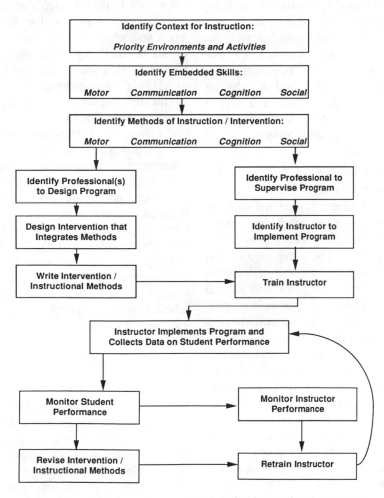

Figure 7.1.   Steps to design comprehensive instructional programs.

of formats for writing procedures and re-cording data. This chapter provides only an introduction to the extensive information currently available on systematic instruction, however, and readers are referred to other sources such as Browder (1991), DeGangi (1994), Johnson, Baumgart, Helmstetter, and Curry (1996), McLean, Bailey, and Wolery (1996), Ottenbacher (1986), Powell et al. (1991), and Snell (1993) for more thorough discussions of instructional strategies, data collection, and data analysis procedures. Guidelines for making decisions about who will provide instruction and how instructors are prepared to provide collaborative in-struction are presented in Chapter 8. The im-portance of home–school communication was discussed in Chapter 3, and this chapter offers examples of how home and school can communicate regularly about the most important and meaningful aspects of the child's performance.

How Often and Where Will Instruction Occur?

As discussed in Chapter 2, students with se-vere disabilities tend to learn new skills slowly and have difficulty transferring learn-ing to new situations. The conclusion of that discussion was that, to be effective, instruc-tion must be provided frequently in natural situations. The traditional approach of pro-viding massed trials (many repetitions in a short time period, e.g., 10 times in 30 min-utes) addressed the need to accelerate learn-ing but usually occurred in artificial con-texts, and thus hampered application and generalization of skills. Distributed trials (repetitions spread over a longer time pe-riod, e.g., 1 day) support instruction in a va-riety of applied settings and are as effective as massed trials to promote skill acquisition if equal numbers of learning opportunities are provided (Mulligan, Lacy, & Guess, 1982). When planning instruction based on

distributed trials, however, there is danger that instruction on priority skills may get lost in the bustle of the daily routine and will not receive sufficient attention. Therefore, the team must plan intentionally to ensure sufficient instruction. An effective planning strategy is to construct a matrix in which skills corresponding to individualized edu-cation program (IEP) objectives are listed on one axis, the day's schedule of activities is listed on the other axis, and instructional op-portunities and considerations are noted in the matrix (Guess & Helmstetter, 1986). An activities–skills matrix for Kristen shows when and where she will receive instruction on all her IEP objectives (see Figure 7.2). Kristen's team found the matrix invaluable to get the "big picture" of how her IEP would be implemented during her daily routine. The matrix also reaffirmed the importance of integrating methods from all disciplines into instruction because sen-sorimotor and communication interventions were needed throughout every day.

For any activity or routine, the team may wish to examine opportunities or priorities more closely and begin planning for instruc-tion. One strategy is to use the same activity or task analysis as was used for the ecolog-ical inventory and student assessment (see Chapter 5). Jamal's team developed a daily schedule listing times of each class or activ-ity, the supports needed for participation (people, materials, positioning), and the ob-jectives to be addressed during each period. This schedule was a logical extension of his IEP, which listed skills to be taught during priority activities (see Chapter 6). A portion of Jamal's schedule is shown in Figure 7.3. Another strategy is to use a related services planning sheet to focus particular attention on the general outcomes of occupational therapy, physical therapy, and speech-lan-guage pathology, which were discussed in Chapter 4. The planning sheet contains col-

Time and Activity	Pants down/up	Use toilet	Pullover top	Say "hi"	Reject task	Request "more"	Make requests	Choose Item	Palmar grasp	Pincer grasp	Sidesit	Stand and kneel	Two hand carry
Objectives from IEP													
8:30 A.M. Arrival	X		X	X	I		help coat						bag
Bathroom		X			I		help wash						
Jobs					I								materials
Free play					I	three times	Ernie, paint	four times (toys)			X	four times	toys
9:00 A.M. Opening				X	I		G	G		X			
9:30 A.M. Story					I		G	G	marker		X	one time	
9:50 A.M. Gross motor					I	G	G				G	two times	G
10:10 A.M. Bathroom	X	X			I		help wash						
10:20 A.M. Fine Motor					I	G	paint	one time	marker	X			G
10:45 A.M. Snack			X	X	I		cookie, cracker, cheese	one time	cup	after wearing splint			materials
11:15 A.M. Bathroom	X	X	X		I		help wash		tooth-brush				
Clean up							Ernie		lotion		X	one time	
11:30 A.M. Departure			G		G		help coat					G	G
Specials			G	G	G		G	G	G		G	G	X

Figure 7.2. Activities–skills matrix for Kristen. (X, provide instruction; I, as incidents arise; G, generalization opportunity.)

Student: Jamal W.   Schedule for: Tuesday/Thursday   Week of:

Time and Activity	Supports	Objectives	Performance	
			Tues.	Thurs.
	Assistant: Jake	Greet friends (loud voice)		
7:15 A.M.	Stretch elbows, shoulders	Relax for coat off (drop head)		
Locker	Hang out with friends	Answer yes/no (gaze 5 sec)		
	Assistant: Jake	Stand 5 sec		
7:30 A.M.	Stretch knees, shoulders	Use toilet (Y/N)		
Restroom	Check appearance	Request assist (scan board)		
	Peer support (informal)	Vocalize for attention		
7:45 A.M.	Position: WC	Answer yes/no (gaze 5 sec)		
Homeroom		Drive WC 100 ft in 3 min (hall)		
	Position: WC	Vocalize for attention		
8:05 A.M.	Peer: Sean	Choose partner		
Spanish	Make script for class; arrange tape recorder and switch	Make requests (scan board)		
		Paddle switch		
9:00 A.M.	Assistant: Jake to drive to class and position in supine stander	Drive WC 100 ft in 3 min (hall)		
		Stand 1 hr		
Home and Careers	Informal peer support in class	Vocalize for attention		
		Make requests (scan board)		

Figure 7.3.   Daily schedule for Jamal. (WC, wheelchair.)

umns to note transitions, positions, participation, comprehension, expression, and social interactions for one student in multiple activities or multiple students in one activity. The planning sheet is particularly useful when teams are either trying to increase the type and amount of instruction during an activity or trying to establish balance among competing needs. Kristen's team used the planning sheet to examine the morning arrival and play routine, which presented so many opportunities for instruction that there was a danger of trying to do too much. Besides Kristen, there are also children with mild disabilities who receive instruction during these routines, so the planning sheet helped the team keep a perspective on the needs of all the children. The priorities to be addressed during this routine are shown in Figure 7.4.

When classroom activities are not sufficiently predictable or detailed for the team to make corresponding plans for students with disabilities, Ryndak (1996) suggests developing "generic instructional plans." These plans offer a menu of options that can be matched to classroom activities as they arise. Ryndak (1996) offered examples of generic plans for academic activities. Similar plans can be developed to address basic sensorimotor and communication needs in a variety of contexts. Figure 7.5 shows generic plans for TJ, an elementary school student with severe physical disabilities. These plans were developed at the start of the school year to remind TJ's new paraeducator of abilities she should expect him to use and strategies she could use to facilitate his academic and social inclusion.

How Will the Student Be Prepared for Instruction?

Preparation for instruction would address each student's abilities and needs related to sensory processing, positioning, movement, and communication. Preparation related to sensory processing would take into consideration both the student's sensory systems and the sensory characteristics of the natural environment in which participation would typically occur, as illustrated in Kristen's assessment in Chapter 5. Dunn (1996) identified qualities of each of the sensory systems that can be used to gain a student's attention (arousal/alerting descriptors) and other qualities that can help organize the student's sensorimotor system to perform functional tasks successfully (discriminating/mapping descriptors). These qualities are outlined in Table 7.1. Although therapists have traditionally addressed sensory needs through isolated therapy, eliciting much criticism from educators (see, e.g., McWilliam, 1996), Dunn points out the feasibility and importance of addressing sensory processing difficulties in the context of everyday activities. Furthermore, the recommended strategies are consistent with "conventional wisdom" and practices upheld by many other disciplines, although rationales often differ because of different knowledge bases. Sensory processing strategies are incorporated into examples throughout this chapter.

Preparing the student might also entail proper positioning for participation. Research shows that even children without identified disabilities perform academic tasks more successfully when they use chairs and desks that fit properly (Sents & Marks, 1989). It is essential that students with physical disabilities have regular position changes and use positions that match the physical demands of activities (Rainforth & York-Barr, 1996). The following questions will help teams identify positions and positioning equipment that are most appropriate for students with severe disabilities:

- What positions do peers without disabilities use when they engage in the activity?

Teachers: Jill and Jan   Activity: Free Play   Time: 8:30 - 9:00

Students	Transitions	Positions	Participation	Interactions	Comprehension	Expression
Kristen	Ask another child to walk with Kristen to toy shelves. Staff prompt her to kneel + stand correctly.	On floor: sidesitting. No w-sitting	Carry baskets and large toys with 2 hands	Continue taking turns by requesting "more" (Involve other children and remind them to use gestural dictionary)	Follow specific directions: Go get —. Give me —. Let's go to —.	Chose activity from 2 pictures (before leaving cubby). Choose one of 2 toys by reaching for preference (Involve other children.)
Turner		Discourage w-sitting (OK occasionally)	Use finger tip grasp and refined release (Provide high visual contrast between toy + play surface.)	Use toys for representational play (e.g., for playing house, dress up, cars)	Respond to verbal directions given to the group.	Tell playmate choice of toys or next activity. (Remind playmate to ask what he wants to play with.)
Rex					Respond to verbal directions given to the group.	Bring toy to another child and ask "Want to play with —?"

Positioning Options	
When members of TJ's group/class	TJ can
sit at desks	sit in his wheelchair at his desk or sit in the adapted classroom chair at his desk
sit at the computers	sit in his wheelchair, with the tray
stand at the sand table	stand straddling your leg (Make sure his feet are resting on the floor, so he can bear weight on his legs.)
sit on the floor	sit on the floor tailor style, with support from you or from friends when they learn how or sit in the red floor sitter, with you moving back so friends can sit near him or lie on the floor, especially when other kids are playing with toys (not board games) (Make sure TJ is in a central spot so he can see and kids are closer to him than adults.)
Mobility Options	
When TJ needs to go somewhere in	TJ can
the classroom	be carried (With the room so crowded, it's harder to lift TJ than carry him, so carry him to another seat rather than pushing the chairs around.) or ride in his wheelchair or roll or crawl (on the rug)
the hallways	use his wheelchair or walk in his walker
Communication Options	
When TJ needs to communicate	TJ can
yes/no	Touch one section of his communication board | No	I need a break	Yes
:(| | :)	 (If he answers too slowly during lessons, ask Mrs. Hill for concepts/language she will ask him about so he can rehearse answering with you before the lesson.)
choices	Gaze at your hand that represents the option he prefers (Say: "TJ, do you want ___ [hold up your right hand to represent his first choice] or ___ [hold up your left hand to represent his second choice]?")
his own ideas	Scan his electronic keyboard with his head pointer

Figure 7.5.   Generic instructional plans for TJ.

Table 7.1. Reasons for incorporating various sensory qualities into integrated intervention programs

Sensory system	Arousal/alerting descriptors	Discriminating/mapping descriptors
For all systems	*Unpredictability:* To develop an increasing level of attention to keep the child interested in the task/activity (e.g., change the position of the objects on the child's lap tray during the task)	*Predictability:* To establish the child's ability to anticipate a programming sequence or a salient cue; to decrease possibility to be distracted from a functional task sequence (e.g., use the same routine for diaper changing every time)
Somatosensory	*Light touch:* To increase alertness in a child who is lethargic (e.g., pull cloth from child's face during Peekaboo)	*Touch pressure:* To establish and maintain awareness of body parts and body position; to calm a child who has been overstimulated (e.g., provide a firm bear hug)
	Pain: To raise from unconsciousness; to determine ability to respond to noxious stimuli when unconscious (e.g., flick palm of hand or sole of foot briskly)	*Long duration:* To enable the child to become familiar, comfortable with the stimulus; to incorporate stimulus into functional skill (e.g., grasping the container to pick it up and pour out contents)
	Temperature: To establish awareness of stimuli; to maintain attentiveness to task (e.g., uses hot foods for spoon eating and cold drink for sucking through a straw)	*Large body surface contact:* To establish and maintain awareness of body parts and body position; to calm a child who has been overstimulated (e.g., wrap child tightly in a blanket)
	Variability: To maintain attention to or interest in the task (e.g., place new texture on cup surface each day so child notices the cup)	
	Short duration: To increase arousal for task performance (e.g., tap child on chest before giving directions)	
	Small body surface contact: To generate and focus attention on a particular body part (e.g., tap around lips with fingertips before eating task)	

Vestibular	*Head position change:* To increase arousal for an activity (e.g., position child prone over a wedge) *Speed change:* To maintain adequate alertness for functional task (e.g., vary pace while carrying the child to a new task) *Direction change:* To elevate level of alertness for a functional task (e.g., swing child back and forth in arms prior to positioning him or her at the table for a task) *Rotary head movement:* To increase arousal prior to functional task (e.g., pick child up from prone [on stomach] facing away to upright facing toward you to position for a new task)	*Linear head movement:* To support establishment of body awareness in space (e.g., carry child around the room in fixed position to explore its features) *Repetitive head movement:* To provide predictable and organizing information; to calm a child who has been overstimulated (e.g., rock the child)
Proprioception	*Quick stretch:* To generate additional muscle tension to support functional tasks (e.g., tap belly muscle of hypotonic muscle while providing physical guidance to grasp)	*Sustained tension:* To enable the muscle to relax, elongate, so body part can be in better position for function (e.g., press firmly across belly muscle while guiding a reaching pattern; add weight to objects being manipulated) *Shifting muscle tension:* To establish functional movement patterns that contain stability and mobility (e.g., prop and reach for a toy; reach, fill, and lift spoon to mouth)
Visual	*High intensity:* To increase opportunity to notice object; to generate arousal for task (e.g., cover blocks with foil for manipulation task) *High contrast:* To enhance possibility of locating the object and maintaining attention to it (e.g., place raisins on a piece of typing paper for prehension activity) *Variability:* To maintain attention to or interest in the task (e.g., play rolling catch with a clear ball that has moveable pieces inside)	*Low intensity:* To allow the visual stimulus to blend with other salient features; to generate searching behaviors because characteristics are less obvious (e.g., find own cubby hole in back of the room) *High similarity:* To establish more discerning abilities; to develop skills for naturally occurring tasks (e.g., scoop applesauce from beige plate) *Competitive:* To facilitate searching; to increase tolerance for natural life circumstances (e.g., obtain correct tools from equipment bin)

(continued)

Table 7.1. (continued)

Sensory system	Arousal/alerting descriptors	Discriminating/mapping descriptors
Auditory	*Variability:* To maintain attention to or interest in the task (e.g., play radio station after activating a switch) *High intensity:* To stimulate noticing the person or object; to create proper alerting for task performance (e.g., ring a bell to encourage the child to locate the stimulus)	*Rhythmic:* To provide predictable and organizing information for environmental orientation (e.g., sing a nursery rhyme while physically guiding motions) *Constant:* To provide a foundational stimulus for environmental orientation; especially important when other sensory systems (e.g., vision, vestibular) do not provide orientation (e.g., child recognizes own classroom by fan noise and calms down) *Competitive:* To facilitate differentiation of salient stimuli; to increase tolerance for natural life circumstances (e.g., after child learns to look when her name is called, conduct activity within busy classroom) *Noncompetitive:* To facilitate focused attention for acquiring a new and difficult skill; to calm a child who has been overstimulated (e.g., move child to quiet room to establish vocalizations) *Low intensity:* To allow the auditory stimulus to blend with other salient features; to generate searching behaviors since stimulus is less obvious (e.g., give child a direction in a normal volume)
Olfactory/gustatory	*Strong intensity:* To stimulate arousal for task (e.g., child smells spaghetti sauce at lunch)	*Mild intensity:* To facilitate exploratory behaviors; to stimulate naturally occurring activities (e.g., smell of lunch food is less distinct, so child is encouraged to notice texture, color)

From Dunn, W. (1996). The sensorimotor systems: A framework for assessment and intervention. In F.P. Orelove & D. Sobsey, *Educating children with multiple disabilities: A transdisciplinary approach* (3rd ed., pp. 70–72). Baltimore: Paul H. Brookes Publishing Co.; reprinted by permission.

- What positions allow for proximity to peers?
- Which of these positions allow easy view of and access to activity materials and equipment?
- Which positions allow or promote the movement needed to perform critical tasks?
- What positions provide alternatives to overused postures or equipment?
- If positioning equipment is required, is it unobtrusive, cosmetically acceptable, and not physically isolating?
- Is the positioning equipment safe and easy to handle?
- Is the equipment selected and modified to match individual needs?
- Is the equipment available in or easily transported to natural environments?

Prior to Jamal's team asking these questions, he had spent nearly his entire school day sitting in his wheelchair. The team quickly recognized that some alternative positioning was necessary. The members also discovered that, contrary to popular opinion, high school students did not sit for hours at a time, and other options were feasible for Jamal. Recommended positions are now included in his daily schedule, under Supports, as shown in Figure 7.3. In addition to position changes that were a natural part of Jamal's personal hygiene routine, the team determined that he could use a sidelying position during Choir and standing position during Home Economics, Horticulture, and Earth Science classes. The team was not satisfied yet with the frequency or duration of alternatives to sitting, particularly on Jamal's work–study days, and was committed to work on creating more options.

Although sidelying is not a normal position for school, the team found that Jamal appreciated the change and the position enabled him to "sing" in Choir. Because Jamal was prone to upper respiratory infections, the team was pleased that the position and activity improved his breathing, even if only temporarily. The Choir teacher was equally pleased that Jamal was able to participate. Once given an explanation, the other students were very accepting of and interested in how Jamal was positioned. Because transporting equipment through the school and changing Jamal's position was easier with extra people, the team recruited classmates for assistance. The occupational therapist and physical therapist established training activities to teach students to help lift and transfer Jamal safely. (See Inge & Snell [1985] for an example of a systematic instructional program that could be used in this way.) The Special Education teaching assistant who accompanied Jamal to Home Economics, Choir, Horticulture, and Earth Science was then able to ask for assistance from a student who had been taught to help lift Jamal. In addition to teaching students and staff a variety of lifting, transferring, and positioning strategies, the occupational and physical therapists devised checklists, diagrams, and photographs as reminders of how to use the strategies properly with various students. The reminders were attached to equipment or posted on walls unobtrusively in the areas where staff would usually reposition students with physical disabilities.

Another way that students with physical disabilities might be prepared for instruction is by normalizing their tone (York & Weimann, 1991). Most frequently, this means that a student with spasticity has his or her tone reduced by some type of slow, rhythmic movement. In isolated therapy models, therapists often have done this by using special equipment such as bolsters or therapy balls. Both Kristen's team and Jamal's team found they could accomplish the same goal in a more integrated fashion. For example, one of Kristen's objectives was to rise to stand

and lower to kneel by stepping up or down with one foot at a time. Without intervention, spasticity caused her to keep both knees together and push her weight over the inner side of her ankles to get on and off her feet. During the kindergarten play routine and other daily activities, Kristen frequently moved between kneeling and standing spontaneously, so the team needed an incidental teaching strategy to normalize her tone and facilitate reciprocal movement. The team agreed on how it would prepare Kristen verbally for the physical intervention (e.g., "Kristen, let me help you stand up, one foot at a time") and how it would reinforce her (e.g., "That was great! One foot at a time"). The physical therapist taught classroom staff to identify when Kristen was getting ready to change positions, separate Kristen's knees to facilitate a normal standing or kneeling position, reinforce the position by pressing down through her hips, hold her knees apart and shift weight as she changed position, and then reinforce the new position by pressing down through her hips (see Figure 7.6). In addition to stick figure diagrams, the physical therapist provided a datasheet to re-

mind staff of the procedures, to record Kristen's performance, and to monitor the number of opportunities provided for Kristen to learn this new pattern (see Figure 7.7). When therapists develop useful diagrams, they may wish to file them for use with other students and staff. Commercial packages of diagrams to guide positioning and handling are also available (e.g., Jaeger, 1987; Ossman & Campbell, 1990).

Jamal was expected to improve use of his arms and hands for tasks such as turning on the tape recorder in Spanish class, stamping mail at Metro Insurance Agency, and driving his wheelchair. After working on these tasks for a few days, team members reported back to the occupational therapist that Jamal continued to be "stiff" and seemed to resist participation. In response, the occupational therapist established a warm-up procedure of tone normalization, stretching, and coactive movement to prepare Jamal to use his arms and hands (see Figure 7.8). To evaluate its effectiveness, the procedure included a system for data collection. As with Kristen, the warm-up was done as an integral part of the activities in which Jamal needed to use

Steps 1, 2, & ✱   Steps 3&4   Steps 5&6   Steps 7, 8, & ✱

Figure 7.6.   Stick figure diagrams to remind staff how to prompt Kristen to rise to stand. Steps 1 through 8 and * are detailed in Figure 7.7.

Student: Kristen F.   Program: Kneel to stand
Initial Instruction: Kristie, go one foot at a time.
Prompts and Scoring:
  3 = spontaneous
  2 = touch/tap body part
  1 = grasp body part, passive move
  0 = grasp body part, resisted movement
Time Delay between Prompts:
          3 seconds

Movement sequence	Prompt at:	9/16	9/23	9/30	10/7	10/14	10/21	10/28
1. Hold furniture with two hands	No physical prompt	3	3	3	3	3	3	3
2. Kneel - knees apart, hips straight	Inner side knees, top front and lower back of pelvis	1	1	1	2	1	2	2

✱ Reinforce position by pressing down on hips for 5 seconds.

3. Shift weight over one knee.	Opposite hip	1	1	2	2	2	2	2
4. Lift opposite knee, place foot in front, keep knee out to side.	Back and inner side leg, just above knee	0	0	0	0	1	1	2
5. Shift weight over forward leg.	Both sides of pelvis	1	1	2	2	2	3	2
6. Straighten front hip and knee, keeping weight forward.	Top front and lower back of pelvis	1	2	2	3	3	2	3
7. Slide other foot forward and place.	Heel	2	2	2	2	3	3	3
8. Stand - knees apart, hips and knees straight	Front and inner sides of knees, back of hips	0	0	1	2	1	2	2

✱ Reinforce position by pressing down on hips for 5 seconds.

POSSIBLE SCORE = 24 TOTAL SCORE =	9	10	13	16	16	18	19
# TIMES TAUGHT TODAY	//// 4	++++ / 6	++++ /// 8	++++ /// 8	++++ /// 8	++++ // 7	++++ /// 8

Figure 7.7.   Performance scoring datasheet for Kristen.

Student:	Jamal
Date:	10-16
Contexts:	Drive wheelchair, stamp mail, clothing on/off, personal care activities, turn on/off tape recorder, and other hand/arm use.

Positioning

Jamal: Standing or sitting, as specified for activity. Right elbow and forearm supported on tray.

Instructor: Standing facing Jamal on his right side. Left hand cupped firmly around top outside part of Jamal's right shoulder. Right hand cupped firmly around underside of elbow and upper forearm.

Preparation

1. While maintaining a firm hold around Jamal's shoulder, gently shake the arm from the elbow until you feel a release of the muscle tension (usually about 2 to 5 seconds).

2. As the tension releases move the shoulder into a rounded forward position, the elbow into a straighter position, and the forearm into a position so the palm of the hand faces downward.

3. Hold the arm in this more forward and elongated position for 2 to 5 seconds. Then allow the arm to relax a little, but maintain a firm hold at the shoulder and elbow.

4. Repeat steps 2-3 until the arm remains in the forward and elongated position. Maintain control at the shoulder only (approximately 5 to 10 repetitions).

5. With your right hand, hold firmly under Jamal's wrist and hand. Shake the hand/wrist gently. As tension releases, continue to move wrist and fingers into a slightly extended position.

Active Movement

1. **Coactive practice**: Maintain firm hold around right shoulder. Initiate movement of his elbow into extension. Pause slightly (but maintain hold) to allow Jamal the opportunity to continue active extension himself. Guide completion of movement as necessary to perform the designated task.

2. Repeat 3 times.

3. **Active movement** (with maintained control at shoulder): Repeat practice sequence but remove control at elbow after Jamal starts to extend his elbow.

4. **Error correction**: Reinstate control from elbow and assist to complete facilitated movement pattern.

Data

1. **Preparation**: Number of repetitions required for relaxed and elongated position to be achieved.

2. **Coactive Practice**: Score (+) for the practice opportunities in which Jamal completes active elbow extension while instructor maintains hold.

3. **Active movement**: Score (+) for the opportunities in which Jamal completes active elbow extension without the instructor maintaining control at elbow.

4. **Function/application**: Score (+) for the opportunities that active extension results in sufficient movement to perform the designated task.

Figure 7.8.   Generic procedure to prepare Jamal to use his arms.

his hands. The occupational therapist worked with all staff members to ensure that they could use the procedure effectively. In the process, they reviewed the written procedure, clarified terminology, and selected key words that would cue staff to remember the most relevant aspects of the procedure.

Another way students might be prepared for an activity is through communication about the day's schedule, upcoming transitions, choices available in an activity, and changes in the routine. Kristen's team determined that she was likely to become upset when she was confused about the sequence of activities, such as on days the class went to special activities. To help communicate these changes to Kristen, she was given a sweatband to wear to gym, bells to wear to music, or a smock to wear to art just prior to leaving for the activity. When Kristen develops an association between the objects and corresponding events, the team will incorporate these cues into a picture schedule (see, e.g., Stremel & Schutz, 1995). The team also started a "gestural dictionary" (Beukelman & Mirenda, 1992) that "defined" Kristen's gestures, facial expressions, and vocalizations and suggested appropriate ways for children and adults to respond to Kristen as a successful communicator before she gets frustrated. Kristen's classmate, Brad (who was not identified as having disabilities), often became upset during the transition from playtime to opening group. The team discovered that he did much better when he could anticipate the end of playtime by being told that cleanup would start in 1 minute, at which time a kitchen timer would go off. The team did not think a formal program was needed for any of these procedures; members simply implemented practices that seemed to assist Kristen and Brad. The procedures enable the students to anticipate upcoming events and participate actively, rather than fight to control confus-

ing events. In Brad's case, the team acted as a classroom support team, preventing the type of crisis that often results in student referral to special education (Hayek, 1987; Pugach & Johnson, 1995).

What System and Types of Cues and Prompts Will Be Used to Elicit the Desired Performance?

There are extensive combinations of verbal, visual, and physical prompts that can be individualized to meet the learning needs of each student. Although verbal prompts are often considered the least intrusive and physical prompts the most intrusive, the number, type, and sequence of prompts that are effective depend on the task to be performed and the type of prompts to which the student responds (see Effgen, 1991; Powell et al., 1991). For example, the movement procedures outlined for Kristen and Jamal in Figures 7.7 and 7.8 rely on a range of physical prompts to elicit the desired performance. Jamal understands verbal directions and Kristen responds well to gestures, but verbal and gestural prompts were not effective to elicit the desired movements, nor would they be easy to fade from tasks of this type. So the occupational and physical therapists, knowledgeable about movement facilitation techniques, worked with the team members knowledgeable about systematic instruction to delineate individualized systems of physical prompts. One of Kristen's communication programs (see Figure 7.9) uses a sequence of a gesture, then an indirect verbal prompt and a gesture, and finally physical guidance. One of Jamal's communication programs (see Figure 7.10) uses an indirect verbal prompt ("Do you want to tell me something?") with a direct but complex verbal prompt ("When I touch what you want, look at my eyes"), followed by a direct verbal prompt ("Look at your board"). One of Jamal's student co-workers at Metro

Student: _____Kristen_____   **Date :** _10-6_____

Program: _____Requests_____

Instructional Procedures

Setting, Grouping, Positioning	• Adults and children should model use of pictures for communication with Kristen throughout daily routines. Classmates should be encouraged to talk about the pictures, touch them, match them to real objects, and so forth.
Equipment/Materials	• Pictures placed around the classroom where corresponding activities occur
Initial Instruction and Prompt	• Teacher announces the activity to all students (natural cue). • When Kristen approaches the activity associated with a picture, an adult directs her attention to the picture by pointing at it.
Correct Response	• Kristen touches the picture.
Time Delay and Correction	• Wait 5 seconds. If no response say, "Kristen, do you want _____?" and point to the picture. • Wait 5 seconds. If still no response, manually guide her hand to touch the picture.
Reinforcement	• Natural consequence-obtain object/activity • Social- Touch the picture while saying, "Great, you touched _____, so here's _____."
Frequency to Teach	• Daily, at least 10 opportunities throughout the day
Frequency of Data	• Tuesdays and Fridays
Type of Data	• Record type of performance for each opportunity provided -- (N)Natural cue only, (P)Point, (V)Verbal prompt, (G)Guide.
Criterion for Change	• Success of plan -- 10 times per day with pointing cue only for 4 out of 5 days • Failure of plan -- physical guidance needed on more than 50% of trials for 4 out of 5 days

Projected completion date: ___11-23_____
Actual completion date: _____
Comments:

Figure 7.9. Communication program for Kristen.

Insurance Agency, whose independence was limited by his reliance on frequent verbal directions, is learning to use a pictorial checklist as the least intrusive prompt to perform his job. In these situations, speech-language pathologists had vital roles in helping their teams identify the type and order of language cues appropriate for individual students.

When using a sequence of increasing assistance, a good rule of thumb is to select two or three prompts for the prompting sequence. The first prompt would be as close as possible to a natural cue; the student may not respond to this prompt at the start of instruction but is expected to learn the prompt during the school year. The second prompt would provide greater assistance but would not consistently elicit the desired performance from the student at the start of instruction. The final prompt in the sequence would increase assistance but provide the

Student:_____Jamal W._____   **Date** : 10-9_____

Program:____Scanning_____

The emphasis of this objective is on learning to scan rather than initiation of communication, which will be addressed at a later date.

Instructional Procedures

Setting, Grouping, Positioning	• Spanish I class in supine stander or w/c, grouping varies with activity. • Daily after the opening exercise (request to move). • Daily after being repositioned for the joke of the day (request tape recorder). • Daily immediately after the joke of the day (request to put tape in bag). • Daily before the team activity (request to move).
Equipment/Materials	• Hinged Plexiglas display, that attaches to his stander or wheelchair, 4 clear plastic pockets attached to the display, object/symbol (e.g., a scrap of fabric from his bag and a picture of his bag) to put on the display
Instruction and Prompt	• Classmate stands near Jamal and announces the next activity. • "Jamal, do you want to tell me something on your board? When I touch what you want, look at my eyes." (Classmate gestures toward his/her eyes.) • Classmate points to the 4 plastic pockets one at a time (3 empty) manually, pausing for 3 seconds at each pocket.
Correct Response	• Jamal looks at the classmate's eyes when he/she touches the object/symbol.
Time Delay and Correction	• If Jamal looks up at the wrong time or doesn't look within three seconds say, "Let's try again, look at your board." Repeat scanning and say, "Here's (object/ symbol)," when the object/symbol is reached. • If Jamal still does not succeed, repeat the above cues along with a slight physical prompt to his chin to lift his eyes to yours.
Reinforcement	• Natural consequences -- Classmate touches the object/symbol again, reiterates Jamal's message, and responds by touching the object/symbol and saying, "Oh you want some help with the tape recorder," and then assisting Jamal with the activity.
Frequency to Teach	• 4 opportunities daily
Frequency of Data	• Tuesdays and Thursdays
Type of Data	• Record type of performance for each opportunity provided -- (+) scanned correctly, (0) error or no response. • Note number correct per day.
Criterion for Change	• Success of plan -- 4 out of 4 correct for 5 consecutive days • Failure of plan -- $\leq$ 2 out of 4 correct for 5 consecutive days

Projected completion date:____11-9_____
Actual completion date: _____
Comments:

Figure 7.10.   Communication program for Jamal. (W/C, wheelchair).

minimum amount needed to ensure the desired performance. Using more than three prompts would make the student wait too long before experiencing success. Another component of a prompting sequence is a time delay, a brief waiting period before giving the next prompt (see Snell, 1993). A time delay may be as little as 1 second for a student who moves quickly and makes frequent errors. A student with a severe physical disability may need as long as 10 seconds to initiate a motor response. A time delay of between 2 and 5 seconds is appropriate for most students and tasks, but individualized decisions are needed even within this range. During initial learning, delays longer than 10 seconds are rarely effective because they encourage distractions. When students have learned skills but do not use them spontaneously, delays of 15 seconds have been used to elicit responses (Halle, Marshall, & Spradlin, 1979).

Although it is best to individualize the prompting sequence to both the student and the objective, some students benefit from a generic prompting sequence that can be used until specific instructional programs are developed. For example, Kristen's classmate, Rex, did not follow directions when expectations were not clear and consistent. After the third day of school, the team agreed to use the following prompting sequence with Rex:

> Give a general verbal instruction to the group (e.g., "It's time to sit in the story circle on the rug").
> Wait 5 seconds.
> Face Rex at eye level; give a specific verbal direction (e.g., "Rex, please go sit on the rug now").
> Wait 5 seconds.
> Tell Rex you will help him; gently take his hands/shoulders and physically guide him if necessary.

The team's intent was not to force compliance but to make sure the members' expectations were expressed clearly and consistently, enabling Rex to choose participation over resistance and confrontation. After 1 week, Rex was responding to specific verbal directions. By the end of September, he was following group directions as consistently as other children in the class.

For his community work experience, Jamal needed varied types and levels of assistance to perform the steps in his job of stamping the mail. Rather than try to determine one prompting sequence for the entire task, the team determined the preferred prompts for each step in the task analysis and noted them on the datasheet (see Figure 7.11). Periodically the team, including the teaching assistant who went to the worksite, reviewed Jamal's performance and updated the preferred prompts. Because the team was also concerned with Jamal's rate of production, the datasheet included space for this information.

There are countless formats for recording information about instructional procedures to ensure that all team members understand and use the same method to achieve an objective. In addition to the prompting sequence, procedures should include the type and schedule of reinforcement, the frequency at which to teach the skill, the frequency at which to collect data, the type of data to be collected, and criteria to revise the instructional procedure.

What Adaptations Will Be Used to Enhance Performance?

Adaptations can take many forms (Baumgart et al., 1982; York-Barr, Rainforth, & Locke, 1996). The form most familiar to therapists involves modifying materials or providing special equipment. Jamal's team had an assistive device built to enable him to stamp mail at Metro Insurance Agency (see Figure 7.12). A pictorial checklist enables Jamal's co-worker to perform his job independently. Jamal's and Kristen's augmentative com-

Position: Sitting in wheelchair at workstation
Materials: Date stamp, adaptation, mail, pictures of materials in plastic pockets

Procedure	Jamal's response	Date	Date	Date	Date	Date
A. SCAN PICTURES TO OBTAIN MATERIALS						
1. Say, "Do you want to tell me something on your board? When I touch what you want, look at my eyes."	Scans for date stamp.					
2. Point to each of 4 pockets (3 empty), pausing for 3 seconds at each.	Scans for adaptation.					
	Scans for stack of mail.					
B. STAMP MAIL						
1. **Preparation:** Refer to generic preparation procedure for arm use. T maintains shoulder and elbow control.	Relaxes arm in elongated position.	# repetitions required ___	# repetitions required ___	# repetitions required ___	# repetitions required ___	# repetitions required ___
2. **Coactive practice:** T initiates movement, maintains shoulder and elbow control.	Completes active movement into elbow extension.					
3. **Active movement:** T maintains shoulder control only.	Initiates and completes active movement into extension.					
4. **Depress stamping adaptation:** T places hand on adaptation, maintains shoulder control only.	Initiates and completes depression of adaptation.					
5. **Slide mail off adaptation:** T places hands on top of pieces of mail, initiates lateral movement, maintains shoulder control only.	Completes lateral movement to slide mail off pile.					

Repeat steps 4-5 until the pile of mail is stamped. If needed, repeat steps 1-30.

Figure 7.11. Community work program for Jamal.

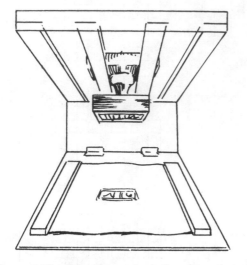

Figure 7.12. Stamping adaptation (Developed by Kathy Zanella Albright; from York-Barr, J., Rainforth, B., & Locke, P. [1996]. Developing instructional adaptations. In F.P. Orelove & D.J. Sobsey, *Educating children with multiple disabilities: A transdisciplinary approach* [3rd ed., p. 147]. Baltimore: Paul H. Brookes Publishing Co.; reprinted by permission.)

munication systems are both adaptations. The options outlined in TJ's generic instructional plans (see Figure 7.5) offer several more examples of adaptations.

Another form of adaptation involves modification of task sequences so steps are skipped or completed with assistance. Jamal is expected to drive his power wheelchair in uncongested hallways, and he is given physical assistance as both an adaptation and a teaching strategy. In congested areas such as classrooms, someone else pushes Jamal's chair. Jamal's team agreed that "put on coat" is not an appropriate goal for Jamal, but members do expect him to partially participate by dropping his head, a position in which his arms relax and others can remove his jacket more easily. (See Snell, Lewis, & Houghton [1989] for full discussion of a similar plan.) Jamal is not expected to point to symbols on his communication board, but when someone else points to the symbol he

wants to communicate, Jamal can confirm that with his eyes. In each of these instances, personal assistance was planned as an adaptation.

Personal assistance can be given by family members, by staff, or, in inclusive settings, by peers without disabilities. Jamal's co-workers at Metro Insurance Agency and his classmates at school are encouraged to provide needed assistance. They were taught when, how, and how much to assist Jamal so he both completes the immediate task and improves his performance over time. Some of Jamal's teachers use cooperative learning groups, a sound instructional strategy that allows Jamal's classmates to achieve their own academic goals while supporting his participation and learning (Hunt, Staub, Alwell, & Goetz, 1994; Thousand, Villa, & Nevin, 1994). Jamal's school also has a formal peer support program, separate from special education, which the team used to support Jamal in some of his classes. (See Fisher & Rodifer [1996] for a description of this system.) Kristen has an IEP objective to carry objects with both hands. During playtime, however, the team has opted both to teach this skill and to encourage her to hand materials to a peer who will carry them for her. Kristen's friends are being taught to help make decisions about which situations are better for each approach. As other issues arise, Kristen's classmates help find solutions while practicing their emerging skills in creative problem solving, a strategy taught district-wide to help all students adapt to a changing world (see, e.g., Giangreco, Cloninger, Dennis, & Edelman, 1994).

Although certain types of adaptations may be associated with particular disciplines, it is the team that decides whether an adaptation is warranted. York-Barr et al. (1996) discussed the following considerations that can assist a team with decisions about adaptations:

- Will the adaptation increase active participation in the activity?
- Will it allow the student to participate in an activity that is preferred or valued by the student, friends, or family members?
- Will it continue to be useful and appropriate as the student grows older and starts using other environments?
- Will it take less time to teach the student to use the adaptation than to teach the skill directly?
- Will the team have access to the technical expertise to design, construct, adjust, and repair the adaptation?
- Will use of the adaptation maintain or enhance related motor and communication skills?

An adaptation is a strategy, like a prompt, that is one component of an instructional procedure. Therefore, when an adaptation is warranted, team members will provide instruction, assess performance, and conduct responsive program modifications (including modifications of the adaptation), just as they do with other instructional procedures. Furthermore, as with other "artificial" strategies, adaptations are faded as soon as it is possible and efficient to do so.

How Will Performance Be Assessed?

Student performance on IEP objectives and the effectiveness of instructional procedures must be assessed regularly through ongoing data collection. Schwartz and Olswang (1996) recommended scheduling data collection into weekly lesson plans and staff assignments. Quantitative data on skill acquisition are collected once a week, often enough to accurately monitor student performance without being burdensome and consistent with the schedule of data collection for students without disabilities (e.g., quizzes, homework in different subject areas). In a collaborative team approach, any

member of a student's team could collect data on motor or communication performance. During individual or small-group instruction, the instructor would usually collect data. During large-group instruction, one adult might lead the lesson while another supports individual students and collects data. One way that therapists can monitor student performance is to review the data that other team members have collected. During their scheduled time with a class, therapists might also collect data as a reliability check. Thus, regular data collection promotes communication about student performance and program effectiveness.

The data collected for an objective should provide relevant information about student performance. Duration, latency, frequency, distance, rate, and number correct all provide relevant information about some types of performance, but not all types. Several instructional procedures presented in this chapter provide information about the type of prompts needed to perform tasks successfully. When a score is assigned to each prompt, this type of data collection is termed *performance scoring*. The advantage of performance scoring over simply recording the type of prompt is that performance on the complete task can be summarized with a numerical score. The total score does not provide information on specific aspects of performance; rather, it shows a trend in overall performance. The datasheet for Kristen's "kneel to stand" program (see Figure 7.7) presents an example of performance scoring. Once data are collected and summarized, graphing the data is recommended for accurate analysis and responsive program modification.

Deciding when to modify an instructional procedure is expedited by establishing two types of performance criteria. The "success criterion" indicates that the student has achieved an intermediate objective and a more challenging procedure or criterion should be established. The "failure criterion" indicates that the instructional procedure has not been effective and must be revised. (*Note:* Because the special education team is responsible for designing effective instruction, it is the procedure that has failed, rather than the student.) These criterion lines are marked on the graph so it is easy to compare desired and actual performance. To be used for responsive decision making, data must be collected, graphed, and compared with criteria regularly (i.e., at least weekly). If data are collected only once a week, the frequency of data collection can be increased temporarily as a student approaches the criterion established by the team. The graph of Jamal's performance driving his power wheelchair illustrates that the first instructional procedure was not effective but that he made steady progress af-

ter the team modified its approach (see Figure 7.13).

A simple strategy for timely communication about student performance is to keep a supply of short fill-in-the-blank notes (see Figure 7.14). When the teaching assistant who worked with Jamal on driving his wheelchair noticed that Jamal was not making satisfactory progress, he completed a program change note and put it in the occupational therapist's mailbox. When the therapist received the note, she made it a priority to observe this program during her next regularly scheduled time with the class. Based on observation and discussion with the teaching assistant, the therapist tried the warm-up procedure discussed previously in this chapter, put the procedure in writing, and circulated the completed program change note to relevant team members. When Jamal reaches the success criterion,

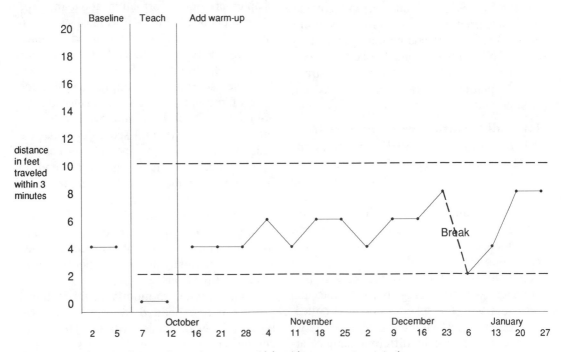

Figure 7.13.   Graph of Jamal's performance driving his power wheelchair.

PROGRAM CHANGE NEEDED	PROGRAM CHANGE MADE
Date: 10-12	Date:
To: Lisa W. (OT)	To:
From: Jake S. (Teaching Assistant)	From:
Student: Jamal W.	Student:
Program: Driving wheelchair	Program:
Reason change is needed: ___ criterion met _X_ no progress ___ other (specify)	Reason change was met: ___ criterion met ___ no progress ___ other (specify)
Comments/suggestions: He's not doing as well as during baseline. He seems interested but he gets real stiff and seems to resist my prompts.	Comments/suggestions:

PROGRAM CHANGE NEEDED	PROGRAM CHANGE MADE
Date: 10-12	Date: 10-16
To: Lisa W. (OT)	To: Jamal W.'s team
From: Jake S. (Teaching Assistant)	From: Lisa W.
Student: Jamal W.	Student: Jamal W.
Program: Driving wheelchair	Program: Stamping mail, driving wheelchair, turning on tape recorder
Reason change is needed: ___ criterion met _X_ no progress ___ other (specify)	Reason change was met: ___ criterion met _X_ no progress ___ other (specify)
Comments/suggestions: He's not doing as well as during baseline. He seems interested but he gets real stiff and seems to resist my prompts.	Comments/suggestions: Jamal does much better when relaxed and stretched before asked to use his hands. I'll work with each of you to use warm-up procedure (attached).

Figure 7.14. Program change notes regarding Jamal.

the teaching assistant will send another note to the therapist so the program can be revised quickly.

Schwartz and Olswang (1996) noted that quantitative data, although an important aspect of ongoing student assessment, may not provide a complete picture of student performance. They advised identifying "systemic" or holistic questions that might be answered through other types of data, such as focused anecdotal reports, daily records of a student's "standouts" (most outstanding performance) and "stickouts" (most problematic performance), periodic interviews, periodic questionnaires or ratings, videotapes, and permanent products. These items are consistent with entries recommended for student portfolios (Wesson & King, 1996). For example, Kristen's team members devised a way to collect quantitative data on pulling to stand. Although they considered videotaping her performance on a regular basis, the quantitative approach seems less intrusive and provides details they want at this point. They did agree to videotape Kristen quarterly, however, to provide a more global view of her motor performance. Jamal's team wants specific information about his ability to scan a communication display, but the members also wonder if developing this ability improves his social integration, so once a month team members ask classmates without disabilities and co-workers at Metro Insurance specific questions about Jamal's communication and social interactions. These videotape and interview data, along with other quantitative and qualitative data, help paint full pictures of student performance and guide decisions about instruction.

How Will Home and School Communicate About Performance?

For Kristen's entire school history there had been daily communication between home and school via a shuttle notebook, and, with all the uncertainties of a transition to public school, Kristen's parents wanted to continue this practice. School personnel could not commit to writing (or reading) long notes every day but soon realized the benefit of regular communication about certain information. The team generated two lists of yes/no questions reflecting home and school priorities, one for Kristen's family to complete, the other for school personnel to complete (see Figure 7.15). These were bound into a journal that looked like the journals other kindergarten students made in language arts. Although it was a bit more time consuming to create this individualized journal, it is easy to use and provides additional analytical and systemic data on Kristen's achievements and needs.

Jamal's mother and foster parents do not desire such frequent or formal communication with school, as is natural when students reach high school. The team at school understands and respects that Jamal's mother was unable to take an active role in his instruction at this time. Jamal's foster family takes a more active role and communicates more frequently about his "standouts" and "stickouts." When needed, home and school team members send notes or make telephone calls. In addition, the school team believes it is appropriate to send home copies of Jamal's weekly schedule (excerpted in Figure 7.3), which has space for data and brief comments on Jamal's performance. Jamal also gets a report card, which looks like that of other high school students and includes a summary of quantitative and qualitative data on IEP objectives, as well as space for comments from each of Jamal's teachers and therapists. As recommended in Chapter 3, both Jamal's and Kristen's teams have worked out communication systems that meet needs of the individual students and their families at a given point in time. By

A: Home-to-School Communication for Kristen

Date 10/15	Yes	No	Comments
Did Kristen do anything special yesterday afternoon/evening or over the weekend?	✓		Kristen's grampa visited. We carved pumpkins and made apple pie, with Kristen's help. She was very proud of herself.
Did she sleep well?	✓		
Did she have a good morning?	✓		
Are there any health concerns or changes?	✓		Seems like she's getting a cold — maybe just tired.
Does Kristen have any doctor or dental appointments coming up?		✓	
Will you be away from home this week? If so, who should we contact in case of emergency?		✓	
Did Kristen use the toilet successfully?		✓	We were really off schedule this weekend.
Did Kristen reject anything with words/gestures?	✓		She told Duke "No!" after Julie scolded him.
Did Kristen request anything with words?	✓		Asked for more pie! (pointed + said "ma")

Additional Comments:

Kristen sat in Grampa's lap while he read stories. She wasn't always looking at the book, but she did seem interested in it. And she doesn't usually sit so long. Would it help her with stories at school if I read the same ones at home?

Anne Fleming
Parent Signature

Figure 7.15.   Individualized home–school communication journal for Kristen: A, home-to-school communication; B, school-to-home communication.

(continued)

Figure 7.15.   *(continued)*

B: School-to-Home Communication for Kristen

Date October 15	Yes	No	Comments
Did Kristen have a good morning?	X		
Were there any special programs?		X	Just Art – made leaf prints
Did buddies help Kristen with any activities?	X		Kaylee at playtime; Josh walking to/from art; Jessie will walk to bus with her.
Were any therapists in class today? PT 8:30-11:30 SLP 8:30-10:00	X		PT worked with all others on staff on facilitating motor skills (grasp, walking) - got a lot done
Did Kristen work on grasp today?	X		pincer grasp - Art, snack palmar grasp - bathroom (pants) play (plastic food in store)
Did Kristen work on standing or walking today?	X		Rise to stand - 4x at free play (SLP + teacher both did at once). Walking passed out materials at art - No HELP!
Did Kristen use words or pictures to request anything?	X		Pictures to choose store for free play. Very intentional! She looked, pointed, then went straight to store
Did Kristen use words or gestures to reject anything?		X	Seemed to like everything today
Did Kristen use the toilet successfully?		X	Sat 2 min. without fussing but no success (3x). Dry until 11:15

Additional Comments:

Kristen seems more interested in stories here, too. It would be great if you could read her a story the day before we do it here. Mrs. March could let you know what she has planned. She will talk with you about it when you come in on Thursday.

Lisa Simpson, PT
Staff Signature

79–118). Baltimore: Paul H. Brookes Publishing Co.

Risley, T. (1996). Get a life! Positive behavioral intervention for challenging behavior through life arrangement and life coaching. In L.K. Koegel, R.L. Koegel, & G. Dunlap (Eds.), *Positive behavioral support: Including people with difficult behavior in the community* (pp. 425–437). Baltimore: Paul H. Brookes Publishing Co.

Ryndak, D.L. (1996). Adapting environments, materials, and instruction to facilitate inclusion. In D.L. Ryndak & S. Alper (Eds.), *Curriculum content for students with moderate and severe disabilities in inclusive settings* (pp. 97–124). Newton, MA: Allyn & Bacon.

Salisbury, C., Mangino, M., Petrigala, M., Rainforth, B., & Syryca, S. (1994). Promoting the instructional inclusion of young children with disabilities in the primary grades. *Journal of Early Intervention, 18*(3), 311–322.

Schwartz, I.S., Carta, J.J., & Grant, S. (1996). Examining the use of recommended language intervention practices in early childhood special education classrooms. *Topics in Early Childhood Special Education, 16*(2), 251–272.

Schwartz, I.S., & Olswang, L.B. (1996). Evaluating child behavior change in natural settings: Exploring alternative strategies for data collection. *Topics in Early Childhood Special Education, 16*(1), 82–101.

Sents, B., & Marks, H. (1989). Changes in preschool children's IQ scores as a function of positioning. *American Journal of Occupational Therapy, 43*(10), 685–688.

Snell, M. (1978). *Systematic instruction of the moderately and severely handicapped.* Columbus, OH: Charles E. Merrill.

Snell, M. (1993). *Instruction of students with severe disabilities* (4th ed.). Columbus, OH: Charles E. Merrill.

Snell, M.E., Lewis, A.P., & Houghton, A. (1989). Acquisition and maintenance of toothbrushing skills by students with cerebral palsy and mental retardation. *Journal of The Association for Persons with Severe Handicaps, 14*(3), 216–226.

Stremel, K., & Schutz, R. (1995). Functional communication in inclusive settings for students who are deaf-blind. In N.G. Haring & L.T. Romer (Eds.), *Welcoming students who are deaf-blind into typical classrooms: Facilitating school participation, learning, and friendships* (pp. 197–229). Baltimore: Paul H. Brookes Publishing Co.

Taylor, S. (1988). Caught in the continuum: A critical analysis of the principle of the least restrictive environment. *Journal of The Association for Persons with Severe Handicaps, 13*(1), 41–53.

Thousand, J.S., Villa, R.A., & Nevin, A.I. (Eds.). (1994). *Creativity and collaborative learning: A practical guide to empowering students and teachers.* Baltimore: Paul H. Brookes Publishing Co.

Udvari-Solner, A. (1994). A decision-making model for curricular adaptations in cooperative groups. In J.S. Thousand, R.A. Villa, & A.I. Nevin (Eds.), *Creativity and collaborative learning: A practical guide to empowering students and teachers* (pp. 59–78). Baltimore: Paul H. Brookes Publishing Co.

Udvari-Solner, A., & Thousand, J. (1996). Creating a responsive curriculum for inclusive schools. *Remedial and Special Education, 17*(3), 182–192.

Watts, N. (1983). Eighteenth Mary McMillan lecture: The principle of choice. *Physical Therapy, 63*(11), 1802–1808.

Wesson, C.L., & King, R.P. (1996). Portfolio assessment and special education students. *Teaching Exceptional Children, 28*(2), 44–48.

Yonemura, M.V. (1986). *A teacher at work: Professional development and the early childhood educator.* New York: Teachers College Press.

York, J., & Weimann, G. (1991). Accommodating severe physical disabilities. In J. Reichle, J. York, & J. Sigafoos, *Implementing augmentative and alternative communication: Strategies for learners with severe disabilities* (pp. 239–256). Baltimore: Paul H. Brookes Publishing Co.

York-Barr, J., Rainforth, B., & Locke, P. (1996). Developing instructional adaptations. In F.P. Orelove & D. Sobsey, *Educating children with multiple disabilities: A transdisciplinary approach* (3rd ed., pp. 119–159). Baltimore: Paul H. Brookes Publishing Co.

III

IMPLEMENTATION STRATEGIES AND ISSUES

The second section of this book (Chapters 4–7) focused on strategies for designing individualized education programs for students with severe disabilities that facilitate current and future participation in integrated school and community environments. Central to the design was the integration of the perspectives, knowledge, and skills of various disciplines into one cohesive and comprehensive program, rather than an educational program composed of independent discipline-referenced segments (e.g., the physical therapy program, the communication program). In order for such integrated educational programs to be implemented, traditional models of service provision must change.

There are organizational, personal, and interpersonal factors that influence the ability to develop new approaches to service provision. Organizationally, there must be structures that allow team members to collaborate with one another and to work with students in their educationally relevant learning environments. There must also exist or be developed cultural norms and expectations for collaboration as a way of life in schools. Individually and collectively, team members must be skilled in their own disciplines, demonstrate effective interpersonal collaboration skills, and create shared purpose about their work together on behalf of students.

The last section of this book (Chapters 8 and 9) focuses on organizational, personal, and interpersonal issues and strategies related to implementing the integrated curricular and instructional design described in Section II. Chapter 8 presents a framework and applications to promote positive interdependence among team members. Specifically addressed are strategies for creating shared purpose, for identifying specific core team members, for scheduling, and for developing collaborative skills. Chapter 9 includes suggestions for moving forward—as individuals and as organizations—toward more collaborative ways of working and learning together. A discussion of current and future issues that influence the realization of collaborative team practices is provided as well.

8

Strategies for Implementing Collaborative Teamwork

Johnson and Johnson (1989, 1994) described a theory of social interdependence that provides a basis for understanding and subsequently designing effective collaborative teamwork strategies. They identified three ways in which people interact—individualistically, competitively, and cooperatively (Table 8.1)—and referred to these ways of interacting as goal structures. In *individualistic* goal structures, people work independently; there is no interdependence (Johnson & Johnson, 1994). The outcome of one person's efforts has no effect on and is not affected by the actions of another person. Each person does his or her own work with students. Frequently, this is how members of educational "teams" function in a school setting. An individualistic goal structure is perpetuated by traditional organizational structures, such as medically oriented funding criteria and rigid schedules of direct therapy in isolated environments (e.g., physical therapy on Tuesday and Thursday from 10:00 A.M. to 10:30 A.M.). Individualistic structures also are perpetuated by personal and interpersonal factors, such as the history and comfort of working privately, negative prior experiences with collaboration attempts, perceptions about efficiency, avoidance of conflict, and clear authority in decision making.

In *competitive* goal structures, there is negative interdependence (Johnson & Johnson, 1994). For one person to achieve his or her goal (i.e., to win), another person must fail to do so (i.e., lose). Sometimes interactions among educational team members unintentionally take this form of win–lose competition. For example, when direct therapy time conflicts with reading class, the therapist and teacher are in competition for time with the student. When the speech-language pathologist feels strongly that social interaction is the instructional priority for a 25-minute lunch period and the occupational therapist insists that promoting more efficient hand use skills is most important, they have competing goals. Lacking

247

Table 8.1. Goal structures that affect team interactions and outcomes

Competitive
- win or lose
- negative interdependence

Individualistic
- work independently
- no interdependence

Cooperative
- help and support others
- positive interdependence

Summarized from Johnson, D.W., & Johnson, R.T. (1989). *Cooperation and competition: Theory and research.* Edina, MN: Interaction Book Company.

skills in perspective taking, conflict resolution, consensus decision making, or facilitating student and family empowerment, many team members are destined for competitive interactions, frequently at the expense of what is best for the student. Developing and working from a unifying curricular orientation, as discussed in Chapter 4, reduces competition among team members because there is a shared vision of desired outcomes as the basis for joint decision making.

In *cooperative* goal structures, there is positive social interdependence (Johnson & Johnson, 1994). Each person's work to achieve his or her goal both depends on and supports other people to achieve their goals. Team members "sink or swim" together. Positive interdependence is an underlying premise of collaborative teamwork among adults, just as it is with cooperative learning among students. Cooperative interactions are promoted by structuring goal interdependence, resource interdependence, and reward interdependence (Thousand & Villa, 1992). *Goal interdependence* occurs when all members of the educational team commit themselves to achieving a mutually agreed-upon goal. *Resource interdependence* occurs when team members commit their respective talents to achieving their mutual goals and when team members divide tasks in an efficient, fair, and agreed-upon manner. *Reward interdependence* occurs when all team members share equally in benefits realized from accomplishing their mutual goal. For example, when a student with severe disabilities develops a friendship with a classmate for the first time, all team members share the feeling of accomplishment just as they shared commitment to the goal and shared resources in achieving the goal. The speech-language pathologist developed an effective method of communication, the occupational therapist adapted the positioning equipment so an upright head position and sustained eye contact were possible, the teacher created and reinforced regular interaction opportunities between the students, and the father facilitated after-school shared time at least once each week. To function as a collaborative educational team, positive interdependence must be structured through mutually determined goals, contribution to goal attainment, and celebration of goal accomplishment.

Making the decision to work as a collaborative team and to design structures to promote positive interdependence does not result immediately in collaboration. Change to collaborative ways of interacting, like all change, involves an evolution in thinking and in behaving. Efficient and satisfying interactions among group members evolve through ongoing interaction opportunities, commitment to work through inevitable differences in perspective, and focused effort to develop effective structures, strategies, skills, and other supports for collaboration. The well-established field of study on small group dynamics offers helpful insight and validation of the complex evolution of effective teams. In 1965, Tuckman introduced a conceptual framework for understanding group development that remains relevant (Tuckman, 1965; Tuckman & Jensen, 1977):

- *Forming* is an initial phase of group interaction in which members try to determine their places in the group and to develop the procedures and rules of the group.
- *Storming* is the period in which conflicts arise. Some members may resist the group influence or rebel against accomplishing the task.
- *Norming* describes the period during which the group establishes cohesiveness and commitment. Members discover new ways to work together.
- *Performing* describes the period in which the group members become efficient at their work and develop more flexible ways of working together.
- *Adjourning* describes the point at which the formal work of the group is completed, thereby removing the central mission. The result is dissolution of the group. This period sometimes involves elements of *mourning* as well, given the changes in relationships among members of the group.

Lacoursiere (1980) presented a similar chronology of group evolution with stages labeled as orientation, dissatisfaction, resolution, production, termination, and negative orientation. Yet another variation of group evolution begins with defining procedures and becoming oriented; then come conforming to procedures and getting acquainted; recognizing mutuality and building trust; rebelling and differentiating; committing to take ownership for goals, procedures, and other team members; and, finally, reaching a period of functioning maturely and pro-

ductively. Termination occurs when the work of the group is completed (Johnson & Johnson, 1994).

Most teams, including individualized education program (IEP) teams, are vulnerable to collapse or disaffiliation when members first encounter the storming (Tuckman, 1965), dissatisfaction (Lacoursiere, 1980), or rebelling and differentiating (Johnson & Johnson, 1994) stages of interaction. Conflict is not to be avoided, however, because it is a necessary and important type of interaction in productive teams. Later in this chapter, benefits that can be realized and strategies for working through differences in perspective are addressed. Teams that constructively work through differences move on to more effective shared work. In the case of IEP teams, the work is rarely completed, but terminations and new beginnings occur as some members leave and as new members join. Changes in other group variables can result in recycling through various stages as well. As teams form and change over time, some people are invigorated while others experience emotions associated with loss (e.g., sadness, disorientation, loneliness, questioning competence) from changes in relationships, meaning, and function. Bridges (1993) explains this psychological impact:

> It isn't the changes that do you in, it's the transition . . . . *Change* is situational: the new site, the new boss, the new team roles, the new policy. *Transition* is the psychological process people go through to come to terms with the new situation. Change is external, transition is internal. (p. 3)

The development of effective collaboration involves an active, ongoing process—sometimes exhilarating, sometimes challenging, and always dynamic. This chapter presents strategies for promoting positive interdependence among team members, resulting in effective support for students. Specifically, the following topics are discussed: 1) moving toward shared purpose by clarifying the functions of collaborative educational teams; 2) identifying specific team members for individual students; 3) structuring opportunities to collaborate, including scheduling related services personnel in integrated educational environments with students and arranging regular opportunities to interact with fellow team members; 4) developing collaboration skills, including exchanging skills among team members, solving problems, and making decisions as a group; and 5) communicating with parents. Chapter 9 discusses ways to move forward with integrating related services and collaborative teamwork.

CREATING SHARED PURPOSE AMONG TEAM MEMBERS

The primary function of collaborative educational teams is to support students with disabilities during their public school years to acquire the knowledge, skills, and dispositions to lead meaningful, contributive lives. This work is given specific focus through each student's IEP. A major responsibility for related services personnel is to support teachers, paraprofessionals, family members, and others who work closely with students on a daily basis. Not all team members come to a team with clarity of purpose regarding educational processes and outcomes or their respective roles and contributions; certainly, not all team members come with *shared* clarity of purpose. As members work together, clarity emerges.

Support Students to Achieve Meaningful, Integrated Life Outcomes

Before effective support can be provided, team members need to know what it is that they are supposed to support and what is, in fact, supportive. *Why* are they working as a

team and *what* do they hope to accomplish? Engaging in a dialogue is one way for team members to develop shared purpose as the basis for collaborative interactions. Senge, Ross, Smith, Roberts, and Kleiner (1994) define *dialogue* as "sustained collective inquiry into everyday experience and what we take for granted" (p. 353). They contrast *dialogue* with the more familiar means of interaction, *discussion,* which involves trying to convince. The focus of dialogue is learning about one's own and others' perspectives, creating understandings, and building common ground. The following questions promote dialogue focused on understanding one another's perspectives, clarifying and potentially changing one's own perspective, and identifying common elements of purpose or direction:

- What do we want the students in our school community knowing, doing, and believing when they leave school? How will they participate and contribute as members of a community?
- What might these outcomes be like for students who present unique capacities and challenges?
- What learning opportunities and supports are important to maximize the likelihood of achieving these outcomes?
- Why do we need to work together to maximize the likelihood of achieving these outcomes for students? What does each of us know? How can each of us contribute? What networks and supports can we tap?
- What matters most in my work? When I am 80 years old and look back on my life as an educator, what do I hope I will have contributed?
- If I/we made significant strides toward these desired student outcomes and collaborative processes, what would my/our school be like as a place to work and as

a place for students next year at this time?

Interactions involving such questions may be most effective in small groups or with partners. Sometimes it is useful for team members to spend individual time reflecting and writing before interacting with others. If staff development time is not allocated for dialogue, team members may choose to spend time together before the school year gets under way by meeting for an extended breakfast or lunch.

In addition to talking about more general purposes of education and roles, team members discuss desired outcomes and roles related to individual students (as discussed in Section II of this book). For example, shared responses to the statement "I believe that an educational program for Roberto (a student with severe disabilities) should result in . . ." might include descriptions of how Roberto participates in family life, whether he has friends to play with in the neighborhood park, and how he makes choices in daily life tasks and activities (e.g., clothes to wear, snacks to eat, messages to share during morning circle). Leaders in the field of special education have conceptualized desirable life outcomes for students with disabilities as presence, participation, accomplishment, contribution, and satisfaction across life domains (National Center on Educational Outcomes, 1995; Ysseldyke & Thurlow, 1994). These broad domains provide a framework from which specific, relevant objectives could be considered during the individualized curriculum development process. Collective purpose and direction among team members are requisites for developing the structures and skills (discussed later in this chapter) to move forward with effective collaborative interactions. For example, if appropriate social interactions during recess is identified as an important and relevant outcome for an individual student, a schedule must be put in place that allows selected team members to be present during recess, and skills must be developed to determine capacities, needs, and interventions that may be appropriate.

Support Fellow Team Members

As part of the collaborative process required to effectively support student learning, team members also support one another. Different types of support that team members provide to one another include 1) resource support (e.g., materials, funding, literature, people); 2) moral support (e.g., listening, encouraging); and 3) technical support (e.g., specific and individualized strategies, instructional methods, adaptations) (York, Giangreco, Vandercook, & Macdonald, 1992). For support to be real, rather than merely perceived, the recipient of the support must, in fact, feel supported. As team members work together to achieve desired student outcomes and to support one another, they should talk about specific actions that support students and each other. Examples of practices that will likely be perceived as supportive and not supportive are presented in Figure 8.1 (York et al., 1992).

The way in which support is operationalized into collaborative teamwork practices, and specifically into individual team member roles and responsibilities, will vary from team to team, building to building, and district to district. For individuals joining an established and effectively functioning collaborative team, responsibilities and expectations can be communicated clearly through written guidelines, dialogue with fellow team members, and observation and experience working in the existing shared work environment. For teams just initiating collaborative teamwork, responsibilities and performance expectations frequently seem vague and poorly defined. Some support

---

Support means . . .

..... helping students and families realize their own vision of a good life

..... listening to and acting on the support needs identified by students, families, and other team members

..... reallocating resources to support efforts to include students in regular school life, including resources for teams to learn and work together

..... remembering that the students are the "stars" and that the educational team members are the supporting actors

..... acknowledging the efforts of fellow team members

..... designing curricular and instructional methods that assist the student to be an active learner

..... designing curricular and instructional methods that assist the classroom teacher to effectively include the student

..... designing curricular and instructional methods that promote positive interdependence among students in the class

..... providing constructive feedback to fellow team members that results in more effective team member interactions and ultimately improved student learning

..... providing enough information, but not too much

..... being around and available enough, but not too much

Support does not mean . . .

..... conducting a classroom observation then writing and depositing notes on the teacher's desk with no opportunity for follow-up discussion

..... giving your opinions, advice, and recommendations then leaving before a discussion can ensue

..... requesting to meet with the classroom teacher during instructional time without making prior arrangements

..... presenting the classroom teacher with a list of skills or activities to be integrated into the class-room day

..... telling the teacher or family what to do

..... giving the classroom teacher a file folder of resources when she asked for problem-solving support

..... hovering near students with disabilities in the classroom

..... doing "therapy" in the back of the room

..... suggesting interventions that interfere with the classroom routine

..... providing more support than is needed

Figure 8.1. Examples of what support means . . . and does not mean. (From York, J., Giangreco, M.F., Vandercook, T., & Macdonald, C. [1992]. Integrating support personnel in the inclusive classroom. In S. Stainback & W. Stainback [Eds.], *Curriculum considerations in inclusive classrooms: Facilitating learning for all students* [p. 104]. Baltimore: Paul H. Brookes Publishing Co.; reprinted by permission.)

during this transition phase can be provided by external sources (e.g., individuals from other teams, written materials, outside consultants). Developing effective means of collaboration among the members of any specific team, however, involves a process and cannot be achieved exclusively through external support.

As team members work together, more effective and comfortable ways of interacting and supporting one another develop. When team members begin to understand more clearly their roles and responsibilities, new job descriptions might be developed that reflect more accurately the role and function of members on a collaborative team. The sample job description in Figure 8.2 includes broad statements of educational outcomes and expectations, as well as operationalized physical/occupational therapist performance expectations. Figure 8.3 outlines supports that speech-language pathologists might offer to address the communication needs of students with severe disabilities in inclusive settings (Calculator, 1994). The checklist in Figure 8.4 outlines competencies that are generic for most members of a collaborative educational team. The checklist can be used as a self-check, as a way to solicit feedback from fellow team members, or as a performance evaluation by an informed and involved supervisor. As with most forms, these are potentially useful only to the extent that they provide a structure around which meaningful communication occurs. That is, independent reading of the responsibilities in no way ensures either relevance to a specific member or collective understanding by the entire team. Instead of actually filling out the form, team members may choose to talk about additions, clarifications, or omissions, and then select questions that form a basis for discussing how well the team is working

and for identifying areas that could use additional attention.

The overarching responsibilities of each member of the collaborative educational team are 1) to contribute knowledge, perspective, and skills so that students achieve their educational goals; 2) to support fellow members of the collaborative team; and 3) to contribute to the overall development of their school communities, where all students and adults are welcomed, valued, supported, and successful.

IDENTIFYING TEAM MEMBERS FOR INDIVIDUAL STUDENTS

In Chapter 2, the concepts of a *core team* and an *extended team* (Giangreco, Cloninger, & Iverson, 1993) were introduced. Also mentioned was the need for flexibility in terms of who functions on the core team, given the priority educational needs of a student at any given point in time. Core team members are those individuals who are most directly involved in designing, implementing, and/or monitoring the daily educational program. The extended team consists of individuals who are available as needed but who do not have frequent and regularly scheduled interactions with students or members of the core team.

Many professional disciplines could contribute to the educational service provision of students with disabilities. The Individuals with Disabilities Education Act (IDEA) of 1990 (PL 101-476) ensures the availability of a variety of special education and related services professionals so that individual student needs can be met. When deciding specifically who should provide support to an individual student, as well as what, when, and how support should be provided, several factors require thoughtful consideration, especially given constraints in the real world of educational practice.

Physical / Occupational Therapist

The following job description delineates responsibilities for physical and occupational therapists who work with students who have moderate, severe, and multiple disabilities categorically referred to here as severe disabilities. This job description was predicated on the following tenets. Physical and occupational therapy services provided in educational settings must 1) address the individual educational needs of each student; 2) be integrated throughout the general education, domestic, recreation/leisure, community, and vocational environments in which students receive instruction and are expected to function; and 3) be coordinated with the services provided by other members of the educational team. Collaboration and communication across disciplines and with family members is essential.

Meeting the comprehensive, varied, and complex educational needs of students with severe disabilities presents a significant challenge for students as well as team members. However, through a collaborative teamwork model, the educational team can move closer toward accomplishing the goal of maximal student participation in regular school and community environments. This job description is intended to present guidelines for the practice of physical/occupational therapists in educational settings such that achievement of this goal can be realized.

The Physical / Occupational Therapist Job Description is divided into four primary areas of responsibility: assessment, program planning, program implementation, and team process.

ASSESSMENT

1. The Physical / Occupational Therapist will participate in assessment of individual students to determine the need for and the type of therapy services that need to be delivered to support the educational program.

2. The Physical / Occupational Therapist will participate in initial assessments performed jointly by an Occupational Therapist and a Physical Therapist. Two types of assessment information will be obtained: environment-referenced information derived from an ecological inventory, and skill referenced information derived from diagnostic assessments. Both types of information can and should be obtained through observation and hands-on interaction in naturally occurring, functional situations to the greatest extent possible.

   a. Environment-referenced information addresses the ability of a student to interact and participate in educational activities under natural conditions. To obtain this information, the Physical / Occupational Therapist will observe students and perform hands-on assessment in the school, home, and community environments intended as priority educational contexts for each individual student. Examples of environments and activities in which assessment might take place include

   School environments: classrooms, rest rooms, cafeteria, hallways and entryways, playgrounds, and bus loading/unloading areas

   Community environments: cars, public buses, grocery stores, shopping malls, restaurants, and worksites

   Home environments: walkways and entryways, yard, kitchen, family room, bathroom, and bedroom

   _____

   (continued)

Figure 8.2. Sample physical/occupational therapist job description. (Adapted from York, J., Peters, B., Hurd, D., & Donder, D. [1985]. *Guidelines for using support services in educational programs for students with severe, multiple handicaps.* Dekalb, IL: Dekalb County Special Education Association; adapted by permission.)

Figure 8.2. (*continued*)

The information that will be obtained in the above environments will be related to the following activity components:

Transition: How does / should the student move between educational environments and activities?

Position: How does / should the student be positioned to enable maximal participation in the educational environments and activities?

Participation: How does / should the student move to engage in educational activities in an efficient and participatory manner?

Adaptation: What equipment, environmental modifications, or adaptive devices are available or could be built / obtained to enhance participation in educational environments and activities?

b. Skill-referenced information in each of the following areas will be obtained:

Gross motor skills, including: methods of mobility, postural control, balance / equilibrium responses, transitions and transfers between body positions, strength and endurance

Fine motor skills, including: functional and cooperative hand use, reach/grasp/release, eye-hand coordination, visual-motor skills, tool use

Oral motor skills, including: drinking, sucking, swallowing, biting, chewing, and other components related to effective eating

Respiratory functioning, including: breathing patterns and efficiency, coughing

Overall neuromotor status, including: joint range of motion, muscle tone, muscle strength, endurance, coordination, efficiency, motor planning, quantity and quality of movement, interfering reflexes, sensorimotor integration and processing

3. The Physical / Occupational Therapist will determine and then share with other team members safe and efficient methods for transitioning, positioning, handling, facilitating movement, and transferring individual students. Methods will incorporate use of proper body mechanics to increase movement efficiency and to minimize physical strain on persons working with the students.

4. The Physical / Occupational Therapist will collaborate with other team members during the ecological assessment process. Because each team member analyzes the abilities and needs of students from a different point of view, a synthesis of observations and viewpoints provides a comprehensive and balanced analysis of student functioning in educational contexts. Therapists and teachers will jointly discuss synthesized analyses of assessment findings leading to collaboration in determining priority of educational goals and objectives.

5. The Physical / Occupational Therapist will contribute to the collaborative team assessment reports by detailing relevant environment-referenced and skill-referenced information. Skill-referenced assessment information that is pertinent to educational programming will be objectively and concisely summarized for parents, physicians, and other team members regarding each student's current motor abilities as part of every 3-year reevaluation. Environment-referenced assessment information will be summarized as part of the collaborative team report on performance in educational environments and activities. This information will be organized into school, community, general community, domestic, recreation / leisure, and vocational areas of functioning. Specific activities assessed in each of these areas will be delineated and commented upon. The IEP goals and objectives will serve as the basis for documenting change in student abilities on an annual basis.

(continued)

Figure 8.2.   (continued)

6. The Physical / Occupational Therapist will engage in ongoing assessment of student abilities in educational environments and activities. This will include both observations of and hands-on interactions with students, as well as implementing and/or monitoring ongoing systems of data collection and analysis.

PROGRAM PLANNING

1. The Physical / Occupational Therapist will participate in a discussion with other team members to prioritize educational goals and objectives to be targeted for instruction during the school year. This requires delineation of educational needs identified during assessment, followed by team discussion of consensus decision making regarding the most important skills to receive instructional emphasis.

2. The Physical / Occupational Therapist will write educationally relevant goals and objectives that are stated in behavioral and measurable terms and that specify performance in educational environments and activities.

3. The Physical / Occupational Therapist will collaborate in the writing of instructional programs and procedures, many of which will be carried out on a regular basis by other team members. The instructional information contributed by the Physical / Occupational Therapist might include
    • Equipment and adaptive devices required
    • The position of the student and a description of how to achieve the position
    • The movements expected of the student for participation
    • The position of the instructor
    • The assistance provided by the instructor
    • Other pertinent antecedents
    • Consequences, both error correction and reinforcement procedures
    • Data collection procedures

4. The Physical / Occupational Therapist will participate in scheduling student and class activities for the purpose of identifying opportunities throughout the week when mobility / transition, positioning, movement, and other movement expectations can be integrated into educational activites that occur in school, home, and community environments.

PROGRAM IMPLEMENTATION

1. The Physical / Occupational Therapist will observe, monitor, and reevaluate student performance during educational activites in school, home, and community environments on a regular basis. The frequency, duration, and location of these interactions will be determined by the educational team based on individual student needs.

2. The Physical / Occupational therapist will provide direct and indirect services as appropriate for each student. To the greatest extent possible, intervention methods designed to improve mobility, posture, and efficient movement will be integrated as part of instruction that occurs on an ongoing basis in educational activities. When most intervention methods are integrated in the educational program, the therapist will still maintain direct, hands-on interactions with students on at least an intermittent basis. This direct interaction can and should occur in a consultative manner in educational contexts.

3. The Physical / Occupational Therapist will make or obtain necessary equipment and adaptive devices required for appropriate mobility, positioning, and optimal participation in educational activities.

(continued)

Figure 8.2.   (continued)

4. The Physical / Occupational Therapist will teach teachers, parents, instructional aides, and others methods of safe and therapeutic physical management of students, including methods for lifting, carrying, transferring and mobility, positioning and use of positioning equipment, normalizing muscle tone, facilitating efficient movement, and using adaptive devices.

5. The Physical / Occupational Therapist will document recommendations, feedback, and program changes after each observation of or interaction with a student in the context of educational activities. This information will be distributed to all team members.

6. The Physical / Occupational Therapist will collaborate with other team members in writing educationally relevant goals and objectives, instructional programs, and data-based assessment procedures. He or she will analyze performance and determine program changes needed based on systematically collected data.

7. The Physical / Occupational Therapist will perform temporary direct therapy services when
    • Hands-on interaction is necessary to determine student progress and effective intervention procedures.
    • Highly specialized and high-risk handling procedures are required, such as immediately after surgery.
    • The functional status of a student is either rapidly progressing or deteriorating so as to warrant frequent direct interactions to determine changing needs. In every situation in which direct services are deemed appropriate, indirect service must be provided also.

TEAM PROCESS

1. The Physical / Occupational Therapist will participate in regularly scheduled team meetings for students when the therapist is a core team member. Participation includes problem solving and brainstorming related to all areas of educational programming. That is, participation is not limited to areas viewed as specific to the therapist's own discipline or areas of expertise.

2. The Physical / Occupational Therapist will be a supportive team member and participate in collaborative educational program planning and implementation as specified previously.

3. The Physical / Occupational Therapist will expand his or her knowledge and expertise in educational and therapeutic advances of relevance to the education of students with severe disabilities by attending in-service training activities, professional conferences, and workshops.

The *number of individuals* on a team is one factor that has an effect on collaboration. Theoretically, involving more people brings more expertise to an individual student. The more people involved, however, the greater the difficulty in coordinating schedules and enabling team members to have access to one another. Communication among all members of the team becomes more difficult. As groups get bigger, individual commitment, accountability, and con-

tribution frequently diminish. Another factor that enters into team member selection is the likelihood of *meaningful* (e.g., frequent and engaged) *access and involvement* of the potential team member. Few would argue that the people who spend the most time with an individual student are the experts about that student. Individuals who are more removed may have important and relevant generalized "expertise," but without knowing the student and the realities of his or her life at

1. Collaborate with others (particularly the classroom teacher) to identify, implement, and then monitor the impact of classroom and curriculum modifications. These supports are designed to assure that the student's educational needs are being addressed within the regular curriculum.
   a. During art class, a classmate will encourage John to show his completed project to another student.
   b. The classroom aide will review the teacher's lesson plan and then program messages on Laura's communication device to make sure she can offer pertinent content when this activity occurs later in the day.
   c. A classmate will offer Sarah a choice of two books, either of which the peer is prepared to read to her, during silent reading.
   d. The classroom teacher is asked by the SLP to purposely mumble two questions to Paul one day, then record Paul's response. Later, the teacher and SLP develop a plan, which incorporates modeling by classmates, to encourage Paul to request clarification and repetition in these and subsequent (actual) situations.
2. Identify communication demands of the curriculum (teacher input, peer input, materials used, responses expected) relative to student's abilities. (Previous chapters have reviewed specific protocol for conducting such analyses.)
3. Identify the need for augmentative communication, and develop an appropriate AAC system (e.g., method of depicting symbols, type of output, type of display, means of accessing the system [e.g., choice of switch]).
4. Collaborate with others (teacher, parents, classmates) to discern the role of the AAC system, relative to extant modes of communication, in enhancing a student's level of participation in school activities. Reinforce the notion that the AAC system is a means and not an end.
   a. John shines a flashlight on a picture denoting that it is "sunny," in response to his teacher's asking the class, "Can anyone tell me what it is like outside today?" Later, he uses a smile vs. frown to respond to yes/no questions. Still later, he points to symbols in his communication book to select a classroom job that he would like to perform that day.
   b. Tara's goal of indicating choices at mealtime is suspended. Classmates have wondered why she has such an opportunity whereas they are expected to eat everything sent from home. In addition, all agree that it is more important that she feed herself than rely on others to provide food in response to her requests. Other times in a day's schedule for addressing choice making are determined (e.g., equipment she would like to be taken to during recess, a musical instrument she wishes to play, a classmate with whom she would like to work). These are all choices that are available to other children as well and choices that arise naturally in her existing curriculum.
5. Purchase necessary supplies and equipment.
   a. Several teachers and related service staff are on the mailing lists of major manufacturers.
   b. Catalogs and other pertinent information are shared with teachers, parents, and other team members.

(continued)

Figure 8.3. Types of communication supports that might be provided by speech-language pathologists (SLPs) (and others) to enhance students' inclusion and participation in general education. (AAC, augmentative and alternative education.) (From Calculator, S. [1994]. Communicative intervention as a means to successful inclusion. In S. Calculator & C. Jorgensen [Eds.], *Including students with severe disabilities in schools: Fostering communication, interaction, and participation: School-age children series* [pp. 183–214]. San Diego: Singular; reprinted with permission.)

Figure 8.3. (*continued*)

c. One person is designated to pursue the purchase of a communication device. The helper contacts vendors and arranges for a demonstration of the device at school.
6. Maintain and service supplies and equipment.
   a. A team member is identified who can help teachers and others troubleshoot when a problem is encountered with Jennie's communication device. This same individual assumes responsibility for communicating with the manufacturer.
   b. A classmate removes Phil's communication board from his lap tray and places it in a safe location when a particular activity counterindicates its use.
7. Continuously monitor the student's motivation and attitudes about his or her communication system.
   a. The teacher maintains a log, for three consecutive days, of situations in which a student uses a communication device. The instructor also notes situations in which use of the device would have been warranted, in that it could have led to more effective and efficient communication, but had not been employed.
   b. The SLP maintains ongoing contact with the student, classmates, and others to identify problems/limitations of the communication system, and to brainstorm possible solutions.
   c. The school counselor develops a procedure for monitoring the student's frequency of socially inappropriate/challenging behaviors. Staff have found these behaviors increase in contexts in which the student is unable to express thoughts and feelings with her present communication system.
8. Collaborate with classroom teacher and aide to identify changes in instructional style and philosophy that can promote increased interaction among students (e.g., cooperative learning).
9. Home–school coordination.
   a. Highlights of the school day are briefly summarized in a notebook that goes home with the student (and is returned, with similar information from home back to school). The communication system provides a means by which Tom can answer questions and provide additional novel information about topics that are briefly alluded to in the notebook.
10. Appropriate and effective methods of interacting with the student are modeled for others. The student takes as active a role in the training of listeners as possible.
    a. Jamal has a recorded message on his augmentative device that politely asks his listener to refrain from interrupting him.
    b. Sheila's communication notebook includes a brief description of her system and some tips on how others can use it with her effectively. She directs both unfamiliar and familiar persons to these instructions.

school, the more distant professional will have difficulty contributing to overall student functioning. In some districts, certain support staff (e.g., physical therapists) simply are not available, despite ongoing attempts to recruit and retain additional staff. Distant professionals must rely on close service providers and family members to make the link between generalized professional expertise (e.g., what an occupational therapist knows about children with spastic quadriplegic cerebral palsy) to individualized

Collaborative Team Member Checklist

Team Member Name:_____ Date:_____

Checklist completed by: (check one)

___Teacher   ___Support Staff   ___Aide   ___Program Supervisor   ___Other

	High 5	4	3	2	Low 1	NA
Participates in the assessment of student abilities in the array of educational environments and activities determined as priorities for individual students:						
•School environments and activities	5	4	3	2	1	NA
•Home environments and activities	5	4	3	2	1	NA
•Community environments and activities	5	4	3	2	1	NA
Effectively communicates educationally relevant assessment information to other team members.	5	4	3	2	1	NA
Participates in writing educationally relevant team assessment reports.	5	4	3	2	1	NA
Participates in team collaboration for determining priority educational goals and objectives.	5	4	3	2	1	NA
Writes educational goals and objectives that are:						
•Educationally relevant	5	4	3	2	1	NA
•Functional	5	4	3	2	1	NA
•Chronologically age appropriate	5	4	3	2	1	NA
•Behavioral	5	4	3	2	1	NA
•Measurable	5	4	3	2	1	NA
Writes clear instructional programs and procedures, including evaluation information.	5	4	3	2	1	NA
When teaching other team members, provides a rationale for the procedures and clear instruction-supportive feedback.	5	4	3	2	1	NA
Incorporates behavior management practices into programs and procedures as appropriate.	5	4	3	2	1	NA
Effectively teaches other team members how to integrate their own expertise into student's daily programming.	5	4	3	2	1	NA
Requests information from other team members.	5	4	3	2	1	NA
Is organized, efficient, and directed during classroom and community consultations.	5	4	3	2	1	NA
Effectively monitors and observes student performance.	5	4	3	2	1	NA
Provides supportive and instructive feedback to other team members regarding expanded roles.	5	4	3	2	1	NA

(continued)

Figure 8.4.   Generic team member performance checklists. (From York, J., Peters, B., Hurd, D., & Donder, D. [1985]. *Guidelines for using support services in educational programs for students with severe, multiple handicaps* [pp. 48–49]. Dekalb, IL: Dekalb County Special Education Association; adapted by permission.)

Figure 8.4.   (*continued*)

	High				Low	
	5	**4**	**3**	**2**	**1**	**NA**
Participates effectively and appropriately in team meetings.	5	4	3	2	1	NA
Participates effectively and appropriately in IEP meeting and annual reviews.	5	4	3	2	1	NA
Maintains a good rapport and interacts appropriately with students.	5	4	3	2	1	NA
Maintains a good rapport and interacts appropriately with family members of students.	5	4	3	2	1	NA
Maintains a good rapport and interacts appropriately with other team members.	5	4	3	2	1	NA
Presents him/herself as a learner and continually attempts to enhance his/her knowledge of educational and specialized professional practices.	5	4	3	2	1	NA
Supports overall development of educational excellence in the school community.	5	4	3	2	1	NA

ADDITIONAL COMMENTS

1. Areas of strength:

2. Areas for improvement:

3. I would like more of:

4. I would like less of:

recommendations (e.g., intervention strategies that integrate methods from varied disciplines shown to be effective with a particular student who has unique abilities and needs related to movement). Another selection factor is *overlap in knowledge and skill* demonstrated by potential team members. Roles and responsibilities of specific professionals and disciplines can vary greatly across districts, school buildings, and even professionals themselves. These variations are due to interests, education, and experience of individual staff, combined with the past and current expectations set at each school.

A starting point for identifying necessary support services is for the team to determine the primary challenges experienced by an individual student in accomplishing his or her educational goals. Next, potential team members with the specific competencies needed to address those challenges and provide support to the student and his or her direct instructional staff are identified. Table 8.2 delineates a range of student challenges and individuals who might provide support (York et al., 1992). The table shows that there are several possible support personnel options for each student challenge. For example, depending on the specific nature of the communication challenges experienced by an individual student, support could be provided by teachers, classmates, speech-language pathologists, occupational therapists, psychologists, or family members.

In selecting the specific support personnel to function on the core team, the following guidelines should be considered:

1. If two or more potential team members have overlapping information and skills related to the challenge area, select only one of the team members to be involved.

An individual audiologist and an individual speech-language pathologist both are knowledgeable about how the classroom teacher can more effectively communicate with Henry, a student with a mild hearing impairment. The team decided that only one of these professionals needed to be involved in designing instructional adaptations for Henry. The other could be consulted as needed, particularly in complex problem-solving and long-range program development activities.

2. If one potential team member is able to address multiple challenges or needs of an individual student, select that team member.

Henry also had some difficulty interacting with classmates. The speech-language pathologist has been very interested and involved in developing social skills curricula. The team, therefore, decided to have the speech-language pathologist, instead of the audiologist, be more directly involved with Henry because she could address both his auditory and socialization challenges.

3. If two or more potential team members have similar competencies but one has more frequent or closer geographical access to the student's school, select the individual who has closer and more frequent access.

Yolanda has a vision impairment that presents particular challenges during her community-based instruction. Both the vision specialist and orientation and mobility specialist have experience teaching students with vision impairments to access community environments. Neither professional currently serves students in the rural high school that Yolanda attends. The vision specialist, however, lives in that community. The team decided that the vision specialist should be part of Yolanda's core team because he would have more frequent access to Yolanda as a result of geographical proximity. The team also decided that the orientation and mobility specialist would consult informally with the

Table 8.2.   Student challenges and respective support personnel

Student challenge	Potential support personnel
Cognitive / learning process	
Curricular / instructional adaptations or alternatives	General educator, special educator, speech-language therapist, occupational therapist, psychologist, vision or hearing specialists
Organizing assignments, schedules	General educator, special educator, occupational therapist, speech-language therapist
Communication / interactions	
Nonverbal communication	Speech-language therapist, special educator, family members
Socialization with classmates	Speech-language therapist, special educator, psychologist, classmates
Behaving in adaptive ways	General educator, special educator, psychologist, speech-language therapist, classmates
Physical / motor	
Functional use of hands	Occupational therapist, physical therapist, special educator
Mobility and transitions	Physical therapist, occupational therapist, orientation and mobility specialist, special educator
Posture (body alignment)	Physical therapist, occupational therapist
Fitness and physical activity	Physical therapist, adaptive physical educator, nurse
Sensory	
Vision	Vision specialist, occupational therapist, orientation & mobility specialist
Hearing	Audiologist, hearing specialist, speech-language therapist
Health	
Eating difficulty	Occupational therapist, speech-language therapist, physical therapist, nurse, special educator
Medications	Nurse
Other health needs	Nurse, physicians, selected health care professionals
Current and future living	
Career and vocational pursuits	Vocational educator, counselor, special educator
Leisure pursuits	Special educator, occupational therapist, recreation personnel
Support from home and community	Social worker, counselor, special educator, general educator

From York, J., Giangreco, M.F., Vandercook, T., & Macdonald, C. (1992). Integrating support personnel in the inclusive classroom. In S. Stainback & W. Stainback (Eds.), *Curriculum considerations in inclusive classrooms: Facilitating learning for all students* (p. 108). Baltimore: Paul H. Brookes Publishing Company; adapted by permission.

vision specialist just prior to each bimonthly regional support group meeting for professionals serving low-incidence student populations.

4. If none of the potential team members has adequate knowledge and skills to address a challenge area, identify one team member who already has ongoing involvement with the student to obtain additional training and support either through student-specific technical assistance or through various forms of continuing education and in-service training (e.g., courses and workshops).

Amy, a 6-year-old, experiences extreme gagging when attempting to eat. Neither the occupational therapist, the physical therapist, nor the speech-language pathologist has experience facilitating oral-motor skills for complex eating challenges. The occupational therapist has been extensively involved in teaching other students to feed themselves and has developed an increased interest in mealtime skills. Because of the occupational therapist's interest and current availability during mealtimes, the team decides that it makes sense for the occupational therapist to take a 3-day workshop on prespeech and eating skills offered at a regional therapy training institute. In the meantime, the administrator supports the team's recommendation to hire a consultant to provide initial and follow-up technical assistance to assist in the assessment and program development related to Amy's specific eating abilities.

5. If two professionals have similar but not overlapping knowledge and skill competencies, provide the opportunity for these two individuals to work together to train one another in complementary skill areas, with the ultimate goal being a divided caseload with each professional having more time to be involved with individual students. This is a capacity-building approach in that the

capacity of one professional to meet more diverse learner needs is being developed. Ultimately, this can result in greater efficiency because the number of people involved with any one student can be streamlined without significant loss of expertise. It also can result in more meaningful involvement because the one therapist will have more time to understand more fully the demands and opportunities experienced by a given student throughout his or her school day.

An occupational therapist and a physical therapist have common competencies related to positioning, handling, and adaptive equipment. In addition, the occupational therapist has considerably more knowledge about hand use. The physical therapist has more experience facilitating mobility. For 4 months they work together with students who have hand use and mobility challenges to train and support one another. They also spend time together sharing resources on their respective new learning topics. After 4 months, they divide their caseloads so that either the occupational therapist or the physical therapist is providing primary sensorimotor support to students with comprehensive physical challenges (including hand use and mobility). They also schedule monthly opportunities to work together with the students.

Selections regarding specific core team members must balance efficiency (e.g., number of team members with whom to coordinate, logistical issues such as regular access and availability), time available to understand how a student functions in his or her daily education, and diversity of knowledge and skill. Selections always focus on matching student challenges and needs with the competencies of individual support personnel. The type and amount of services provided continue to be accurately documented on the IEP. Our experience has been that, in the vast majority of situations, if there are reasonably positive and trusting relationships in place and if the reasons for more integrated, flexible, and collaborative approaches to service provision are explained, most parents are supportive of such decisions. Arrangements must also be made so that students do not lose access to relevant disciplinary expertise. For example, when a physical therapist and an occupational therapist assume the role of primary sensorimotor therapist, the two individuals must have ongoing opportunities to have access to and learn from one another. Keep in mind that specific competencies are not ensured by a given discipline label. There is tremendous variability in the knowledge and skill among professionals with the same discipline label. As professionals advance in their careers, it is not unusual for them to expand their knowledge and practice base within and outside their own discipline. Furthermore, there is tremendous overlap in the knowledge and skills of some professionals who have different discipline labels. In making the best possible decisions regarding support personnel to meet individual student needs, the following myths about professional discipline labels must be dispelled (York et al., 1992):

Myth 1: *The most important variable for team member effectiveness is competence within one's own discipline. For example, a clinically superb physical therapist will also be an excellent team member in a public school setting.* (Competence is a necessary but not sufficient criterion of team member effectiveness.)

Myth 2: *There are well-defined boundaries between disciplines. For example, there is no overlap between what teachers and occupational therapists know and do.* (Such boundaries only exist in the mind of the naive professional.)

Myth 3: *Each individual trained in the same discipline has the same competencies. For example, all speech-language pathologists have competence in augmentative communication.* (Preservice preparation programs—classroom and clinical experiences—vary enormously nationwide; professional practice and development opportunities and expectations vary as well.)

Myth 4: *Professionals with a specific discipline label "own" their respective area of discipline expertise. For example, only the physical therapist can be knowledgeable about mobility.* (Thankfully, knowledge is a commodity available to anyone. In the best case scenario for children, each team member continually learns and incorporates more about his or her discipline contributions and about those of other disciplines.)

These discipline myths expose some of the perceived "truths" we hold in making decisions about support and personnel needs. Focusing on the labels of professionals, instead of on the specific competencies and interests of an individual professional, can create inefficiencies and inadequacies in service provision (just as labels and resulting generalizations ascribed to children conceal individual assets and interests). Defining roles by discipline label can also be stifling and result in team member dissatisfaction. Individual people with their unique contributions, only some of which relate to an ascribed discipline label, are what make collaborative teams work. Playing a game called "Discipline Myths and Truths" at an initial team meeting can help team members begin talking about what each knows, does, and wishes to learn as they work together to support students (Figure 8.5).

DEVELOPING STRUCTURES THAT PROMOTE COLLABORATION

When educational teams are just starting to design and implement a collaborative approach to service provision, more time is needed to interact than in later stages of implementation. By definition, the acquisition stage of learning is inefficient and, therefore, requires more effort, time, and opportunities to practice. One of the most frequently asked questions is "How are we supposed to function as a collaborative team when we have no time to interact?" The answer is simply "You cannot." Time must be allocated for team members to work together. Because

---

Discipline Myths and Truths

Instructions: This is a screening tool for determining your *DISCIPLINE OUTLOOK*. For each of the following statements, mark "M" for MYTH or "T" for TRUTH. If you work with other people to discuss the statements, add an additional 5 points to your score. If you work in isolation subtract 5 points from your score.

(M) There are well defined boundaries between disciplines. For example, there is no overlap between what teachers and occupational therapists know.

(T) No single discipline encompasses sufficient knowledge and skills to effectively meet the needs of all students.

(T) Many of the skills considered unique to a particular discipline can, in fact, be taught to people who do not have the particular discipline label.

(M) There are genetic and identifiable brain differences between people with differing discipline labels.

(M) The most important requisite for team member effectiveness is competence within one's own discipline. For example, a clinically superb psychologist will also be an excellent team member in a public school setting.

(M) Each individual trained in the same discipine has the same competencies. For example, all speech-language therapists have competence in augmentative communication.

(T) Disciplines involved in educational teams exist to support students to participate in and contribute to family, school, and community life . . . now and in the future.

(M) Professionals with a specific discipline label "own" their respective area of discipline expertise. For example, only the occupational therapist can be knowledgeable about hand function; only a nurse can know about seizure disorders.

(T) There are many areas of overlapping knowledge and skills among disciplines.

(T) The most important consideration in determining who should provide support to a student is knowledge and skills, not discipline label.

Figure 8.5.　A game to elicit discussion about roles and responsibilities of various disciplines.

obtaining more work time (or more personnel) is not a viable option in most circumstances, the task becomes that of making changes in how time is currently spent. If implementing a collaborative approach to the provision of related services is determined to be a priority, time must be allocated for therapists to work with students in integrated learning environments and to collaborate with other members of the educational team. Strategies for scheduling services in integrated learning environments and meetings with team members are discussed here.

Schedule Related Services Personnel in Integrated Educational Environments

In traditional multidisciplinary or interdisciplinary service provision models, each professional spent individual or small-group time with students focusing on a specific skill or challenge. For example, a physical therapist might have worked with a student on improving walking skills by using parallel bars in a separate therapy room. A speech-language pathologist might have spent individual time increasing a child's response to greetings by engaging in massed practice trials in a one-to-one therapy session. Greater inclusion of students with disabilities in general education classes and other integrated learning environments has created the need for support personnel to change their traditional approaches to scheduling service provision. Specifically, structures that allow support personnel to observe and work with students in the context of the ongoing educational programs are *essential* to ensure educational relevance of their support. The need to observe how students function in daily life at school in general education classes and in other integrated school and community environments cannot be overemphasized. In order to make such

observations, however, flexible approaches to scheduling are required. Two strategies for flexible scheduling are *block scheduling* and *coteaching*.

Block Scheduling One alternative to traditional scheduling of related services time (i.e., back-to-back direct therapy sessions of 30–45 minutes twice a week in a separate environment) is the use of block scheduling (Benson, 1993; Rainforth & York, 1987; York, Rainforth, & Wiemann, 1988). Block scheduling refers to allocating longer periods of time than usual (e.g., a half or full day instead of 30–45 minutes) to provide the time and flexibility needed to work in and move between the learning environments in which students with disabilities are integrated. The amount of time spent providing services using a block-scheduling approach usually is about the same as in a more traditional approach to scheduling. For example, in a more traditional approach, a speech-language pathologist might have spent a total of 12 hours per month with three students, seeing each student for 30 minutes twice a week. Using a block-scheduling approach and assuming there are 6 hours of school each day, the same speech-language pathologist might spend 1 half day per week or one full day every other week in an elementary school in which three students with intensive challenges are integrated. Each student will continue to receive 4 hours of service per month. The major difference between the approaches is not how much time is spent supporting students, but where and how that time is spent. Most, if not all, of the time is spent in integrated learning environments by observing how students participate, determining context-specific needs and capacities, working directly with the student, and working indirectly with other staff who work directly with students on a regular basis.

There are countless ways to design block schedules. The specific design will vary given the array of demographic, student, district, and team member variables. As mentioned previously, a block-scheduling model results in less frequent interactions with students, but the interactions are for longer periods of time. This longer time block provides the flexibility for the therapist to interact with students in a number of educational environments and activities. Two examples of how a block schedule might look for an individual therapist are provided in Figures 8.6 and 8.7.

In the first example (Figure 8.6), the schedule for Ms. Jackson, a speech-language pathologist who works in an urban high school, is shown. There are two speech-language pathologists at the high school. One has a caseload of students with mild disabilities and speech/language needs only. The other therapist, Ms. Jackson, has 10 students with mild disabilities and 20 students with severe disabilities (students labeled as having moderate, severe, or profound mental retardation) in her caseload. Ms. Jackson now provides support through block scheduling (designated as A on the schedule) for most of the students with severe disabilities in integrated general education classes and off campus in community-based instructional sites. Because block-scheduled services are relatively new for Ms. Jackson, her students with mild disabilities (B) will continue with a more traditional schedule and model of services for this school year. There are five students with severe disabilities in each grade. One half-day block of time is allocated to each different class (e.g., freshmen, sophomores, juniors, seniors) to facilitate interactions with staff assigned to the respective grade levels during the block of scheduled time. Because some of the high school classes meet every other day, the schedule rotates to provide opportunities to work with students on different days of the week. Two flex days are scheduled every month for students with severe disabilities to provide the opportunity to work in environments missed during the regularly scheduled block times and to consult with other school and community personnel.

The second example (Figure 8.7) shows the schedule for Mr. Wiley, a physical therapist working as the primary sensorimotor therapist for a physical–occupational therapist team. (A primary therapist approach is described in greater detail later.) Mr. Wiley provides services in a three-county rural cooperative education district. Some of the same scheduling strategies are used for this rural-based therapist as for the urban high school therapist: Allocate half- or full-day blocks of time for a designated group of students; add a rotating element to the schedule to allow work on different days; and add "flex" time to get back to missed activities and to consult with other team members. Therapists in rural areas usually have smaller caseloads spread over large geographic areas, requiring considerable time for travel. Because of the low-incidence factor, the scheduling options for this rural therapist were to see every student for a short block of time on a weekly basis or to see every student for a longer block of time but less frequently, about every other week. The teams decided that longer blocks of time every other week would provide more meaningful interactions than shorter blocks of time every week. Because this full-time physical therapist is working as a primary sensorimotor therapist, his caseload is about half of what it would be if both the physical and occupational therapist tried to provide ongoing support to every student. The physical–occupational therapist team decided that, for most of the students, one ther-

Ms. Jackson's Schedule for 1996–97 School Year

	Monday	Tuesday	Wednesday	Thursday	Friday
Week 1	A (freshmen) · · · · · A (sophomores)	B	A (juniors) · · · · · A (seniors)	B	A flex
Week 2	B	A (freshmen) · · · · · A (sophomores)	B	A (juniors) · · · · · A (seniors)	flex
Week 3	A (freshmen) · · · · · A (sophomores)	B	A (juniors) · · · · · A (seniors)	B	A flex
Week 4	B	A (freshmen) · · · · · A (sophomores)	B	A (juniors) · · · · · A (seniors)	flex

Central High School
•1,500 students grades 9-12

•80 students receiving speech-language support:
  60 students with mild disabilities or **speech-language** needs
  20 students with moderate/severe disabilities

•Caseloads of 2 full-time speech-language therapists:
  •Ms. Romando: 50 students with mild disabilities or **speech-language** needs
  •Ms. Jackson: A blocks - 20 students with moderate/severe disabilities and **speech-language**
                  needs (5 freshmen, 5 sophomores, 5 juniors [including Jamal], 5 seniors)
                  B blocks - 10 students with mild disabilities and/or **speech-language** needs

Figure 8.6.   Sample block schedule for a speech-language pathologist in an urban high school.

Mr. Wiley's Schedule for 1996–97 School Year:

	Monday	Tuesday	Wednesday	Thursday	Friday
Week 1	HS (5 students)	MS (2 students) • • • • • • • • • • E1 (2 students)	E2 (2 students)	E3 (2 students)	flex
Week 2	E6 (1 student) • • • • • • • • • • E7 (1 student)	E1 (2 students) • • • • • • • • • E8 (1 student)	E4 (2 students)	E5 (2 students)	flex
Week 3	E1 (2 students) • • • • • • • • • MS (2 students)	HS (5 students)	E3 (2 students)	E2 (2 students)	flex
Week 4	E8 (1 student) • • • • • • • • • E1 (2 students)	E7 (1 student) • • • • • • • • • E6 (1 student)	E5 (2 students)	E4 (2 students)	flex

•Mr. Wiley functions as the primary therapist for an OT/PT team. Opportunities for Mr. Wiley and his OT complement are available on flex days and by overlapping schedules in the same regions on the same days.

•22 students in 10 different school buildings receive integrated motor support from Mr. Wiley:

Union Junior / Senior High School	(HS)	5 students
Wawiag Middle School	(MS)	2 students
East Wawiag Elementary School	(E1)	2 students
Central Elementary School	(E2)	2 students
Duncan Elementary School	(E3)	2 students
Farmington Elementary School	(E4)	2 students
Elliott Elementary School	(E5)	2 students
Horace Elementary School	(E6)	2 students
Grant Elementary School	(E7)	2 students
West Union Elementary School	(E8)	1 student

Figure 8.7.   Sample of a block schedule for a physical therapist (functioning as a primary therapist for an occupational–physical therapist team) in a rural cooperative district.

apist or the other could meet the sensori-motor needs, as long as both therapists had initial and ongoing opportunities to learn with and from one another.

Most frequently applied to the provision of occupational and physical therapy services, a *primary therapist model* involves designating either the physical or occupational therapist as the primary "sensorimotor therapist" for individual students (in the same way that more special educators are beginning to work cross-categorically). A physical therapist and an occupational therapist are teamed to have ongoing access to one another. They work together during assessments and during initial team discussions about the design of the educational program and selection of educational priorities. Ongoing consultation and support to students and teachers is provided by one therapist or the other. Usually on a monthly basis, the physical therapist and occupational therapist are scheduled to work together on individual student issues or other relevant aspects of service provision and support. Adoption of a primary therapist model of service provision is predicated on recognition that many physical therapists and occupational therapists have overlapping areas of expertise, particularly in the area of developmental disabilities. When areas of expertise do not overlap, they can learn from one another, just as when professionals learn new skills from members of their own discipline, and just as special educators and related services personnel expect general educators to expand their repertoire of skills to effectively support students when no additional professional support is present in integrated learning environments.

There are numerous advantages to a primary therapist model. First, teachers, parents, students, and other members of the teams know whom to consult when "sen-sorimotor" issues arise. Second, there are fewer team members among whom coordination must occur. Third, therapists usually can spend nearly twice the time with any one student because caseloads are condensed. Fourth, therapists are forced to look comprehensively at students' sensorimotor needs, the impact of those needs on educational performance, and priorities for instructional intervention and management. Fifth, therapists have an opportunity for ongoing professional growth and learning. Sixth, therapists have a way to structure ongoing (albeit infrequent) access to another therapist. This is particularly advantageous for therapists who are isolated from one another in rural areas. The primary disadvantage in the initial stages of implementing a primary therapist model can be somewhat lower knowledge and skill related to certain aspects of student performance given that there are unique areas of expertise between physical and occupational therapists. Diminished expertise in the short term, however, usually is considered a reasonable cost for long-term efficiency and effectiveness in meeting holistic, context-specific student needs.

On days that therapists have time blocked to spend with students, they typically work in a range of educational environments. Before school on a block-scheduled day, usually the therapist meets briefly (10–15 minutes) with the teacher(s) of the students to be seen during the day to identify priorities for the therapist to address for each student and to determine where the therapist needs to be and when in order to attend to the priorities. With priorities identified, a schedule for the block time is developed. Figure 8.8 shows an example of one such schedule.

Activities engaged in during the block-scheduled time can include collaborating with teachers, the student, and paraprofessionals to establish priorities that must be

Time	Location	Instruction	Students and Activities/Priorities for Therapist	
7:45-8:00	Homeroom (Room 106)	Nancy A. (teacher)	Andy:	Greetings Conversation book
			William:	Initiate and maintain conversation
8:05-8:55	Spanish (Room 247)	Trish G. (teacher)	Jamal:	Vocalize for attention Choose a partner Make requests by scanning
			Sue:	Initiate appropriate conversation Choose a partner Maintain conversation (turntaking)
9:15-12:00	Community Work Experience (Metro Insurance Agency)	Jake S. (teaching assistant)	Andy:	Greetings Conversation book Indicate need for assistance
			Jamal:	Vocalize for attention Make requests by scanning Tell a joke with the tape recorder
			William:	Initiate and maintain conversation Request assistance Indicate when work is finished
12:40-1:30	Art Class (Room 117)	Brian K. (teacher)	Denise:	Choose art materials Request assistance Show project to a classmate
			Sharla:	Greetings Follow directions for project tasks Secure listener attention before communicating
1:35-2:25	Home Economics (Room 106)	Jane M. (teacher)	Sue:	Initiate appropriate conversation Maintain conversation (turntaking) "Read" the list of ingredients in an adapted recipe to a classmate
			Sharla:	Greetings Secure listener attention before communicating Follow directions from a peer for a cooking task
			James:	Greetings Give color-coded utensils to a classmate upon request Maintain conversation by responding to a question from a classmate

Figure 8.8. Sample blocked schedule for speech-language pathologist assigned to high school students.

addressed; observing and working directly with students in educational contexts to determine the effectiveness of interventions and the need to make program changes, expansions, or deletions; providing support to primary instructors in terms of training, problem solving, and providing feedback and reinforcement; recording data on student performance; and documenting decisions made. Many teams designate regularly scheduled meeting times on some of the block-scheduled days to reduce the time that therapists spend traveling between school buildings on any given day. Although meeting to establish priorities and plan interventions is essential for an effective collaborative team approach, team members are cautioned about letting meetings encroach on time that was originally allocated for working directly with students.

One challenge encountered when implementing a block-scheduling approach is to develop an accountability or monitoring system so that priority needs of students are not inadvertently forgotten. Figures 8.9 and 8.10 provide two formats that can be used to keep track of priority student needs supported by the therapist. Figure 8.9 presents a worksheet format used to identify and monitor priority needs for each educational context. The specific example shows a partial listing of the priority needs of students with severe disabilities in the junior class (of which Jamal is a member) that will be addressed in collaboration with the physical/occupational therapist. This type of worksheet can be used as a guide for teachers and therapists to identify priorities for the therapist during each block-scheduled time. For example, before school on the day that the therapist is scheduled to observe and work with the Xavier High School juniors with severe disabilities, the therapist and teacher would meet and circle items on the worksheet that were priorities for the therapist to observe on that day. The Comments column provides space to write notes about the specific issues to address and about observations made or follow-up needed. On subsequent visits, the therapist and teacher can look back over past worksheets to determine which needs have

not been attended to and should, therefore, be priorities for subsequent consultations/observations. Depending on the specific format used, the worksheets with comments can be copied and disseminated to other members of the team as well.

Figure 8.10 presents a different consultation/monitoring format, especially useful when more than one student with support needs is located in the same or an adjacent class. In this example, 4 of 22 students in Kristen's kindergarten class required the support of a speech-language pathologist. Before school on block-scheduled days, the teacher and therapist identify needs to be addressed during that day using the chart as an organizational framework. There is room to write comments at the bottom of the worksheet. As with the other worksheet, this worksheet provides an organizational structure to cue team members as to priority needs to be addressed, provides space to write comments, and serves as an ongoing way to monitor attention to priority needs.

Coteaching   A second way to consider scheduling time for related services personnel in general education learning environments is referred to as coteaching. Most frequently described as an approach for general and special education teachers to share responsibility for direct instruction (Bauwens & Hourcade, 1995; Friend & Cook, 1996), the application for related services providers is apparent in some situations as well (Rainforth & England, 1997). When coteaching, the classroom teacher and support person jointly design and implement instruction. For example, an occupational therapist and preschool teacher may coteach for half days in an integrated preschool class. Using a variety of centers as a primary means of instruction, the two teachers determine the desired outcomes, activities, and learning methods that will be employed at each center. Then each professional may

Consultation/Monitoring Worksheet

School: Xavier High School   **Grade**: 11th (junior)
Students: JW, MR, YI, RJ, SN
Support Schedule: Week 1 Monday morning   **Support person**: Ms. Adams
                       Week 2 Tuesday morning   **Team meeting**: Week 3
                       Week 3 Monday afternoon   Monday 2:45 - 3:45 PM
                       Week 4 Tuesday afternoon

Student	Context	Priority	Comments	Student	Context	Priority	Comments
JW	School	Inside mobility		YI	School	Rate of mobility	
	Classes	Positions			School	Transfers	
	Classes	Movement sequence			School	Carrying belongings	
	Classes	Arm use			School	Locker use	
	Classes	Adaptation			School	Coat	
	Comm.	Other			School	Gym clothes change	
	Comm.	Outside mobility			School	Gym participation	
	Comm.	Arm use			School	Location in class	
	Comm.	Head/neck position			School	Organization of materials	
	Comm.	Other			Comm.	Rate of mobility	
	Work	Inside mobility			Comm.	Inclines	
	Work	Positions			Comm.	Doors	
	Work	Arm use			Comm.	Elevators	
	Work	Head/neck position			Comm.	Carrying	
	Work	Other			Comm.	Car transfer	
	Home	Positions			Comm.	Other	
	Home	Movement sequence			Home	Floor mobility	
	Home	Arm use			Home	Position transfers	
	Home	Adaptations					

Figure 8.9. Partial sample consultation/monitoring worksheet of educationally relevant priorities to be addressed by a physical/occupational therapist.

assume primary responsibility for creating specific centers. Both would facilitate instruction of all students as they rotate through the centers. In this way, both

Consultation/Monitoring Worksheet

Date: _____   Support by: _____

Daily Kindergarten Schedule	Instructional Priorities Requiring Speech–Language Support for:			
	Kristen	Yolanda	Turner	Rex
Arrival and Free Play				
Opening Group (at tables)				
Story (on rug)				
Gross Motor/Perceptual Activity (or specials)				
Fine Motor/Perceptual Activity (or specials)				
Snack				
Free Play				
Dismissal				
Other				

Comments / notes: _____

_____

_____

_____

_____

Copy and disseminate to: _____

_____

_____

_____

Figure 8.10.   Sample consultation/monitoring worksheet for identifying instructional priorities supported by a speech-language pathologist.

the occupational therapist and preschool teacher are tied to daily, direct instructional responsibilities.

Drawing on the integrated instructional program example involving Kristen, Figure 8.11 illustrates one specific structure for implementing a coteaching approach. In this situation, the team decided to have the speech-language pathologist spend the first half of every morning (1½ hours) coteaching with the teacher in Kristen's kindergarten class and the second half of the morning coteaching in another kindergarten class. In Kristen's class, there were three other youngsters who were known to require speech/language support to benefit from their educational programs. There were several students considered to be at risk for de-velopmental delays but not identified as needing special services. There were also two students for whom English is not a primary language. With consultation from the English for Speakers of Other Languages (ESOL) teacher to the speech-language pathologist and kindergarten teacher, these students benefited from the presence of another teacher during the morning kindergarten session (although the ESOL students received direct instruction to learn English). In the afternoon, the speech-language pathologist implemented more of a block-scheduling approach to support students by spending each afternoon block of time with a different grade level. A paraeducator assumed a classroom support role with primary responsibilities for Kristen when the speech-language

Ms. Jan M.'s Speech-Language Weekly Schedule

	Monday	Tuesday	Wednesday	Thursday	Friday
Before-school meetings			WK 1: Multiage Class A WK 2: Multiage Class B	Kindergarten coteachers (meet weekly)	WK 1: Grade 1 WK 2: Grade 2
Morning 8:30-10:00	Coteach in kindergarten A	Coteach in kindergarten A	Coteach in kindergarten A	Coteach in kindergarten A	Coteach in kindergarten A
Morning 10:15-11:45	Coteach in kindergarten B	Coteach in kindergarten B	Coteach in kindergarten B	Coteach in kindergarten B	Coteach in kindergarten B
Afternoon	Multiage Class A (grades 1-3)	Multiage Class B (grades 1-3)	Grade 1 Team	Grade 2 Team	Afternoon kindergarten

Figure 8.11.   Sample speech-language pathologist schedule combining coteaching and block scheduling. (WK, week.)

pathologist was not present. (At the beginning of the school year, the paraeducator was paid to spend additional hours with the speech-language pathologist to learn how to effectively support Kristen and to function as a learning facilitator for all members of the class.) The schedule shown also provides the flexibility to schedule opportunities for the therapist to work with students individually or in small groups in the afternoon as needed for assessment or short-term intensive intervention. Finally, the schedule in Figure 8.11 indicates a brief before-school meeting schedule made possible because the school administration is committed to no schoolwide morning meetings, preferring after-school meeting times instead. The speech-language pathologist is scheduled to meet weekly with her coteachers and every other week with the afternoon classroom teachers.

Considering Use of Block Scheduling, Coteaching, or a Combination of Both There are distinct advantages and disadvantages in selecting block scheduling, coteaching, or a combination of the two approaches. Block scheduling offers the flexibility to learn about and indirectly support student learning needs across a variety of learning activities and environments. However, therapists would typically see students less frequently and would rely heavily on an indirect model of service provision. Coteaching offers the opportunity to regularly (e.g., three to five times each week) provide direct instruction and to share equally with the teacher in instructional design, facilitation, and evaluation. Another advantage is acquiring the distinction of being a "real teacher" in the eyes of all the students by establishing a wider circle of relationships. As a result, students with unique needs are less likely to feel singled out. A primary disadvantage of coteaching exclusively is the inability for a therapist to be present in other

learning environments because he or she is tied to providing direct instruction. This means, for example, if the speech-language pathologist is scheduled to coteach for a 2-hour language arts block every morning, he or she would not be available to observe and indirectly support any other students during that time.

The block-scheduling and coteaching approaches are both intended to provide more contextually relevant instructional support to students in their educational programs. Both require an expanded repertoire of knowledge, perspective, and skill versus more traditional and familiar means of service provision. As mentioned previously, special educators have used coteaching more widely than related services personnel. Among related services providers, this option has been used primarily by speech-language pathologists in elementary schools and by occupational therapists in preschool classrooms. Given current incidence, caseload, and geographic distribution of students with severe disabilities, block scheduling is likely to be the more frequently adopted approach for occupational therapists and physical therapists. Block scheduling may be more appropriate when a speech-language pathologist has major responsibility for students with severe disabilities, but coteaching may be more appropriate when heterogeneous groups of students require support in inclusive classrooms. At the secondary level, coteaching will be most successful when related services are individually matched with general education teachers and classes. In high school, for example, there may be language arts classes that provide excellent learning opportunities for students with reading and language challenges in which the support of a speech-language pathologist would be appropriate. Another example might be home and community living classes in which students would benefit greatly from the regular support of an occupational therapist. As more related services personnel work toward integrating their support, more will be learned about the scheduling and service provision options that are most effective in unique situations.

Schedule Regular Meeting Times for Team Members to Reflect and Plan

Opportunities to collaborate, learn from, and support teammates in their work with students occur informally and continuously throughout the shared experiences working with students in everyday activities. In fact, as team members share work space, responsibilities, and instruction of students, the need to meet outside of those times often decreases. When team members work in isolation from one another, a considerable amount of meeting time is necessary for teachers to explain the context in which students are experiencing difficulty and for support personnel to suggest how unique learning challenges might be interfering and to recommend potentially useful interventions. Sharing common experiences in the instructional context results in more efficient interactions among team members. The need to get a team member "up to speed" about the context is alleviated. The focus of collaborative meeting times then shifts to long-range planning, focused problem solving regarding very complex and difficult challenges, and broadening the scope of disciplines (e.g., the school psychologist attends to provide input on a perplexing problem). For at least these reasons, regularly scheduled meetings with select team members, in addition to IEP meetings and staff development sessions, are necessary.

The authors strongly recommend that, at the beginning of each school year, a year-long schedule for meetings be established. Meetings can always be canceled, but they are very difficult to schedule, especially when many people are involved. Some professionals respond negatively to the notion of regularly scheduled meetings. Much of this negative response stems from a history of meetings that do not result in useful outcomes. Questioning the benefit of these types of meetings is understandable. The purpose of regularly scheduled interactions among members of the collaborative educational team is to provide support to other team members in meeting the needs of students. As team members begin to realize benefits from the supportive interactions, they are usually less opposed to the regular interactions. In fact, many team members have come to enjoy and look forward to team member interactions because they provide a sense of community among co-workers, in addition to enhancing the quality of their work.

The way in which team members carve out regularly scheduled meeting times depends largely on a range of local logistical factors. Certainly, the easiest structure for which to plan regularly scheduled team meetings was that of students with severe disabilities attending only self-contained special education classes. Team meetings could then address the needs of multiple students with disabilities from the same (separate) class at the same time. As more students become fully included in general education and other integrated learning environments, scheduling meeting opportunities becomes more complex because of the decentralized student population, the increased number of team members involved (i.e., general education staff), and the great number of children with whom each general education teacher is involved. Allocating time to meet poses an even greater challenge at the secondary level than at the elementary level because of frequent class changes, dramatically increased numbers of service providers, and organization of teachers by curricular content area instead of by grade or class. Despite these challenges, or perhaps because of them, team members must work to find time to collaborate so that educational programs are designed and implemented in the most coordinated way possible. Some strategies that may be useful are presented here.

When initiating a change to greater inclusion of students with severe disabilities or to greater collaboration among staff, teams frequently will focus on one or two students as a pilot effort. Sometimes this has resulted in teams scheduling meetings to discuss only the targeted students. Certainly, such intensive scheduling may be necessary during the transition process. It is rarely possible, however, to maintain such a high level of interaction for individual students when increasing numbers of students become involved. Therefore, it is suggested that existing meeting structures (e.g., grade-level team meetings) from which to expand be identified, that interaction structures that will have maintenance potential be developed, or both, because increasing numbers of students will have needs that must be addressed in a collaborative way.

In some schools the focus of preexisting meeting structures has been expanded to include attention to the needs of students with disabilities. For example, many elementary and middle schools have regularly scheduled grade-level team meetings. Special education and related services personnel become participants in these meetings. In this way, they learn more about general education and they can serve as resources to a broader array of children. One special education or related services professional can be assigned to each grade-level team to serve as a primary liaison. The special education and related services personnel may then meet on their own as a support team to exchange information across grade levels. Not infre-

quently, special education teachers are assigned to grade-level teams and related services personnel work through the special educator because there are almost always more special educators than members of any other related service. Furthermore, the student caseload of a special educator is not spread as widely as are the caseloads of students assigned to each related services provider.

In addition to grade-level interactions in elementary and middle schools, time is usually required to focus on issues specific to individual students or classrooms. These interactions usually occur between the classroom teacher, the special education support teacher, and, depending on the needs of the student(s), select related services personnel. During the initial stages of working together, these meetings typically occur at least every other week for at least 30 minutes. Of great support to a related services provider are meetings scheduled on the days he or she will be at a particular building—frequently before school, after school, over lunch, or during prep periods. When junior high schools embrace the philosophy of a middle school with its teaching teams, significant periods of daily or weekly planning time are built in. Sometimes the issues that involve related services personnel must be channeled through the special education teacher because of his or her more frequent access to the general education classroom teacher. At other times the nature of the discussions must involve the related services personnel directly. In general, classroom teachers seem more receptive to meetings when there is the potential to discuss issues related to more than just the labeled student with severe disabilities.

Scheduling regular meetings among team members at the secondary level presents a significant challenge because of the number of different teachers who may be involved with any particular student. It is helpful to develop a master schedule of prep periods for each of the general education classroom teachers. Frequently, the special education teacher meets with the general education classroom teachers during prep periods or for a few minutes before or after classes. The nature of these consultations is specific to the student's participation in the respective class. The flexibility offered through a block-scheduling strategy and through the provision of flex days provides related services personnel with the opportunity to meet with classroom teachers during prep periods as well. To reduce fragmentation, especially at the secondary level, it is useful to conceptualize support teams that comprise special education and related services personnel. These support teams provide support to a number of students and general education teachers across classes and grades.

Nationwide, educational teams of various sorts (not just those supporting students with severe disabilities) are finding creative ways to schedule meeting time. Summarized here are suggestions from our own experiences with school teams and suggestions compiled from a variety of sources (Dettmer, Dyck, & Thurston, 1996; Hanft & Place, 1996; Raywid, 1993):

- Increase each school day by 5 minutes to create 5 early release days.
- Adjust daily student schedule by adding 15 minutes on 4 days each week, resulting in an early release 1 day per week.
- Schedule common lunch 1 day a week, preferably back-to-back with a common prep period.
- Hold monthly or bimonthly special events (all school or all grade), facilitated by community members or nondirect service personnel.

- Combine classes for one period each week to free up one of the classroom teachers.
- Stagger compensatory time throughout the week so paraprofessionals can join meetings.
- Use staff development funds to hire a consistent person to be a rotating substitute teacher, freeing classroom teachers.

Unfortunately, many of these strategies are designed on the premise that time to meet and plan with colleagues is in addition to a full teaching or service provision load. We join with education reform advocates who assert the need for reflection, learning, and development to be an integral and valued part of a professional day. Unfortunately, there are economic and cultural expectations that limit progress in the area of providing educators with significant, regular opportunities for reflection, learning, and development among colleagues. Furthermore, related services providers rarely have "substitutes" and may believe that meetings are not an acceptable use of their limited time. Although meetings cannot be allowed to "eat up" time needed with students, therapists may need to feel support from their team (and administrators) to participate in team meetings as an investment in effective instruction.

DEVELOPING EFFECTIVE COLLABORATION SKILLS

An assumption of collaborative teamwork is that an open exchange of information, made possible through effective communication, results in the best possible educational programs for individual students. Effective communication has been repeatedly identified as essential for collaboration (Bauwens & Hourcade, 1995; Dettmer et al., 1996; Friend & Cook, 1996; Johnson & Johnson,

1994; Nowacek, 1992; West & Cannon, 1988). A central question then develops: What facilitates open communication and effective team member interactions? Trust among team members is essential. Trust behaviors include expressing appropriate warmth and liking of others; expressing support and acceptance; lack of ridicule, rejection, put-downs, and silences; listening to others; and praising others (Thousand & Villa, 1992). Early in its work together, each team is encouraged to establish its own set of ground rules for interaction by having each team member write down answers to the following question: "What would it take for me to feel safe communicating openly and honestly in this group?" The responses are compiled anonymously into a list of ground rules for the group. Effective communication also is enhanced when team members demonstrate both task and relationship skills required for collaboration (Johnson & Johnson, 1994; Kruger, 1988; Thousand & Villa, 1992) (see Figure 8.12). To remain effective, collaborative educational teams must maintain a balance between accomplishing the work or tasks of the group and maintaining positive and reinforcing relationships among team members.

Collaboration skills are learned. Some team members may be more inclined to demonstrate collaborative tendencies, but all team members can learn specific collaboration skills, given the commitment, support, and opportunity. Five skill areas are identified here as being central to effective collaboration: 1) facilitating effective team meetings; 2) exchanging information and skills (e.g., engaging in role release, teaching one another); 3) solving problems as a group; 4) making decisions by consensus; and 5) working through differences in perspective (e.g., conflict resolution). Some team members are familiar with these skill areas.

Most can benefit from further exposure and application. This section briefly addresses each of these five skill areas, emphasizing specific application to integrating related services. Interested readers are urged to refer to the resources cited in our discussion and to the extensive array of literature and professional development opportunities widely available.

Facilitating Effective Team Meetings

As discussed previously, scheduling regular opportunities for team members to meet poses a challenge for many teams and schools. Once scheduled, significant effort is almost always necessary to maximize the effectiveness and outcomes of time allocated to collaboration. The authors know of many teams that invested enormous effort (e.g., year-long planning) to schedule regular meetings but, within weeks after the meetings started, members began to disaffiliate. Individuals can become disillusioned and disappointed when an effective, efficient, and supportive group process does not immediately result. Why? Providing a schedule to meet was only the first step toward creating effective and productive meetings. Team members need to develop meeting facilitation and small-group interaction skills. The following guidelines are adapted from York-Barr, Kronberg, and Doyle (1996) and are offered to increase the efficiency and effectiveness of scheduled meetings. Over time, skills develop and small-group work can become a rewarding means of supporting students in their educational programs.

Establish Expectations and Standards Many teams find it helpful to discuss, establish, and periodically revisit shared expectations and standards for meeting disposition and behavior. Expectations might include

- Team meetings begin and end on time. When people arrive late, everyone's time

Task Skills	Relationship Skills
•Offering information	•Encouraging participation
•Offering opinions	•Offering a tension reliever
•Acting as an information seeker	•Being a communication helper
•Acting as a summarizer	•Being a process observer
•Diagnosing group difficulties	•Being an active listener
•Coordinating work	•Offering support to ideas
•Acting as a recorder	•Offering personal support
•Acting as a timekeeper	•Being a praiser
•Giving help	•Being a harmonizer and compromiser
•Asking for help	•Being an interpersonal problem solver
•Asking questions	

Figure 8.12. Examples of task and relationship skills required for collaborative teamwork. (From Thousand, J., Fox, T.J., Reid, R., Godek, J., Williams, W., & Fox, W. [1986]. *The Homecoming Model: Educating students who present intensive educational challenges within regular education environments* [p. 36]. Burlington: University of Vermont, Center for Developmental Disabilities; reprinted by permission.)

is wasted. When people leave early, contributions are lost and momentum decreases. Collective "team time" ends when one member leaves, unless that member does not have a central role in remaining items.

- Team meeting times are honored and take priority over most work functions. If a member is unable to attend, he or she notifies the facilitator or other team member. Preference will be to reschedule instead of cancel if urgent issues requiring broad input are pressing.
- If there is an agenda item of critical importance, the team will allocate sufficient time to address the item. Decisions will not be hastily made without adequate input and process and careful consideration of possible outcomes.

- Team members actively listen to the perspectives expressed by others.
- Team members are prepared for meetings.
- Team leadership is shared and group roles are rotated.
- Team discussions and decisions are student focused.

Some teams decide to record and post (e.g., on the back side of meeting agenda forms) agreed-upon standards so they are easily reviewed at meetings.

Prepare for Team Meetings Preparation maximizes meeting efficiency and effectiveness of the valuable time members have allocated to collaborative interactions. Suggestions include

1. Jointly establish meeting times, locations, and expectations (as discussed

previously). If possible and agreed upon, create a schedule of meetings for the entire school year.

2. Generate an agenda prior to the meeting using a process that allows any member to contribute. Agenda items include those held over from prior meetings as well as new items submitted by members. Members can contribute new items on an agenda posted in a common or easily accessible location (classroom) or by communicating items over the telephone, by voice mail, or by e-mail. Submitted agenda items should include a brief description of the item, the name of the person who submitted the item, preparation that is needed by other team members, the desired outcome of the discussion, and an estimated amount of time required to address the item. Agenda items should be submitted sufficiently in advance of the meeting to allow time for the facilitator to make copies and for members to prepare for items as needed. Some teams choose to list something fun, new, or interesting as the first agenda item for each meeting. A sample agenda format is provided in Figure 8.13.

3. Assign group roles prior to meetings so that members know the roles for which to be prepared. Assigned roles frequently include *facilitator, recorder, timekeeper,* and *process observer.* Roles can be rotated and assigned months, or even an entire school year, in advance. If meetings are scheduled in advance, preassigned roles can be listed on the master schedule. On both the sample agenda (Figure 8.13) and sample meeting minutes (see Figure 8.14) forms there are spaces provided to indicate who will be performing specified roles.

4. Extend meeting invitations to additional people (nonregular team members) who

are needed to move forward on designated agenda items. For example, a building principal may be needed to assist with making changes in schedules that have an impact on other teams or elements of school functioning.

5. Finally, and optionally, there are teams that adopt rituals of varying sorts that take on important meaning for the group. Many teams bring food or some type of treat. One team the authors know begins every meeting with the ritual of reading one another's horoscope. Many times, individual team members bring quotes or readings of interest and relevance to the group. Each of these team member contributions and connections facilitates building a sense of community.

Conduct Team Meetings When run well and participated in fully, team meetings can be a vehicle for meaningful, productive, and supportive collaborative interactions. Following are basic guidelines for conducting team meetings:

1. When meeting dates and group roles have been scheduled in advance for a school year, meeting roles are already designated and the meeting can begin. If not, the following roles must be assigned:

Facilitator

- provides structure and focus during the meeting
- supports team members in sharing responsibility for the process and outcomes of the meeting
- encourages participation of each member (and ensures that visiting members are introduced to the group

Team Meeting Agenda

Team meeting for:_____ Date:_____ Time:_____

Location of meeting: _____

Facilitator:_____ Recorder: _____

Agenda Items and Description	Outcomes Desired	Time
1. Something fun, new, or interesting 2. Follow-up items		

Figure 8.13.   Sample team meeting agenda format.

Team Meeting Minutes

Team meeting for:_____   Date:_____
                                             Start time:____ Finish time:_____

Participants: _____
_____

Facilitator:_____   Recorder: _____

Priority Sequence	Agenda Items and Key Points	Follow-up Needed: Who? What? When?
1. 2.	Anecdote: Follow-up:	

Next meeting:
Date/time: _____   Location:_____
Facilitator:_____   Recorder:_____
Agenda items:_____

Figure 8.14. Sample team meeting minutes format.

with their reason for participation articulated as well)

- clarifies individual and group communication, including taking the lead in facilitating more structured problem-solving and decision-making processes
- summarizes discussion and decisions or asks that another member do so

Recorder

- documents key information
- brings closure to topics by summarizing decisions reached, clarifying people responsible, and identifying time lines for follow-up activities
- copies and distributes meeting minutes to all team members

Timekeeper

- monitors efficient use of time
- informs team when predetermined time allocations are nearing
- assists the team to negotiate new time allocations as needed

Process Observer

- attends to overall group process
- observes the use of interpersonal and task skills among team members
- shares observations and reflections related to the group process, particularly related to preestablished standards or areas of group process difficulty (e.g., shared responsibility for follow-up, active listening when there are differences of opinion)

2. At the beginning of each meeting, the facilitator leads the team in a process of prioritizing agenda items so that the an-

ticipated discussion lasts no longer than the predetermined time. (The authors suggest limiting meetings to 30, 45, or 60 minutes. Focused interactions for set amounts of time can be very productive, especially after teams have evolved to more efficient ways of interacting.) Follow-up responsibilities from previous meetings also are reviewed by the facilitator. After reviewing the agenda items, estimate the amount of time required to address each item. Assign ranks, being sure to put the most important items early in the meeting. At times, team members may agree to adjust a predetermined agenda or schedule if urgent issues arise. Such adjustments should be made judiciously, however, so that crisis and reactive work does not become a group norm.

3. Create and disseminate notes from the meeting. For each item, delineate follow-up activities, assign people to be responsible for completion, and determine an appropriate time line for follow-up. A sample format for keeping minutes of the meetings is provided in Figure 8.14. It may be possible to make copies on site immediately following the meeting and disseminate copies before team members leave.

4. Leave sufficient time (5–10 minutes) to process information on group functioning at the end of the meeting. Reflecting on how group members work together promotes continuous improvement and effectiveness (Johnson & Johnson, 1994).

Process and Bring Meetings to Close Particularly during the early formation of a specific team of individuals, processing is useful at the end of each meeting. Processing time is allocated to elicit individual perceptions from each team member about how the group functioned during the meeting. Such ongoing attention to group process and expectation for individual feedback bring an important degree of attentiveness to individual and group skills and styles of interaction. As teams evolve, decisions to engage in formal processing less frequently, less formally, or both may be made. Any team member, however, should provide feedback whenever deemed necessary to maintain effective task and relational aspects of group functioning. Teams often discuss the following topics:

- Identify a component of the meeting that went well.
- Share a circumstance during the meeting that felt uncomfortable.
- Describe an interaction between team members that might have been handled differently.
- Note the overall tone of the meeting and consider why that tone was present.
- Acknowledge and celebrate improvements of individual or group skills.

After processing such items, some teams choose to close the meeting more informally by engaging in a "whip" or "sweep" in which each member states a word or phrase that captures his or her current thoughts about the meeting or desires for future meetings or work together.

Exchanging Information and Skills
To implement an integrated approach to the provision of related services, information and skills are exchanged among team members. As discussed in Chapter 7, intervention methods are contributed from various team members and integrated into one instructional plan, usually for each educational activity. Implementation of the instruction is then carried out by a designated primary instructor, usually a teacher or paraprofes-

sional. Sometimes, the student him- or herself may be responsible, with others monitoring. Effective implementation of the integrated instructional plans requires that team members become effective teachers and learners. Given the availability of therapists for only portions of a school day or week, frequently they assume the role of teaching others specific methods of intervention. In this way, they function in a consulting capacity. Hanft and Place (1996) offer six general strategies to enhance the roles of therapists when they function as consultants:

1. Work as an equal, not an authority.
2. Participate in school routines.
3. Nurture relationships with teachers and other team members.
4. Expect to learn from others and acknowledge when you do.
5. Incorporate principles of adult learning.
6. Ask for feedback about your consultation.

West and Cannon (1988) conducted a survey of 100 people judged to be experts in collaborative consultation, representing 47 states, regarding the knowledge, skills, attitudes, and characteristics for effective collaborative consultation. Several of the competencies considered most essential were communicating clearly and effectively in oral and written form, using active ongoing listening and responding skills, giving and soliciting continuous feedback, giving credit to others for their ideas and accomplishments, managing conflict skillfully so as to maintain collaborative relationships, and willingness to say, "I don't know. Let's find out." Central to the art of teaching and consultation is effective communication. Mutuality and respect are prevalent themes. Therapists, as consultants, are not hierarchically superior to or more expert than other team members. They simply know different material and must maximize their contributions to student learning through teaching and role release.

When therapists are unsuccessful in teaching others to develop and use new skills, it is often due to two preventable situations. First, the recipient of training did not understand or share the therapist's intention or goal for the student. The need for shared goals and strategies for eliciting them have been discussed throughout this book. The second preventable situation is that the therapist did not teach effectively. Often therapists demonstrate strategies, ask trainees if they understand, and incorrectly assume that an affirmative response means learning has occurred. Most effective in the teaching–learning partnership is interaction focused on student-specific naturally occurring situations. Providing general information (e.g., an in-service program on cerebral palsy) is rarely perceived as responsive to or effective in meeting the needs of the adult learner. Primary implementors benefit most from specific demonstration, explanation, and coaching in the actual student performance context. Figure 8.15 presents a multistep teaching sequence that the authors have found effective. This sequence can be adapted for individual circumstances. Another framework team members might find useful was created by York-Barr and colleagues (1996) for use among team members working in inclusive schools (Figure 8.16). Their framework assumes that both the learning and teaching team members share responsibility for effective interactions and that question asking and context analysis skills facilitate positive and mutual interactions.

Like all instruction, the specific strategies employed when team members teach one another intervention methods will depend on a number of variables, including the complexity of the skills to be taught, the risks involved in demonstration of the skill, the experience of the teacher, the experience of the learner in the skill area, and unique characteristics of the student with disabilities. The decision regarding when the team member in the role of learner is considered sufficiently skilled to implement interventions will depend on a number of factors as well. Ensuring the safety of both the team member who will implement the interventions and the student with disabilities is the most important consideration. Specific to meeting the physical and health care needs of students with disabilities, many professionals, professional organizations, and agencies set forth guidelines to assist in making such determinations.

Implemented in a supportive environment, exchanging information and skills among team members can be a source of positive personal and professional growth. In summary, the following principles may be used to guide teaching–learning interactions among team members:

1. *Be approachable and supportive.* Welcome questions and assist the adult learner to formulate the questions when difficulty arises. Assume responsibility for unclear expectations. Do not be too serious—use humor. Be respectful but have fun.

2. *Communicate clearly and watch for signs of understanding.* Interventions are learned and implemented most effectively when the adult learner knows not just the specific procedures and the desired student outcomes, but a rationale as well. Signs that the learner has a clear understanding of the expectations and rationale frequently are exhibited through nonverbal feedback (e.g., head nodding, smiling). Lack of understanding frequently is evident in facial expressions and body language as well.

1. Specify the desired student behavior/outcome and explain why the behavior is important for the student.

2. Outline the intervention sequence and provide a rationale for its design.

3. Explain the sequence and steps to the team member learner. Emphasize no more than two or three of the most important aspects of the intervention.

4. Demonstrate the intervention sequence in the situation in which the intervention will actually be used.

5. Ask the team member learner to review the demonstration and written sequence. Assist in reinforcing critical aspects of the intervention.

6. Provide an opportunity for the team member learner to demonstrate the intervention sequence at least three times. It may be helpful to try the intervention with another team member and/or in a simulated setting. For teaching to be complete, however, the learner must demonstrate the intervention with the student in the setting where support is required.

7. Provide instructive feedback and reinforce successive approximations. Provide specific and positive feedback about correct intervention procedures. Provide corrective feedback only on the critical aspects of the intervention that were not demonstrated correctly.

8. Review, discuss, and revise the written procedures so they function as a useful prompt for correct implementation of the intervention.

9. Ask if the team member learner has any questions or concerns or if he or she would like to demonstrate the procedures again.

10. Encourage the team member learner to initiate contact if questions or comments arise. Arrange for follow-up interactions.

Figure 8.15.   A sample sequence for teaching other team members (role release).

3. *Use an experiential learning approach.* To the greatest extent possible, especially in the early stages of learning new information, provide the adult learner with opportunities to understand through direct experience. It has been estimated that people retain 10% of what they hear, 15% of what they see, 20% of what they see and hear, 40% of what they discuss with others, 80% of what they experience directly and practice, and 90% of what they teach to others (National Training Lab, n.d.). After an experiential base is established, the adult learner has an emerging construct with which to apply new pieces of information.

4. *Increase and build from an awareness of the learners' own movement.* When assisting other team members to understand and facilitate movement, demonstrate and explain how their bodies work. For example, when teaching principles of effective seating, ask that they move their hips forward in the chair and identify what happens to their trunk, shoulder, neck, and head alignment. This simple exercise for teaching about interconnectedness of body alignment provides the adult learner with a "built-

You as the Learner

1. **Describe the situation:**

   a. Where or what is the location of the class/activity?

   b. Who is doing the teaching?

   c. What is being taught?

   d. How is it being taught (e.g., grouping, instructional delivery, use of media and materials)?

   e. What is expected of the students?

2. **Describe how the student is doing in this situation:**

   a. What is going well?

   b. What is not going well? Why?

3. **Formulate your questions:**

   a. What do you feel like you need to know?

   Short term:

   Long term:

   b. Who do you think has that information?

   c. How will you best learn the information?

   d. What other support do you need to be effective with this student?

4/56c

You as the Teacher

1. **Describe what you know about the student:**

   a. What are the student's strengths?

   b. How can you best maximize those strengths?

   c. What seems to be unpleasant for the student?

   d. What helps minimize unpleasant events or behavior?

2. **Describe what you know about learning strategies and learning contexts for this student:**

   a. What has worked well in the past?

   b. What has not worked very well?

   c. What would you recommend trying again? What would you try again, but with modifications?

   d. What kinds of environments bring out the best in the student?

   e. What kinds of environments are challenging for the student?

3. **Describe how you might teach someone else:**

   a. How will you most effectively communicate what you know?

   b. Who else might contribute to the teaching?

   c. How can you most effectively show another person what to do?

   d. How might you offer ongoing support?

4/56d

Figure 8.16. Teacher and learner questions. (From York-Barr, J., Kronberg, R.M., & Doyle, M.E. [1996]. *Creating inclusive school communities: A staff development series for general and special educators: Module 4. Collaboration: Redefining roles, practices, and structures.* Baltimore: Paul H. Brookes Publishing Co.; reprinted with permission.)

in" means of analyzing posture and movement. Teach the learner to use him- or herself as a reference as appropriate.

5. *Affirm and provide meaningful reinforcement.* An errorless learning approach is advocated for children to promote the confidence that accompanies success and to minimize the defeatist attitude that accompanies repeated failure. Adults also benefit when success is maximized. Many adults are uncomfortable when faced with a situation in which new learning is required while other adults are around. Reinforcing successive approximations and providing positive, meaningful feedback about performance create a positive working relationship. Returning to the seated positioning example, once the adult learner has correctly aligned a child's pelvis in the child's wheelchair, point out how far back on the chair seat the hips are positioned, show how far the backs of the child's knees are from the front edge of the seat (e.g., two fingers can be inserted between back of knees and seat), and indicate how the trunk is vertically aligned with the shoulders resting back so the neck and head are upright. Teach two or three critical "checkpoints" by which the adult learner can self-evaluate his or her own work. Sometimes it is useful to ask what "checks" make the most sense to the learner and to use the learner's insights, language, and learning style.

Solving Problems/ Addressing Issues as a Group

Group problem-solving strategies are considered advantageous over individual problem-solving efforts for the following reasons: 1) more diverse knowledge and perspectives are brought to bear on the problem, 2) greater interest is stimulated in the problem as a result of attention by numerous individuals, 3) there is a cumulative effect of individual contributions, and 4) poorly conceived individual contributions are rejected (Johnson & Johnson, 1994; Kruger, 1988). There are many strategies for group problem solving. Most have their origins in the well-established literature on group dynamics. Based on this literature, Johnson and Johnson (1994) describe a five-component process that is summarized briefly here (an example is provided in Figure 8.17):

1. *Define the problem or issue.* Before a problem can be addressed in an effective way, it must be clearly and completely defined in the most objective way possible. This requires specification of the desired state of affairs (including a concrete description of people, places, events, and other definitive aspects) and validation of the existing state of affairs. Commitment to solving the problem rests with agreement as to the existence of the discrepancy between current and desired circumstances and an understanding of its importance.

2. *Gather information about the problem, focusing on context-specific capacities and barriers.* The next step is to gather information about the problem to understand as accurately as possible why it exists. It is useful to list the restraining forces (or barriers) that must be overcome and the helping forces (or capacities) that can assist with problem resolution. The forces identified are unique to the specific context in which the problem exists. For example, local barriers and facilitators related to scheduling a speech-language pathologist into a specific fourth-grade language arts class will vary from school to school.

DEFINE THE PROBLEM

Current State

Wanena has difficulty participating in morning meeting with peers in her group—positioning and communication seem to be major challenges.

Desired State

Wanena is positioned to see and interact with peers; she has information to contribute; she looks at peers as they communicate; peers encourage and support her involvement.

IDENTIFY CAPACITIES AND BARRIERS

Capacities

Wanena
- seems to enjoy being in group with peers
- when positioned well and stable in her chair, she can maintain an upright head/neck position

Peers
- seem to like Wanena
- used to encourage her participation

Team
- parent would gladly provide home support needed to prepare for sharing during morning meeting
- lead speech-language pathologist (SLP) is highly experienced with augmentative communication options
- primary therapist (OT/PT) interested and knows family from previous school setting

Context
- morning meeting has flexibility to accommodate individualized approaches to support participation

Barriers

Wanena
- is tight and slumped in her chair during morning meeting
- has limited experience with systematic communication
- hesitates to participate unless paraprofessional is present
- has no reliable means to communicate message to peers

Peers
- decreased prompting of Wanena's participation, possibly as a result of perception that Wanena does not repond

Team
- paraprofessional moves between two students during the first hour of school and is not always available to assist with positioning before morning meeting
- primary therapist (OT/PT) is scheduled in Wanena's room for afternoon blocks

Context
- (no barriers)

GENERATE AND CONSIDER STRATEGIES

- Change paraprofessional schedule to work with Wanena before meeting so that Wanena is relaxed and well positioned for the morning meeting.
- Schedule a consultation with lead SLP to determine best means for Wanena to share during morning meeting.
- Talk with parent about supporting Wanena by contributing a ``message'' about after-school/evening/weekend activities with family.
- Switch a scheduled afternoon and morning block for the OT/PT so she can observe and work directly with Wanena during a morning meeting.
- Talk with peers in morning group to obtain their suggestions and recruit their participation.

(continued)

Figure 8.17. Example of problem-solving process.

Figure 8.17.   (*continued*)

DECIDE AND IMPLEMENT STRATEGIES

- Within 2 weeks, schedule OT/PT and lead SLP to be present with Wanena at the same time during a morning meeting for the purpose of determining sensorimotor and communication support needs. During that classroom consultation, also ask Wanena's group peers for their ideas.
- Schedule follow-up meeting with teacher, paraprofessional, and parent to share and then finalize positioning and communication strategies; then map out tasks, time lines, responsibility for putting strategies into place.
- Check with principal and classroom teacher of the other student supported by paraprofessional to examine possibility of changing the support schedule so paraprofessional works with Wanena in preparation for morning meeting.
- Revisit this issue at next scheduled team meeting in November.

EVALUATE THE SUCCESS OF STRATEGY

- Revisit this issue at monthly team meetings.
- Schedule follow-up in-class consultation by OT/PT and SLP to examine:
    positioning to maximize participation
    effectiveness/progress using augmentative communication method (e.g., microswitch to activate pre-recorded message)
    facilitation of peer support
- Check in with parent about best way to contribute messages about activities that occur after school and on weekends.

---

3. *Generate and consider alternative strategies.* The third step is to generate strategies aimed at reducing the restraining forces, increasing the helping forces, or both. Reducing the restraining forces such that existing helping forces can be applied usually is more effective than exclusive effort to increase helping forces. In group problem solving, one of the greatest restraining forces can be resistance of member(s) to change. Resistance usually is lessened when the member(s) are involved in problem diagnosis. During this step, group members should come up with as many ways as possible to reduce each identified restraining force as well as ensure at least maintenance of helping forces.

4. *Decide and implement strategy.* To decide on which alternative strategy to implement, team members go through a process of discussing the benefits for each alternative, identifying resources (e.g., people, time, money) needed to implement each alternative, and discussing the likelihood of success. There are a number of decision-making approaches that teams can use for final selection of a strategy to implement. A consensus decision-making approach is advocated in most circumstances and is discussed later. A consensus decision-making strategy results in greater commitment by the team to follow through with implementation. Implementation of the strategy selected proceeds when

specific actions, people responsible, and time lines are developed.

5. *Evaluate the success of the strategy.* Evaluation involves determination of the success of the implementation process (was the strategy implemented at all and, if so, was it implemented correctly?) and the outcome (is the current state of affairs now closer to the desired state of affairs?). If the outcome is closer but not close enough, other alternatives may need to be considered.

Giangreco, Cloninger, Dennis, and Edelman (1994) discuss a similar process for teams and recommend teaching it to children to enlist their help in solving day-to-day classroom and instructional challenges.

In addition to identifying a process for problem solving, Johnson and Johnson (1994) discussed eight blocks to problem solving. These are lack of clarity in stating the problem; not getting the needed information; poor communication within the group; premature testing of alternative strategies; a critical, evaluative, competitive climate; pressures for conformity; lack of inquiry and problem-solving skills; and inadequate motivation. When teams experience inefficient or ineffective problem-solving efforts, it is likely that the difficulty stems from one of these blocks.

Making Decisions by Consensus

Integral to solving problems is the ability of the collaborative team to make decisions. There are a number of different means by which decisions can be made (Johnson & Johnson, 1994): by a person in authority (with or without group discussion), by a person considered an expert in the relevant area, by majority vote, by averaging the individual opinions of group members, by a minority composition of the group (e.g., an executive committee structure), and by consensus. For most decisions that are made by a collaborative educational team, consensus decision making is recommended. Consensus is generally considered to represent the collective opinion of the group, arrived at through open communication of perspectives and opinions. It is not always possible for all members to agree on a decision, but the greater the level of agreement the greater the shared commitment to implementation. Making decisions through consensus is a time-consuming activity and necessarily involves some degree of conflict, but the benefits of a high-quality decision resulting from the sharing of diverse perspectives and shared commitment to the decision and its implementation are worth the investment of time and energy for important team decisions.

Johnson and Johnson (1994) offered the following guidelines for making decisions through consensus among group members:

1. *Avoid arguing blindly for your own opinions.* Present your position as clearly and logically as possible, but listen to other members' reactions and consider them carefully before you press your point.
2. *Avoid changing your mind only to reach agreement and avoid conflict.* Support only solutions with which you are at least somewhat able to agree. Yield only to positions that have objective and logically sound foundations.
3. *Avoid conflict-reducing procedures,* such as majority voting, tossing a coin, averaging, and bargaining.
4. *Seek out differences of opinion.* They are natural and expected. Try to involve everyone in the decision process. Disagreements can improve the group's decision because they present a wide range of information and opinions, thereby creating a better chance for the group to hit upon more adequate solutions.
5. *Do not assume that someone must win and someone must lose* when discussion reaches a stalemate. Instead, look for

the next most acceptable alternative for all members.

6. *Discuss underlying assumptions,* listen carefully to one another, and encourage the participation of all members. (pp. 243–244)

As with attempts to solve problems, teams also can run into blocks when making decisions. The blocks identified by Johnson and Johnson (1994) include lack of group maturity, conflicting goals of group members, failure to communicate and use information, egocentrism of group members, concurrence seeking within the group, lack of sufficient heterogeneity, interference, inappropriate group size, no need for deliberations, leaving work to others, power differences and distrust, premature closure and dissonance reduction, and lack of sufficient time.

Specific to the practice of integrating related services, Giangreco (1994, 1996) and his colleagues have created and field-tested the Vermont Interdependent Services Team Approach (VISTA) to making decisions when planning the type, mode, and frequency of related services for students with special education needs. Although Giangreco and colleagues recognize and support the potential contributions of related services, their decision-making process is grounded in the underlying value base of *only as special as necessary.* They assert that too much special support has drawbacks, including decreasing time with peers in regular activities and increasing communication difficulties among professionals and with families when large numbers of providers are involved. There are five major features of VISTA: 1) shared understanding of a student's educational program, 2) analysis of the function of related services providers, 3) decision-making criteria consistent with the federal definition of educationally related services, 4) consensus decision mak-

ing, and 5) matching related services to educational needs. Findings indicate that, after engaging in the VISTA process, team members knew more about the specific functions of related services providers, were more confident in their group's teamwork practices, and were more satisfied with their decision-making process. Readers are encouraged to learn more about this promising application of consensus decision making for educationally related services.

Working with and Through Differences in Perspective

Whenever two or more individuals are gathered with a shared work agenda, differences in perspective inevitably emerge. Many have learned to view differences and the conflict they induce as negative. Only recently has a broader understanding emerged that difference and conflict are potentially positive and growth enhancing when individuals are properly equipped—with attitudes and with skills—to work with differences and address conflict in a healthy and productive manner. Recall that a primary reason for group, as opposed to individual, problem solving is that differences in perspective can result in higher quality solutions to complex challenges. A colleague of the authors has gone so far as to assert (and mean it), "Conflict is our friend." Thomas Jefferson once remarked, "Difference of opinion leads to inquiry, and inquiry to truth" (as quoted in Johnson & Johnson, 1994, p. 306).

In the past decade, there has been a substantial increase in resources available on conflict resolution. A large body of literature focuses on children learning to peacefully resolve conflict (see, e.g., Drew, 1987; Duvall, 1994; Hill & Hill, 1990; Johnson & Johnson, 1991, 1995; Wade, 1991). There is also an abundance of literature that focuses on constructively working with conflict among members of collaborative work teams (see, e.g., Hocker & Wilmot, 1995; Long, Morse, & Newman, 1996). Hocker and Wilmot (1995) define *conflict* as "an expressed struggle between at least two interdependent parties who perceive incompatible goals, scarce resources, and interference from others in achieving their goals" (p. 21). For example, the mother of a 6-year-old child who bunny-hops wants the educational team to begin teaching her son how to walk. The physical therapist on the team asserts that walking is inappropriate and the child must first learn reciprocal crawling. Another example is a father who wants his daughter to work on speech and not spend time using augmentative forms of communication support. The speech-language pathologist and teacher believe it is more appropriate to also augment attempts at speech. Often, conflicting perspectives stem from different belief systems and values that are highly personal. The highly personal nature of conflict makes attempts at resolving conflict exceedingly more difficult than attempts to solve problems (such as the example outlined in Figure 8.17). Early in the process of learning to address conflict, it is not unusual for teams to benefit from a mediator.

The authors make no attempt to provide a comprehensive discussion of conflict resolution here. Instead, we return once again to Johnson and Johnson (1994) as a resource and outline their research-based guidelines for constructive controversy:

1. Emphasize your common ground of making the best possible decision.
2. Look for opportunities to engage in controversy.
3. Prepare the best case possible for your position.
4. Advocate your position forcefully but with an open mind.
5. Encourage others to advocate their positions forcefully but with an open mind.
6. Understand, then challenge opposing ideas and positions.
7. Do not take personally other members' disagreements and rejection of your ideas.
8. Ensure that there are several cycles of differentiation (bringing out differences in opinion) and integration (combining several positions and creating a new position).
9. Put yourself in the other member's shoes.
10. Follow the canons of rational argument.
11. Synthesize the best ideas from all viewpoints and perspectives.

In this process, we emphasize the importance of listening to and understanding others' perspectives to at least an equal degree as clarifying one's own position. Both are necessary but require different states of mind. If one is in the psychological state of needing to be heard, it is difficult to listen well. Covey (1989) has suggested that seeking first to understand the perspectives of others and then sharing one's own perspective is a habit of effective interpersonal communication and relationships. Stepwise sequences are a helpful guide but must allow for effective and valuing exchanges. The purposes of engaging different perspectives are to clarify one's own perspectives, to learn from different perspectives, to examine one's own perspectives, to be open to challenge, and to collectively generate best combinations of responses.

Complementing linear strategies and procedures that frequently emphasize only skill development is attention to the psychological realities and challenges of working through conflict (Bauwens & Hourcade,

1995; Covey, 1989). Elevating this perspective is validating and appreciated by many team members who on a daily basis work in the complex arena of interpersonal dynamics of collaboration. One of the greatest barriers to constructively addressing conflict is the inability to communicate openly and honestly. Many hold concerns about being rejected because of their perspectives and about having diminished value if their positions are not adopted by the group. When anticipating such psychological threat, it is unlikely that individuals will choose to take the risks involved in both expressing honestly one's own opinion or in truly understanding another's opinion. When actively listening, one is open to being influenced by another. Team members must feel understood and accepted as people, regardless of the particular perspectives on an issue being explored by the team. Creating an atmosphere of mutual respect in which the safety and integrity of each individual are ensured is essential for effective communication to occur. Readers are encouraged to develop a more in-depth understanding of their own responses to conflict and effective ways for members of their teams to understand one another's perspectives, and work together to create high-quality solutions to the complex issues they face in their work. Some of the many resources available on this topic were cited as this section was introduced.

COMMUNICATING
OPENLY WITH PARENTS

In Chapter 3, the central role of home–school–community partnerships in the educational program of students with severe disabilities was emphasized. This final section of Chapter 8 addresses specific issues that sometimes arise when interacting with parents about integrating related services. Parents, like most people, are highly influenced by their history and experiences. Frequently, parents' initial interactions with therapists are in a hospital or clinic setting, such as a clinic-based early intervention program. Some infants and toddlers receive therapies as their only early intervention services. Clinical settings typically define therapist roles such that therapists provide the traditional direct and isolated intervention and rarely work with children in naturally occurring daily routines. Although there is increasing emphasis on home-based early intervention programs and integrating "therapy" interventions as part of family daily routines (Hinojosa & Anderson, 1991; Montgomery, 1994; Rainforth & Salisbury, 1988), many families reach public school programs with the experience of their child receiving only direct and isolated therapy. Interactions with classmates and participation in an ongoing schedule of educational activities is not the focus of clinical early intervention programs. Therefore, it is understandable that the introduction of a more integrated approach to therapy is not always embraced. Following are suggestions to consider when discussing with parents a more integrated approach to therapy services in the educational program.

Learn What Parents
Want for Their Child

Parents of students with disabilities, like all parents, want what is best for their child. If they are asking for a particular type of service or program, the professional realizes that in almost every situation the request reflects what they honestly believe would be best for their child. Team members must focus on the desired outcomes first, rather than on the process or method of service provision. They must provide parents with the opportunity to state their perspectives and desires. To ensure that parent desires are correctly understood, the other team members should restate what they believe to be the parents' perspective. Parents should be asked to identify the outcomes they would like for their child as a result of therapy or assisted to identify desired outcomes. Team members should always emphasize where and in what activities (i.e., the context) the parents desire improved functioning of their child. For example, if a parent wants his son to use his hands better, the occupational/physical therapist should ask for specification about the daily routines and activities in which improved hand use would facilitate greater participation and success. If a parent wants her daughter to articulate better, the speech-language pathologist should determine specific situations in which and people with whom improved communication would be especially important. Some parents, like therapists, have learned to focus on improved skills without equal or greater attention to function in naturally occurring daily environments and activities.

Find Out the Specific Concerns About Integrated Therapy

Until the parents' specific concerns or fears about integrating therapy throughout daily routines are identified, it is impossible to address those concerns. Some of the most commonly expressed concerns of parents are that 1) team members other than therapists do not have sufficient expertise, 2) intervention will be "watered down," 3) the therapy will not get done because of the other demands in the classroom, 4) the child needs isolated and direct intervention to really focus on improving skills, 5) therapists will not remain involved in the educational program, and 6) services are being reduced because the potential of child benefit or growth is being questioned. Some parents also believe that an integrated approach to therapy is an administrative device to decrease the number of therapists required. With the actual concerns identified, information can be

provided and services designed to minimize the concerns.

Explain Why Integrated Therapy Frequently Is Appropriate and Least Restrictive

Therapy services provided through the public schools must be implemented so as to support the educational program. It is difficult, if not impossible, to determine educational relevance when assessment and intervention occur in environments removed from the educational context. Therapy integrated into daily routines not only results in opportunities to learn and use new skills in functional situations, but it also avoids removal of the child from his or her educational program and peers. When students are removed to a therapy room, they miss participation with classmates in the typical, ongoing activities. For these reasons, integrating therapist knowledge and skill into the educational program is a logical first choice of service provision, whether or not isolated services are provided. Readers should review the comprehensive rationale provided in Chapter 2 and consider which of the reasons may be most important to share with parents. Particularly relevant to share may be research in the area of motor learning that suggests that facilitation of motor skills in the absence of a functional context is not likely to result in improved movement in naturally occurring situations.

Share Research-Based Information About Various Models of Service Provision

There is an emerging research base supporting the effectiveness of interventions applied in contexts that are most relevant to daily life (Campbell, McInerney, & Cooper, 1984; Giangreco, 1986; Peck, Killen, & Baumgart, 1989) and the idea that therapy integrated in naturally occurring contexts is preferable to that provided in isolation (Dunn, 1990; Karnish, Bruder, & Rainforth, 1995). Given the limited depth of research specific to integrated related services, perhaps the most compelling research related to the effects of collaborative teamwork can be derived from an extensive body of literature (more than 520 studies in the past 90 years) that indicates that cooperative goal structures provide many advantages over either individualistic or competitive goal structures (Johnson & Johnson, 1994). Clearly, effective collaboration among team members is a cooperative effort.

Develop Clear Procedures to Ensure Accountability for Integrated Services

The student's daily or weekly schedule should indicate the times when instruction will be provided to assist the student to move, use his or her hands, or communicate better. The instructional methods to be used and the way in which performance data will be collected can be outlined there. Also, the schedule should indicate who will assist the student (e.g., the classroom teacher, paraprofessional, classmate) and when the therapist will be present to train and support the primary implementor. Professionals should share with parents the way that team members teach one another to implement intervention methods (see Figures 8.15 and 8.16). The consultation/monitoring worksheets (Figures 8.9 and 8.10) presented previously in this chapter provide another means of demonstrating accountability. These are necessary implementation details to address and can be communicated to parents. The type and quantity (e.g., duration, frequency) of related services must be documented on the IEP as well (see Chapter 6).

If a Team Decides that Direct and Isolated Therapy Is Needed to Supplement Integrated Therapy, Clarify the Intent of the Service and Develop Criteria for Discontinuation

There are at least three circumstances in which the provision of short-term direct and isolated therapy may be appropriate for individual students. First, when a student presents a particularly unique, complex, or challenging combination of capacities and needs, a therapist may need to conduct an expanded and longitudinal assessment to determine interfering influences and successful intervention methods. A therapist cannot teach others how to work with students before he or she has had a chance to determine what will be effective, which requires hands-on, direct interactions. A second circumstance could involve a student just returning to school after undergoing orthopedic or oral surgery. Postoperative interventions can require a high degree of sophistication and evaluation during implementation. Safety of the student and ensuring continued progress are central to the decision making regarding type and amount of therapy support. A third circumstance in which direct and isolated therapy might be considered is when a student is in a period of tremendous growth or regression and therefore requires frequent changes in intervention. It is important to note that in each of these circumstances there would still be people (who are not therapists) who interact with the students throughout the school day. Therefore, integrated therapy is always a support provided by therapists in educational settings. Short-term direct and isolated therapy services are decreased or eliminated when the mitigating circumstances no longer exist.

When Disagreements Arise, Implement a Data-Based Approach to Making Decisions

Occasionally, team members cannot resolve disagreements through discussion. There are simply opposing viewpoints that cannot, and arguably should not, be resolved in the absence of experience by the individual student. In these circumstances, implementation of a data-based approach to making decisions can render a more objective, ex-

perienced-based, and student-centered resolution. For teams that routinely implement a
systematic and data-based instructional approach, disagreements can be easily addressed in this way. For teams that do not
have such an approach instituted, assistance
may be necessary to specify the desired student outcome, to operationalize the opposing intervention methods, and to design an
implementation schedule that can result in
reasonable attribution of change in student
behavior (or lack of it) to one of the methods
or a combination of the methods (see, e.g.,
Ottenbacher, 1986). Team members should
agree on the desired outcomes and how to
determine when the outcomes are met.

Invite Parents to Visit
the Classroom and School
Part of parental concern about changing to
an integrated model of service provision
stems from a lack of experience with the
new model and the resulting lack of clarity
about what it would look like. The shift, as
many therapists have learned, is a significant
change in paradigms. For example, how
could working on a transitional movement
sequence from sidesitting to standing be integrated as part of the routine in reading
class? Parents should be invited to visit, to
see what their child's classroom is like and
how their son or daughter participates. A
"come and see" attitude also reduces the
fear that school personnel are hiding the
"real reasons" for changing models of service provision. Many parents fear that
school personnel have given up on their children and, therefore, are shifting to a less intense model of service provision. Most
therapists realize that to effectively integrate
services requires *more,* not less, time (Effgen, 1995). Even so, the concern prevails
that the real reason behind an integrated approach to therapy is to diminish services and
save money. By being open and welcoming,

it becomes clear that there is nothing to hide.
Because it is not yet commonplace for parents and other community members to be
present and involved in schooling in general
education, the only precaution associated
with the "come and see" strategy is to avoid
making visits obtrusive or uncomfortable for
the student.

When Families Request
Therapy Services that Are Not
Educationally Relevant, Assist
Them to Obtain Supplemental Services
Some families want their children to receive
frequent, direct, hands-on therapy by a therapist. Sometimes such service is not educationally relevant. (Questions that address the
educational relevance of therapy services
were provided in Chapter 2; also see Giangreco, 1996.) At other times, such services
may be determined to be educationally relevant but, because removal from integrated
learning environments would be necessary,
families decide to arrange direct therapy services as an after-school activity, rather than
remove the child from the program. In those
situations in which therapy is not educationally relevant or is not an educational priority,
school personnel should assist parents in
their search for supplemental services from
local agencies or therapists in private practice. Parents have the right and responsibility
to pursue activities they view as beneficial
to their children, and school personnel
should respect these pursuits.

CONCLUSION
This chapter has provided general strategies
and specific examples related to some of the
many organizational, professional, interpersonal, and key developmental issues that
arise in the process of integrating related
services into IEPs for students with severe
disabilities. One of the challenges in providing these strategies and examples has been

to ensure relevance to a wide range of readers. The strategies presented can be adapted, expanded, and replaced to fit specific circumstances. The next chapter provides suggestions for initiating or continuing the process of collaborative teamwork. Also discussed are current and emerging critical issues that are likely to influence the design and implementation of collaborative teamwork for students with severe disabilities. As teams work together, the change process can be a source of great personal and professional growth.

REFERENCES

Bauwens, J., & Hourcade, J. (1995). *Cooperative teaching: Rebuilding the schoolhouse for all students.* Austin, TX: PRO-ED.

Benson, S. (1993). Collaborative teaming: A model for occupational therapists working in inclusive schools. *AOTA: Developmental Disabilities Special Interest Newsletter, 16*(4), 1–4.

Bridges, W. (1993). *Managing transitions: Making the most of change.* Reading, MA: Addison-Wesley.

Calculator, S. (1994). Communicative intervention as a means to successful inclusion. In S. Calculator & C. Jorgensen (Eds.), *Including students with severe disabilities in schools: Fostering communication, interaction, and participation: School-age children series* (pp. 183–214). San Diego: Singular.

Campbell, P.H., McInerney, W., & Cooper, M.A. (1984). Therapeutic programming for students with severe handicaps. *American Journal of Occupational Therapy, 38*(9), 594–602.

Covey, S.R. (1989). *The seven habits of highly effective people.* New York: Fireside.

Dettmer, P.A., Dyck, N.T., & Thurston, L.P. (1996). *Consultation, collaboration and teamwork for students with special needs* (2nd ed.). Newton, MA: Allyn & Bacon.

Drew, N. (1987). *Learning the skills of peacemaking.* Rolling Hill Estates, CA: Jalmar Press.

Dunn, W. (1990). A comparison of service provision models in school-based occupational therapy services. *Occupational Therapy Journal of Research, 10*(5), 300–320.

Duvall, L. (1994). *Respecting differences: A guide to getting along in a changing world.* Minneapolis, MN: Free Spirit Publishing.

Effgen, S. (1995). The educational environment. In S.K. Campbell (Ed.), *Physical therapy for children* (pp. 847–872). Philadelphia: W.B. Saunders.

Friend, M., & Cook, L. (1996). *Interactions: Collaboration skills for professionals* (2nd ed.). White Plains, NY: Longman.

Giangreco, M.F. (1986). Effects of integrated therapy: A pilot study. *Journal of The Association for Persons with Severe Handicaps, 11*(3), 205–208.

Giangreco, M.F. (1994). Effects of a consensus-building process on team decision-making: Preliminary data. *Physical Disabilities: Education and Related Services, 13*(1), 41–56.

Giangreco, M.F. (1996). *Vermont interdependent services team approach (VISTA): A guide to coordinating educational support services.* Baltimore: Paul H. Brookes Publishing Co.

Giangreco, M.F., Cloninger, C.J., Dennis, R.E., & Edelman, S.W. (1994). Problem-solving methods to facilitate inclusive education. In J.S. Thousand, R.A. Villa, & A.I. Nevin (Eds.), *Creativity and collaborative learning: A practical guide to empowering students and teachers* (pp. 321–346). Baltimore: Paul H. Brookes Publishing Co.

Giangreco, M.F., Cloninger, C.J., & Iverson, V.S. (1993). *Choosing options and accommodations for children (COACH): A guide to planning inclusive education.* Baltimore: Paul H. Brookes Publishing Co.

Hanft, B.E., & Place, P.A. (1996). *The consulting therapist.* San Antonio: Therapy Skill Builders.

Hill, S., & Hill, T. (1990). *The collaborative classroom: A guide to co-operative learning.* Portsmouth, NH: Heinemann.

Hinojosa, J., & Anderson, J. (1991). Mothers' perceptions of home treatment programs for their preschool children with cerebral palsy. *American Journal of Occupational Therapy, 45*(3), 273–279.

Hocker, F.J., & Wilmot, W.W. (1995). *Interpersonal conflict* (4th ed.). Madison, WI: Brown & Benchmark.

Individuals with Disabilities Education Act (IDEA) of 1990, PL 101-476, 20 U.S.C. §§ 1400 *et seq.*

Johnson, D.W., & Johnson, R.T. (1989). *Cooperation and competition: Theory and research.* Edina, MN: Interaction Book Company.

Johnson, D.W., & Johnson, R.T. (1991). *Teaching students to be peacemakers.* Edina, MN: Interaction Book Company.

Johnson, D.W., & Johnson, F.W. (1994). *Joining together: Group theory and skills* (5th ed.). Englewood Cliffs, NJ: Prentice Hall.

Johnson, D.W., & Johnson, R.T. (1995). *Reducing school violence through conflict resolution.* Alexandria, VA: Association for Supervision and Curriculum Development.

Karnish, K., Bruder, M.B., & Rainforth, B. (1995). A comparison of physical therapy in two schoolbased treatment contexts. *Physical & Occupational Therapy in Pediatrics, 15*(4), 1–25.

Kruger, L. (1988). Programmatic change strategies at the building level. In J.L. Graden, J.E. Zins, & M.J. Curtis (Eds.), *Alternative educational delivery systems: Enhancing instructional options for all students* (pp. 491–512). Washington, DC: National Association of School Psychologists.

Lacoursiere, R. (1980). *The life cycle of groups: Group developmental stage theory.* New York: Human Sciences Press.

Long, N.L., Morse, W.C., & Newman, R.G. (1996). *Conflict in the classroom: The education of at-risk and troubled students* (5th ed.). Austin, TX: PRO-ED.

Montgomery, P. (1994, March). Frequency and duration of pediatric physical therapy. *Physical Therapy Magazine,* pp. 42–47, 89–91.

National Center on Educational Outcomes. (1995). *Foundations for NCEO's outcomes and indicators series.* Minneapolis: University of Minnesota, National Center on Educational Outcomes.

Nowacek, J.E. (1992). Professionals talk about teaching together: Interviews with five collaborating teachers. *Intervention in School and Clinic, 27,* 262–276.

Ottenbacher, K. (1986). *Evaluating clinical change: Strategies for occupational and physical therapists.* Baltimore: Williams & Wilkins.

Peck, C.A., Killen, C.C., & Baumgart, D. (1989). Increasing implementation in special education instruction in mainstream preschools: Direct and generalized nondirective consultation. *Journal of Applied Behavior Analysis, 22,* 197–210.

Rainforth, B., & England, J. (1997). Collaborations for inclusion. *Education and Treatment of Children, 20*(1).

Rainforth, B., & Salisbury, C. (1988). Functional home programs: A model for therapists. *Topics in Early Childhood Special Education, 7*(4), 33–45.

Rainforth, B., & York, J. (1987). Integrating related services in community instruction. *Journal of The Association for Persons with Severe Handicaps, 12*(3), 193–198.

Raywid, M.A. (1993). Finding time for collaboration. *Educational Leadership, 51*(1), 30–34.

Senge, P., Ross, R., Smith, B., Roberts, C., & Kleiner, A. (1994). *The fifth discipline fieldbook: Strategies and tools for building a learning organization.* New York: Currency Doubleday.

Thousand, J., Fox, T.J., Reid, R., Godek, J., Williams, W., & Fox, W. (1986). *The Homecoming Model: Educating students who present intensive educational challenges within regular education environments* (p. 36). Burlington: University of Vermont, Center for Developmental Disabilities.

Thousand, J.S., & Villa, R.A. (1992). Collaborative teams: A powerful tool in school restructuring. In R.A. Villa, J.S. Thousand, W. Stainback, & S. Stainback (Eds.), *Restructuring for caring and effective education: An administrative guide to creating heterogeneous schools* (pp. 73–108). Baltimore: Paul H. Brookes Publishing Co.

Tuckman, B.W. (1965). Developmental sequence in small groups. *Psychological Bulletin, 63,* 384–399.

Tuckman, B.W., & Jensen, M.A.C. (1977). Stages of small group development revisited. *Group and Organizational Studies, 2,* 419–427.

Wade, R.C. (1991). *Joining hands: From personal to planetary friendship in the primary classroom.* Tucson, AZ: Zephyr Press.

West, J.F., & Cannon, G.S. (1988). Essential collaborative consultation competencies for regular and special educators. *Journal of Learning Disabilities, 21,* 56–63.

York, J., Giangreco, M.F., Vandercook, T., & Macdonald, C. (1992). Integrating support personnel in the inclusive classroom. In S. Stainback & W. Stainback (Eds.), *Curriculum considerations in inclusive classrooms: Facilitating learning for all students* (pp. 101–116). Baltimore: Paul H. Brookes Publishing Co.

York, J., Peters, B., Hurd, D., & Donder, D. (1985). *Guidelines for using support services in educational programs for students with severe, multiple handicaps*. Dekalb, IL: Dekalb County Special Education Association.

York, J., Rainforth, B., & Wiemann, G. (1988). An integrated approach to therapy for school aged learners with developmental disabilities. *Totline, 14*(3), 36–40.

York-Barr, J., Kronberg, R.M., & Doyle, M.B. (1996). *Creating inclusive school communities:*

A staff development series for general and special educators: Module 4. Collaboration: Redefining roles, practices, and structures. Baltimore: Paul H. Brookes Publishing Co.

Ysseldyke, J.E., & Thurlow, M.E. (1994). What results should be measured to decide whether instruction is working for students with disabilities. *Special Services in the Schools, 9*(2), 39–49.

9

Moving Forward with Collaborative Teamwork

So far this book has provided a foundation of collaborative teamwork for students with severe disabilities in inclusive settings and has described strategies and examples for designing individualized curriculum and instruction and for supporting the efforts of collaborating team members. This final chapter presents perspectives and suggestions to consider in moving forward with collaborative teamwork. The unique collection of people and circumstances represented by the readers of this book warrants individual consideration of the information that follows to determine what will work best for each person. A lesson the authors continue to learn in their work with school teams is that general principles of change may hold constant for most teams, but the specific starting points and strategies for moving forward are unique to each combination of people and their respective work circumstances.

PERSPECTIVES ON MOVING FORWARD

The following perspectives represent the authors' collective learning and insight from

working with practicing educators and related services personnel, families, students, and colleagues. Also reflected is a current understanding about change—personal and organizational—drawn from numerous written and experiential sources that are now integrated knowledge applied in our daily work. We offer both broader contextual perspectives and more narrowly focused personal learning perspectives. To us, all these perspectives contribute to our decisions about why and how to move forward in facilitating collaboration among professionals in schools to more effectively support students with unique learning capacities and needs.

The Broader Context of Inclusive Education

It is hard to believe that, only a decade ago, the language of inclusion as it pertained to students with disabilities in public schools was unfamiliar or without much meaning to most educators and families. Today, articles about inclusion are featured in national magazines, such as *U.S. News and World Report,*

McCall's, Sesame Street Parent, and *Reader's Digest*. It also has been the topical focus for entire issues of professional journals, such as *Educational Leadership, School Administrator, Phi Delta Kappan*, and *Remedial and Special Education*. In addition, there are literally hundreds, if not thousands, of books, manuals, articles, and videotapes related to inclusion in education.

Not only have the quantity and sources of information about inclusion changed dramatically, but so too has the content focus of the information. Initially, much of the literature consisted of success stories and descriptions of strategies that emerged from isolated local efforts to more fully integrate students with severe disabilities. Historically, these students had been excluded from mainstreamed educational opportunities. Individual families decided they did not want their children to grow up in a separate world, attending separate education programs. Many families persevered to create positive change for their children and effectively opened doors previously closed to other children and families as well.

Presently, inclusion is increasingly viewed by many as an approach to schooling in which students with a wide range of abilities and interests learn together in heterogeneous classrooms and schools. Inclusion is not just about "special ed kids" anymore. Various school restructuring themes, such as holistic and student-centered approaches to learning and collaborative interdisciplinary teaching, are common to the practices in both general and special education. Increasing student diversity combined with a rapidly changing world has led to widespread awareness and action to re-create the culture of schooling.

Why this discussion of the broader context of inclusion? Many special educators and related services personnel have chosen to work in schools because they want to work with students who have disabilities. Their arena of practice in schools, however, is rapidly changing. Not too long ago, therapists could expect to work in a therapy room in a school in much the same way they did in rehabilitation or hospital environments. The context for practice has expanded from the therapy room to the special education classroom to general activity areas in and around the school to general education classrooms and the surrounding local community. An expanded context of practice also has meant an expanded and more varied cast of players. To achieve meaningful inclusion in these more typical environments requires partnerships with the people therein. More than ever before, a foundation of quality education is formed from the relationships among many different people in schools. Effective partnerships grow from shared purpose. Shared purpose is about more than students with disabilities—it is about how to most effectively prepare all students for life in a complex, diverse, dynamic world. Reciprocity, mutual benefit, and shared responsibility are predicated on interest and commitment to the entire educational enterprise. This does not mean that special educators and related services personnel abandon their primary charge of supporting students with disabilities, but it does mean contribution at some level to the broader school community. The more support personnel or programs are viewed as contributing to the educational enterprise, the more open this dominant culture (i.e., general education) will be to involving students with disabilities.

As special educators and related services personnel move forward with collaborative teamwork, they need to recognize areas of shared interest and establish partnerships with individuals outside their particular disciplines and beyond the domain of special education. Team members should learn about what is happening in general education and consider how they or their "program," through their work with students who have disabilities, can contribute to overall positive change in classrooms or even the broader school community. Contributions can range from being a positive presence by greeting people by name as one passes in the hallways to sharing instructional responsibilities to serving on schoolwide work groups. There are many ways to contribute to creating a positive learning community.

Research on Collaborative Teamwork

In almost every circumstance in which the authors discuss issues of collaboration and inclusion related to students with severe disabilities, someone inquires about the empirical basis of their work. Typically, this inquiry is raised in some variation of the following question: "What empirical, systematic, controlled, data-based, quantitative, longitudinal research supports are you recommending?" To the best of our knowledge, we have provided references throughout the book that support the information presented. Much of the information, however, is based on our collective applied work as members of collaborative educational teams and as external facilitators with individuals currently working as members of teams in educational settings. There is extensive research both on effective collaborative group processes and on effective instruction of students with severe disabilities (see Chapter 2). In this book, we have indicated ways these bodies of research apply to integrating education and therapy in educational settings for students with severe disabilities. Unfortunately, there is little empirical research that either supports or negates the specific practices set forth in this book. There also is no empirical research that supports the traditional practices of direct, isolated therapy by members of loosely organized teams. We can be sure of one empirical pursuit: No additional facts and figures are necessary to indicate that changes are needed in our current system of education.

To define the arena from which to pose research questions of interest, we must ask, "What do we want to know?" To a large extent, the answer to this question is directed by what each of us values. Some people want to know whether or not inclusion and collaboration are good ideas or effective practices. Other people want to know how to collaborate effectively to achieve positive inclusive learning experiences and outcomes. The *whether or not* question is substantially different from the *how to* question. The authors are interested in the latter question and have chosen to pursue research and practice efforts focused on the conditions (personal and organizational) and processes that support collaborative and inclusive practices. The research questions of interest to us reflect a desire to learn *how to* collaborate best and *how to* educate students most effectively in inclusive school communities. How can learning be maximized in heterogeneous and inclusive schools? How should we design and implement structures so that schools are environments in which adults and children maximize the human resource potential to learn and grow throughout life?

Each of us, as individuals, chooses the types of knowledge-seeking questions he or she asks. Our choices directly influence our learning and professional practice endeavors. The authors believe that collaboration will be necessary to an even greater degree as our world becomes more and more complex. Some people disagree. We believe that children with diverse abilities and challenges must grow up and learn together in inclusive school communities in order to best prepare all children for complex and heterogeneous community life. Some people disagree.Readers should consider what they believe and are interested in learning and how that has influenced decisions they have made about where and how they choose to practice. How might one's beliefs influence future decisions about one's life at work?

Resources

Another perspective influencing decisions about how to move forward with collaborative teamwork concerns the resources available to facilitate collaborative practices for inclusive schooling. Generally, the authors assume there will be no additional fiscal resources available to schools—at least not in the near future. We choose to proceed, therefore, with the perspective that our option in moving forward necessarily involves changing how existing resources are used. The largest existing resource is people, most of whom would agree they cannot do *more* than they are currently doing. This leaves the option of doing *differently* from what they are doing. Numerous examples of *doing differently* have been provided throughout this book. With scheduling, for example, instead of spending three 1-hour sessions providing pull-out speech-language services, the speech-language pathologist could spend one 3-hour session each week in the general education classroom. Instead of occupational and physical therapists directly working with the same students with multiple disabilities, they could adopt a primary therapist model of support, resulting in more time spent with each student. Instead of one paraprofessional being assigned to support one student, he or she could be assigned to support a program or grade level, cofunded by special and general education monies.

When change is posed, the usual request is for *more* people. This is not a very realistic option in these times of diminishing resources. We must consider how to do *differently* by stepping back and taking a comprehensive look at current practices and structures. We must begin asking ourselves and one another "How about if we . . .?" or "Why couldn't we . . .?" We must be creative, explore many possibilities, and resist the pull to stay rooted in the realities of current structures and expectations. As we enter into these "What if . . .?" sessions, we must adhere to the rule that *"yeah buts . . ."* are not allowed. Team members are the experts on their particular daily arenas of practice and are in an advantaged position to think about *doing differently*. Sometimes, however, it is helpful to obtain external perspectives as a way to foster divergent thinking. The team may want to consider inviting an experienced outsider to join it or visiting other schools that work differently.

Organizational Change

Many practicing educators might consider the term *organizational change* an oxymoron. Although the realities of organizational change may seem daunting, in the past 10 years, volumes of research findings have been published about effective change in schools. Here we offer just a few perspectives on organizational change in schools to consider as professionals move forward with collaborative teamwork. First, school change is a complex, interdependent process. Change in one part of the organization affects change in other parts of the organization. Curricular changes affect scheduling. Scheduling affects service time and location. Initial change efforts may appear "self-contained," but institutionalized change affects all components of schooling. We should not be surprised when seemingly small, self-contained efforts give rise to unanticipated systems issues. We work in an interdependent social system.

Second, an emphasis on purpose, as opposed to structure, must be maintained for substantial and sustained change to result. In an attempt to remove some of the inevitable and uncomfortable ambiguity of change, there is a tendency to focus on the structural components of the change process. For example, therapists may view collaborative teamwork as changing from a back-to-back schedule of direct therapy to long blocks of time in classrooms. Once the schedule is changed, however, they may not know what to do in the new structure ("Now that I am in the classroom, why is it that I am here? What is it that I am supposed to do?"). Similarly, teams may expend enormous effort to set up a master schedule of team meetings. Once everyone is in the room, it is not uncommon for team members to wonder, "Now that we are here, why did we decide we needed to meet? What are we supposed to do?" The importance of keeping in mind *why* structural change is occurring cannot be overemphasized. Structures are tools that help address a need or achieve a goal in a particular context. They are not ends in themselves. Furthermore, the structures that emerge in any one school are likely to be different from those in other schools. Replication of another team's or school's structure does not ensure replication of that team's or school's success. Structure is put into place to allow team members to function in new ways. If a team visits a school, then comes back and establishes the same schedule in its school, team members should not be surprised if they do not experience the same results. Considerable interaction and conscious effort is required to make use of the structures put into place. Once team members are scheduled in a classroom, for example, it will take them awhile to figure out their new roles—how they will practice differently. Once the team is drawn together in a meeting, it will take time to work through how to effectively interact to address student and classroom issues.

Third, change involves the hearts and minds of the people involved. Change is highly personal and relational. Personally, those involved are affected by changes in roles and relationships. As the context of practice and roles evolves and changes, people must disaffiliate with their previous notions of who they were at work and what they did. As they move forward, they create new meanings and attachments of who they are in their work. This transition from old to new frequently engenders mixed feelings of loss, excitement, disorientation, and fun. Relationally, old relationships sometimes become altered as new people become part of work life. Making changes in established relationships and creating new relationships is effort of the heart and mind. We must proceed, knowing that organizational change is ultimately necessary to best support our work, but also proceed knowing that organizational change begins with personal change.

Personal Change

At the heart of organizational change is personal change. *Why do people change?* People change because there is something that they care enough about that they are willing to invest the energy and take the risks necessary to change. Some people also consider change because of their relational affiliation with another person or people contemplating change. They may experience a growing realization that some kind of change in their practice of work feels important or even urgent. They begin to sense dissonance between current reality and desired reality. This dissonance is responsible for their personal initiation of change. They become internally motivated to reduce the dissonance and its associated discomfort by moving toward constructive action.

How do people change? One of the greatest facilitators of personal change is experience. Another is open dialogue with trusted, respected, and valued colleagues.

Despite the recognition that experience and dialogue facilitate change, "convincing" and "manipulating" and "mandating" approaches to school changes are all too prevalent. Sharing stories and strategies of other people doing differently usually is effective only when a listening person is at a point of openness to consider doing differently. With some initial direction and support in place, people should be encouraged to go for it! *Learning through doing with ongoing reflection* greatly influences perspective, thought processes, and action. This is why, in part, attempting to reengage people in a change process that previously failed is exceedingly difficult. Through experience, they learned "it doesn't work" and, probably, "all that effort is for nothing!" If we take the time to ask why an individual is feeling resistant to engage in a change process, listening to his or her response can be illuminating. Frequently, failed attempts result from poorly supported efforts. A key question in analyzing change efforts is "What support is necessary to facilitate change?"

Personal change through experience is further enhanced by *learning with others* and *learning in a safe place*. The usefulness of learning with others is self-evident when considering more collaborative ways of working to support students with severe disabilities. Partnerships provide support for change by helping to sustain momentum during inevitable periods of discouragement and low energy. Interactions with colleagues stimulate creative thinking and problem solving and serve as a safe harbor for retreat when the course of action must be changed or when particularly challenging events arise.

Personal change also involves developing new skills and talents. For example, the perspective and skills required when observing students in inclusive environments to determine needs are different from administering a developmental inventory in a separate environment. Making decisions by consensus is substantially different from making decisions alone. Interacting directly with children all day is substantially different from interacting with adults. As we become aware of the need for new perspective and skills in our work, we might find ourselves seeking external "how to" information. There are many excellent resources to be tapped. If we choose one of the generic "team-building skills" workshops readily available in most communities, we should not be surprised when generalization of skills addressed during a workshop does not readily emerge in the context of our daily work. When skills are taught devoid of context or meaning, they seem deceptively simple to adopt. It is easy to go through the five-step process for consensus decision making when we are not particularly interested or invested in what the decision is. When we become emotionally attached to decisions, as each of us does related to our daily work realities, the step-by-step process is exceedingly more difficult to move through. Suffice it to say, skill development frequently is an integral element in the process of personal change but is not always used easily in the fast-paced, emotionally charged, interpersonal context of daily work. Perspective and practice are necessary to integrate new skills into a readily obtained repertoire of behaviors.

To change the way our school or team functions, we must begin with ourselves. We can only change what we can influence directly. We need clarity of purpose. We need safe opportunities to learn by doing. Ultimately, we need to join with others. For these reasons, the section that follows focuses on ways an individual person might choose to move forward with collaborative teamwork.

SUGGESTIONS FOR GETTING STARTED

As we consider getting started, or restarted, we must realize that we are never done. The evolution toward more collaborative ways of working together in schools has a beginning, but it has no end. When we get close to what we envisioned as the desired future state, we begin to envision a new desired state that was not possible to envision previously. As mentioned previously, the dissonance we feel between what presently exists and what we desire creates a personal need to learn more and to change.

We must pay attention if we begin to feel that we, or our team or school, are "done." On the positive side, reaching a point where we feel ready and excited to share with others our accomplishments and open our school to visitors is a wonderful and important time of affirmation and celebration. Too much investment in the present ways of working, however, ultimately can lead to protectiveness, defensiveness, complacency, and even suppression of feelings of dissonance that are largely responsible for initiating efforts to make important changes in our ways of work. Most of us can readily identify moments in our professional lives in which we felt we had "arrived." Finally, we knew the best way to provide services or the most important ways for students to learn. All too soon, it seemed, there always emerged another perspective to consider. For example, in our zest to achieve a "functional only" curriculum, we enthusiastically ventured into community-based instruction with *everyone*, including 5-year-olds. Albeit this was an improvement over nonfunctional tasks in an isolated special education room, it was not long before we realized the children were missing out on important social and developmental experiences with peers in general education. Ooops! Continually, we must critically question our directions, the

basis for our decisions, and the outcomes we achieve.

Creating effective approaches to learning for complex children and learning about personal and interpersonal effectiveness are lifelong pursuits—work in progress, the authors believe, for as far as can be seen into the future. Our suggestions for getting started do not assume that readers have not already begun. Wherever we are in our process of becoming more collaborative and inclusive, we can step back and reconsider what we think is most important in our work, how well we are aligning our thoughts and actions with these most important directions, and how we might proceed from the present to create a new future. Following are five interrelated suggestions for moving forward with collaborative teamwork.

Deciding What Matters Most

In *Alice's Adventures in Wonderland* (1865), Lewis Carroll's Cheshire Cat told Alice that choosing a path "depends a good deal on where you want to go; if you don't know where you want to go, it doesn't matter which way you go." A necessary starting place for moving forward is to decide what matters most to each of us. This sounds simple enough but is surprisingly difficult. The realities of daily practice—intense schedules, on-the-fly meetings, designated content to cover, unanticipated events—can result in a state of exhaustion just in time for after-school meetings on a new curricular innovation, schedule changes to accommodate a pep rally, revised procedures for petty cash allocation, soup label and T-shirt fund-raising opportunities, or various other issues deemed necessary for faculty attention. The authors know of numerous professionals who have developed a fondness for their time alone in their cars as they drive home, only to face a different set of demands and commitments. Sound familiar?

Although deciding what matters most does not require a 3-day retreat in the woods, it does require deliberate consideration of personal desires to make a difference and the wide range of possibilities for how. Some people draw or write. Some think without tools and contemplate as they sit, rock, walk, or drive. Some choose to talk with a spouse, a sibling, a respected colleague, or a trusted friend. Whatever our means of securing quiet space for reflection, we should consider the following questions:

- If I could redesign how we work with children and families, what would that look like? Why would that be important? Where and how would we interact with one another and with the students?
- For a particular child and family, what is the most important contribution I could make? What could I do to make their lives just a little bit easier, a little more fun, or a little more peaceful? How could I learn more about this child and figure out the best way to increase participation? How can I listen well, to really hear what families want and need for their children?
- What do I care about enough to make the commitment and expend the effort required to change? What am I interested in enough to take the risks involved when venturing out into unknown territory?
- What feels most lonely, frustrating, or challenging about my work? What would make it better?
- What do I need to learn more about to understand how I can best support students to interact effectively in their classroom environments?

Although we may engage with others to consider possibilities for change, ultimately, the meaning created and direction chosen must matter to each of us individually. Early on, our desires and directions may seem vague. For example, a speech-language pathologist might want to somehow become more involved in the jobsites of several high school students because he or she learned that many experience communication difficulties and social isolation at work. An occupational therapist may want to work more closely with the kindergarten teachers of students with severe disabilities so they can learn early how to more independently manage the routines of the day. A physical therapist may react strongly to the separation of children with mobility challenges during recess and gym. As we work from a point of formulating initial desires and directions through engaging in an action-oriented process, our desires and directions become more clear.

Find a Partner

With some clarity about our desires and direction, we can consider who might join us in the process. Are there obvious partners given their central role in what we have targeted? For example, the speech-language pathologist might seek out a job coach. The occupational therapist might identify one kindergarten teacher. The physical therapist might approach the adapted physical education teacher. Is there someone we think might share some of our beliefs and desires? We can survey our work environment to see if there might be someone we know well or someone we do not yet know but for whom we have a good feeling. We can get to know the person, stop by his or her classroom, share our ideas, and see if the person is interested and why. Does he or she have space in his or her life right now to consider taking on a new challenge?

We each can create much on our own but can create much more with another. Collaborating to create more inclusive school communities is not an individual endeavor, it is a team endeavor.

Identify a "Piece" that We Can Directly Influence, Then Figure Out What Comes Next

To be effective in our desire to continuously learn and improve our work, we must stay focused on what we can influence. By doing so, we are empowered to act and we expand our ability to influence others. Many people get stuck immediately by choosing to focus their energy on issues over which they have little or no control. This is a sure path toward disempowerment, frustration, and hopelessness. We should start small by talking about ways we will work together. When will we be together? How do we want to share space? What are our individual pet peeves? What roles do we anticipate assuming with students and with one another? What concerns or anxieties do we each have? We should explicitly state our shared recognition that there will be rocky points along the way and that we want to be sure to connect about those challenging experiences. Such interactions maximize the likelihood of experiencing some degree of success. Others will observe and join in efforts that result in increased student learning and greater connections and support among adults.

Do It, Reflect on It, Adjust the Course

Just do it! Some people remain in a perpetual state of planning and never get to doing. With a supportive partner and manageable "piece" identified, we must begin our process of learning by doing and then reflecting on what we do. If team members are working together in the same environment (e.g., a general education classroom), they will undoubtedly interact in the process of teaching together and sharing space. In addition,

they may consider allocating regular (e.g., weekly), even if only brief, periods of time to connect with their teammates about how things are going. Such meetings can be fun if team members have coffee, go for a walk after school, or meet for breakfast. They can talk about how things are going: What is working well; what's not? Why? How are the students doing? What else might be tried? Are there other people we should bring in as resources? As experience grows with these reflective interactions, initial discomfort about shared reflection decreases and the rich learning opportunities available through connection with teammates become a source of renewal and support.

Take Time Out to Celebrate Movement Forward!

Although it is usually the lowest priority on an extensive "to do" list in a tightly scheduled life, time out to recognize and celebrate movement forward serves many important functions. Creating a pause provides refreshing relief in daily cycles of high-paced doing. Recognizing movement forward contributes to a sense of personal capacity and power. Celebrating movement affirms one's choices and gives rise to consideration of future desires and directions. Knowing that we have contributed toward making schooling a more positive, inclusive, and successful experience for individual students enhances the personal meaning gained through our lives' work.

CLOSING THOUGHTS

Increasing complexity and diversity, combined with diminishing resources, have created a crisis in public schooling. As with most crises, both challenges and opportunities emerge. Each of us chooses his or her perspective and response to the crises around us. Some of us choose the status quo and wait to act until more resources are available—which is likely to be a very long wait. Some of us choose to advocate persistently and, we hope, convincingly for more resources—which is an important position for long-term change. Some of choose to join with others and do things differently with the resources currently available—which is a pragmatic position within our immediate capacity to influence. As we move forward with collaboration, we learn of its paradox. Collaboration offers support yet instills pressure and accountability. It is a source of creative energy and can also feel overwhelming. It is sometimes efficient and sometimes laborious and burdensome. So, why collaborate? In the words of Skrtic (1994), "out of chaos and confusion can emerge defensiveness and isolation or mutual collaboration." Scharge (1995) contends that we collaborate "not only because we don't really have a choice—but because it is the best choice we've got!" (p. 130). The authors agree.

Fortunately, it is very apparent that many educators, related services professionals, family members, and communities are choosing to collaborate in the important work of educational and social change. Many have realized that the capacity to better support all students is realized when creative, talented, and committed educators join with students and families to share experiences and perspectives, and to cocreate new and flexible instructional supports in today's heterogeneous schools. For many of us, inclusion has moved beyond the effort to establish membership and facilitate learning for students with severe disabilities in general education settings. It has expanded to be both a process and an outcome of an effective education. Inclusion means providing equal educational opportunity by cocreating learning communities in which unique needs and diverse capacities are recognized, understood, accepted, and valued. It is about meaningful collaboration and professional growth for the varied education and related services providers who have previously worked in relative isolation from one another. It is about attempting to create positive social change through the experience of public education.

In our work, the authors see many hopeful and inspirational efforts by individuals and by teams to create positive learning experiences for students with severe disabilities in inclusive settings. We believe strongly that individuals can and do make a difference but must join with others to maximize their effects. Since the first edition of *Collaborative Teams for Students with Severe Disabilities: Integrating Therapy and Education* was published in 1992, the authors have seen and heard many educators and related services personnel tell their stories about students learning, socializing, and contributing in inclusive classrooms. These individuals' sense of efficacy, knowing that they made a positive difference in the lives of individual children, is an evident and essential part of the stories. In a reality of practice that sometimes seems complex and harried, these individuals serve as an ongoing source of inspiration and hope. As we make the personal decision to move forward and to work and learn with others who share our desires, we may be confident that we are joining with countless others whom we may not know but who share our beliefs and commitments. There is an intangible but real interconnected web of people involved in positive efforts to reculture schools. As we share your stories and continue to learn from the stories of others, the connections and support will be more fully realized for all of us. The authors wish for our readers good energy as they continue on their journey toward more inclusive and collaborative educational realities for today's children and youth. We offer an affirmation of their choice to join with others in this journey:

Congratulate yourself on selecting such an important area for your life's work—educating today's young people and exploring the possibilities for maximizing the learning potential of each child.

You have not chosen an easy, unobstructed path on which to journey,

But your journey will be rich in meaning, purpose, and discovery.

Know that it is possible to make significant positive differences in the lives of children and youth in our public schools.

When the children know you care about them, they will learn to trust.

When they trust, they will share responsibility for their education.

Embrace the inevitable challenges that lie ahead.

They are necessary hurdles to overcome.

They present opportunities for great personal and professional growth.

Continue to ask yourself,

"What is most important for students to understand, to be, and to do?" and

"How can we most effectively facilitate their learning and growth?"

Do not let yourself become isolated and alone.

Create a circle of friends and colleagues who support your continuous learning by listening, offering different perspectives, fostering creativity, encouraging risk taking, helping you address challenges, and having fun!

Choose to be a positive spirit in your community of practice.

Recognize and celebrate each success, yours and others, no matter how small it might seem.

Refuse to be a victim of circumstance by assuming a proactive attitude on life.

Allocate space and time to keep your spirit renewed.

Maintain balance and perspective in life by not letting your work consume you, by nurturing your mind and body health, and by laughing a lot.

Keep clearly in mind a happy, invigorating, rich vision of diverse and inclusive community life,

in which all members, regardless of their unique capacities and challenges, are valued and contribute to caring, cooperative community life.

Never doubt that, through our efforts, individual and collective, successive approximations of this vision can be realized.

REFERENCES

Carroll, L. (1865). *Alice's adventures in Wonderland*. London: Macmillan.

Scharge, M. (1995). *No more teams! Mastering the dynamics of creative collaboration*. New York: Doubleday.

Skrtic, T. (1994, December). *A political and economic justification for inclusive education*. Presentation at the Annual Conference for The Association for Persons with Severe Handicaps (TASH), Atlanta, GA.

Appendix
Blank Forms

What Does Your Family Consider Important About School Contacts?

Parents have different ideas about the kinds and amounts of information they want to get from school about their child. The list below contains different ways you and your child's teacher might communicate with each other. Please circle the number to the right of the phrase to show how important each type of contact is to you.

		NA	not at all					extremely	RANK	COMMENTS
1.	Written notes	0	1	2	3	4	5	6	____	
2.	School newsletters	0	1	2	3	4	5	6	____	
3.	Parent/teacher conferences or individualized education program (IEP) meetings	0	1	2	3	4	5	6	____	
4.	Open house	0	1	2	3	4	5	6	____	
5.	Informal contacts	0	1	2	3	4	5	6	____	
6.	Parent / Teacher Organization (PTO) meetings	0	1	2	3	4	5	6	____	
7.	Classroom observation	0	1	2	3	4	5	6	____	
8.	Other, please specify:	0	1	2	3	4	5	6	____	

Using the above list, place the numbers 1, 2, or 3 next to the three most important ways of communicating between your family and your child's teacher.

A. How much contact do you want to have with your child's teacher after your child begins public school?
   ___Daily   ___Once a week   ___Once a month
   ___Once a semester ___Other (specify)

B. Would you prefer
   ___to initiate most of the contacts with your child's teacher?
   ___the teacher to initiate contacts with you?
   ___or both?

Source: Unknown

What Is Important for Your Child To Learn at School?

Parents want their child to go to a classroom where he/she will make progress. Children can make progress in different areas, and some areas may be more important than others. The list below contains different areas your child may progress in next year. Please circle the number to the right of the phrase to show how important it is for your child to progress in this area next year.

	NA	not at all					extremely		RANK
1. Learn basic concepts such as colors, numbers, shapes, etc.	0	1	2	3	4	5	6		_____
2. Learn prereading and reading skills such as letters.	0	1	2	3	4	5	6		_____
3. Learn to use a pencil and scissors.	0	1	2	3	4	5	6		_____
4. Learn to listen and follow directions.	0	1	2	3	4	5	6		_____
5. Learn to share, and play with other children.	0	1	2	3	4	5	6		_____
6. Learn to be creative.	0	1	2	3	4	5	6		_____
7. Learn more communication skills.	0	1	2	3	4	5	6		_____
8. Learn confidence and independence.	0	1	2	3	4	5	6		_____
9. Learn to work independently.	0	1	2	3	4	5	6		_____
10. Learn to climb, run, and jump.	0	1	2	3	4	5	6		_____
11. Learn self-care such as toileting, dressing, feeding.	0	1	2	3	4	5	6		_____
12. Learn to follow classroom rules and routines.	0	1	2	3	4	5	6		_____

Using the above list, place the numbers 1, 2, and 3 next to the three most important areas for your child to progress in next year.

_____

Source: Unknown

IEP Worksheet

Life Domains: Environments, Activities, and Routines

School	Home/Domestic	Recreation/Leisure	Vocational	General Community

Embedded Skills

Motor	Communication	Social	Other

Adapted from York, J., & Vandercook, T. (1991). Designing an integrated education through the IEP process. *Teaching Exceptional Children,*

Assessment of Student Participation in General Education Classes

Student: _____

Classroom Teacher: _____

Assessment Completed by: _____

Grade, Subject, and Class Period: _____

Prep Periods: _____ Room Number: _____ # of Students in Class: _____

Date: _____

Instructions:
1. After the student attends the specific general education class for approximately one week, the team reviews all the skills identified in Sections I and II of this assessment tool.

Score:	+	for items that student consistently performs;
	+/-	for items that student does some of the time but not consistently;
	-	for items that student never or very rarely performs; and
	NA	for items that are not appropriate for the student/class

2. Circle about 5 items that the team identifies as priorities for instructional emphasis for the individual student.
3. Write objectives for each of the circled items, then design related instructional programs.
4. Review student progress on all items at least 2 more times during the school year. Revise as needed.

I. CLASSROOM ROUTINES AND ACTIVITIES

Date: _____   Date: _____

1. Gets to class on time							
2. Gets seated in class on time							
3. Performs transitional activities during class in response to situational cues (e.g., changes in seating, activity)							
4. Begins tasks							
5. Stays on task							
6. Participates in some regular class activities without adaptations							
7. Terminates tasks							
8. Tolerates out-of-the-ordinary changes in classroom routine							
9. Follows class rules							
10. Locates / brings materials to class as needed							
11. Shares materials with peers when appropriate							
12. Uses materials for their intended purpose							
13. Puts materials away after use							
14. Uses classroom materials and equipment safely							
15. Works cooperatively with a partner							
16. Works cooperatively with a small group							
17. Performs competitive learning tasks							
18. Readily accepts assistance							
19. Evaluates quality of own work (given a model)							
20. Copes with criticism/correction without incident and tries an alternative behavior							

II. SOCIAL AND COMMUNICATION SKILLS

Date: _____   Date: _____

21. Interacts with peers
   a. responds to others
   b. initiates

22. Interacts with the classroom teacher
   a. responds to the teacher
   b. initiates

23. Uses social greetings
   a. responds to others
   b. initiates

24. Uses farewells
   a. responds to others
   b. initiates

25. Uses expressions of politeness
   (e.g., please, thank you, excuse me)
   a. responds to others
   b. initiates

26. Participates in joking or teasing
   a. responds to others
   b. initiates

27. Makes choices and indicates preferences
   a. responds to others (cue or question)
   b. initiates

28. Asks questions
   a. asks for help
   b. asks for information (e.g., clarification, feedback)

29. Follows directions
   a. for curricular tasks
   b. for helping tasks/errands
   c. given to the student individually
   d. given to students as a group

30. States or indicates
   a. don't know / don't understand
   b. when finished with an activity

31. Orients toward the speaker or other source of input

32. Secures listener attention before communicating

33. Maintains eye contact with the listener when speaking

34. Takes turns communicating in conversation with others

35. Gives feedback
   a. gives positive feedback
   b. gives negative feedback

36. Uses appropriate gestures and body movements when interacting with others

37. Uses appropriate language / vocabulary / topic of conversation

38. Uses intelligible speech (volume, rate, articulation, etc.)

Comments:

From Macdonald, C., & York, J. (1989). Regular class integration: Assessment, objectives, instructional programs. In *Strategies for full inclusion*. Minneapolis: University of Minnesota, Institute on Community Integration; reprinted by permission of the authors.

Communication Environment Checklist

Student _____

Environment _____

Rating Scale: 1 = Not provided in current environment; needs intensive intervention
2 = Provided on a limited basis; needs expansion and refinement
3 = Generally provided; needs some refinement
4 = Provided consistently; needs no intervention

Dates

I. OPPORTUNITIES: Something To Communicate About

1. Consistent routines are present to allow students to learn natural cues.
2. Communication opportunities are integrated into daily routines.
3. Multiple opportunities to communicate are provided within activities that have multiple or repetitive parts (e.g., turntaking).
4. Natural opportunities to communicate are not eliminated by others in the environment (i.e., by guessing the student's wants and needs before they can be expressed).
5. Additional opportunities to communicate are created by delaying action on wants/needs and by interrupting daily routines.

II. MOTIVATION: The Desire To Communicate

6. Instructional routines and activities utilized have a high reinforcer value for the student, especially at first.
7. Instruction ensures the student is reinforced by natural consequences of communication acts.
8. Reinforcement is of high frequency and/or duration in order to provide success.

III. MEANS: Partners and Tools for Conveying Messages

9. Communication partners who are familiar with the student's means of communication are accessible at all times as listeners, conversation partners, and models.
10. There are many opportunities for communication with same-age peers in the environment.
11. Others in the environment recognize and respond to/reinforce alternate forms of communication used by the student (especially nonverbal).
12. If an augmentative means of communication is used by the student, it is accessible at all times.

IV. MAINTENANCE, GENERALIZATION, AND SPONTANEITY: Varying Contexts and Fading Cues

13. Spontaneous, initiated communication is agreed upon as the ultimate goal of communication.
14. Opportunities for practice of specific communication skills continue to be available even after skills are "mastered."
15. Cues and prompts are individualized and faded to "natural" cues as soon as possible.
16. Communication partners are familiar with the hierarchy of cues and prompts for an individual student and know the student's current level.
17. Partners use directives and questions sparingly to increase initiation, independence, and problem solving.
18. Opportunities are available for practicing communication skills in a variety of environments and with a variety of people.

Rainforth, B., & York-Barr, J. (1997). *Collaborative teams for students with severe disabilities: Integrating therapy and educational services* (2nd ed.). Baltimore: Paul H. Brookes Publishing Co.

Sensory Characteristics of Task Performance

Routine/Task Sensory Characteristics		What does the task routine hold? A B C	What does the particular environment hold?	What adaptations are likely to improve functional outcome?
Somatosensory	light touch (tap, tickle)			
	pain			
	temperature (hot, cold)			
	touch–pressure (hug, pat, grasp)			
	variable			
	duration of stimulus (short, long)			
	body surface contact (small, large)			
	predictable			
	unpredictable			
Vestibular	head position change			
	speed change			
	direction change			
	rotary head movement			
	linear head movement			
	repetitive head movement—rhythmic			
	predictable			
	unpredictable			
Proprioceptive	quick stretch stimulus			
	sustained tension stimulus			
	shifting muscle tension			
Visual	high intensity			
	low intensity			
	high contrast			
	high similarity (low contrast)			
	competitive			
	variable			
	predictable			
	unpredictable			
Auditory	rhythmic			
	variable			
	constant			
	competitive			
	noncompetitive			
	loud			
	soft			
	predictable			
	unpredictable			
Olfactory/ Gustatory	mild			
	strong			
	predictable			
	unpredictable			

Task Components   A=   B=   C=

From Dunn, W. (1996). The sensorimotor systems: A framework for assessment and intervention. In F. Orelove & D. Sobsey, *Educating children with multiple disabilities: A transdisciplinary approach* (3rd ed., p. 67). Baltimore: Paul H. Brookes Publishing Co.; reprinted with permission.

Related Services Planning Sheet

Teacher:

Activity:

Time:

Students	Transitions	Positions	Participation	Interactions	Comprehension	Expression

Rainforth, B., & York-Barr, J. (1997). *Collaborative teams for students with severe disabilities: Integrating therapy and educational services* (2nd ed.). Baltimore: Paul H. Brookes Publishing Co.

Performance Scoring Datasheet

Student: **Program:**
Initial Instruction:
Prompts and Scoring:

Time Delay between Prompts:

Dates

Movement Sequence Prompt at							
1.							
2.							
3.							
4.							
5.							
6.							
7.							
8.							
9.							
10.							
POSSIBLE SCORE= **TOTAL SCORE=**							
# TIMES TAUGHT TODAY							

Rainforth, B., & York-Barr, J. (1997). *Collaborative teams for students with severe disabilities: Integrating therapy and educational services* (2nd ed.). Baltimore: Paul H. Brookes Publishing Co.

Instructional Program Format

Student:_____   **Date** :_____

Program:_____

Instructional Procedures

Setting, Grouping, Positioning	
Equipment/Materials	
Instruction and Prompt	
Correct Response	
Time Delay and Correction	
Reinforcement	
Frequency to Teach	
Frequency of Data	
Type of Data	
Criterion for Change	

Projected completion date:_____
Actual completion date: _____
Comments:

Rainforth, B., & York-Barr, J. (1997). *Collaborative teams for students with severe disabilities: Integrating therapy and educational services* (2nd ed.). Baltimore: Paul H. Brookes Publishing Co.

Adaptations Worksheet for Students with Physical Disabilities

Environment: _____
Period: _____

Activities of Peers Without Disabilities	Typical Methods and Acceptable Alternatives		
	Transitions / Mobility	Positions	Participation

TYP: indicates typical methods displayed by peers without disabilities.
ALT: indicates alternatives that may be acceptable.

Rainforth, B., & York-Barr, J. (1997). *Collaborative teams for students with severe disabilities: Integrating therapy and educational services* (2nd ed.). Baltimore: Paul H. Brookes Publishing Co.

Program Change Notes

PROGRAM CHANGE NEEDED	PROGRAM CHANGE MADE
Date:	Date:
To:	To:
From:	From:
Student:	Student:
Program:	Program:
Reason change is needed: _____ criterion met _____ no progress _____ other (specify) Comments/suggestions:	Reason change was met: _____ criterion met _____ no progress _____ other (specify) Comments/suggestions:

Rainforth, B., & York-Barr, J. (1997). *Collaborative teams for students with severe disabilities: Integrating therapy and educational services* (2nd ed.). Baltimore: Paul H. Brookes Publishing Co.

Collaborative Team Member Checklist

Team Member Name:_____ Date:_____

Checklist completed by: (check one)

___Teacher   ___Support Staff   ___Aide   ___Program Supervisor   ___Other

	High				Low	
	5	4	3	2	1	NA
Participates in the assessment of student abilities in the array of educational environments and activities determined as priorities for individual students:						
•School environments and activities	5	4	3	2	1	NA
•Home environments and activities	5	4	3	2	1	NA
•Community environments and activities	5	4	3	2	1	NA
Effectively communicates educationally relevant assessment information to other team members.	5	4	3	2	1	NA
Participates in writing educationally relevant team assessment reports.	5	4	3	2	1	NA
Participates in team collaboration for determining priority educational goals and objectives.	5	4	3	2	1	NA
Writes educational goals and objectives that are:						
•Educationally relevant	5	4	3	2	1	NA
•Functional	5	4	3	2	1	NA
•Chronologically age appropriate	5	4	3	2	1	NA
•Behavioral	5	4	3	2	1	NA
•Measurable	5	4	3	2	1	NA
Writes clear instructional programs and procedures, including evaluation information.	5	4	3	2	1	NA
When teaching other team members, provides a rationale for the procedures and clear instruction-supportive feedback.	5	4	3	2	1	NA
Incorporates behavior management practices into programs and procedures as appropriate.	5	4	3	2	1	NA
Effectively teaches other team members how to integrate their own expertise into student's daily programming.	5	4	3	2	1	NA
Requests information from other team members.	5	4	3	2	1	NA
Is organized, efficient, and directed during classroom and community consultations.	5	4	3	2	1	NA
Effectively monitors and observes student performance.	5	4	3	2	1	NA
Provides supportive and instructive feedback to other team members regarding expanded roles.	5	4	3	2	1	NA

(continued)

Collaborative Team Member Checklist *(continued)*

	High 5	4	3	2	Low 1	NA
Participates effectively and appropriately in team meetings.	5	4	3	2	1	NA
Participates effectively and appropriately in IEP meeting and annual reviews.	5	4	3	2	1	NA
Maintains a good rapport and interacts appropriately with students.	5	4	3	2	1	NA
Maintains a good rapport and interacts appropriately with family members of students.	5	4	3	2	1	NA
Maintains a good rapport and interacts appropriately with other team members.	5	4	3	2	1	NA
Presents him/herself as a learner and continually attempts to enhance his/her knowledge of educational and specialized professional practices.	5	4	3	2	1	NA
Supports overall development of educational excellence in the school community.	5	4	3	2	1	NA

ADDITIONAL COMMENTS

1. Areas of strength:

2. Areas for improvement:

3. I would like more of:

4. I would like less of:

Adapted from York, J., Peters, B., Hurd, D., & Donder, D. (1985). *Guidelines for using support services in educational programs for students with severe, multiple handicaps* (pp. 48–49). DeKalb, IL: DeKalb County Special Education Association; revised and reprinted by permission.

Consultation Schedule for Blocked Therapy Time

Time	Location	Instruction	Students and Activities/ Priorities for Therapist

Rainforth, B., & York-Barr, J. (1997). *Collaborative teams for students with severe disabilities: Integrating therapy and educational services* (2nd ed.). Baltimore: Paul H. Brookes Publishing Co.

Consultation/Monitoring Worksheet

School:_____   Grade:_____
Students:_____
Support Schedule:_____   Support person:_____
_____   Team meeting:_____
_____
_____

Student	Context	Priority	Comments	Student	Context	Priority	Comments

Rainforth, B., & York-Barr, J. (1997). *Collaborative teams for students with severe disabilities: Integrating therapy and educational services* (2nd ed.). Baltimore: Paul H. Brookes Publishing Co.

Consultation/Monitoring Worksheet

Date: _____   Support by: _____

Daily Schedule	Instructional Priorities Requiring Speech-language Support for:			
	Student: _____	Student: _____	Student: _____	Student: _____
Other				

Comments / notes: _____
_____
_____
_____
_____

Copy and disseminate to: _____
_____

Rainforth, B., & York-Barr, J. (1997). *Collaborative teams for students with severe disabilities: Integrating therapy and educational services* (2nd ed.). Baltimore: Paul H. Brookes Publishing Co.

Team Meeting Agenda

Team meeting for:_____ Date:_____ Time:_____

Location of meeting: _____

Facilitator:_____ Recorder: _____

Agenda Items and Description	Outcomes Desired	Time

Rainforth, B., & York-Barr, J. (1997). *Collaborative teams for students with severe disabilities: Integrating therapy and educational services* (2nd ed.). Baltimore: Paul H. Brookes Publishing Co.

Team Meeting Minutes

Team meeting for:_____   Date:_____

Start time:_____ Finish time:_____

Participants: _____

_____

Facilitator:_____   Recorder:_____

Priority Sequence	Agenda Items and Key Points	Follow-up Needed: Who? What? When?
1. 2.	Anecdote: Follow-up:	

Next meeting:

Date/time: _____   Location:_____

Facilitator:_____   Recorder:_____

Agenda items:_____

Rainforth, B., & York-Barr, J. (1997). *Collaborative teams for students with severe disabilities: Integrating therapy and educational services* (2nd ed.). Baltimore: Paul H. Brookes Publishing Co.

Index

Page numbers followed by "t" denote tables; those followed by "f" denote figures.

American Occupational Therapy Association
    position on inclusion, 10
    areas of expertise of, 46, 47t
    as core team member, 45
    as coteacher, 273–276
    primary therapist model for, 271
    sample job description for, 253, 254f–257f
Olfactory system, 145t, 148t, 224t
"Only as special as necessary" concept,
    212–213
Organizational change, 308–309
Outcomes
    educational, 24–25
    life, 251

PALS, see Program for the Acquisition of Language with the Severely Impaired
PARC v. Pennsylvania, 40t
PARC v. Pennsylvania Consent Decree of Enforcement Petition in Fialkowski v. School District of Philadelphia, 40t–41t
Parents, see Families/parents
Part H program, 61
Partnerships, 312–313
    home–school, 36t, 57–82
Peabody Developmental Motor Scales, 141–142
Peer relationships, 4, 24, 35
Perceptions, 65–67
Performance
    adaptations for enhancement of, 232–235,
        233f, 234f
    assessment of, 235–238, 236f; see also
        Assessment
    collecting data on, 235
    communication about, 236–238, 237f
        between home and school, 238–241,
            239f–240f
    cues and prompts to elicit, 229–232, 230f,
        231f, 233f
    motor, see Motor performance
Performance scoring, 235
Performance Scoring Datasheet, 227f, 326f
Performing phase of group interaction, 249
Personal assistance, 234
Personal change, 309–311
Perspective, differences in, 26–28, 295–297
Physical therapist, 1, 2, 5, 11, 15, 22, 39, 109,
    200
    areas of expertise of, 46, 47t
    block scheduling for, 268, 270f
    as core team member, 45
    primary therapist model for, 271

sample job description for, 253, 254f–257f
PL 94-142, see Education for All Handicapped Children Act Amendments of 1975
PL 99-457, see Education of the Handicapped Act of 1986
PL 101-476, see Individuals with Disabilities Education Act (IDEA) of 1990
PL 102-119, see Individuals with Disabilities Education Act Amendments of 1991
Placement Checklist, 149, 151t
Planning, 23, 70
    of assessment, 131–134
        examples of, 155–156, 169
    development of ecological curriculum,
        94–120
    for development of individualized education program, 191
    for related services, 216, 219, 220f
    transition, 36t, 103
Policy development, 70
Positioning, 110–111
    to prepare student for instruction, 219, 225
    teaching strategies required for, 225
Postural control, 111
    assessment of, 139–142
Pragmatic approach to communication instruction, 115–116
Preservice training programs, 16
Primary therapist model, 271
    advantages of, 271
    block scheduling for, 268–271, 270f
Problem solving, 291–294
    barriers to, 294
    group strategies for, 291
    process for, 291–294, 292f–293f
    see also Conflict resolution
Professional constraints, 67
Program Change Notes, 236–238, 237f, 329f
Program for Infants and Toddlers with Disabilities, 61
Program for the Acquisition of Language with the Severely Impaired (PALS), 149, 151t
Prompts, to elicit desired performance,
    229–232, 230f, 231f, 233f
Proprioception system, 145t, 146t, 223t
Psychological safety of educational setting,
    10–11

Reciprocal interactions, 117
Recommended educational practices, 33–37, 36t
    characteristics of good schools for all children, 35